Computer Integrated Construction Project Scheduling

WITHDRAWN from collection

John Buttelwerth

Cincinnati State Technical and Community College

PEARSON

Prentice Hall

Upper Saddle River, New Jersey
Columbus, Ohio

Library of Congress Cataloging-in-Publication Data
Buttelwerth, John.
   Computer integrated construction project scheduling / John Buttelwerth.
     p. cm.
   Includes index.
   ISBN 0-13-111465-4 (alk. paper)
  1. Building–Superintendence–Data processing.   2. Production scheduling–Data
processing.   I. Title.

TH438.4.B88   2005
690'.068'5–dc22

                                  2004011896

Executive Editor: Ed Francis
Editorial Assistant: Jennifer Day
Production Editor: Holly Shufeldt
Project Coordination: Carlisle Publishers Services
Design Coordinator: Diane Ernsberger
Cover Designer: Tom Mack
Cover art: SureTrak is a registered trademark of Primavera Systems, Inc. Reprinted with permission from Primavera Systems, Inc.
Production Manager: Deidra Schwartz
Marketing Manager: Mark Marsden

This book was set in Berkeley by Carlisle Communications, Ltd. It was printed and bound by Courier Kendallville, Inc. The cover was printed by Phoenix Color Corp.

Pearson Education Ltd.
Pearson Education Singapore Pte. Ltd.
Pearson Education Canada, Ltd.
Pearson Education—Japan

Pearson Education Australia Pty. Limited
Pearson Education North Asia Ltd.
Pearson Educación de Mexico, S.A. de C.V.
Pearson Education Malaysia Pte. Ltd.

10 9 8 7 6 5 4 3 2
0-13-111465-4

Dedication

This book is dedicated to my loving family: my wife, Cheryl, and our children, Tasha, Johnnie, Rhea, and Julie. Thank you for your love, patience, and encouragement.

Preface

In the summer of 1990, I was leading a group of construction management students on a field trip through a thirty-five-story building. When talking to the project manager in the job trailer, I asked if they used a CPM schedule for the project. He answered, "Yeah, we use it every day." I was feeling pretty good, because I had just told my students about the importance of CPM schedules in our previous class. He then pointed to the bottom of the office door, where the CPM schedule was folded over about twenty times and stuffed under the door. It was being used as a doorstop!

Well, times have changed. Computer integrated, critical path method (CPM) scheduling is used as a management tool on nearly every commercial, industrial, and institutional project today. Over the last five years, many construction companies have moved from an office in which one or two people acted as the company "schedulers," to an office in which every project manager is expected to create and update computer-generated CPM schedules for every project they run.

I wrote this book to provide a textbook that covers all the relevant information and topics necessary for students to learn how to create and monitor the types of project schedules that are used throughout the construction industry today. This textbook offers a comprehensive examination of the following three key areas that the student must learn before starting a professional career in the construction industry:

- How to plan and schedule, including the determination of project activities, logic, and durations
- How to skillfully and confidently draw precedence network diagrams and to manually calculate CPM schedules
- How to create and update computer-generated schedules and schedule reports

In addition,

- The student will bring this knowledge together in a textbook *capstone project* where the student develops, draws by hand, manually calculates, and creates in the SureTrak a detailed construction schedule for a mixed-use commercial project.

I believe this is the first textbook to combine a full exploration of all three of these crucial areas into one text. It provides a complete curriculum, including numerous exercises in all three previously described areas.

The text is written in a style that is meant to be open and inviting to the reader with shorter paragraphs and interesting illustrations, rather than page after page of dense, uninviting text.

WHO IS THE TEXT INTENDED FOR?

The text is intended to be used as the sole textbook for the lecture and lab of a one-semester scheduling course in a baccalaureate or associate degree program. The text is also well suited to be used as the text for an online project scheduling course.

In addition, this text is well suited to be used by construction practitioners in the industry as an independent study guide to learn scheduling at their own pace, on their own time schedule, and in the comfort and convenience of their home or office. Later, the text can be used as a reference manual for the practitioner.

SCOPE OF THE TEXT

The first four chapters of the text are intended to provide the necessary framework and background for the student to learn scheduling terminology and gain an understanding of the environment and landscape that exists when the construction project schedule is created.

These chapters take the student from the general to the specific, starting with an overview of the construction industry in Chapter 1, including coverage of project delivery systems and types of construction contracts. Chapter 2 discusses who's who in the construction industry, detailing the relationships that exist between the various parties. Chapter 3 follows the evolution of the project from the owner's idea to the grand opening. Chapter 4 analyzes the concepts of planning and scheduling in detail, covers the different types of construction schedules that are used, introduces the critical path method (CPM), and explains the use of fast-tracking in construction.

The next four chapters of the text teach the students how to skillfully and confidently create construction schedules. Chapter 5 begins this process with an in-depth discussion of the determination of project activities, their logic, and durations using actual projects for examples and student exercises. In Chapter 6, the student learns how to draw, by hand, network diagrams of the schedule using the precedence diagramming method—the only method that supports Start-to-Start and Finish-to-Finish activity relationships, which are so important to creating real-world schedules. In Chapter 7, the student learns how to manually calculate the schedule using the CPM method, thereby gaining an intuitive knowledge of the CPM process. In Chapter 8, the students are taken step-by-step through the creation of the first draft of a construction project schedule, then through the revision of that schedule. The exercise accurately portrays the typical development and refinement of a construction schedule.

The second half of the text presents computer integration using SureTrak. Employing a module-driven format, it teaches the student how to use the software. SureTrak and P3e comprise a large majority of the construction scheduling software market, with SureTrak being the more common (2:1) of the two among construction companies. For that reason, it was chosen as the software to use in the text. The text is written to the 3.0b version of the software, which is the most current release and is nearly identical to the 3.0 version. The text could also be used with the 2.0 version of the software with little difficulty.

What's different about this text and its approach to teaching the software is that it feeds the information to the students in the appropriate order and in appropriate amounts. This approach does not overwhelm the students with too much information at one time nor does it try to cover every corner of the software and every arcane detail. (I have taught the SureTrak software for fifteen years at the college level and as a consultant to the construction industry.)

This module-driven approach allows the instructor to customize the text to his or her course and also allows individuals in industry to cover only the topics that they need to know, without going through the entire text.

Finally, the modules include *Schedule Analyses* that the students perform to measure not only if they have learned the software, but also if they understand the schedules they are creating with it.

TEACHING FORMAT

The text works best when taught in a lecture/lab format; however, it is partitioned to fit nearly any existing course format, allowing the instructor to skip around and customize it to fit his or her particular course or to choose to teach only certain parts of the material. The three major topics can be taught sequentially or concurrently. The more common practice might be to teach the chapter topics in the lecture and the modules in the lab. Regardless, it is recommended to teach Chapters 5, 6, 7, and 8 in sequential order.

TOPICS RARELY COVERED

This text includes some of the more challenging (and more interesting) topics that are rarely, and in some cases never before, covered in other textbooks. They include teaching true precedence diagramming rather than activity-on-node, using Start-to-Start and Finish-to-Finish activity relationships including their calculations with lags, using hammock and milestone activities, calculating and analyzing the free float of activities, and stressing the importance of hand-drawing network diagrams.

Additional topics rarely covered in other texts that are fully explored in the Sure-Trak modules consist of the use of multiple calendars including a four-tens calendar, assigning various resources to the schedule, creating multi-phase schedules, activity coding, updating the schedule to show progress, lookahead schedules, and creating customized schedule reports. All of these topics are used every day throughout the construction industry, but are rarely discussed in other texts.

Feel free to contact me with questions/comments about the text at (513) 569-1758 or john.buttelwerth@cincinnatistate.edu .

I look forward to your comments.

Acknowledgments

I would like to acknowledge the following people for their inspirations and contributions to this book. First, I want to thank the tremendous faculty and staff at Cincinnati State, whose dedication to changing lives has taught me the meaning of vocation.

I would like to thank Ken Jones of Turner Construction for the use of what he calls "the Who's Who? molecule" and his perspective on our business; Andy Lorenz of Messer Construction for his help with the schedules and his perception of what the students should be taught; and Bob Smyth of HGC Construction for his help with the schedules and continued support and dedication to my students. I would also like to thank Messer Construction for their commitment to the Civil Engineering Technology program at Cincinnati State over the years and to their dedication to the prospect that we all learn from each other.

I am thankful to Champlin/Haupt Architects, Cincinnati, for the use of the Delhi Medical Building project and to Integrated Architecture, Grand Rapids, for the use of the USA Volleyball Centers project.

I would like to thank my editor, Ed Francis, for his valued guidance throughout the entire process. In addition, particular thanks are due to Terry L. Anderson; Flynn L. Auchey, Virginia Tech; Jay Christofferson, Brigham Young University; and John Schaufelberger, University of Washington; for their assistance with the text review.

Contents

CHAPTER 1 The Construction Industry 1

The Construction Industry 1
Risky Business 2
Project Delivery Systems 5
Types of Construction Contracts 15
Individual Project Arrangements 20

CHAPTER 2 Who's Who? 21

Who's Who? 21
The Project Team 21
Owner Groups 24
Subconsultants 26
Trade Contractors 30
Other Trade Contractors 31
Material Suppliers 33

CHAPTER 3 What Is a Project? 35

What Is a Project? 35
Evolution of the Project 35
Predesign Phase 36
Design Phase 40
Construction Phase 47
Start-Up Phase 49
Grand Opening and Property Management Phase 50

CHAPTER 4 Planning and Scheduling 53

Planning versus Scheduling 53
Planning 54
Scheduling 56
Types of Schedules 62
What Is CPM? 67
What Is Fast-Tracking? 68

CHAPTER 5 Activities, Logic, and Duration 75

Identifying Activities 76
Logical Sequencing of the Activities 87
Activity Duration 95
In-Class Exercise #1, 105

In-Class Exercise #2, 112
In-Class Exercise #3, 115
In-Class Exercise #4, 118
Student Exercise #1, 120
Student Exercise #2, 120
Student Exercise #3, 121
Student Exercise #4, 122

CHAPTER 6   Network Diagrams   123
Importance of Drawing the Network 123
What Is a Network Diagram? 124
Drawing the Precedence Network Diagram 128
In-Class Exercises: Drawing the Network Diagrams 134
    In-Class Exercise #1, 134
    In-Class Exercise #2, 136
    In-Class Exercise #3, 138
Student Exercises: Drawing the Network Diagrams 141
    Student Exercise #1, 141
    Student Exercise #2, 142
    Student Exercise #3, 143
    Student Exercise #4, 143
    Student Exercise #5, 144
    Student Exercise #6, 145

CHAPTER 7   CPM Calculations   147
CPM Calculations 148
Forward Pass 148
Backward Pass 156
The Critical Path 166
In-Class Exercises: Calculating the CPM Network 173
    In-Class Exercise #1, 174
    In-Class Exercise #2, 178
    In-Class Exercise #3, 182
Student Exercises: Calculating the CPM Network 186
    Student Exercise #1, 187
    Student Exercise #2, 189
    Student Exercise #3, 191
    Student Exercise #4, 193
    Student Exercise #5, 195
    Student Exercise #6, 197

CHAPTER 8   Creating Construction Schedules   201
Document Review 201
Identify the Up-Fronts 210
Creating Construction Schedules 212
Schedule Analysis—First Draft Construction Schedule 219
Revising the Schedule 221
Schedule Analysis—Revised Construction Schedule 227
Capstone Project—USA Volleyball Centers 229

MODULE 1   Drawing the Schedule by Hand   239
Drawing the Network Schedule 239

MODULE 2   Creating a Project   242
Opening the Software 242

Creating the Project 244
Saving the Project 246

MODULE 3   Adding Activities   249
Adding Activities 249
Using Spellcheck 252
Changing Activity Types 253

MODULE 4   Adding Logic (Successors)   256
Relationship Types and Lag 256
Adding Logic 257
Adding Buttons (Icons) to the Toolbar 261
Creating Screen-Captures and Window-Captures 263

MODULE 5   Printing the Schedule   264
Printing the Schedule 264

SCHEDULE ANALYSIS—MODULES 1–5 267

MODULE 6   Saving and Closing a Project   269
Saving the Project to the Hard Drive 269
Saving the Project to a Disk 269
Saving the Project under a Different Name 271
Saving the Project to a Different Folder 272
Automatic Save Feature (and a Word about the Undo and Redo Buttons) 272
Closing the Project 272

MODULE 7   Opening a Project   273
Opening a Project 273

MODULE 8   Delhi Medical Building—Bid Package Schedule   275
Draw the Schedule 275
Create the SureTrak Schedule 276

MODULE 9   The PERT View   284
Changing the Project Window to the PERT View 284

SCHEDULE ANALYSIS—MODULES 8–9 291

MODULE 10   Layouts—Saving, Applying, and Creating   293
What Is a Layout? 293
The Default Layout 293
Saving Changes to the Layout 293
Applying an Existing Layout 294
Creating a New Layout 297

MODULE 11   Formatting Columns   300
Formatting Columns 300

MODULE 12   Sorting by Early Start   305
Sorting by Early Start 305

MODULE 13   Formatting the Footer   308
Formatting the Footer 308

MODULE 14   Formatting the Header   313
Formatting the Header 313

SCHEDULE ANALYSIS—MODULES 10–14 315

MODULE 15   Renaming a Project   317
Renaming a Project 317
Renaming the Number/Version, Project Title, and Layout 317

MODULE 16   Working with Calendars   320
Global Calendar 320
Normal Workweek Calendar 320
Adding Holidays to Calendars 322
Creating a Calendar (Six-Day Workweek) 324
Assigning Calendars to Activities 326
Creating a Calendar (Four-Tens) 328

SCHEDULE ANALYSIS—MODULE 16 333

MODULE 17   Activity Codes   335
Rename the GARG Project 337
Defining Activity Codes 337
Assigning Activity Codes 340
Grouping the Activities by Activity Codes 343

MODULE 18   Budgeted Costs   348
Assigning Lump Sum Costs to Activities 348

MODULE 19   Resources   353
Defining Resources 353
Assigning Resources to Activities 355
More on Assigning Resources 360

MODULE 20   Resource Profiles   363
Project Cash Flow 363
Printing Resource Profiles 366
Other Resource Profiles 368

MODULE 21   Resource Tables   372
Project Cash Flow 372
Printing Resource Tables 374

Other Resource Tables 377
Combined Resource Profiles and Tables 381

SCHEDULE ANALYSIS—MODULES 17–21 383

MODULE 22   Target Schedules   385
Renaming the Project 385
Creating the Target Schedule 386

MODULE 23   Reports   390
Applying a Pre-Built Report 390
Classic Schedule Report 392
Reports and Layouts 394
Schedule Status Report 395
Three-Week Lookahead Report 397
Run Report Menu 401

SCHEDULE ANALYSIS—MODULES 22–23 403

MODULE 24   Multi-Phase Projects   405
Create the Project 405
Transferring Resources 406
Copying Activities 408
Adding Activities to an Existing Project 413
The Logic of a Multi-Phase Project 414

SCHEDULE ANALYSIS—MODULE 24 425

MODULE 25   Updating the Schedule   427
Naming and Saving Conventions for Updates 427
Tracking Project Progress 429
What Is the Data Date? 429
Begin the Update 433
Updated Schedule Status Report 439

SCHEDULE ANALYSIS—MODULE 25 445

MODULE 26   Revising Schedules   449
Revising Schedules 449

MODULE 27   Capstone Project   450
Capstone Schedule 450

APPENDIX A   463

INDEX   491

Drawing list

The following schedules and drawings have been included at the back of the text. They are listed below with the chapter(s) and/or module(s) in which they will be used.

Delhi Medical Building

Construction Scheduling (First Draft)	Chapter 8 and Module 26
Construction Scheduling (Revised Schedule)	Chapter 8 and Module 26
Elevations (A6)	Chapters 5, 6, 7, and 8 and Modules 8, 9, and 26
Site Plan Detention (A1)	Chapters 5, 6, 7, and 8 and Modules 8, 9, and 26
Site Plan (ME1)	Chapters 5, 6, 7, and 8 and Modules 8, 9, and 26
First Floor Plan (A2)	Chapters 5, 6, 7, and 8 and Modules 8, 9, and 26
Second Floor Plan (A3)	Chapters 5, 6, 7, and 8 and Modules 8, 9, and 26
Building Sections (A7)	Chapters 5, 6, 7, and 8 and Modules 8, 9, and 26
Wall Sections (A8)	Chapters 5, 6, 7, and 8 and Modules 8, 9, and 26
Wall Sections (A9)	Chapters 5, 6, 7, and 8 and Modules 8, 9, and 26
Foundation Plan/Second Floor Framing Plan/Misc. Details (S1)	Chapters 5, 6, 7, and 8 and Modules 8, 9, and 26
Roof Framing Plan/Misc. Details (S2)	Chapters 5, 6, 7, and 8 and Modules 8, 9, and 26

USA Volleyball Centers

Main Level Floor Plan (Sheet 2 of 7)	Chapter 8 and Module 27
Upper Floor Plan (Sheet 3 of 7)	Chapter 8 and Module 27
Exterior Elevations (Sheet 5 of 7)	Chapter 8 and Module 27
Building Sections (Sheet 6 of 7)	Chapter 8 and Module 27
Wall Sections (Sheet 7 of 7)	Chapter 8 and Module 27

CHAPTER 1
The Construction Industry

To fully understand the concepts and importance of planning and scheduling, it is important for the student to have a basic knowledge of the construction industry. This chapter presents an overview of the construction industry and will provide a background and context to prepare the student for the concepts of planning and scheduling that follow in the remainder of the text.

In this text, the phrase *construction industry* will encompass the entire scope of the industry including all design and engineering professionals, material suppliers, involved governmental agencies, and related organizations, as well as the many companies that perform and manage the actual construction.

THE CONSTRUCTION INDUSTRY

Construction has been, currently is, and will continue to be one of the greatest and most consuming human endeavors. We still marvel at the skills of the ancient builders of monuments such as the pyramids of Egypt, the highways of Rome, the Great Wall of China, and the cathedrals of Europe, to name only a few. These projects consumed tremendous amounts of time, labor, material, equipment, and wealth. They were built with a workforce of thousands over many years who hauled materials, such as huge cut stones, sometimes hundreds of miles over water and land. In the case of the pyramids, the stones were rolled up massive earth-built, temporary ramps and put in place.

Equally impressive are more recent projects such as the Trans-Continental Railroad and the Panama Canal. Even within the past fifty years we have witnessed the construction of remarkable projects such as the tunnel beneath the English Channel (often referred to as the Chunnel), which now connects Europe with Great Britain, and the U.S. Interstate Highway System which consists of nearly 45,000 miles of highway throughout the United States and is considered the largest construction project ever built.

Over the last half century, the construction industry has ranked first or second as the leading U.S. industry in terms of employment and gross national product. With the currently aging infrastructure and this country's propensity for building new rather than renovating, there is every reason to believe that the strength of the construction industry will sustain this position in the economy for the foreseeable future. However, an even larger market for the century to come will grow outside the U.S. border.

The twentieth century has seen a tremendous leap in technology and human sophistication that has led to a rapid pace of development in science and industry. Add to that the tremendous advances in communication, including most recently the Internet, and the world has seemingly become a single village. Remember that as recently as last century, communication from Europe was carried by ship across the Atlantic. Today, of course, communication is instant from one corner of the world to any other. From all this, we have begun to see, and will continue to see, an economic revolution centered in Asia, followed by South America, and eventually Africa. The people from the nations in these areas have embraced capitalism with a passion and are aggressively filling the

1

consumption needs of the developed nations. This is leading to their own rapid development, including a need to establish their own infrastructure. Construction companies from around the world will be called upon to fill this need.

In the coming decades, the construction industry will have to tackle the challenge of rebuilding the deteriorating infrastructure, as well as industrial, production, and other facilities of the developed countries, and the construction of new communities, infrastructure, and industrial/production complexes in the developing world.

An added challenge, particularly in the United States, is the lack of a skilled construction craft workforce and construction management workforce. Fewer and fewer high school students are entering the industry as carpenters, electricians, plumbers, and so forth. The stark reality is that in our high-tech world, these types of careers are viewed as "low-tech," dirty, and meant for below-average students. How many parents are proud to say that their son or daughter is going to be a construction worker? The image of a construction worker is usually ranked quite low in surveys taken by high school students. The construction industry has worked quite hard over the last five to ten years to try to counteract this image and bring more students into the crafts. The construction management profession has the benefit of a better image than the craft field. However, the profession usually requires a two-year or four-year college education that often includes some studies in math, physics, and engineering technology. This scares away many of today's students, thereby causing a shortage in the construction management profession as well.

The construction industry must overcome these obstacles to meet the needs of the future.

RISKY BUSINESS

Construction is risky business. In fact, it is one of the riskiest, and maybe *the* riskiest, business to be in. The following list details various characteristics of the construction industry, many of which are particular only to that industry, that make it inherently more risky than other types of business:

- Uniqueness of projects (no prototype)
- Lack of repetitiveness
- 3-D object from 2-D plans
- Design by multiple entities
- Built by numerous companies
- Product built outdoors
- Enormity of size
- Price locked-in prior to construction
- Cash flow problems
- Small companies
- Safety concerns
- Contract value relative to company size

UNIQUENESS OF PROJECTS (NO PROTOTYPE)

When a manufacturer produces a product such as a lamp or automobile, it will eventually build thousands of them. Before the manufacturer begins to mass-produce the product, it builds numerous prototypes of the product to refine, perfect, and help improve and streamline the production. Conversely, when a construction company builds a project, it has most likely never built it before. You cannot build a prototype. There may be a prototype or mock-up built for testing or viewing a particular item of the project such as a curtain wall system or finish material. However, the contractor has just one shot at building the project and getting it right.

LACK OF REPETITIVENESS

Due to the uniqueness of construction projects, the repetitiveness that results from mass production and assembly line production is not present—or, at least, is greatly diminished. The contractor is not able to get accustomed to the work and gain speed performing it and therefore risks low productivity. Some projects do have repetitive processes within them, particularly projects with multiple phases of the same work. For example, most of the floors of a multistory building are often very similar to each other, so once you install ductwork on one floor, it will be the same on the next, and the next, and so on. The contractor is able to establish a learning curve with some work, but usually never gets the chance to build the same building (or roadway, gymnasium, or power plant) again.

3-D OBJECT FROM 2-D PLANS

The end product of the construction project is a three-dimensional structure. However, the plans used to build the project are two-dimensional. Building a 3-D object from 2-D plans can present unique problems such as the various interferences that often occur. For example, the plumbing drawings show the location of a floor drain needed for a piece of equipment. When the plumbing contractor goes to install the required 8-inch diameter sleeve in the concrete deck for the drain, he or she discovers that the sleeve is located directly above a 12-inch-wide concrete floor beam. That is a typical example of an interference. So how do you solve it? The plumbing contractor will probably write up a Request for Information (RFI) or bring the interference to the attention of the construction manager. There are two probable solutions: either move the location of the drain or somehow fit it through the beam. Moving the drain location may require moving the piece of equipment it serves, which may disrupt the design and layout of that space. Fitting the floor drain through the beam will require a redesign of the beam by the structural engineer. If the beam is already formed and the rebar is in place, there would be a rework charge in addition to the cost of the redesign.

One promising solution to interference and other problems caused by the 3-D/2-D nature of the industry is to perform all design in one integrated three-dimensional, object-oriented format. So when the mechanical designer begins locating floor drains, he or she will start with a 3-D model that already includes the building's structural frame and other components. The construction/design industry has been slow to implement this technology, so few projects have been designed and built this way.

DESIGN BY MULTIPLE ENTITIES

Rarely does one company design an entire project. In addition to the architect, most projects have a structural engineer design the foundation and frame of the building, a mechanical engineer design the heating, ventilation, and air conditioning (HVAC) and plumbing, and an electrical engineer design the electrical components of the building. Many other design disciplines may also be involved including a soils engineer, site engineer, fire protection specialist, landscape architect, acoustical engineer, and so forth.

The challenge is to coordinate these various designs together without conflicts. Currently this is done through the use of two-dimensional layers of computer-aided (CAD) drawings, with each discipline having its own layer. Unfortunately, this technology will not detect conflicts. As previously mentioned, the use of an object-oriented, integrated three-dimensional design model may help prevent conflicts and interferences.

BUILT BY NUMEROUS COMPANIES

Rarely are construction projects built by one single contractor. Rather, they are often built by numerous (typically ten to twenty or more) specialty contractors. A specialty contractor performs a particular part of the work, such as electrical. Specialty contractors are also called trade contractors or subcontractors (subs) because they often sign a subcontract with the general contractor. Additionally, specialty contractors often subcontract out part of their work to other specialty contractors, which might, in turn, get subbed-out again. Add to that the scores of material suppliers that furnish materials to the job, and even a small project may have well over 100 different companies somehow involved in the project. Therefore, it is not uncommon for medium to large projects to have hundreds of companies involved in the project. With this many companies, careful coordination of the project is imperative. Planning and scheduling will help greatly in this effort.

PRODUCT BUILT OUTDOORS

Most products are produced indoors in a controlled environment. The construction project has to be built in its final resting place, which means that it has to be built outdoors, exposed to the elements. This obviously creates many potential problems that must be overcome including the effect on productivity, the complete stoppage of work due to in inclement weather, and many others.

ENORMITY OF SIZE

Construction projects are the largest manmade—and handmade—objects built. Compared to other manufactured products, construction projects are enormous. Their size inherently creates special problems. The lifting and placement of materials requires some type of crane for a portion of the job. Large projects necessitate a significant area to lay down materials. Buildings built in an urban setting often require materials to be lifted directly from trucks since there is a very limited lay down area. This requires the precise scheduling of just-in-time deliveries. The heights of multistory projects dictate that strict safety practices are adhered to. These factors and others greatly affect the project schedule and productivity.

PRICE LOCKED-IN PRIOR TO CONSTRUCTION

When most products are produced, the manufacturers know what they can charge for the product and have a good idea of what their profit will be. Since construction projects are often unique and never previously built, the contractor does not know what the actual project cost will be until the project is complete. However, there is a good chance that the contractor has committed to a locked-in lump sum price for the work. This is very risky since the contractor will have to pay, out of pocket, to finish the project if it goes over budget. Even if the contractor has built a similar project in the past and therefore knows what the project should cost, the many other risk factors previously listed could significantly alter the cost of the work.

CASH FLOW PROBLEMS

Contractors are usually paid thirty to ninety days after they perform work on a project. However, they usually have to pay their expenses within thirty days or less. This is a cash flow problem for the contractor, and the only solution is to accumulate enough cash to get through that period. This is so critical to contractors that it becomes the controlling factor in the amount of work they can perform. Mismanaging cash flow is the leading cause of contractors going bankrupt. Generally, larger, more mature contractors have learned how to manage cash flow. However, even large companies can overextend themselves and get into trouble or even go bankrupt because of cash flow.

SMALL COMPANIES

The construction industry is made up of a large number of relatively small companies. A large percentage of all companies in the construction industry have twenty-five or fewer employees. Construction companies can start up rather easily. You really need only a few tools and the willingness to take on the risk of a job to get started. For that same reason, however, they also go out of business rather easily.

There are two major factors, previously discussed, that put small construction companies at risk. The first is the fact that the contract amount of one project is often greater than the entire value of the business. Therefore, when a project goes bad, the construction company often goes under. The second is the problem of cash flow. Small and immature companies are particularly susceptible to this problem.

SAFETY CONCERNS

Construction is intrinsically a dangerous business and there are numerous risks, financial and otherwise, that come with that danger. The construction industry has worked hard over many years to reduce the level of danger on the job and has been relatively successful. Construction now ranks at, or often below, the manufacturing industry in terms of overall safety. So while the construction industry, relative to all other industries, is still less safe, it has come a long way to improve safety.

CONTRACT VALUE RELATIVE TO COMPANY SIZE

It is very common for the contract amount of one project to be greater than the entire value of the contractor's business. The following scenario details why this is a problem. A small homebuilding contractor gives a lump sum, locked-in contract price of $300,000 to build a house for a customer. The total value of the contractor's business including tools, equipment, a truck, and cash in the bank is $45,000. The project is built and, due to various factors, goes over budget by 5 percent ($15,000 dollars). The contractor has to pay for this $15,000 overrun out of his or her pocket. The contractor just lost one-third of the company. If the overrun had been 15 percent, the entire company would be lost.

This example illustrates the tremendous risk of the contracting business. As a comparison, imagine the value of General Motors relative to the cost of producing one car.

In conclusion, when the typical construction project is built, the end product is a wholly unique, never before built, very large three-dimensional object built from hundreds of pages of two-dimensional plans and specifications designed by numerous firms conforming to many different codes referencing hundreds of different standards. The project is built, by hand, outside in the weather, in its final resting place by hundreds of different companies that may have never worked together before, employing craft from many different trades, for a price that is locked-in up front, regardless of difficulties encountered, risking the entire value of the company, for probably less than 10 percent profit. Sounds like a great deal!

PROJECT DELIVERY SYSTEMS

In the past twenty-five years, the construction industry has seen a remarkable evolution of project delivery systems in response to increasing owner requirements, urgency of schedules, heightened demands for safety and quality, and the critical necessity of reducing adversity in construction (Dorsey, 1997, p. xi). In those years, various project delivery systems have evolved to meet those needs.

Project delivery system is a general term that describes the process used to design and construct a project. Choosing the project delivery system is one of the first decisions that the owner will have to make when pursuing the project. It is an important decision because it will dictate which parties become involved in the project and at what times.

The intent of all these systems is to deliver to the owner a successfully completed project. There is no one system that is better than the rest. Each system has its own characteristics that may or may not make that system suitable for a particular project. The following project delivery systems are the more frequently used systems. Their characteristics, advantages, and disadvantages will be examined in this section.

- General contracting
- Agency construction management
- At-risk construction management
- Design/build
- Hybrids

GENERAL CONTRACTING

General contracting is the traditional method of contracting. Also referred to as *design-bid-build,* this has been the predominant method of contracting for more than 100 years. While other project delivery systems have gained a significant share of the construction market, the traditional method is still the most widely used project delivery system.

This method is called general contracting because the general contractor is the centerpiece of the construction phase of the project. The term *design-bid-build* properly lays out the sequence, and more importantly, the true nature of the separation of these phases in this delivery system. Under general contracting, the owner hires an architect to design the project and help administer the bidding phase of the project. The general contractor enters the project at the bidding phase and carries out the construction from there.

The general contractor enters into a contract with the owner.

A contract between the owner and a contractor is called a **prime contract.**

Therefore, the general contractor is acting as a *prime contractor.*

Rarely do general contractors build the entire project with their own forces. They will often hire various trade contractors, sometimes referred to as *specialty contractors,* who specialize in a particular portion of the work to build part or most of the project. In fact, sometimes the general contractor will not perform any of the work. The trade contractors will enter into a contract with the general contractor.

A contract between two contractors is called a **subcontract.**

That is why many trade/specialty contractors are very often referred to as *subcontractors,* or simply *subs.* Additionally, trade contractors may hire other trade contractors to do part of their work. They would also sign a subcontract and may be referred to as subcontractors.

Figure 1.1 shows a model of the different parties that are involved in the general contracting project delivery system. Obviously, not all the parties are shown. The model is intended to illustrate the relationships that exist down through the project. The type of contract signed (in parentheses) is listed beneath the contractors.

The following lists display the characteristics, advantages, and disadvantages of the general contracting project delivery system.

Characteristics
- The traditional method of contracting
- Also known as design-bid-build or the traditional method

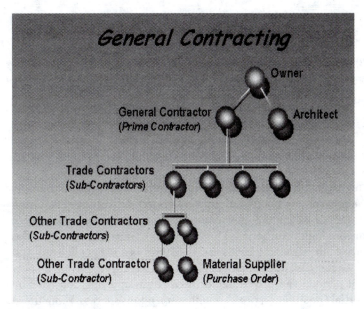

FIGURE 1.1
The general contracting project delivery system.

- Clear separation between design and construction
- Architect plays a prominent role as the owner's representative
- Usually competitively bid
- Typically uses a lump sum contract type
- Contractual relationships often require completed design with final documents prior to bidding

Advantages

- The most common project delivery system—most understood
- Preferred system by many—less-complicated relationships
- Owner holds only one construction contract
- Thought by many to provide the maximum competitive price
- Avoids favoritism
- Owner has good idea of the final cost at the start of construction
- General contractor carries the cost risk of construction indicated on drawings (owner's advantage)
- Higher markup and profit for the general contractor (general contractor advantage)
- Owner has good idea of final product at the start of construction
- Clear system of checks and balances

Disadvantages

- Leads to potential adversarial relationships between team members
- General contractor may work on their behalf first, then on the behalf of the owner
- Construction expertise not present during design

- Scheduling expertise not present during design
- Estimating expertise not present during design
- Budget overruns may not appear until bid day
- Usually cannot fast-track the project
- May require more time and involvement from the owner
- May lead to multiple markups on work passed on through multiple subs

AGENCY CONSTRUCTION MANAGEMENT

Agency construction management is often referred to simply as construction management. *Construction management* was the first alternative project delivery system. Originally developed and practiced by the U.S. government on large projects such as those carried out by the Tennessee Valley Authority (TVA) during the Great Depression, it was borrowed by the private sector in the late 1950s and the 1960s as a project delivery system used to build the very complex nuclear power plants that were springing up all over the country during that period. The private sector then began applying construction management to commercial construction projects with tremendous success. From there, it has gained momentum to become the second most used project delivery system, next to the traditional method of general contracting.

The hallmark of agency construction management is the agency relationship that exists between the owner and the construction manager (CM). Many of the same firms who perform general contracting also perform construction management. They are attracted by the limited liability for the total project cost that agency construction management offers, even though the fees they earn as CMs are not nearly as high as what they might earn as general contractors. Under agency construction management, the construction firm enters the project team, along with the owner and architect, as a teammate rather than a potential adversary. The greatest advantage of construction management is the introduction of construction, estimating, and scheduling expertise into the predesign, design, and bidding phases of the project.

> The predesign, design, and bidding phases of the project are commonly referred to in total as the preconstruction phase of the project.

During the predesign and design phases of the project, the CM serves as a consultant to the project team while the architect leads the project team. The architect will call the meetings, set the agenda, and run the project team meetings throughout the design of the project. Specific tasks that the CM performs during these phases include development of the budget, the project plan, and project schedules, in addition to performing value engineering, the constructability review, and preparing for the bid.

After the design is complete, the project is ready to bid out. At this point, starting with the bidding phase, the CM leads the project team throughout the remainder of the project with the architect now serving in the consultant role.

Under agency construction management, the actual construction of the project is performed by the same trade contractors that might be hired under general contracting; however, in this system, there is no general contractor. The trade contractors are in direct contract with the owner and take direction from the construction manager. The trade contractors enter into a contract with the owner and, therefore, are acting as *prime contractors* (even though they are often still referred to as subs). As is the case in general contracting, trade contractors will often hire other trade contractors to do part of their work. These second-tier trade contractors will enter into a subcontract.

The name for this project delivery system was poorly chosen, as *construction management* implies that the CM is involved in the construction phase only. For this reason,

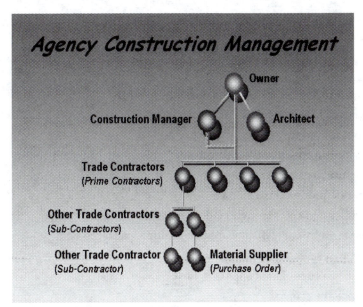

FIGURE 1.2
The agency construction management project delivery system.

many in the construction industry are still confused and only recognize the construction phase services as being construction management. In fact, the greatest advantage of the construction management project delivery system may be the construction manager's involvement in the project from its very inception. A better name for this delivery system might be *project management*. Regardless, the name *construction management* is probably here to stay.

Figure 1.2 shows a model of the different parties that are involved in the agency construction management project delivery system. Obviously, not all the parties are shown. The model is intended to illustrate the relationships that exist down through the project. Notice the dashed line leading from the construction manager to the trade contractors. This indicates that these trade contractors, and all the other contractors beneath them, work under the direction of the construction manager even though they are not in contract with the CM. The type of contract signed (in parentheses) is listed beneath the contractors.

The following lists display the characteristics, advantages, and disadvantages of the agency construction management project delivery system.

Characteristics
- Sometimes referred to as "pure" construction management
- Construction management firm hired about the same time as architect
- Project team of the owner, architect, and CM formed
- Construction manager acts as the owner's agent
- Construction manager acts as consultant throughout project design
- Architect leads the team during the predesign and design phases
- Construction manager leads the team from the bidding phase to the end of the project
- Multiple construction contracts are held by the owner
- Construction manager directs the construction effort
- Construction manager has no risk for the cost of the project

■ Project can be fast-tracked

■ Architect plays a less prominent role during the bidding and construction phase

Advantages

■ Construction manager acts as agent of the owner

■ Absence of adversarial relationship

■ Fosters team approach to the project

■ Construction expertise present during design

■ Scheduling expertise present during design

■ Estimating expertise present during design

■ Budget may be more accurate throughout design—no surprises on bid day

■ Allows for advantages from breaking work into multiple packages

■ Potential project cost savings for the owner

■ Reduces multiple markups of subcontractor work

■ Ability to fast-track the project

■ Ability to fast-track the project with competitively bid, lump sum contracts

■ Requires less time and involvement from the owner

■ Allows owner to purchase materials directly for the project

■ Potential reduction of design fee since many of the traditional architectural duties performed during the construction phase are taken over by the CM

Disadvantages

■ Owner holds multiple construction contracts—more risk to the owner

■ Less common project delivery system—sometimes misunderstood

■ No single, lump sum contract—many little, lump sum contracts

■ Perception of added cost

■ Responsibility without authority for CM—not in contract with prime contractors

■ Potential bonding problems, with trade contractors acting as prime contractors

AT-RISK CONSTRUCTION MANAGEMENT

At-risk construction management is an offshoot of agency construction management. Many owners want the numerous advantages of agency construction management but also the security of a single, lump sum contractor to be responsible for the project. Similarly, some construction firms are interested in the possibility of greater profits associated with taking the risk of the project cost. From these two mutual interests, the at-risk project delivery system was formed.

At-risk construction management is very similar to agency construction, except that the construction manager also holds the contract for construction. The CM performs all the preconstruction services as they normally would perform them with agency construction management; however, they also take on the risk of performing the construction project, including the cost. From the construction phase on, at-risk construction management is very similar to the traditional method of general contracting, where the architect performs many of the duties that he or she would normally perform under the traditional method and the construction manager performs the duties that the general contractor would normally perform.

The construction manager often works under a negotiated, guaranteed maximum price contract which has less of a chance to lead to an adversarial relationship.

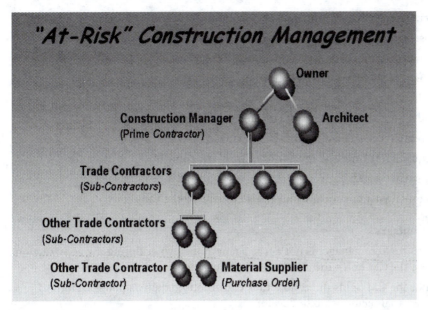

FIGURE 1.3
The at-risk construction management project delivery system.

Figure 1.3 shows a model of the different parties that are involved in the at-risk construction management project delivery system. Obviously, not all the parties are shown. The model is intended to illustrate the relationships that exist down through the project. The type of contract signed (in parentheses) is listed beneath the contractors.

The following lists display the characteristics, advantages, and disadvantages of the at-risk construction management project delivery system.

Characteristics
- Construction management firm is hired at about the same time as architect
- Project team of the owner, architect, and CM formed
- Construction manager acts as the owner's agent throughout the preconstruction phases
- Construction manager acts as consultant throughout project design
- Architect leads the team during the predesign and design phases
- Construction manager leads the team from the bidding phase to the end of the project
- Single construction contract held by the owner
- Construction manager responsible for the construction of the project
- Construction manager often works under a negotiated, guaranteed maximum price contract
- Construction manager takes the risk of the cost of the project
- Architect has a similar role during the bidding and construction phase as in the traditional method of general contracting

Advantages
- Construction manager acts as agent of the owner throughout the preconstruction phase

- Generates smoother and quicker transition from design to construction
- Fosters a team approach to the project
- Construction expertise present during design
- Scheduling expertise present during design
- Estimating expertise present during design
- Budget may be more accurate throughout design—no surprises on bid day
- Potential project cost savings for the owner
- Requires less time and involvement from the owner
- Less adversarial
- Allows owner to purchase materials directly for the project

Disadvantages

- Construction manager is not a true agent of the owner during the construction since the CM holds the contract for construction
- Since the CM holds the contract for construction, there is potential for an adversarial relationship to develop
- Less common project delivery system—sometimes misunderstood
- Perception of lack of competition

DESIGN/BUILD

Design/build is the newest of the major project delivery systems. While delivery methods similar to design/build have been around for many years, its prominence as a major delivery system only dates back to the early 1990s. Actually, design/build has its roots in what was the predominant delivery system of the nineteenth century—the master builder. The master builder was part designer, part builder who oversaw and administered the entire project from start to finish. More recently, design/build has evolved out of a delivery system known as *turnkey construction*. In turnkey construction the design/builder takes care of everything for the owner from finding the land for the project and securing financing to equipping and stocking the building so it is ready for occupancy—the design/builder simply turns the keys over to the owner.

The design/build project delivery system consists of a single entity providing both the design and construction of the project under one contract, thereby creating a single source of responsibility. In design/build, the design/build entity could be one company that performs design and construction in-house; it could be two separate companies that form a joint venture to design and build the project, both sharing in the risk; but most often it is a contracting company that takes the risk of the project and hires a design firm to perform the design. Design firms typically do not take the financial risk on design/build teams because they often do not have the financial resources to secure loans and bonds or take the risk of the construction. Therefore, the design firm is usually working under the direction of the contractor when they combine to form a design/build team.

Some consider the design/build project delivery system to have a major flaw. The owner has no one who is unbiased looking out on their behalf. This is compounded by the lack of checks and balances between the designer and contractor that normally exist under other delivery systems. However, many of these potential problems are mitigated if the owner has worked with the design/builder in the past and has developed a trusting relationship.

Figure 1.4 shows a model of the different parties that are involved in the design/build project delivery system. Obviously, not all the parties are shown. The model is intended to illustrate the relationships that exist down through the project. The type of contract signed (in parentheses) is listed beneath the contractors.

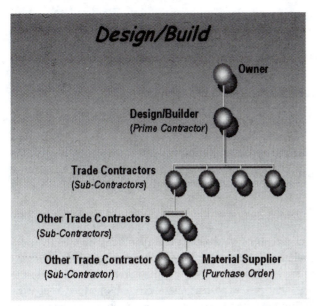

FIGURE 1.4
The design/build project delivery system.

The following lists display the characteristics, advantages, and disadvantages of the design/build project delivery system.

Characteristics

- Design and construction are provided by a single source
- Project team of the owner and design/builder formed
- Design/build entity is often two separate companies that come together to perform a single project
- Contractor usually takes the financial risk of the project
- Design/build team is usually headed by the contractor, with the design firm taking direction from the contractor
- Follows the master builder and turnkey delivery concepts

Advantages

- Single source of responsibility
- Results in a quicker delivery of the project
- Early cost commitment
- Potential benefits from a closer working relationship between designer and contractor
- Smoother and quicker transition from design to construction
- Construction expertise present during design
- Estimating expertise present during design
- Scheduling expertise present during design
- Ability to fast-track

Disadvantages

- No one who is unbiased is representing the owner throughout the project
- Potential for adversarial relationship exists between the owner and design/builder
- Conflict may arise between the designer and the builder
- Less common project delivery system—sometimes misunderstood
- Perception of lack of competition
- Lack of checks and balances
- Potential for collusion between the designer and builder that exists due to their contractual relationship

HYBRIDS

Many hybrids of the major project delivery systems exist and new ones are created every day. It is the owner's choice as to what delivery system to use for the project and, therefore, he or she can create a variation to any of the systems. For example, the owner may want to use an agency construction management system with a general contractor added to give the owner a single, competitively bid, lump sum contract for the construction of the project.

Figure 1.5 shows a model of the different parties that are involved in a hybrid project delivery system that has a general contractor added to an agency construction management system. Obviously, not all the parties are shown. The model is intended to illustrate the relationships that exist down through the project. The type of contract signed (in parentheses) is listed beneath the contractors.

FOR THIS TEXT

To avoid confusion, *the discussion in the remainder of the text will presume that an agency construction management project delivery system exists on the projects discussed.* Therefore, presume that a construction manager is brought on board at the inception of the project. Many examples will be used in the text that presume a construction management presence from predesign throughout the entire project.

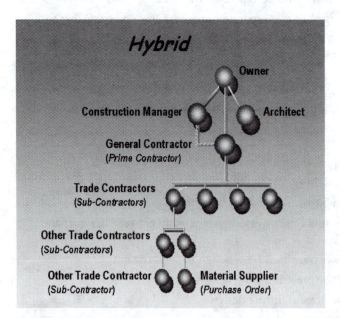

FIGURE 1.5
Hybrid project delivery system (general contractor added to agency construction management).

Therefore, it will be presumed throughout the text that a CM is on board from start to finish on the project and that the CM will perform the many typical preconstruction services associated with this delivery system.

TYPES OF CONSTRUCTION CONTRACTS

There are many different types of construction contracts, distinguished primarily by the method of determining the final contract price. Regardless of the method used, the goal is the same: quality construction completed on time and to all specifications for the lowest possible price while allowing the contractor an opportunity to make a fair profit. To encourage the parties to meet this goal, several different types of contracts have evolved (Fisk, 2003, p. 423).

The type of contract chosen may depend on several factors, including the identity and relationship, if any, of the owner and contractor; the completeness of the design and its complexity; the type of work being done; and the need or desire of competitive bidding (Fisk, 2003, p. 424).

It is important for the student to have a basic knowledge of the different types of contracts that are used in the construction industry before continuing in the text. The most frequently used contract types in construction consist of:

- Lump sum
- Guaranteed maximum price
- Unit price
- Cost plus a fee
- Time and material
- Combinations

LUMP SUM

The lump sum contract is also referred to as a stipulated sum or fixed price contract. It is the most commonly used type of contract because it offers the most protection and least risk for the owner. The following is a definition of the lump sum contract:

> Contractor agrees to perform work in accordance to the contract documents, regardless of difficulties encountered, for an exact fixed price.

Changes to the price of a lump sum contract must be agreed upon by the owner and the contractor and can sometimes become a point of contention. The architect's role is to represent the owner in these matters, and therefore he or she is often put in-between the two parties. Theoretically, the only time the price of the lump sum contract should change is if there is a change in the project's scope, such as the owner choosing a different material, encountering unforeseen solid rock, or an interference between two systems that requires rerouting of one of the systems. Because each change to the contract needs to be negotiated individually, this type of contract can lead to an adversarial relationship between the owner (and to some extent the architect representing the owner) and the contractor.

The contractor is locked-in to the price, regardless of difficulties. As an example, if the price of a material goes up that is part of the contract, the contractor would have to pay the difference—not the owner. If their crews are not as productive as they estimated and budgeted for, they will have to make up the difference. If the entire project ends up costing more than the contract amount, the contractor will have to pay for the difference from out of his or her own pocket. This is the main reason that this type of contract carries the greatest risk to the contractor and the least risk for the owner.

The following is a list of some of the general characteristics common to most lump sum contracts. However, it must be noted that, considering the particular circumstances of any given project and the imagination of the owner and contractor, the actual terms and conditions of a contract can vary widely.

Characteristics

- Greatest risk is with the contractor
- Total project cost is known before construction begins
- Contract price is based on known scope of work and completed design documents
- Usually competitively bid
- Selection criteria of contractor is based mostly on price
- Does not allow for fast-tracking with single lump sum contract
- Potential for adversarial relationship between owner and contractor exists
- Owner does not know the profit of the contractor

GUARANTEED MAXIMUM PRICE

The guaranteed maximum price contract is also referred to as a guaranteed max or GMP contract. It offers nearly the same protection and risk level to the owner as a lump sum contract, but greatly removes the potential for an adversarial relationship to develop between the owner and contractor. The selection of the contractor is based more on trust than on price. The following is a definition of the guaranteed maximum price contract:

> Contractor agrees to perform work in accordance to the contract documents, regardless of difficulties encountered, for an exact fixed maximum price.

A guaranteed maximum price contract is often used in combination with a cost plus contract, with the GMP contract being open book. *Open book* means that the owner sees all the contractor's costs of the project and, if the total project cost comes in below the maximum, the difference is split between the owner and the contractor. This type of contract is based on a more trusting relationship between the owner and the contractor and is usually negotiated, rather than competitively bid out.

Changes to the scope are handled in the same way as a lump sum contract and the contractor is still locked-in to the price, regardless of difficulties. If the project cost exceeds the maximum price, the contractor still pays for the difference.

The following is a list of some of the general characteristics common to most GMP contracts. However, it must be noted that considering the particular circumstances of any given project and the imagination of the owner and contractor, the actual terms and conditions of a contract can vary widely.

Characteristics

- Most of the risk is with the contractor
- Total project "ceiling" cost is known before construction begins
- Contract price is based on the known scope of work and completed design documents
- Usually negotiated contract

- Selection criteria of contractor is based primarily on trust and secondarily on price
- Typically does not allow for fast-tracking
- Contract is based on trust; therefore, there is a low potential for an adversarial relationship to develop between the owner and contractor
- Owner knows the overhead and profit of the contractor since the contract is open book

UNIT PRICE

A unit price is a price per unit of a material, which includes the purchase and installation of that particular material. The unit price includes the material and labor, equipment, tools, or anything else necessary to install it. An example of a unit price is $23 per square yard of asphalt paving or $68 per ton of gravel.

A unit price contract can be used on any type of project but is particularly suited for projects whose quantities of materials are difficult to measure. The classic example is a roadwork job where the exact amount of materials such as earthwork, gravel, asphalt, and so forth is difficult to determine until they are actually installed. The contractor will bid on the project to perform various units of work based on estimated quantities of materials taken-off by the design engineer. The following is a definition of the unit price contract:

> Contractor agrees to perform units of work in accordance to the contract documents, regardless of difficulties encountered, for an exact fixed unit price for each unit of work.

The unit price contract is very similar to the lump sum contract in that the contractor is locked-in to exact unit prices of work, regardless of difficulties encountered, and changes to the project's scope are handled the same way. If the actual unit price exceeds the contracted unit price, the contractor pays for the difference out of his or her pocket. However, in the unit price contract, the total cost of the project is not known until the project is complete. This is a risk that the owner takes with this type of contract, relying only on the estimated total project cost that is based on the unit prices and the estimated quantities of work to be performed. As quantities are installed, the actual installation quantities are recorded and the actual contract price is determined from quantities actually installed.

The unit price contract may be used on projects that are not completely designed. A contractor, for example, does not have to see a completed design to lock into a unit price of work. The contractor will want to have an idea of the overall scope of the project to be able to gauge the economies of scale. For instance, a contractor would quote a different price for 200 feet of guardrail installation versus 2 miles of guardrail or quote a different price for 2 miles of guardrail on a flat rural road versus 2 miles of rail installed on a winding mountain pass. The greatest asset of the unit price contract is that it allows for competitively bid prices on a project whose design is not complete and whose scope is only broadly defined. For that reason, this type of contract is usually competitively bid.

The following is a list of some of the general characteristics common to most unit price contracts. However, it must be noted that considering the particular circumstances of any given project and the imagination of the owner and contractor, the actual terms and conditions of a contract can vary widely.

Characteristics

- Shared risk between the owner and the contractor
- Total project cost is *not* known before construction begins

- Contract unit prices are based on a broadly defined scope of work but not always on completed design documents
- Usually competitively bid
- Selection criteria of contractor is based mostly on price
- Allows for fast-tracking with competitively bid prices
- Potential for adversarial relationship between owner and contractor exists
- Owner does not know the profit of the contractor
- Allows for competitively bid prices on uncompleted design
- Field verification of installed quantities is required

COST PLUS A FEE

The cost plus a fee contract is often simply referred to as a cost plus contract. It is fundamentally different from the three contract types discussed so far. The following is a definition of the cost plus a fee contract:

> Contractor agrees to perform work in accordance to the contract documents and is reimbursed for its actual costs and paid a fee for this service.

Most of the risk falls to the owner with the cost plus contract. The contractor is reimbursed for all actual costs of performing the work, regardless of the difficulties that might be encountered. Therefore, if the price of a material goes up or if the contractor's crew is not as productive as was estimated, the contractor is still reimbursed for the actual cost. If the entire project ends up costing more than what was estimated, the owner will pay for the difference. To help alleviate some of the risk from the owner, a cost plus contract may often also have a guaranteed maximum price added to it. This gives the owner a worst-case ceiling cost to plan by and establishes an additional check and balance for controlling the project cost.

Like the GMP, the cost plus contract is open book. This type of contracting relationship is based on trust and the contract is usually negotiated. The contractor's fee is based either on a percentage of the total reimbursed cost or is a fixed amount.

The following is a list of some of the general characteristics common to most cost plus a fee contracts. However, it must be noted that considering the particular circumstances of any given project and the imagination of the owner and contractor, the actual terms and conditions of a contract can vary widely.

Characteristics

- Most of the risk is with the owner
- Total project cost is *not* known before construction begins; however, the contract may have a GMP added to it
- Contract is based on a broadly defined scope of work but not always on completed design documents
- Usually negotiated contract
- Selection criteria of contractor is based mostly on trust
- Allows for fast-tracking
- Contract is based on trust; therefore, there is a low potential for an adversarial relationship to develop between the owner and contractor
- Owner knows the fee paid to the contractor

■ Fee is a percentage of actual reimbursed costs or a fixed amount

TIME AND MATERIAL

The time and material contract is often simply referred to as a T&M contract. The following is a definition of the T&M contract:

> Contractor agrees to perform work in accordance to the contract documents and is paid a marked-up price for work performed.

The owner takes the greatest risk of the five contract types with time and material. Since the contractor is paid a marked-up price for work performed, even the profit is guaranteed. For example, the contractor may buy a metal stud for $1.70 per stud but charge the owner $2.25 per stud. Or the contractor may pay the carpenter $17.00 per hour to install metal studs but charge the owner $25.00 per hour for the carpenter's time. If the price of studs goes up, the contractor raises the price to the owner, or if the carpenter takes a bit longer to install the stud, the contractor still gets paid for the carpenter's time regardless of the productivity rate. The contractor's profit is already built into the prices. The owner has very little control over project costs with this type of contract.

Why would an owner ever use T&M? Sometimes cost is less important than other issues, such as time or safety. When a power plant goes down unexpectedly, the utility begins to immediately lose money with every minute it is not generating electricity.

Unlike the cost plus contract, time and material is not open book. The owner has no idea what the contractor pays for time and material. This type of contracting relationship is based on trust and the contract is usually negotiated.

The following is a list of some of the general characteristics common to most time and material contracts. However, it must be noted that considering the particular circumstances of any given project and the imagination of the owner and contractor, the actual terms and conditions of a contract can vary widely.

Characteristics

- Greatest risk is with the owner
- Total project cost is *not* known before construction begins
- Contract can be based on unknown scope and absent design documents
- Usually negotiated contract
- Selection criteria of contractor is based mostly on trust
- Allows for fast-tracking
- Contract is based on trust; therefore, there is a low potential for an adversarial relationship to develop between the owner and contractor
- Contractor is paid a marked-up price for work performed.

COMBINATIONS

These contract types are sometimes combined together to achieve a particular arrangement for the owner. The cost plus contract is often combined with a guaranteed maximum price contained within it. Lump sum contracts will often have a portion of the work performed using unit prices, cost plus, or time and material. As mentioned earlier, considering the particular circumstances of any given project and the imagination of the owner and contractor, the actual terms and conditions of a contract, including combinations of different types of contracts, can vary widely.

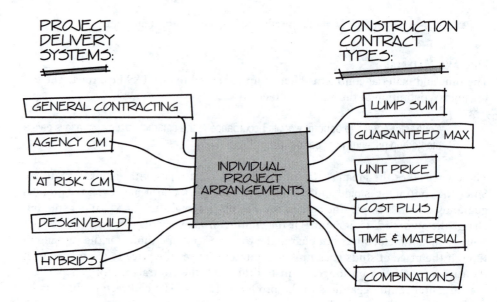

FIGURE 1.6
Individual project arrangements.

INDIVIDUAL PROJECT ARRANGEMENTS

Every project is unique with its own contractual needs and idiosyncrasies that may dictate a specific individual arrangement for that project. Therefore, it is important to note that any project delivery system can be used in conjunction with any one (or more) of the construction contract types to form various individual project arrangements.

Figure 1.6 shows how different project delivery systems will join different construction contract types to form individual project arrangements.

As stated earlier, the phrase *construction industry* encompasses the entire scope of the industry including all design and engineering professionals, material suppliers, involved governmental agencies, and related organizations, as well as the many companies that perform and manage the actual construction. When drawn together for an individual project, there may be hundreds of different companies working on a construction project from the owner down through the smallest material supplier. This next section will define the many parties that are commonly involved in a project and illustrate the relationships that exist between them. These parties can be grouped into the following:

- The project team
- Owner groups
- Subconsultants
- Trade contractors
- Other trade contractors
- Material suppliers

THE PROJECT TEAM

The project team meets regularly throughout the life of the project. Various other parties may also be included on the project team on a regular basis or brought in for their expertise, specifically to address a particular issue. The project team is typically made up of the owner, architect, and builder. The primary members include:

- Owner
- Architect
- Builder (CM/GC)

OWNER

The owner is the most important party on the project—and not only because the owner pays the bills. The owner is the client and customer of the construction industry, and sets the tone for the project. He or she has to live with the project long after the rest of the project team is gone. There are three main owner objectives on every project: time, cost, and quality. The owner wants to minimize the construction time and cost of the project while maintaining the quality that was specified in the contract documents.

There is an old joke in the industry: "Good, fast, and cheap—pick any two!" There is some truth to the joke because, on some projects, one of the three owner objectives may suffer to achieve the other two. Over the last few decades the construction industry has done a better job at satisfying the owner as it has shifted from a contracting industry to more of a construction management industry.

The owners of construction projects can be divided into two distinct groups: public and private.

Public

A public owner can be defined as the owner of a project completely or partially funded with public funds. Public funds would be any funds raised or levied by a public entity, such as taxes, fees, and so forth. Examples of public owners are federal, state, city, county, and township governments, school boards, park commissions, transit authorities, and so on.

Public projects must follow open bidding procedures. Each of the various public governments passes bidding laws to be used for their jurisdiction. These bidding procedures are intended to ensure the complete fairness of the bid; since the money for a public project comes from the public, everyone in the public should have a fair and equal chance to be awarded the job. All bids are publicly open and the job is awarded to the *lowest responsive and responsible bidder* (the exact award criteria may change slightly from jurisdiction to jurisdiction).

Additionally, public projects are often subject to prevailing wage laws, which state that individuals working on these public projects must be paid a wage that *prevails* in the area (a wage that would be typical for that type of work in that area). Over the years, the prevailing wage has aligned itself with the local union wages. Today, most prevailing wage laws use the local union wage scales. The minimum wage that is in law today, and periodically increased, was first passed by the federal government as part of the Davis-Bacon Act in 1931. Eventually most state and local governments passed their own prevailing wage laws. In the past ten years, prevailing wage laws have come under scrutiny. Opponents of the laws argue that the prevailing wage, as set by the union scale, is artificially high since union construction encompasses only approximately 18 percent of all construction. They state that it adds approximately 20 percent to the total cost of a project. Some of these laws have been abolished.

Another requirement of public projects in many jurisdictions is the use of *set-aside packages,* an affirmative action policy intended to help minority-owned and/or female-owned businesses that have often been shut out of construction awards in the past receive construction contract awards. With this policy, the project team reserves certain contract packages to be bid on by only minority-owned and/or female-owned businesses. The set-aside packages represent a percentage of the total project, often ranging from 10 to 20 percent. Like the prevailing wage laws, in recent years set-aside requirements have also come under scrutiny. Opponents argue that they are a type of reverse discrimination.

Private

A private owner can be defined as the owner of a project completely funded with private funds. Private funds would be any funds that *are not* raised or levied from the public. Examples of private owners are individuals, corporations, utilities, or institutions such as hospitals, private schools, and so forth.

The many rules, laws, and procedures that apply to public projects *do not* apply to private projects. Private project bids do not have to be publicly open. They do not have to award the job to the lowest bidder. They do not have to pay prevailing wages or utilize set-aside packages. However, many companies, particularly larger corporations, use set-aside packages as a course of company policy.

ARCHITECT

The architect heads the design team and is ultimately responsible for preparing the contract documents that include, among other things, the drawings and specifications. The architect, one of the three primary members of the project team, is sometimes referred to as the *associate*. The architect serves as an advocate for the owner throughout the project.

The architect, usually the first firm hired by the owner when the owner gets an idea for a project, guides the owner through the predesign phase of the project, helping the owner identify their needs and wants and develop the program for the project. The architect may develop the early budget and schedule for the project if a construction manager is not present.

Architects rarely design the entire project in-house. Most of the engineering design on the project is subbed-out to engineering firms. Other specialty design elements, such as fire protection, acoustics, telecommunications, and so on, are usually performed by other design firms, as well. These other design and engineering firms are typically referred to as subconsultants.

The architect usually performs about half of the project design. About half of the pages of the job drawings are *A pages,* which stands for Architectural. The subconsultants design the remaining pages.

During the early design stages, the architect performs the schematic design. Decisions made during this phase include the overall shape or *footprint* of the building, potential locations for the building on the site, the number of stories, and ideas for the exterior skin materials. Some interior building spaces may be roughly laid out. Additionally, the architect will be discussing choices for the structural, mechanical, and electrical systems with the subconsultants.

The next phase of design, called design development, is where the design is refined and developed further—hence the name. At the start of design development, the design is sketchy and still very open to change. The architect completes much of the interior space design, begins to outline the specifications, and addresses the many safety measures for the building, in addition to supervising the design being performed by the subconsultants. By the end of design development, most of the design decisions are made and the majority of the design yet to be completed is the actual drafting of the documents.

The final design phase is called the construction document phase. In this phase the architect completes the drawings and specifications and collates them with the design performed by the subconsultants into one complete set of bidding documents.

The architect performs other nondesign duties throughout the project, including ensuring the quality of construction through periodic inspections and supervising material testing. If a construction manager is not present on the project team, the architect will perform many of the duties normally handled by the construction manager. Some of these duties include supervising the bid and award of the construction contracts, processing contractor payments, estimating the construction phase, handling change orders, and monitoring the budget and schedule.

BUILDER (CM/GC)

The final primary member of the project team is the builder. The builder of the project may be either a construction manager (CM) or general contractor (GC), depending on which project delivery system the owner chooses for the project. Project delivery systems were discussed in the previous chapter. If the owner chooses construction management for the delivery system, the construction manager will become involved in the project early on, often before the design begins. If the owner chooses general contracting, the general contractor typically does not become involved in the project until the time of the bid, after the design is complete.

There are many differences and some similarities between construction management and general contracting, as discussed in detail in the previous chapter. The

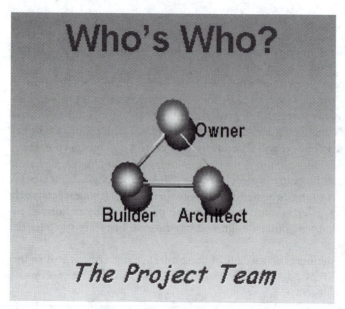

FIGURE 2.1
Primary parties of the project team.

construction manager and general contractor perform much of the same work during the construction phase of the project. They both have knowledge of the entire construction process and both are responsible for running the job during construction. However, the construction manager becomes involved in the project long before the general contractor. The construction manager lends its expertise throughout the predesign and design phases of the project and acts as an agent, or representative, of the owner.

Figure 2.1 shows the three *primary* parties that make up the project team.

OWNER GROUPS

The owner of a project may be represented by more than one entity. The following list shows four examples of different owner groups, all of whom may be involved in the project in some capacity. You cannot expect these different groups to always speak with one voice. For this reason it is important that one individual be assigned as the spokesperson for the owner and be the liaison to the project team.

- Tenant
- Board
- End users
- Owner's representative

TENANT

A tenant is an individual or company that rents or leases a space from the owner of the building. For example, it could be a person that rents an apartment on a month-to-month basis or a large company that signs a twenty-year lease for multiple floors of a high-rise office building. In the latter case, the tenant would most likely be involved in the design of their space and might possibly be involved in the overall design of the building. Some tenants who are leasing large portions of a building can negotiate for separate, dedicated entrances, special parking arrangements, and so forth. If a tenant is

FIGURE 2.2
The demonstration kitchen of the Midwest Culinary Institute at Cincinnati State while under construction.

leasing the majority of a building, he or she could be involved in all aspects of the building's design. In this case the tenant may have as much clout as the project's owner.

BOARD

Most companies and institutions have a board of directors or board of trustees that help guide and direct the company or institution. Since a building project is such a large undertaking, the boards are usually somehow tied into the approval process. This is important to know for planning and scheduling the project's design. The design of the project is reviewed and approved at three or four different intervals during the design. Since boards meet only monthly, or sometimes less often than that, it is important to try to align the various approvals with the board meetings.

Additionally, the boards are going to be very interested in monitoring the budget and schedule as the project is designed and built.

END USERS

As mentioned earlier, the owner has to live with the project long after the rest of the project team is gone. So how do you ensure that the owner, in the end, gets the best project? Architects are very good at helping owners determine what they need and want in a project, but they must also rely on representative groups of end users from the owner's company to help provide input into the project. As an example, the maintenance and operation unit of a company would be asked to provide significant input into the various building systems.

The Advanced Technology and Learning Center at Cincinnati State was designed to house the college's Midwest Culinary Institute and includes eight teaching kitchens and a 200-seat demonstration kitchen/auditorium (see Figure 2.2). The subconsultant brought in to design the kitchens worked with the institute's faculty, on a daily basis at times, to "get it right."

Owners are wise to realize that a high level of involvement throughout the predesign, design, and construction of the project will help guarantee a very high level of satisfaction with the end product.

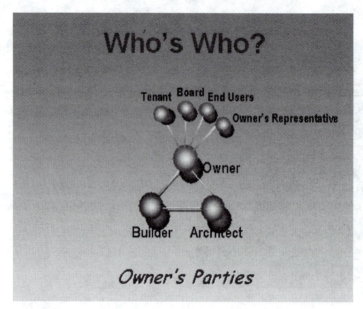

FIGURE 2.3
The project team with the owner groups added.

Owner's Representative

The typical project owner has little knowledge of design and construction. However, their investment in a project can be sizable, often the largest investment the company will make. For this reason, they may decide to hire an owner's representative to advise them throughout the project.

The owner's representative, often referred to simply as the *owner's rep,* is an individual or company that is hired directly by the owner to work strictly and exclusively on behalf of the owner throughout the project. While one of the duties of the architect is to serve as the owner's advocate throughout the project, and the *agency* construction manager serves as an agent of the owner, some owners find it appropriate to hire their own representative that works directly for them and is paid directly by them to ensure that they receive nonbiased advice.

In addition to providing nonbiased advice, the owner's representative can represent the owner in project meetings. Designing and building a project is a long and time-consuming commitment for any owner. There are numerous meetings that the owner must attend to ensure the success of the project. The owner's rep can attend many of these meetings in place of the owner, thereby saving the owner significant time.

The cost of hiring an owner's rep can be viewed as an extra cost to the project for an additional layer of management. However, that cost might quickly be recouped by averting one or two bad decisions, let alone the additional time the owner has recouped. The owner's rep fee on a large, multimillion dollar project may be less than one-half percent of the total project cost. On smaller projects, the cost might range from one-half percent up to 2 or 3 percent, depending on the duties assigned.

Figure 2.3 shows the project team with the additional parties that represent the owner of the project.

SUBCONSULTANTS

As mentioned earlier, architects rarely design the entire project in-house. Most of the engineering design on the project is subbed-out to engineering firms and other specialty design firms. These design and engineering firms are typically referred to as subconsultants. The architect usually performs about half of the design on a project. About half of the pages of the job drawings are **A** pages, which stand for Architectural. The subconsultants design the remaining pages.

Additionally, a project may require specialty design work in areas such as acoustics, telecommunications, culinary, fire protection, information technology, and so forth. Sometimes one firm may perform design in multiple areas, such as a mechanical engineer designing the HVAC, plumbing, and fire protection or an electrical designer performing the electrical and telecommunications design.

Subconsultants work under the direction of the architect and report directly to them: therefore the architect typically hires the subconsultants. Occasionally on some jobs, the owner will ask to have input into the hiring of the subconsultants, but in general, it is better to let the architect have total control, since the architect is ultimately responsible for the entire design.

The following is a list of some subconsultants that are commonly found on most projects.

- Site
- Structural
- HVAC
- Electrical
- Plumbing
- Interiors
- Other specialty design

SITE

The site engineer designs everything outside of the footprint of the building. The *footprint* can be thought of as the building's perimeter. This design includes the placement of the building on the site, the layout of the parking, and the design of the earthwork (cut and fill) required. The site engineer also locates and designs the utility runs from the tie-in to within five feet of the building. Utilities include electrical, gas, water, sanitary sewer, storm sewer, telecommunication lines including cable and phone, and so on. Landscaping and walkways may be designed by site engineers if they have landscape architecture capabilities; otherwise, this might be performed by an individual landscape architectural firm or by the architect. The construction work that results from this design is often referred to as *sitework*.

STRUCTURAL

The structural engineer designs the foundation and superstructure of the building. The building's foundation includes the foundation walls, footings, and any piles, piers, or caissons the footings may rest on. In addition, the foundation may require retaining walls and specialized drainage systems.

The superstructure is also called the *frame,* or skeleton of the building. One of the early decisions the project team has to make, usually with the guidance of the structural designer, is what type of system should be used for the building frame. The two standard choices for buildings are structural steel or reinforced concrete. Wood frame construction is usually not a viable choice for buildings. However, although wood has been the predominant material for residential frame construction for years, metal studs have recently become a popular alternative to wood frame construction.

When the structural engineer designs the building frame, he or she will calculate loads and select appropriate members for the structure. The design of the connections is usually performed by the fabricator's shop, which also physically produces the connections. The connection drawings, referred to as *shop drawings,* are sent to the structural engineer for approval. It is the structural engineer who stamps all drawings and, therefore, is ultimately responsible for all structural design.

HVAC

The HVAC system, which stands for heating, ventilation, and air conditioning, consists of the facilities and equipment necessary to produce and distribute heating, cooling, and ventilating air throughout the building. While the method of production may vary with different systems, there is almost always a need for vast distribution lines of ductwork to carry air throughout the building. The HVAC is a significant part of the design and construction of a project and, combined with the other mechanicals and electrical, usually comprise about 40 percent of the project.

One of the early decisions in the project design is the choice for the HVAC system. This choice needs to be made early due to its potential impact on other components of the design. For example, if chillers are used, the decision has to be made early on as to their placement. If they are to be placed on the building's roof, structural considerations must be made to account for this weight. Additionally, a false wall may be needed to hide the chillers from view. This will force changes to be made to the design to accommodate the wall.

ELECTRICAL

The major components of the electrical design include the power requirements of the building, the power risers throughout the building, the circuit feeds within the building, and the lighting design. The electrical design must also take into account the need to provide power to the many other pieces of equipment designed and/or provided by others, such as HVAC equipment, office equipment, kitchen equipment, and other equipment particular to the owner or the use of that building.

The electrical designer may also design phone and cable wiring, other telecommunications, security, and exterior lighting, to name a few.

PLUMBING

Plumbing design is often referred to as mechanical design, as is the HVAC design, and one engineering firm will often design both. The designer is usually referred to as the mechanical engineer.

Plumbing design includes all supply side plumbing, as well as fixtures and equipment throughout the building and the disposal of that water through the sanitary piping and into the sewer. The design of the floor drains and roof drains are also included. The design of the supply of natural gas to various equipment and the proper flue ventilation from the equipment is usually performed by the mechanical engineer.

In addition to the standard piping found in buildings, hospitals and industrial facilities require tremendous amounts of additional piping to supply various types of fluids and gases. For example, nearly every hospital room built has an oxygen line running to it. Industrial facilities such as chemical plants, power plants, and paper mills have miles and miles of different types of piping running throughout them.

INTERIORS

One of the last project components to be designed is the building's interior. Occasionally, the interior design is not included in the scope of the original design, and the interior of the building may be left as a shell until a tenant is brought on board; that space is then designed and built-out. Alternatively, the interior design might be combined with the selection of furnishings, fixtures, and equipment. This package of design is referred to as furnishings, fixtures, and equipment (FF&E).

Regardless, the interior design is comprised of selecting colors and materials to provide the finish for all floors, walls, and ceilings. It may also include the selection of interior furniture such as office desks and chairs, filing cabinets, and so forth; mounted fixtures; and office equipment.

OTHER SPECIALTY DESIGN

In addition to the design scope previously detailed and commonly found on most projects, there may be a need for a specialized design that is not common to most projects. Some examples of specialty design include fire suppression, security, acoustical, telecommunications, culinary, environmental, landscape, and many more.

These specialized designs must be integrated into the total design effort to prevent interferences and conflicts. A good example to illustrate this is acoustical design. While considering the acoustics of any project is important, it usually does not require a special design. The arrangement and finishes of most spaces provide for adequate acoustics. However, if you are designing an auditorium as part of a project, you may want to bring in an acoustical designer to design the shape, finishes, and sound system for that space. This design may affect other elements of the design. For instance, when air moves through a duct at a high rate of speed, it makes a lot of noise. To move air with less noise, you must slow it down. Therefore, to move the same amount of air at a slower rate, the volume (and therefore the duct size) has to increase. Running larger duct may require greater floor-to-floor height, which would, in turn, trigger other design changes.

Another example is the design of kitchens in a building. Kitchens require the obvious need for additional plumbing such as supply and waste water piping and floor drains. They require additional electrical wiring for equipment, special finishes such as tile, and different HVAC loads. Beyond this, kitchens may call for other special equipment and requirements such as a walk-in cooler, which normally necessitates a recessed slab as well as other design considerations.

Figure 2.4 shows the project team with added subconsultants that are commonly used. Notice that the subconsultants are branched off of the architect since they work directly for the architect.

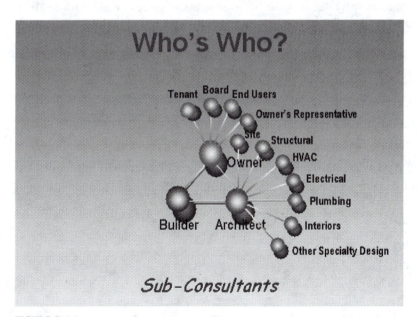

FIGURE 2.4
The project team with the subconsultants added.

TRADE CONTRACTORS

A trade contractor performs a particular type of work or a type of work related to a particular trade. For example, an electrical contractor is a trade contractor that performs electrical work. Trade contractors are sometimes referred to as *specialty contractors* because they perform a special or particular type of work. More often, however, trade contractors are referred to as subs or subcontractors because they sign a subcontract with the general contractor. This name may not be correct.

Strictly speaking, a subcontractor is a contractor that is in contract with another contractor. Therefore, on a project that is using general contracting as the project delivery system, trade contractors usually are subcontractors to the general contractor and rightly could be referred to as subs. However, on a project that is using construction management as the project delivery system, the trade contractors are in direct contract with the owner and, strictly speaking, are *prime contractors*. If this is confusing, refer back to the section on project delivery systems in Chapter 1.

Regardless of what they are called, trade contractors are the front line of the construction industry. They perform the work. That is, they and their crews actually build the job. They have the greatest expertise in their particular field of work—greater than the GC/CM and greater than the architect. They know the materials and methods used in their field and stay current with the related codes and standards. They are the best source for pricing, and have the clearest perspective on the future of their trade. They are often brought into the project design to help solve a problem because of their expertise. They are also often asked to perform constructability review and value engineering on projects.

Trade contractors are the best source to turn to when confronted with a problem. A good example of the value of their expertise is demonstrated in Chapter 8. In Chapter 8 the Delhi Medical Building is scheduled, then revised in an effort to compress the schedule. With the input of the electrical, plumbing, and foundation trade contractors, a plan was devised that took twenty-one *workdays* out of the schedule in one area alone, all stemming from their detailed knowledge of equipment, design, and construction processes.

Trade contractors also take on most of the risk of the job. The owner passes most of its risk to the general contractor, who then passes most of it on to trade contractors.

Trade contractors will often sub-out (subcontract out) some of their work to other trade contractors; in turn, that trade contractor may sub-out part of that work. This may continue until the original trade contractor's work is spread out through four or five (or more) contractors. These relationships are illustrated in more detail in the next section.

The following is a list of trade contractors that are commonly found on most projects:

- Sitework
- Foundation
- Structure
- Curtain wall
- Roofing
- Masonry
- Interiors
- Plumbing
- Electrical
- HVAC

Figure 2.5 shows the project team with some of the trade contractors that are commonly found on most projects. Notice that these contractors are branched off of the

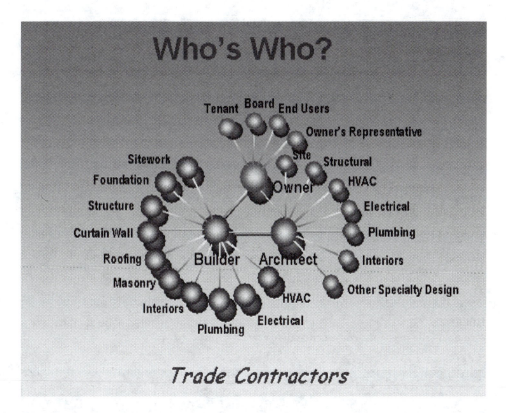

FIGURE 2.5
The project team with the trade contractors added.

builder, indicating that they work for the builder. This would be different on a job that is using agency construction management, as discussed in the previous chapter.

OTHER TRADE CONTRACTORS

As previously mentioned, a trade contractor will often sub-out some of the work to other trade contractors, and in turn, those trade contractors might sub-out part of that work. This may continue until the original trade contractor's work is spread out through four or five (or more) contractors. To fully understand "who's who" on a project, you have to understand this relationship. Here is an example.

> A foundation trade contractor is awarded the contract for the foundation of a building and has signed a subcontract with the builder. Included in the foundation contract is the shoring for the foundation. Since the foundation contractor does not do shoring, they sub this work out to a shoring company. However, part of the shoring work is the excavation. Since the shoring contractor does not do excavation, they sub the excavation work out to an excavating company. But part of the excavation work is to truck in gravel, and the excavating contractor does not own the trucks to do this. Therefore, the excavating contractor subs out the gravel hauling to a trucking company. And finally, the trucking company purchases the gravel from a gravel yard.

This example demonstrates the extent to which work on a project may be subbed-out. Figure 2.6 shows the *sub tree* that can be drawn from the previous example.

The following is a list of other trade contractors that are commonly found on projects. While this group of trade contractors are shown as subs in Figure 2.7 to the trade

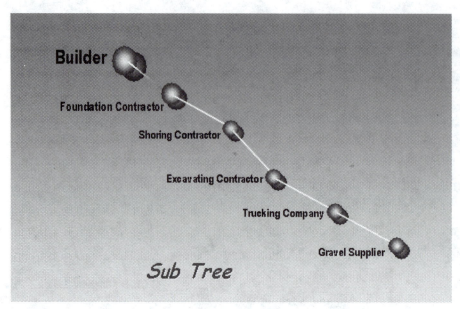

FIGURE 2.6
A common sub tree in the construction industry.

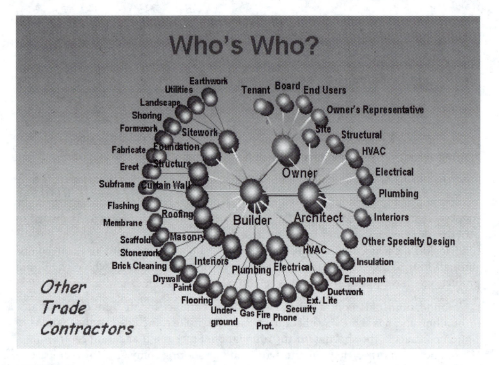

FIGURE 2.7
Other trade contractors as subcontractors to the original trade contractors.

contractors previously listed, they could also serve as a subcontractor working directly for the builder, or even as a prime contractor in direct contract with the owner.

Earthwork	Landscaping
Utilities	Shoring

Formwork	Flooring
Steel fabrication	Underground plumbing
Steel erection	Gas piping
Subframe	Fire protection
Flashing	Phone wiring
Membrane	Security
Scaffolding	Exterior lighting
Stonework	Ductwork
Brick cleaning	Install equipment
Drywall	Insulation
Painting	

Figure 2.7 shows the project team with the other trade contractors added as subcontractors to the original group of trade contractors.

MATERIAL SUPPLIERS

Material suppliers make up a large majority of the parties involved in any project. This becomes evident when you consider that the typical project will have numerous trade contractors and each trade contractor has multiple material suppliers. Material suppliers might also provide equipment and tools for rent or purchase such as lifting equipment, welding machines, scaffolding, and so on.

Approximately 50 percent of the direct cost of a construction project is spent on materials. Most materials for the job are purchased by the trade contractor who is contracted to install the material and, therefore, are part of the contract.

Some material items are produced specifically for the project and require careful planning and scheduling to ensure their delivery in time for installation. These items are referred to as *long lead items*. For example, if the frame of the building is to be built with structural steel, the steel frame members must be fabricated before being delivered to the job. Each piece must be produced in the fab shop with the appropriate connections, so when they are delivered to the job, they can be quickly erected. The fabrication cycle will take ten to fifteen weeks or longer in busy times.

Windows are usually produced specifically for the job and often require up to ten weeks for delivery. If the windows include special glass such as color-tinted glass or *low-E* glass, the delivery time could easily double. The project team must be aware of these long lead items and plan accordingly.

Other long lead items include brick; major pieces of equipment like air handlers, transformers, and switchgear; and anything that is custom produced for the job such as carpet, tile, or window coverings.

Figure 2.8 completes the image of who's who on a typical project.

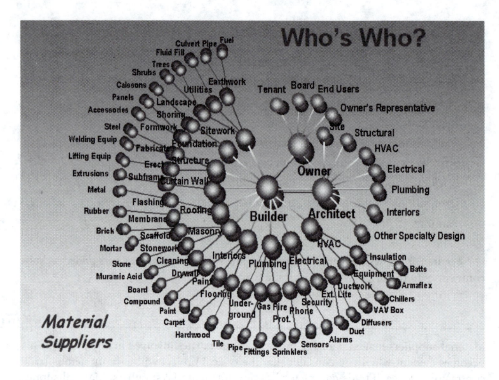

FIGURE 2.8
Material suppliers added to complete the image of who's who in the construction industry.

CHAPTER 3
What Is a Project?

A *project* can be defined in many different ways. Projects and the use of planning and scheduling can be abundantly found outside the world of construction. For our purpose, the discussion will be limited to construction projects. Most construction projects have the following similar characteristics:

- Construction projects include some type of physical work. It may consist of only the demolition of a building or the clearing of land, but it normally includes the building of some type of structure.
- The physical work is performed in accordance to designed construction documents that have been approved by the jurisdiction where the work is taking place.
- Each project has defined goals and objectives established by the owner and project team and are reflected in the construction documents that are intended to meet the needs and wants of the owner.
- The project has a defined start and finish based on its goals and objectives.
- The project normally has a target budget that may or may not be fixed or guaranteed.
- Each project follows a similar life cycle as it evolves from its conception (when the owner gets an idea) through to its completion.

EVOLUTION OF THE PROJECT

Each project follows a similar life cycle as it evolves from its conception (when the owner gets an idea) through to its completion, grand opening, and day-to-day operation. The evolution of a project can be divided into the six phases listed below. These phases are routinely separated into two distinct groups: *preconstruction* and *construction,* since the project is typically viewed in terms of these two construction stages. It is important for the reader of the text to understand this division and to know what phases they include.

Preconstruction Phases
- Predesign phase
- Design phase
- Bidding phase

Construction Phases
- Construction phase
- Start-up phase
- Grand opening and property management phase

PREDESIGN PHASE

The predesign phase of the project is often overlooked in discussions concerning the project. However, it is an extremely important time relative to the success of the project. If a project does not meet its schedule or budget goals, quite often the reason or reasons can be traced back to events of its design or predesign phase.

In the predesign phase, the owner will begin the preliminary evaluation of both the project's technical and economic feasibility.

A project starts when an owner gets an idea. It could be a married couple planning to build a home, a manufacturer building an addition onto their production plant, or a city council deciding to build a park. The owner may want to perform market research to help determine if there is a need for the project. The market research may be performed directly by the owner or by a hired research firm.

Once a clear need is established, the owner will begin the process of evaluating the different aspects of the project. The owner typically does not have the expertise in-house to make these evaluations, so they will enlist the services of various professionals for help. Usually the first firm hired is the architect. If the project is going to use a construction manager, he or she would be hired soon after the architect.

The architect is very experienced at directing the activities of the predesign phase and particularly skilled to begin and direct the program evaluation. The program evaluation is defined below.

> The program evaluation, often referred to simply as the program, is a formal process undertaken to determine the goals and objectives of the project and to identify the needs and wants of the owner.

Architects have been trained to perform this exercise. The first step is to gather input from the owner.

It is important to gather input from as large of a spectrum of end users as possible. This will ensure that many different points of view are heard. Of course, those many different points of view must eventually be honed into a consistent plan that everyone can agree too. That is the challenge of creating a successful program.

A successful program evaluation will also include an assessment of the existing facilities if they are at all related to the new project. This system-wide assessment will provide a complete view of the owner's needs and wants and possibly provide innovative solutions and a more efficient project design. Figures 3.1 and 3.2 show two examples of a classroom utilization study. Figure 3.1 shows utilization by day, then by hour, for a particular classroom while Figure 3.2 shows a matrix of the utilization of four different rooms by the courses taught in those rooms each week.

The program is developed from the general to the specific. Initially, the major goals and objectives of the project are defined. Eventually, when complete, the program will list very specific project parameters. For example, a goal of a project might be to create more office space. When complete, the program will list the total square footage intended for the various uses of the project and how it is to be divided into individual spaces.

Figure 3.3 is a graphical comparison of spaces dedicated to various uses in a program evaluation prepared toward the end of the programming process. The smaller spaces to the right represent individual spaces of the various program uses. The larger square spaces on the left show the accumulation of the smaller spaces into one mass per program use. This allows the owner to quickly visualize utilization of the program as it currently exists. This type of graphic can be enlightening. A quick look reveals that the largest space is dedicated to the *IT: Technology Center.*

In conclusion, the program evaluation is usually not completed during the predesign phase. The program continues to evolve as more project information is gathered.

At this point in the project, the land for the project may not be identified. The owner might seek the help of a realtor, attorney, and/or planner to investigate different poten-

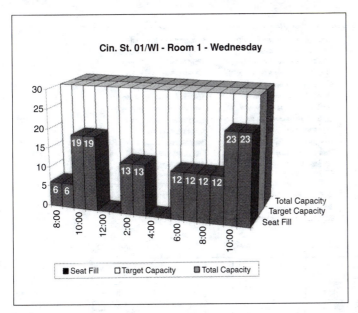

FIGURE 3.1
Program evaluation showing room utilization by day, then by hour, of a particular college classroom.
(Burt Hill Kosar Rittelmann Associates)

tial sites. If the site is known, it must be properly zoned and free of legal and environmental issues or problems. If the owner owns or controls the land, this information may already be known.

During the predesign phase, some preliminary design takes place. There is a rough idea of the size, number of floors, and mass of the building. From this an estimated square footage of the building's area can be calculated. With these very basic design decisions, preliminary budgets and plans can be developed. The first draft of a feasibility study is created along with the first draft of the project plan. The feasibility study will measure project benefits (revenues) against project costs. The project plan provides an overall strategy to accomplish the project goals and addresses issues such as fast-tracking the project, selection of the project delivery system, and potential milestone dates for the project. At this point, it would be too early to start to develop a detailed construction schedule.

The owner will consult with its banker and accountant to help determine if the project is feasible and worth pursuing. Both the feasibility study and the project plan are necessary to take the project to the next phase, which is the start of the project design. This is an important juncture, because the design of the project often costs between 5 percent to 10 percent of the total project budget. The owner will not want to commit to the design—and its cost—without a firm belief that the project will eventually be built.

To help determine the feasibility of the project, a budget must be developed. The accuracy of the budget is directly correlated to two factors: the amount of information known about the project at the time the budget was estimated and the amount of time spent performing the estimate. During the predesign phase there is very little information known about the project. It is estimated that by the end of the predesign phase, maybe **5 percent** of the project information is known. However, the owner needs to have a good idea about the budgeted cost of the job before deciding whether to proceed on with the project into the design phase. This is the *classic dilemma* of the owner—and project team—during the entire preconstruction phase of the project.

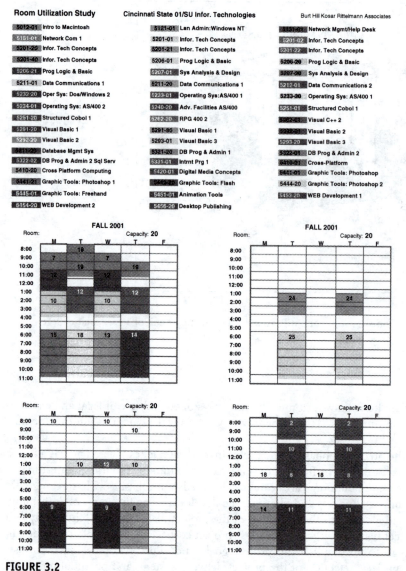

FIGURE 3.2

Program evaluation matrix used to analyze the room utilization of four different college classrooms by the courses taught in those rooms each week.
(Burt Hill Kosar Rittelmann Associates)

Since there is very little information known, the construction manager, or architect if a CM is not being used, will use his or her past experiences and unit cost(s) to estimate the budget at this time. A *unit cost* is a single, all-encompassing cost per item or unit. For example, a typical unit cost per square foot for a hospital is approximately $250 per square foot, where a square foot is equal to one square foot of floor space. A budget will be developed by the end of the predesign phase and will have an accuracy somewhere in the neighborhood of plus or minus **25 percent**.

Table 3.1 describes some common activities that typically occur during the predesign phase of the project and lists the involved parties of each activity, showing the lead (responsible) party for each activity first. At the bottom of the table is an approximation of the accuracy of the budget and the completeness of the design at this point in the project (the end of this phase).

CSTCC Program

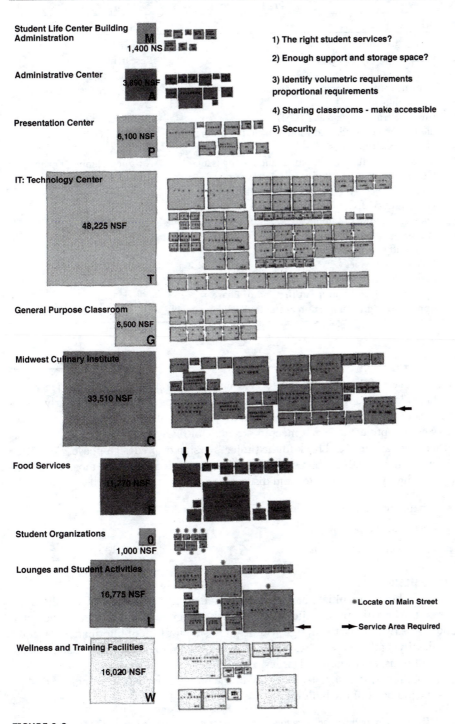

FIGURE 3.3
Graphical comparison of spaces dedicated to various uses in a program evaluation.
(Burt Hill Kosar Rittelmann Associates)

TABLE 3.1 Activities of the predesign phase of the project.

	Predesign Phase	
No.	*Activities*	*Parties (Leads listed first)*
1	Owner gets idea	Owner
2	Perform market research	Research Co., Owner
3	First draft of feasibility study	Owner, CM, Accountant
4	Consult with accountant and banker	Owner, Accountant, Banker
5	Hire architect	Owner
6	Hire construction manager (CM)	Owner, Architect
7	Identify owner needs and wants (begin the program)	Architect, Owner, CM
8	Identify potential sites	Realtor, Owner
9	Investigate legal, environmental, and zoning issues	Attorney, Planner, Owner
10	Preliminary design:	Architect, Owner, CM
	- type of project (e.g., home, plant, park)	
	- rough square footage of project	
	- possible number of floors	
	- massing of structure	
11	First draft of project plan	CM, Owner
12	Conceptual budget (25%)	CM
13	Commit to the project	Owner
	Approx. Budget Accuracy at the End of Phase = ±25%	
	Approx. Design Completion at the End of Phase = 5%	

DESIGN PHASE

The design phase of the project is also an extremely important time in the project's evolution. Many large and irrevocable project design decisions are made in the early stages of design, and the initial project budget and project end date are set early on in the design as well. If a project does not meet its schedule or budget goals, quite often the reason or reasons can be traced back to the project's design or predesign phase.

There are three distinct phases of a project's design as recognized by most in the construction industry. They are listed and discussed as follows:

- Schematic design
- Design development
- Construction document

SCHEMATIC DESIGN

Schematic design is the initial phase of the project design. Before the design evolves too far, it is best to have the project site selected and the program evaluation well developed. Without these two items, the design will begin to stall for lack of information. In addition to identifying the project site, it is important to begin to investigate the site relative to soil conditions, environmental issues, and utilities.

Most of the major design decisions about the project are made in schematic design, such as the footprint of the building.

> The footprint of the building is the term used for the overall perimeter shape of the building. It could be thought of as the outline of the building when looking down on the building in plan view.

A study of various potential building locations on the site is examined. Various systems for the building are investigated such as the foundation, structural frame, and HVAC systems. Different exterior skin materials are considered and narrowed down, and the interior spaces of the building are roughly laid out in what are called *bubble diagrams*. An example of a bubble diagram of an office layout can be seen in Figure 3.4.

In addition to the design aspects of the project, the specifications for the project are started in the schematic phase and are referred to early on as the *outline specifications*.

The project budget is updated in the schematic phase since more information is known about the project. It is estimated that by the end of the schematic design, approximately **25 percent** of the project information is known. A schematic design budget is performed by the construction manager at the end of this phase and has an accuracy of approximately plus or minus **15 percent**.

The first draft of the project schedule is developed by the construction manager and is called a master schedule or milestone schedule. The milestone schedule is not a detailed construction schedule, but rather a schedule that plans the expected start and finish of major milestones of the project.

> A milestone is a significant event that highlights a turning point in a project.

Milestones might include events from the three design phases and the bidding phase, as well as various construction milestones such as getting the building out of the ground, topping out, enclosing the building, finishing the interior, moving in, and the grand opening. A more expanded list of typical milestones can be found in Chapter 4, where milestone schedules are discussed in detail. The detailed construction schedule will ultimately evolve from the milestone schedule. An example of a milestone schedule can be seen in Figure 3.5. This example shows a project broken into four phases of design and construction with each phase having its own bid package; that is, each phase is bid out separately.

The schematic design concludes as the feasibility study is refined and updated with new budget, schedule, and project information. The schematic design plans are reviewed and commented upon by the owner before the design moves on to the next phase.

Table 3.2 describes some common activities that typically occur during the schematic design of the project and lists the involved parties of each activity, showing the lead party for each activity first. At the bottom of the table is an approximation of

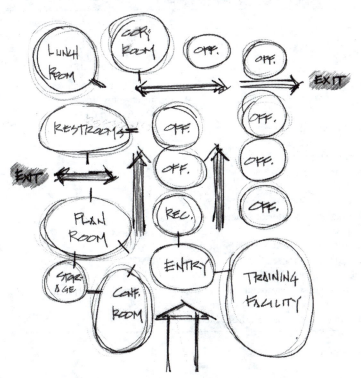

FIGURE 3.4
Rough layout of interior office spaces shown using a bubble diagram.

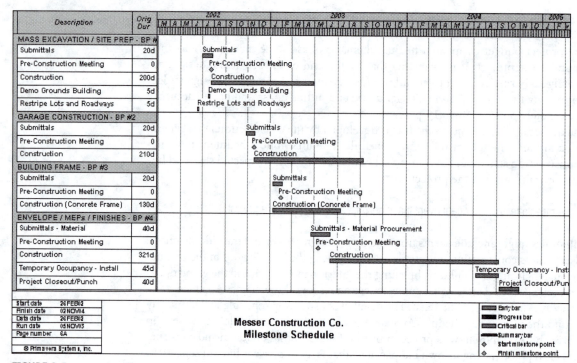

FIGURE 3.5
Project milestone schedule.
(Messer Construction)

TABLE 3.2   Activities of schematic design.

No.	Activities	Parties (Leads listed first)
Design Phase (Schematic Design)		
1	Secure project site	Realtor, Owner
2	Perform soil analysis	Soils Engineer, CM
3	Finalize the program	Architect, Owner, CM
4	Schematic design:	Architect (sometimes with intervening feedback from Owner and CM)
	- develop footprint of building	
	- study various site locations for building	
	- select foundation system	
	- select structural frame system	
	- select HVAC system	
	- review possible exterior skin materials	
	- develop bubble diagrams of interior spaces	
5	Develop outline specification	Architect
6	Develop draft of milestone schedule from project plan	CM
7	Develop schematic design budget ($\pm15\%$)	CM
8	Update and refine feasibility study	CM, Owner
9	Schematic design phase plans approved	Owner (Board and End users)
	Approx. Budget Accuracy at the End of Phase = $\pm15\%$	
	Approx. Design Completion at the End of Phase = 25%	

the accuracy of the budget that is prepared at the end of this phase and the completeness of the design at this point in the project, (the end of this phase).

DESIGN DEVELOPMENT

The next phase of the design is called design development. In this phase the design is developed further—hence its name. At the start of design development, the design is sketchy and still very open to change. By the end of design development, most of the design decisions have been made and the majority of work to be completed is the actual drafting of the construction documents. It is usually the longest of the three design phases.

The location of the building must be finalized early in design development, and the sitework design, such as the earthwork cut and fill and location of utilities, begins. The design of the various building systems is continued throughout design development. These systems include the foundation, structural frame, and MEP systems.

> MEP is an acronym often used in the industry that stands for **m**echanical, **e**lectrical, and **p**lumbing. The term **mechanical** is another name that is used for HVAC (heating, ventilation, and air conditioning).

One of the most significant segments of design development is the design of all interior building spaces. The architect performs this design with periodic input from the owner, CM, and other parties that may need to be consulted. There are normally multiple submittals of ideas by the architect and reviews by the project team before the layout of all the spaces is finalized. In conjunction with this, the exterior skin materials are reviewed and selected. As the architect is presenting floor plans and elevations as part of this review, other architectural pages are beginning to be filled with sections, details, and schedules while the project specification is continuing to be developed as more and more materials are being identified.

The milestone schedule is finalized and approved during the design development phase and, from it, the construction manager will sketch out the first draft of what will eventually become the bid package schedule. The project team will perform value engineering as needed to investigate the variety of design issues that inevitably arise.

The project budget is updated in design development as well and may be updated more than once. By the end of design development, most of the design decisions are made; therefore, quite a bit of information is known about the project although probably much of it is not drafted into the documents yet. It is estimated that by the end of this phase, approximately **66 percent** of the project information is known, resulting in a design development budget with an accuracy of approximately plus or minus **10 percent**.

The feasibility study is refined and updated with new budget, schedule, and project information. The design development plans and specifications are reviewed, commented upon, and approved by the owner.

Table 3.3 describes some common activities that typically occur during the design development of the project and lists the involved parties of each activity, showing the lead party for each activity first. At the bottom of the table is an approximation of the accuracy of the budget prepared at the end of this phase and the completeness of the design at this point in the project (the end of this phase).

CONSTRUCTION DOCUMENT

Construction document is the final phase of the project design. When complete, the project should be ready to go out for bid. At the start of this phase, most of the design decisions have already been made, but have yet to be reflected in the documents. The majority of the work to be performed in this phase is the actual drafting of the construction documents. The construction documents are often referred to as *CDs* and include all drawings and specifications, as well as the bidding documents.

TABLE 3.3   Activities of design development.

No.	Activities	Parties (Leads listed first)
	Design Phase (Design Development)	
1	Begin permit review	Architect, Owner, CM
2	Design development:	Architect (with periodic input from Owner, CM, and possibly others)
	- finalize location of building on site	
	- begin site design	
	- develop foundation design	
	- develop structural frame design	
	- develop MEP (mechanical, electrical, and plumbing) design	
	- select exterior skin materials	
	- finalize layout of all interior spaces	
	- begin drawing sections, details, and schedules	
	- begin evaluating interior finish materials	
3	Continue to develop specification	Architect
4	Perform value engineering	CM, Architect, Others
5	Finalize and approve milestone schedule	CM, Owner, Architect
6	First draft bid package schedule	CM
7	Design development budget ($\pm 10\%$)	CM
8	Update and refine feasibility study	CM, Owner
9	Design development plans approved	Owner (Board and End users)
	Approx. Budget Accuracy at the End of Phase = $\pm 10\%$	
	Approx. Design Completion at the End of Phase = 66%	

Some design items are usually still left to be performed and/or finalized in this phase. The site design needs to be finalized, including walkways, paving and parking, site lighting, and landscaping. The selection of most of the interior finishes will be made in this phase.

A very important exercise performed throughout the construction document phase is resolving the many conflicts and interferences that will ultimately occur when designing a building with the numerous systems involved. For example, the HVAC ductwork needs to run without interfering with the structure of the building. The potential for conflicts and interferences is significant; however, if they can be avoided, or at least detected and resolved, during design rather than in the field, the cost and time savings can be tremendous. Figure 3.6 shows this relationship.

Since the project design is nearing completion, the project team must prepare for construction. The process of applying for various permits will begin. Long lead items must be identified, and possibly ordered. The construction manager should perform a constructibility review with the help of different trade contractors. The owner will secure the construction loan and begin to identify and narrow down sources for the permanent financing of the project.

The CM will expand the milestone schedule. At this point, the entire construction of the project is probably shown in one long construction activity. This work will be divided into numerous activities roughly equal to the different trade contracts that will be bid out. The resulting schedule is often referred to as a bid package schedule and will be added to the bidding documents, so the bidders will have an idea when their portion of the work will take place.

The project budget is usually updated one more time near the end of the construction document phase. At this point the documents are thought to be 95 percent complete with only design *punchlist* items left to complete. The budget performed at this

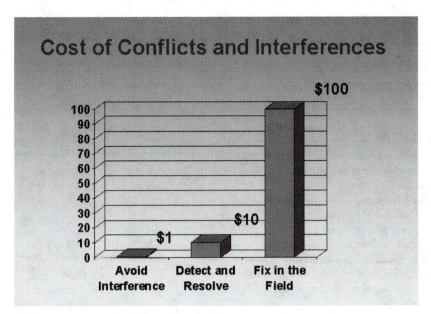

FIGURE 3.6
Influence on the project cost by detecting and resolving conflicts and interferences during design.

point is sometimes referred to as the *95 percent budget* and is thought to have an accuracy of approximately plus or minus **5 percent**. The construction documents at the end of this phase are theoretically 100 percent complete; however, it is better to think of them as approximately ($\approx$) **100 percent** since items may have been left out.

The feasibility study is refined and updated with the new budget, schedule, and project information. The construction document documents are reviewed, commented upon, and approved by the owner. Preparations are then made to bid out the project.

Table 3.4 describes some common activities that typically occur during the construction document phase of the project design and lists the involved parties of each activity, showing the lead party for each activity first. At the bottom of the table is an approximation of the accuracy of the budget prepared at the end of this phase and the completeness of the design at this point in the project (the end of this phase).

BIDDING PHASE

Once the design of the project is complete, it can be bid out for the award of contract(s). The process used to bid out a project is very different depending on whether the owner is public or private. These differences were previously discussed in Chapter 2. Regardless of the process, there are certain events and activities that typically occur during the bidding phase. The bidding phase can be broken into two distinct segments: the bidding period and the award period.

The bidding period is usually four weeks long and starts when the bid advertisement first appears and ends on the due date of the bids. The construction documents are combined with other documents such as the instructions to the bidders and the bid package schedule, then assembled together to form the bidding documents. Once the bids are awarded, these same documents become the *contract documents*. The bidding documents are normally available at the office of the owner, architect, and CM as well as at local plan rooms.

As the bidders review the bidding documents, they will normally find some discrepancies in them. They are encouraged to bring these discrepancies to the attention of the architect and/or CM. The indirect benefit of bidding the job out is the thorough and

TABLE 3.4   Activities of the construction document phase.

	Design Phase (Construction Document)	
No.	*Activities*	*Parties (Leads listed first)*
1	Apply for various permits	Architect, Owner, CM
2	Construction document:	Architect (with periodic input from Owner, CM, and possibly others)
	- complete site design including landscaping	
	- identify and resolve conflicts and interferences detected between and within the various building systems	
	- select all interior finish materials	
	- complete all design documents	
3	Complete specifications	Architect
4	Perform constructability review	CM, Trade Contractors
5	Update construction schedule	CM
6	Identify long-lead items for procurement	CM, Architect, Owner
7	Determine construction document or 95 percent budget ($\pm 5\%$)	CM
8	Update and refine feasibility study	CM, Owner
9	Construction document approval	Owner (Board and End users)
10	Secure construction loan	Owner, Banker, CM
11	Identify sources for permanent financing	Owner, Banker, CM
12	Prepare bidding documents	Architect, CM
13	Secure bid advertisement	CM, Owner
	Approx. Budget Accuracy at the End of Phase = $\pm 5\%$	
	Approx. Design Completion at the End of Phase $\approx 100\%$	

exhaustive examination of the documents performed by the bidders as they prepare their bids, and the best part is that it is free. About halfway through the bidding period, a formal prebid conference is held. The conference is an open meeting attended by the bidders and the project team where further instructions can be given to the bidders and where questions about the project will be answered.

If changes need to be made to the bidding documents during the bidding period, as they often do, they will be communicated in the form of an *addenda*. All bidders who are registered with the project team holding the bidding documents will be sent the addenda.

An addenda is a change to bidding documents.

Once the bids are received, opened, and reviewed, the bidding period ends and the award period begins. A bid analysis is performed to ensure that the bids are in order and to help determine which bid to accept. When this is determined, the contractor receiving the award is notified. The two parties then meet to review the contract and eventually sign it.

Other non-bid-related activities continue to take place during the bidding phase. Long lead items are ordered if necessary. The project team continues to secure permits and pursue project financing.

After this stage, the budget for the project can now be compiled from the awarded bid(s). This will become the official project budget that the project cost will be measured against. It is more accurate than the previous budgets, all of which were based on estimates, because it is based on actual contract commitments. However, due to the risky nature of construction and the potential for unknowns, the accuracy of the budget remains at approximately plus or minus **5 percent**. To plan for these potential unknowns, a contingency fund of **5 percent** is added to the project budget. When an unknown cost arises, it is paid for from this fund.

TABLE 3.5 Activities of the bidding phase of the project.

No.	Activities	Parties (Leads listed first)
	Bidding Phase	
1	Advertise for bid	CM, Owner
2	Issue addendums (if necessary)	Architect
3	Answer bidders' questions	Architect, CM
4	Hold prebid conference	CM, Architect, Owner
5	Receive bids	CM
6	Open and review bids	CM, Architect, Owner
7	Perform bid analysis	CM, Architect, Owner
8	Notify contractors of awards	CM, Owner
9	Prepare project budget from bid results ($\pm 5\%$)	CM
10	Update and refine feasibility study	CM, Owner
11	Contract award approval	Owner (Board)
12	Secure construction loan	Owner, Banker, CM
13	Identify sources for permanent financing	Owner, Banker, CM
14	Prepare contracts for construction	CM
15	Sign contracts	Owner, Contractors
16	Order long-lead items	CM, Owner
17	Continue to secure permits	Architect, Owner, CM
	Approx. Budget Accuracy at the End of Phase = $\pm 5\%$	
	Approx. Design Completion at the End of Phase $\approx 100\%$	

Contingency is an amount of money (usually 5 percent of the total project budget (TPC)) added to the project budget to pay for unknown costs that may arise during construction.

The feasibility study is refined and updated using the numbers from the project budget and other new project information that may be known.

Table 3.5 describes some common activities that typically occur during the project's bidding phase and lists the involved parties of each activity, showing the lead party for each activity first. At the bottom of the table is an approximation of the accuracy of the budget prepared at the end of this phase and the completeness of the design at this point in the project (the end of this phase).

CONSTRUCTION PHASE

The construction phase of the project is usually its longest phase. The roles of the construction manager and general contractor are very much the same throughout the construction phase. The big difference between using construction management versus general contracting as the project delivery system occurs long before construction begins in the preconstruction phases of predesign, design, and bidding.

If a construction management project delivery system is used for the project, as has been described in Chapter 1, the construction manager is on board from the start of the project. If a general contracting project delivery system is used, the general contractor and all the other trade contractors will not arrive to the project until the start of construction. All the activities and tasks performed by the CM that have been described up to this point would have been performed by the architect, or not at all. This early involvement by the CM in the project, and with it the existence of construction expertise throughout the predesign, design, and bidding phases of the project, are considered by many to be the prime reason to choose construction management over general contracting as the project delivery system.

One of the first tasks of the construction manager is to develop the construction schedule. The construction schedule is the detailed schedule that will be used in the field to build the project. At this point in the project, most if not all of the trade contractors have been identified. Using their input, the construction schedule can be developed. This exercise is usually performed right after the contracts are awarded in the early days of the construction phase. Even if a contractor has not signed the contract yet, they will typically participate in scheduling meetings. They do not want to lose the opportunity to impact the schedule that they will eventually have to adhere to.

There are two distinct advantages of waiting to develop the schedule using the input of the job's trade contractors. The first is that the end result will be a more accurate construction schedule because you will have a fresh set of eyes reviewing the activities, durations, and logic by the trade contractors who know better than anyone how their work normally progresses. However, care must be taken by the construction manager to not allow the trade contractors to overinflate their activity durations in order to give themselves extra time to do their work. The second advantage is the *buy-in* to the schedule that the project team gets from the trade contractors. When they are included in the development of the schedule and asked to sign-off onto the final schedule, they are committing themselves to the schedule.

The project team is still quite busy during the construction phase. Immediately after the contracts are signed, contractors will begin to submit for approval of materials they propose to use on the project. Specifications usually specify more than one material for the same purpose. This allows bidders to shop among different manufacturers for the best price to lower their bids. Public projects often require a minimum of three sources to be listed for all materials in the specifications. Once a contract is signed, one of the first things the contractor does is submit samples, cut-sheets, or other information about the materials that they have included in their bid for the architect's approval. These are called *submittals*.

Another time-consuming activity of the construction phase is dealing with RFIs and project changes.

> RFI stands for Request for Information and can be issued by any party on the project about any item that is unclear.

Often a measure of how well construction drawings are put together is how many RFIs are issued on the job. When an RFI is issued, it is sent to the project team and then channeled to the appropriate party to be answered. The resolution of the RFI may result in a change to the project. If this is the case, a change order will be written.

> A change order is a change made to the contract documents. It may modify, add to, delete from, or otherwise alter the work set out in the contract documents.

Change orders may, or may not, change the price of the contract. It is often a full-time job for one person to deal with RFIs, change orders, and submittals.

The construction manager coordinates and supervises all activities of the construction process and leads the project team in monitoring and inspecting the project. The project progress as well as the project budget is monitored as the physical project is inspected for quality and conformance to the contract documents. The project team also has to process contractor payments each month to ensure that the work they are getting ready to pay for was actually completed in accordance with the contract documents.

The feasibility study continues to be refined and updated using the most recent project budget numbers based on changes that may have occurred to the project during construction. Permanent financing should, by now, be secured as the project is coming to a

TABLE 3.6 Activities of the construction phase of the project.

No.	Activities	Parties (Leads listed first)
	Construction Phase	
1	Gather construction schedule input from contractors	CM, Trade Contractors
2	Finalize construction schedule	CM, all other parties
3	Process project submittals	Architect, CM, Owner
4	Continue to secure permits	Architect, Owner, CM
5	Coordinate and supervise construction activities	CM
6	Inspect the project	Architect, CM, Owner
7	Monitor and update the budget	CM
8	Monitor and update the schedule	CM
9	Process RFIs, change orders, bulletins, etc.	CM, all other parties
10	Process contractor progress payments	CM, Owner
11	Perform construction phase estimating	CM
12	Update and refine the feasibility study	CM, Owner
13	Secure permanent financing	Owner, Banker, CM

close, as the owner will be anxious to pay off the higher interest rate of construction loan with the lower interest rate of permanent financing.

Table 3.6 describes some common activities that typically occur during the construction phase of the project and lists the involved parties of each activity, showing the lead party for each activity first.

START-UP PHASE

Start-up is the name given to the project phase when the construction is nearing completion and the building is being turned over to the owner. This phase is sometimes referred to as the turnover or commissioning phase. On a small project, the start-up phase may be as simple as developing and resolving the punchlist, then handing the keys over to the owner. On a large project such as a power plant, the start-up phase may take over a year, or even two, and include the testing, training of plant operations personnel, and turnover of numerous systems and the transfer of raw materials.

For most buildings constructed, the start-up phase begins when systems in the building are complete and are ready to be checked out and tested. An example is the testing and air balancing of the HVAC system in a building. There are numerous other systems in a building that require testing. After the systems are tested, the owner's plant operation personnel are often trained by the contractor installing the system before it is turned over to the owner. This same process of testing, training, and turnover is applied to the many pieces of equipment that are installed in a building but not part of any particular system, such as kitchen equipment. Sometimes systems are turned over long before the rest of the project is complete. This may require the owner to have a maintenance crew on-site during construction.

A good example of this situation comes from the power industry. A power plant has a piece of equipment called a rotor, a long steel shaft about forty feet long and two to three feet in diameter. It is magnetized and spun at about 3,000 rpms inside a field of wires called the stator. This is where the electricity is actually generated in a power plant. (Whenever you spin wires around a magnet or magnets around wires, electricity is created.) The rotor is brought on-site and placed well over a year before it will actually be used. If it just sits there for that time, it would sag and not spin true. Therefore, it is turned over to the power plant operations group after it is installed and they are responsible for

TABLE 3.7 Activities of the start-up phase of the project.

No.	Activities	Parties (Leads listed first)
	Start-Up Phase	
1	Check out systems	Trade Contr., CM, End users
2	Prepare the punchlist	CM, all other parties
3	Train end-user and turnover systems	Trade Contr., CM, End users
4	Assemble warranty information	CM, Trade Contractors
5	Begin project closeout	CM, Trade Contractors
6	Begin owner move-in	Owner, CM
7	Update and refine feasibility study	Owner, CM
8	Receive certificate of occupancy	CM, Owner

continually spinning it at low rpms until it is put to use. This operation is referred to as *turning gear* and is normally considered to be a milestone on the construction schedule.

As systems, and ultimately the entire project, are tested and reviewed for completion, problems or deficiencies are often detected. To help catalog and resolve the problems and to track their resolution, a *punchlist* is generated. The punchlist is simply a list of problems that need to be fixed. Punchlists are often generated on *walk-throughs* through the building by the owner, architect, and construction manager. The project is not complete until all the punchlist items are resolved.

As the project nears completion, the owner will be given access to certain completed areas where they can begin to move in. At the same time, the trade contractors and the construction manager assemble warranty information to be turned over to the owner with the building. This warranty information is placed in large binders and includes manufacturers' operating instructions, technical specifications, and maintenance schedules as well as the warranties. As each trade contractor finishes his or her work, the punchlist is resolved, and the warranty information is assembled, the contract will be ready to be closed out and the project closeout will begin. Eventually all the contracts on the job will have to be closed out. While project closeout starts in the start-up phase, it may not be completed until several months after the project is complete.

Eventually the project is completed and the owner can occupy the building, but not until a certificate of occupancy is received. The owner may still want to update the feasibility study. At this point most of the numbers that populate the study on the cost side will be actual costs. However, the ultimate feasibility, and economic success, of the project will *not* be known until the project begins to generate revenue.

Table 3.7 describes some common activities that typically occur during the start-up phase of the project and lists the involved parties of each activity, showing the lead party for each activity first.

GRAND OPENING AND PROPERTY MANAGEMENT PHASE

When the project is complete, it is ready for the grand opening. Grand openings are often held a few weeks after a facility actually opens for business. This delay is planned for a few reasons. While the facility is open for business, it might not be completely finished and the delay gives the project team a few weeks to put the finishing touches on the facility and to get the bugs out. From a marketing point of view, delaying the grand opening to a few weeks after the facility is actually opened gives the community more time to hear and learn about the facility and will help generate a buzz about the business, thereby making the grand opening an even bigger success.

TABLE 3.8 Activities of the grand opening and property management phase of the project.

Grand Opening and Property Management Phase	
No.	Activities	Parties (Leads listed first)
1	Closeout project	CM, Trade Contractors
2	Complete punchlist	CM, all other parties
3	Move-in	Owner, CM
4	Grand opening	Owner, CM
5	Update and refine feasibility study	Owner, CM
6	Property management	CM

During this phase, start-up activities that were not completed in that phase, such as project closeout and punchlist, are completed. The owner is moved into the facility and the finishing touches are put on the project. The feasibility study is updated once again, with actual costs and early projections of estimated revenues based on the business that may have occurred.

Some construction management firms have the capability of performing property management and offer that service, staying on after the project is complete to maintain the property.

Table 3.8 describes some common activities that typically occur during the grand opening and property management phase of the project and lists the involved parties of each activity, showing the lead party for each activity first.

CHAPTER 4
Planning and Scheduling

The Northridge earthquake in southern California on January 17, 1994, severely damaged a roadway that carried 217,000 car and truck trips per day. The California Department of Transportation awarded a contract to a Sacramento contractor to repair the roadway that had significant incentive clauses for early completion. The company's base bid was $14.9 million, with an incentive of a $200,000 bonus per day for every day it completed the project under the 140-day deadline. The contractor put together a plan that accelerated construction, using multiple shifts, expediting materials, modularizing components of the roadway, and keeping key equipment constantly on standby. That plan resulted in a construction schedule that successfully completed the project in eighty-four days—fifty-six days ahead of schedule. The contractor earned a bonus of $11.2 million (75 percent of the original contract amount) and 217,000 drivers got their road back two months sooner than they expected.

The Northridge road job demonstrates the power of planning and scheduling. The success of a construction project can be judged by many factors. The three predominant measures of a project's success are time, cost, and quality. This chapter stresses the important role that project planning and scheduling play in the successful completion of a construction project. The chapter also provides an overview of the planning and scheduling process, illustrating how effective construction planning and scheduling can optimize project time, cost, and quality.

PLANNING VERSUS SCHEDULING

What is the difference between planning and scheduling? Most textbooks and many individuals use the two words interchangeably. However, they really encompass two distinct functions.

> Planning provides an overall strategy to accomplish a goal.

> Scheduling entails the individual activities or tasks necessary to carry out the plan.

The schedule is an extension of the plan—it evolves from the plan. If the plan is the *idea,* the schedule is the *tool* to implement the idea.

Using the Northridge road project as an example, the following strategies are examples of the *plan* used to repair the road. The Northridge team:

- Influenced the design of the roadway repair to take full advantage of materials and methods that could be expedited and modularized.

  > Modularization in construction is the method of building some parts of the project in components, usually off-site, and delivering them to the project to be lifted into place.

This method saves significant amounts of construction time.

- Formed a construction team of trade contractors and material suppliers that had the capability to expedite the work and create a plan to share and distribute any bonus money that may be earned.
- Analyzed various workday and shift combinations to take advantage of the 24-hour workday.
- Investigated and resolved the impediments that arose from a continuous workday.

The plan is always developed before the schedule, or at a minimum, concurrently with the schedule. The plan should begin to be developed as early as possible in the life of the project, preferably before the design begins. The earlier it is developed, the greater the ability to be creative and influence the project. The modularized component of the roadway, in the previous example, would not have been possible had the idea not been suggested very early in the design. The plan then is refined as the project matures.

Using the Northridge road project as an example, the following are some *schedule* activities necessary to carry out the plan. The Northridge team:

- Scheduled the fabrication of the items that were to be modularized so they were completed in time to be delivered to the project and lifted into place.
- Scheduled the delivery of expedited materials so that they arrived on time.
- Scheduled the supply and maintenance of key pieces of equipment including standby equipment.
- Scheduled all site activities on a 24-hour, seven-day-per-week calendar.
- Analyzed the schedule to identify critical activities and potential areas of schedule compression to save even more time on the project.
- Updated the schedule periodically with actual progress to analyze the effect on the overall project and the project end date.

The schedule is more detail oriented than the plan because it includes the individual activities necessary to carry out the plan. Because of this reliance on the details of the project, it is created later in the project's life when more details about the project are known. Nevertheless, both the plan and schedule must be complete before any portion of the construction begins.

PLANNING

If a construction project fails to be completed on time or within budget, more often than not, it is because of things that happened—or didn't happen—before construction ever began.

For example, most projects have a detailed construction schedule prepared to help control the time of construction. However, how many projects have a detailed design schedule to help control the time of the design? And how often does the design of the project go longer than expected, delaying the start of the construction? The predesign, design, and bidding phases of the project are extremely important to the success of the project. Too much goes on, and there are too many important decisions made during these phases, to not treat them with the same level of planning and scheduling as the construction phase.

The construction industry has, for years, separated the design phase from the construction phase and viewed them as two separate functions. Rather, they should be seen as one continuous and integrated function. The advent of construction management over the past three decades, and design/build over the last decade, as alternative project delivery systems has helped frame the project as a single continuous function. In this

FIGURE 4.1
Advanced Technology and Learning Center on a college campus, an example of a project with a scheduled construction expenditure requirement of $85,000 per day.

light, it is important to create a plan that spans the entire life of the project from pre-design through the grand opening.

To illustrate the need for a plan, consider a project with a duration of eighteen months and budget of $33,000,000 of direct construction cost. If the project duration is eighteen months, the project will have approximately 390 working days, assuming no seasonal shutdowns. Therefore, on average, the project must put in place nearly $85,000 of construction each workday. This example is from a real project that can be seen in two views in Figure 4.1.

This is a staggering amount of work to be performed each day. It is equal to the construction cost of building a small home—each day. The inefficient use of time, equipment, labor, material, space around the building site, and other similar items can quickly add up and have a devastating impact on the budget and schedule. The way to protect against this is to develop a well-thought-out plan for the project that eventually evolves into a detailed project schedule.

Developing a plan for the project allows the project team to design and construct the project on paper before committing resources to it. That is, it allows the project team to "live through" the project. Through this perspective, the project team should be able to analyze the project and avoid major pitfalls. Listed below are some of the more common considerations that apply to a typical building design and construction project. The project team will investigate these and other questions as it develops the plan for the project:

- *How will this project interface with existing conditions?* Rarely are projects built in a vacuum. That is, they are rarely built out in the middle of some field where no other entity, party, or project is affected. Projects are often built on sites where other operating buildings exist or a project might involve the renovation of an existing facility. Road construction is almost always done on roads as they continue to carry traffic. Rarely are roads built from scratch. In these cases, the project team needs to create a plan for building the project that will cause the least amount of disruption to the existing conditions as possible. This requires a creative, careful, and deliberate plan.

- *What project delivery system will be used for the project?* This is important to decide up front to determine who will be included on the project team. Both the construction management and design/build project delivery systems bring construction expertise to the project team during preconstruction; that is, during the predesign, design, and bidding phases of the project. This is considered probably the single most important advantage of both systems.

- *Will the project be fast-tracked?* Fast-tracking allows for the construction to begin while the project is not completely designed, starting the construction considerably earlier and thereby completing the project considerably earlier. This decision has a significant impact on many other components of the plan. (Fast-tracking will be discussed in more detail later in this chapter.)

- *What will be set as the initial completion date of the project?* The owner always has an idea, and sometimes a strict requirement, as to when they hope to complete the project. The project team has to analyze this date to see if it is realistic to use as the initial completion date of the project. This determination can be difficult since it is made so early in the life of the project and so little information about the project is known at this time. Be aware that the owner seems to always remember the initial end date and often judges the project's completion against it—no matter how often the scope of the project may have changed after the date was set. From the end date, the project team will work backwards to establish other milestone dates such as the start of construction, the start and finish of the bidding period, and the start and finish of the three phases of design.

- *What will be set as the initial budget of the project?* The owner is always interested in the early estimates for the price of the job and may have a strict set price for the project budget. The project team has to estimate the budget and weigh it against the intended scope of the project to see if it is realistic. This determination can be difficult since it is made so early in the life of the project with so little information known about the project at this time. Like the schedule, the owner always seems to remember the initial price they hear and judges the project cost against it—no matter how often the scope of the project may have changed after the price was set.

- *What other considerations need to be studied?* There are many other considerations specific to each project that may need to be addressed. Some examples are access to the site, availability of site lay-down area, traffic issues, placement of office trailers and tool trailers, parking for construction workers, availability of craft workers, utility interruptions and temporary utilities, procurement of long-lead items, security, safety issues, and many more. Any and all of these considerations may need to be addressed in the project plan.

SCHEDULING

As stated earlier, planning provides an overall strategy to accomplish a goal. Scheduling entails the individual activities or tasks necessary to carry out the plan. The previous discussion provided concrete examples of issues and considerations that are addressed by, and affect, the plan. The discussion that follows will begin to define the schedule.

The schedule is an extension of the plan. It was stated earlier in the text that the typical construction project has hundreds of different parties involving thousands of separate operations. Each operation is sequenced in-between the other operations. So how is the construction accomplished? Does everybody just *know* what to do?

Don't count on it. These operations have to be coordinated and orchestrated. That is what the schedule does. It is the written blueprint for the coordination of these many operations.

EVOLUTION OF THE SCHEDULE

The project schedule evolves from the plan, which is created and refined in the early stages of the project. The plan includes the overall strategy for completing the project with estimated dates for the start and finish of the project. From this information, the construction manager, with input from the project team, begins the development of the schedule. Like the project design and project budget, the evolution of the schedule goes from the very broad and very general to the specific. That is, the schedule goes from including only a few milestone events such as design complete, construction start, and construction complete to the very specific details of a construction activity such as *Finish Drywall—Room 222*. As the schedule evolves, it goes through the following three steps:

- Milestone schedule
- Bid package schedule
- Construction schedule

Milestone Schedule

The first schedule created for the project is the milestone schedule.

> Milestones are significant events that highlight a turning point in the project.

A milestone may be marked for the start of an event, its finish, or both. A milestone schedule is sometimes referred to as a master schedule because it sets the parameters of the schedule that eventually become the detailed construction schedule.

The first draft of the milestone schedule is created by the construction manager toward the end of the schematic design phase when most of the major project design decisions have been made and the scope of the project (that is, the scale and size of the project) is pretty well defined. If a construction manager is not on board and the project team consists only of the owner and architect, the architect will draft the milestone schedule.

The following is a list of the many different milestones that may be found on a milestone schedule:

- Begin programming
- Complete the program
- Start design
- Complete schematic design
- Complete design development
- Complete construction documents
- Complete design
- Owner approval of design
- Secure financing
- Advertise for bids
- Bid opening
- Award contracts
- Receive permits
- Groundbreaking
- Notice to proceed
- Construction start
- Building out of the ground
- Topping out
- Building enclosed
- Under roof
- Owner move-in

- Substantial completion
- Punchout
- Certificate of occupancy
- Grand opening
- Project closeout
- Project complete

Not every previously listed milestone will always be used in a milestone schedule. Different combinations of these may work better for certain projects. The dates assigned to the milestones are based on the estimates prepared by the project team. The architect will estimate the time needed to reach most of the preconstruction milestones. The construction manager will estimate the rest of the dates with the exception of those milestones that are controlled by the owner, such as approvals of design and construction contracts. The project team members have to rely on their past experience, intuition, and analysis of each milestone to come up with these dates.

Once established and laid out, the milestone schedule will be viewed as a whole and analyzed by the project team for legitimacy. They will see if the schedule matches their gut feeling for the project. As unscientific as this may sound, the many years of combined project experience on the team will provide them with an overall feel for the schedule's accuracy. Based on this review, adjustments and refinements may be made.

As the design continues, the schedule may change. The schedule is like the budget in the fact that it is often being updated based on new information that becomes known as the project evolves. However, the project team will want to lock-in the major milestones like the end of design and the start and end of construction. The milestone schedule itself is usually finalized and approved sometime midway through the project design.

An example of a milestone schedule can be seen in Figure 4.2.

Bid Package Schedule

Once the milestone schedule is finalized and approved, the construction manager will begin to develop the bid package schedule, the intermediate step between the very broad milestone schedule and the very specific construction schedule. For example, the milestone schedule summarizes the entire construction of the project into *one* single all-encompassing activity from beginning to the end. The bid package schedule divides this work into numerous activities roughly equal to the different trade contracts that will be bid out. The resulting schedule consequently is often referred to as the bid package schedule and will be added to the bidding documents so the bidders will have an idea when their portion of the work will take place.

The following is a list of typical construction activities that might be found in a bid package schedule. The list is by no means all inclusive:

- Earthwork
- Site utilities
- Excavation
- Footings
- Foundations
- Slab
- Structural frame
- Floors
- Building skin
- Roof

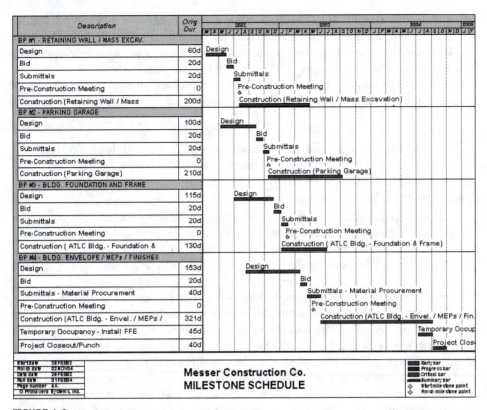

Description	Orig Dur	2002	2003	2004	2005
BP #1 - RETAINING WALL / MASS EXCAV.					
Design	60d	Design			
Bid	20d	Bid			
Submittals	20d	Submittals			
Pre-Construction Meeting	0	Pre-Construction Meeting			
Construction (Retaining Wall / Mass	200d	Construction (Retaining Wall / Mass Excavation)			
BP #2 - PARKING GARAGE					
Design	100d	Design			
Bid	20d	Bid			
Submittals	20d	Submittals			
Pre-Construction Meeting	0	Pre-Construction Meeting			
Construction (Parking Garage)	210d	Construction (Parking Garage)			
BP #3 - BLDG. FOUNDATION AND FRAME					
Design	115d	Design			
Bid	20d	Bid			
Submittals	20d	Submittals			
Pre-Construction Meeting	0	Pre-Construction Meeting			
Construction (ATLC Bldg. - Foundation &	130d	Construction (ATLC Bldg. - Foundation & Frame)			
BP #4 - BLDG. ENVELOPE / MEPs / FINISHES					
Design	153d	Design			
Bid	20d	Bid			
Submittals - Material Procurement	40d	Submittals - Material Procurement			
Pre-Construction Meeting	0	Pre-Construction Meeting			
Construction (ATLC Bldg. - Envel. / MEPs /	321d	Construction (ATLC Bldg. - Envel. / MEPs / Fin.			
Temporary Occupancy - Install FFE	45d			Temporary Occup	
Project Closeout/Punch	40d			Project Clos	

Start date: 28FEB02
Finish date: 02NOV04
Data date: 28FEB02
Run date: 01FEB04
Page number: 6A
© Primavera Systems, Inc.

Messer Construction Co.
MILESTONE SCHEDULE

Early bar
Progress bar
Critical bar
Summary bar
◇ Start milestone point
◇ Finish milestone point

FIGURE 4.2
Project milestone schedule for a phased, fast-tracked project.
(Messer Construction)

- HVAC rough-in
- Electrical rough-in
- Plumbing rough-in
- Interior partitions
- Interior finishes
- Sitework
- Landscaping
- Punchout
- Project closeout

The bid package schedule is developed, reviewed, and refined as the design of the project continues. Specifically, this occurs during the design development and into the construction document phase of the design. It needs to be finalized and approved before the project is bid out so it can be included in the bid documents.

In addition to refining the milestone schedule, the development of the bid package schedule serves a second purpose. It initiates the exercise of work packaging.

> Work packaging is the task of dividing up the construction work of the project into individual packages of work. These packages become the contract packages that are eventually bid out later in the project to the various trade contractors.

It should be noted that the breakdown for the work packages do not always match up directly with the breakdown of activities for the bid package schedule. Often the work of multiple schedule activities will be covered by a single work package; occasionally, multiple work packages will be covered by a single activity.

Here is an example of how the breakdown bid package schedule *activities* and the breakdown of the *work package* may vary in two different ways using the same items of work:

1. *Three activities grouped into one work package.* The schedule breaks the foundation of the building into three activities, Excavation, Footings, and Foundation. These three activities are often covered by a single foundation work package.

2. *One activity covered by three work packages.* The schedule has one activity called *foundation* that includes the excavation, footing, and foundation of the building. This work is covered by three work packages: an excavation work package, a foundation work package, and a footing work package.

How the construction manager decides to break down the work into activities and into packages may depend on many different factors including factors related to the project, factors related to the local bidding environment, the construction manager's own preferences, or a number of other factors. Regardless of how they are broken down, there is a definite correlation and strong relationship between the two.

It must be noted that if the traditional method of general contracting is used as the project delivery system, there is only one contract package and it encompasses the entire construction work. A bid package schedule is not developed. Rather, the general contractor, just recently being chosen and signed to a contract, starts to develop the construction schedule and skips over the intermediate bid package schedule.

An example of a bid package schedule can be seen in Figure 4.3. Compare this to the milestone schedule in Figure 4.2. Notice that in the milestone schedule the work for bid package #4 was summarized in one activity called construction and that that activity had a duration of 321 days spanning from June of 2003 into September of 2004. The bid package schedule for bid package #4 breaks this work up into approximately thirty-two activities, now spanning from April of 2003 to mid-October of 2004. That's an additional two and a half to three months added to the bid package milestone schedule for this same portion of work.

Why did the schedule change? The work is starting two months earlier, but is still ending about a month later. There could be many factors but usually the main reason for differences as the schedule evolves simply reflects the fact that more information is known about the project. When the milestone schedule was developed, the design was only about one-third complete. Bid package schedules are developed toward the end of the design when the scope and complexity of the project is well defined.

Construction Schedule

The construction schedule is a refinement of the bid package schedule. It is the schedule that will be used on a day-to-day basis by the contractors to build the project. Since this is the schedule that the contractors are going to be expected to follow, it is imperative that they participate in its development. Including the contractors in this process will help develop and foster a team approach to the project, create a buy-in to the schedule, and generate a sense of ownership of the schedule by all.

The construction manager leads the effort to develop the detailed schedule through a series of meetings with the contractors. The group will start with the broad activities of the bid package schedule. Each activity on the bid package schedule will be assigned to the appropriate contractor that was contracted to perform that work. The contractors

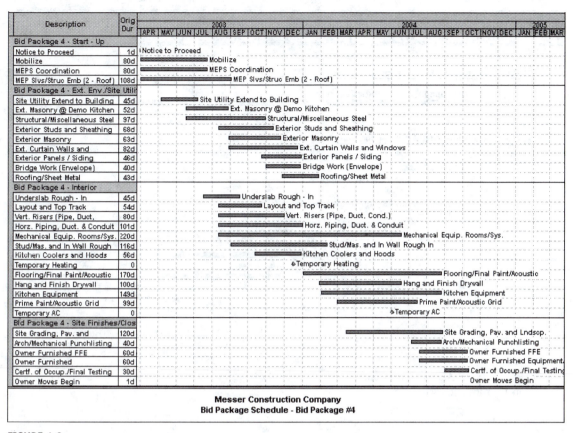

Description	Orig Dur	2003 APR MAY JUN JUL AUG SEP OCT NOV DEC	2004 JAN FEB MAR APR MAY JUN JUL AUG SEP OCT NOV DEC	2005 JAN FEB MAR
Bid Package 4 - Start - Up				
Notice to Proceed	1d	Notice to Proceed		
Mobilize	80d	Mobilize		
MEPS Coordination	80d	MEPS Coordination		
MEP Slvs/Struc Emb (2 - Roof)	108d	MEP Slvs/Struc Emb (2 - Roof)		
Bid Package 4 - Ext. Env./Site Utili				
Site Utility Extend to Building	45d	Site Utility Extend to Building		
Ext. Masonry @ Demo Kitchen	52d	Ext. Masonry @ Demo Kitchen		
Structural/Miscellaneous Steel	97d	Structural/Miscellaneous Steel		
Exterior Studs and Sheathing	68d	Exterior Studs and Sheathing		
Exterior Masonry	63d	Exterior Masonry		
Ext. Curtain Walls and	82d	Ext. Curtain Walls and Windows		
Exterior Panels / Siding	46d	Exterior Panels / Siding		
Bridge Work (Envelope)	40d	Bridge Work (Envelope)		
Roofing/Sheet Metal	43d	Roofing/Sheet Metal		
Bid Package 4 - Interior				
Underslab Rough - In	45d	Underslab Rough - In		
Layout and Top Track	54d	Layout and Top Track		
Vert. Risers (Pipe, Duct,	80d	Vert. Risers (Pipe, Duct, Cond.)		
Horz. Piping, Duct. & Conduit	101d	Horz. Piping, Duct. & Conduit		
Mechanical Equip. Rooms/Sys.	220d	Mechanical Equip. Rooms/Sys.		
Stud/Mas. and In Wall Rough	116d	Stud/Mas. and In Wall Rough In		
Kitchen Coolers and Hoods	56d	Kitchen Coolers and Hoods		
Temporary Heating	0	Temporary Heating		
Flooring/Final Paint/Acoustic	170d	Flooring/Final Paint/Acoustic		
Hang and Finish Drywall	100d	Hang and Finish Drywall		
Kitchen Equipment	149d	Kitchen Equipment		
Prime Paint/Acoustic Grid	99d	Prime Paint/Acoustic Grid		
Temporary AC	0	Temporary AC		
Bid Package 4 - Site Finishes/Clos				
Site Grading, Pav. and	120d	Site Grading, Pav. and Lndsop.		
Arch/Mechanical Punchlisting	40d	Arch/Mechanical Punchlisting		
Owner Furnished FFE	60d	Owner Furnished FFE		
Owner Furnished	60d	Owner Furnished Equipment		
Certf. of Occup./Final Testing	30d	Certf. of Occup./Final Testing		
Owner Moves Begin	1d	Owner Moves Begin		

Messer Construction Company
Bid Package Schedule - Bid Package #4

FIGURE 4.3
Project bid package schedule for Bid Package #4.
(Messer Construction)

will then be asked to break the broad activity into the detailed activities needed to accomplish that work. Here is an example.

On a bid package schedule one of the broad activities might be HVAC rough-in. The HVAC contractor will be assigned this broad activity and asked to identify the detailed activities required to complete the HVAC rough-in. Additionally, the contractor will need to determine the duration of each detailed activity and how they fit logically together with each other and with the detailed activities from other contractors. Figure 4.4 shows the broad HVAC rough-in activity along with the detailed activities of the same work beneath. The activity duration is indicated by the length of the bar, and the connecting arrows demonstrate logical ties to other activities.

The contractors will be given time—a few days or maybe longer—to come up with their detailed activities. At the next meeting, the detailed activities will be reviewed, input into the schedule, and tied logically to the other activities. The construction manager will take the results of all this input and turn it into a formal, reproducible schedule. At the final meeting, all the involved parties will gather to review and discuss possible improvements to the schedule. Changes or adjustments suggested by the participants are discussed then. The schedule as defined will be understood to be accepted by all members.

The result is a finalized detailed construction schedule of the project. The final version, sometimes called the *target schedule,* is the schedule against which the eventual progress of the project will be measured. It is also the schedule that the contractors will sign-on to and agree to meet.

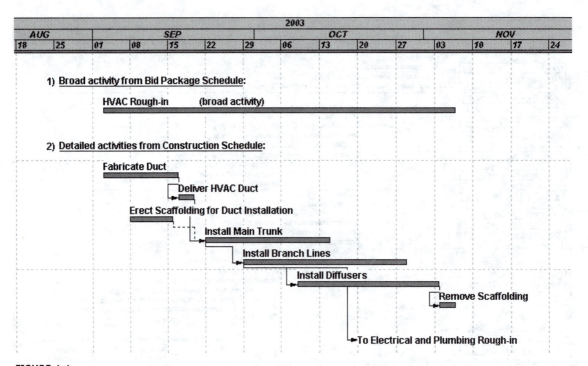

FIGURE 4.4
The broad activity (**HVAC rough-in**) from the bid package schedule along with the detailed activities of the same work from a construction schedule.

An example of the construction schedule is shown in Figure 4.5. It is a small segment of the same project that is shown in the bid package schedule. The activities shown are from the interior of the building and match up with the interior section of the bid package schedule, but are much more detailed, as would be expected.

TYPES OF SCHEDULES

Construction scheduling has been around since man has been building colossal projects such as the pyramids in Egypt or the Great Wall in China (the only manmade object visible from space). These projects could not have been built without some sort of schedule. More recently, in the last 100 years, schedules have been used frequently on projects. The types of construction schedules that are commonly used today include the following:

- Bar chart (Gantt chart)
- PERT
- Time-scaled logic diagram

These are the three predominant methods used to graphically display the schedule. They should not be confused with either CPM scheduling or various diagramming methods known as AOA, AON, or Precedence.

Critical path method (CPM) scheduling is a mathematical algorithm used to calculate the schedule. It will be discussed in more detail later in this chapter and used throughout the text. (It should be noted that PERT, in addition to being a method to graphically display the schedule, is also a computational method like CPM). AOA stands

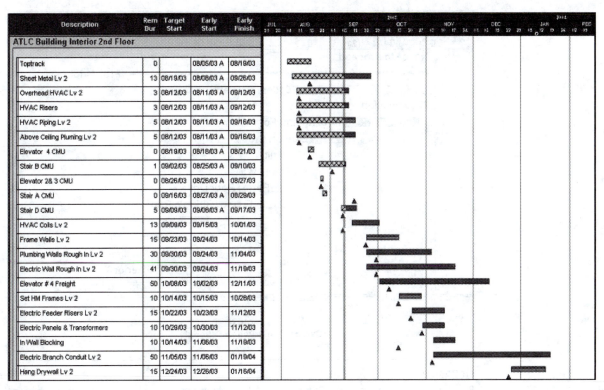

FIGURE 4.5
Segment of the construction schedule from the same project that the bid package schedule was taken from, showing the same area of work.
(Messer Construction)

for activity-on-arrow and AON stands for activity-on-node. These, along with the Precedence method, are the three predominant methods used to hand-draw diagrams of the schedule network. They will be discussed later in Chapter 6.

When you create a construction schedule, it is first best to hand-draw it, in pencil, on a big piece of paper—thereby allowing you plenty of room and the opportunity to erase and revise. When you draw it you could use one of the three previous methods: AOA, AON, or Precedence. The next step is to calculate the critical path (and other information) of the schedule. You will use CPM to do this either manually or with a computer software program, like SureTrak. The software package will also be using CPM to do the calculations. The last step is to graphically represent the results of the schedule. You will choose one of the three types of schedules previously listed (bar chart, PERT, or time-scaled logic diagram) to graphically represent the schedule. You can either draw it manually, which rarely happens anymore, or use computer scheduling software to print it out.

Bar Chart (Gantt Chart)

The bar chart is sometimes called a Gantt chart. Henry L. Gantt and Frederick W. Taylor first popularized the bar chart in the early 1900s. Henry Gantt used a bar chart to represent the duration and sequence of construction activities of U.S. Navy shipbuilding, hence the name Gantt chart. The greatest advantage of bar charts is that they are very easy to read and use. They can be understood by every party involved with the project from the owner and banker down to the layman on the street. They are also easy to prepare. Because they are such good communications tools, most scheduling software allows you to generate the schedule in a bar chart view.

The major disadvantage of the bar chart is that it does not show the relationships that exist between activities. Therefore, it is difficult to determine what effect, if any, one

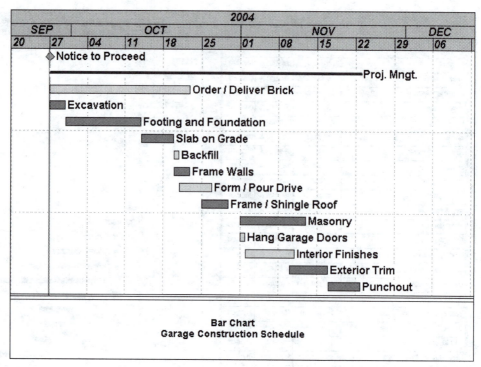

FIGURE 4.6
Bar chart of the garage schedule that will be scheduled in the SureTrak modules later in the text.

activity will have on others nearby. It is also difficult to determine the effect of an unexpected event on the overall project. This is a detriment to the project manager trying to control the project schedule and makes the bar chart less of a management tool. However, this is less of a disadvantage today than it was in the past, when the bar chart was often used as a stand-alone graphical tool to control the project and there was no CPM calculated schedule behind it. Today when you see a bar chart used on a project, there is a very good chance that that bar chart was derived from a calculated CPM schedule and presumably the CPM schedule is updated periodically to measure the effect of events on the schedule, even if they are not reflected on the bar chart hanging on the wall.

Figure 4.6 shows an example of a bar chart. It is the schedule of the construction of a small garage and is the first project schedule the students will create using the SureTrak software later in the SureTrak modules.

PERT

PERT (program evaluation and review technique) can be defined in two ways. It has become known as the name of a graphical technique used to display a schedule and it is also the name of a method used to compute and evaluate the schedule. PERT was developed by the U.S. Navy in the mid-1950s to help in the production of the Polaris Missile program. The PERT computational procedure allows the scheduler to compute the schedule network using variable durations for the activities, usually a high, medium, and low; and even variable logical relationships between activities. The result of the computation is a probability of the project completion by a certain date, rather than an exact date. This will be compared to the CPM (critical path method) later in this chapter.

Over the years, the name *PERT* has often been attributed to AON and/or Precedence network diagrams. The AON and Precedence diagrams are very similar to each other and were often used in conjunction with the PERT computational method to create and evaluate schedules, so the name *PERT* became associated with these two diagramming methods. While initially a misnomer, the name has stuck as a type of graphical display of the schedule. As other textbooks and many scheduling softwares, including SureTrak, refer to these diagrams as PERT charts, this textbook will also use that name for this type of graphical display.

The major advantage of the PERT chart, and of the AON and Precedence diagrams as well, is the easily identifiable relationships between activities. The flow of the activities and their logical ties to each other can easily be seen. Because they communicate the interrelationships that exist between activities, they can be used to reflect changes in the project schedule that occur due to the impact of various unforeseen events as the project progresses.

There are two major disadvantages to these diagrams. Since a node represents the activity and the nodes are all the same size, there is no visual way to quickly detect the duration of each activity as there is with bar charts (the length of the bar). The other disadvantage is that the activities are not time-scaled; that is, they are not tied to a calendar like they are on a bar chart, where you can look directly above the bar to the calendar to see when the activity is to be performed. Another minor disadvantage of PERT charts and AON and Precedence diagrams is that very large and complex schedules often are difficult to read and follow, particularly if they are not laid out on large paper.

Figures 4.7a and 4.7b show what many call a PERT chart. It is the same schedule that was shown as a bar chart in Figure 4.6. Generated from SureTrak, it is the schedule of the construction of a small garage and is the first project schedule the students will create using the software in the SureTrak modules later in this text.

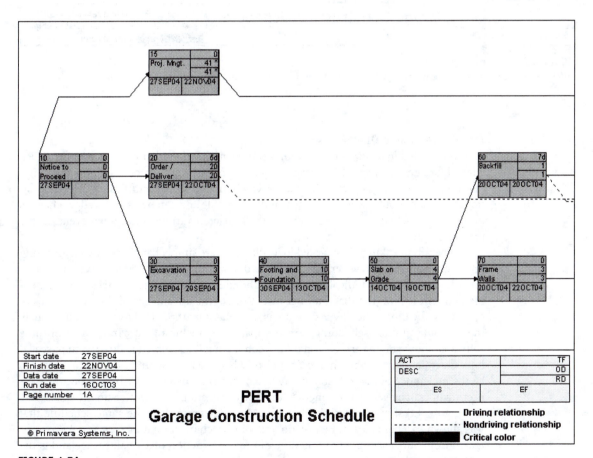

FIGURE 4.7A
PERT chart of the garage schedule that will be scheduled in the SureTrak modules later in the text.

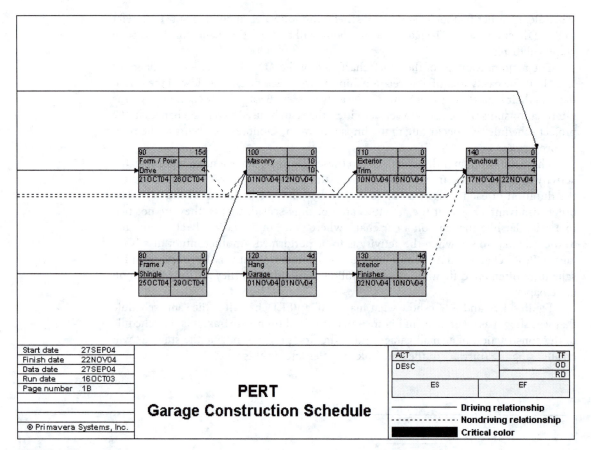

FIGURE 4.7B
PERT chart of the garage schedule that will be scheduled in the SureTrak modules later in the text.

TIME-SCALED LOGIC DIAGRAM

The time-scaled logic diagram combines the strengths of the bar chart and of the PERT chart. Like the bar chart, it is very easy to read and use and can be understood by anyone involved in the project. Like the PERT chart, it also communicates the interrelationships that exist between activities on the schedule and can be used to reflect changes in the project schedule that occur due to the impact of various unforeseen events as the project progresses.

Generally speaking, time-scaled logic diagrams are simply bar charts with connecting lines from bar to bar. However, they are derived from a calculated CPM schedule and therefore can be updated periodically to measure the effect of the project progress on the schedule and reflect it on the diagram. Because it offers the advantages of the other types of schedules, the time-scaled logic diagram is the default method used to graphically display the schedule in most scheduling software packages, including SureTrak. Most of these softwares allow you to turn on and off the connecting lines, which makes the time-scaled logic diagram look very much like a bar chart when the lines are turned off. This seems to be the preference of the industry, because schedules are usually shown without the connecting lines. The general comment is that the connecting lines clutter-up the schedule.

Figure 4.8 shows a typical time-scaled logic diagram. It is the same schedule that was shown as a bar chart in Figure 4.6 and a PERT chart in Figures 4.7a and 4.7b. Generated from SureTrak, it is the schedule of the construction of a small garage and is the first project schedule the students will create using the software in the SureTrak modules later in this text.

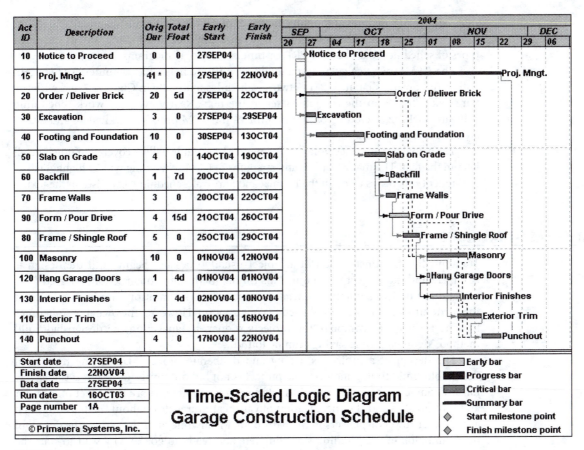

Act ID	Description	Orig Dur	Total Float	Early Start	Early Finish
10	Notice to Proceed	0	0	27SEP04	
15	Proj. Mngt.	41 *	0	27SEP04	22NOV04
20	Order / Deliver Brick	20	5d	27SEP04	22OCT04
30	Excavation	3	0	27SEP04	29SEP04
40	Footing and Foundation	10	0	30SEP04	13OCT04
50	Slab on Grade	4	0	14OCT04	19OCT04
60	Backfill	1	7d	20OCT04	20OCT04
70	Frame Walls	3	0	20OCT04	22OCT04
90	Form / Pour Drive	4	15d	21OCT04	26OCT04
80	Frame / Shingle Roof	5	0	25OCT04	29OCT04
100	Masonry	10	0	01NOV04	12NOV04
120	Hang Garage Doors	1	4d	01NOV04	01NOV04
130	Interior Finishes	7	4d	02NOV04	10NOV04
110	Exterior Trim	5	0	10NOV04	16NOV04
140	Punchout	4	0	17NOV04	22NOV04

Start date	27SEP04
Finish date	22NOV04
Data date	27SEP04
Run date	16OCT03
Page number	1A

© Primavera Systems, Inc.

**Time-Scaled Logic Diagram
Garage Construction Schedule**

Early bar
Progress bar
Critical bar
Summary bar
◆ Start milestone point
◆ Finish milestone point

FIGURE 4.8
Time-scaled logic diagram of the garage schedule that will be scheduled in the SureTrak modules later in the text.

WHAT IS CPM ?

Critical path method (CPM) it is the universal method used in the construction industry to calculate and evaluate project network schedules. It is also the predominant method used in other industries that manage projects through the use of network scheduling methods. With the input of certain project information, the CPM will calculate the minimal possible time needed to complete a project in addition to start and end dates of the activities, the total project duration, and the project's critical path. The critical path, or paths if there is than one, is the path or chain of activities through the project whose activities must be completed on time; otherwise, the end date of the project will be delayed.

The CPM method, developed in the late 1950s as a joint effort by the E.I. duPont de Nemours Company (known to most as DuPont) and the Remington Rand Corporation, is similar to the PERT method.

The PERT computational procedure allows the scheduler to compute the schedule network using variable durations for the activities, usually a high, medium, and low; and even variable logical relationships between activities. The result of the computation is a probability of the project's completion by a certain date, rather than an exact date. CPM uses a single duration for its activities and does not allow for variable logical relationships between activities. The result is a single, exact completion date for the project.

Technically speaking, CPM is a mathematical algorithm used to calculate the early start, early finish, late start, late finish, total float, and free float of all the project's activities and the total project duration and critical path or paths of the project. It can be calculated using any one of the three methods of network schedule diagramming: AOA, AON, or Precedence. The results can be graphically displayed using any of the three types of schedules: bar charts, PERT, or time-scaled logic diagrams.

The CPM can be calculated manually or with the help of a computer. The student will learn how to calculate CPM network schedules manually in Chapter 7 and with the SureTrak software in the modules later in the text. Nearly every network scheduling software package, including SureTrak, utilizes the CPM process to calculate and evaluate the project schedule.

The actual process of creating a CPM network schedule will be covered in much detail later in the text. The many features and strengths of CPM scheduling will be highlighted as the student progresses through the manual and SureTrak scheduling exercises in the text.

WHAT IS FAST-TRACKING?

Traditionally, the construction of a project usually does not begin until the design is complete and the project is bid out. This timing method in construction, referred to as design-bid-build, or sometimes linear construction, is the traditional timing method and the predominant timing method used in construction. However, the owner is sometimes looking for ways to complete the projects sooner. By analyzing the design-bid-build method, significant time savings can be found.

The design of a project is a long and deliberate process. Under the traditional design-bid-build timing method, the project is not bid out until the design is *completely finished*. Some of the last items of the design to be completed are the selection of floor and wall finishes and the specification of various fixtures throughout the building such as the paper-towel dispensers in the bathroom. Meanwhile, months earlier, the design of the foundation of the building was complete and ready to go. So why wait to start the job? With fast-tracking, you don't wait.

Fast-tracking, also called phased construction, is the process of beginning a phase (or phases) of construction *before the design is complete*. The construction will start sooner; therefore, the project will be completed sooner. Since the design usually takes less time than the construction, there isn't the worry of the construction catching up with the design.

Fast-tracking is often used on projects when completion is extremely important. Other factors, such as the budget and quality of the construction, are still important and closely monitored; yet, the completion is the first priority. Here are examples where the project completion might be the top priority: (1) A major metropolitan area is adding a terminal to its airport and wants to disrupt the operation and safety of the airport for as short a time as possible. (2) A city has decided to build a new sports stadium for its professional team and has to have it open in time for the start of the season. (3) A major interstate highway bridge needs to be replaced, which affects not only the city that it is located in, but also an entire region of the country. (4) On a smaller scale, a manufacturer needs to expand its plant in order to meet the demand for their product. (5) A local school district has to have its new high school open in time for the coming school year. (6) On a much smaller scale, a young couple hope to create a nursery before the arrival of their baby.

Figure 4.9 shows the relationship that exists between linear and phased construction (fast-tracking) on a fictitious project. There are a few things to point out. First, notice that the project starts at the same time under both timing methods. The phased project has been broken into six phases. This number will vary depending on the nature of each project. After the sitework is designed, it is bid out and construction begins. This marks the start of the project construction and occurs about halfway through the design of the project under the linear model, and obviously much earlier than the start of construction on the linear model. Soon after the sitework design begins, the foundation design follows and the structural design after that. The phases continue in this cascading fashion until the project is complete.

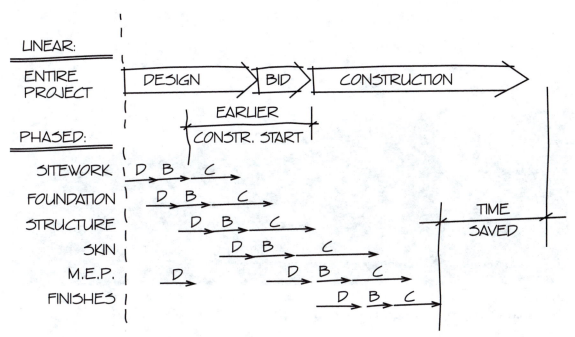

FIGURE 4.9
Relationship that exists between linear and phased construction, also known as fast-tracking.

FIGURE 4.10
Two air-handling units on top of a building early in its construction.

Notice that the MEP design starts and stops. Under fast-tracking, this is not uncommon. In this case, the designers had to decide where the air handlers and chillers are to be located. If they are to be located on the roof of the building, then the structure and foundation of the building need to be designed to support this weight. Once that decision is made, the MEP design will stop for a while and then start back up when the design is further along and there is more information. Additionally, if the air handlers or chillers are located on the roof of the building, certain scheduling considerations will also have to be made. They will have to be ordered early enough to be delivered on time to be lifted onto the top of the building soon after the structural frame is complete. This will allow the enclosure to be built around them since they are so big. Figure 4.10 shows

FIGURE 4.11
The Advanced Technology and Learning Center at Cincinnati State was fast-tracked with four phases.

two air-handling units on top of the structural frame of a building early in the construction of a building. Notice the enclosure is beginning to be built around them.

Finally, the most important aspect shown in Figure 4.9 is the significant time savings with the phased construction. It should be noted that the project was completed earlier solely because it was started earlier. Some believe that fast-tracking accelerates the construction or that the productivity is somehow improved under fast-tracking. This is not true. It simply moves the window of construction up sooner.

Another example of the use of fast-tracking can be taken from the Advanced Technology and Learning Center (ATLC) at Cincinnati State shown in Figure 4.11. The project consists of a massive retaining wall, a 700-space parking garage, and the 225,000 square foot learning center. The garage was built into the hillside and required a forty-foot tall, concrete retaining wall that can be seen to the left of the garage. The learning center sits on top of the hill adjacent to the garage. The college wanted to complete the project as soon as possible, so they chose to fast-track the job. They created four phases that were built in this order:

- Retaining wall and mass excavation
- Parking garage
- ATLC building foundation and structural frame
- ATLC building envelope / MEPs / finishes

Figure 4.12 shows the fast-track schedule for this project. It is the same example used for the milestone schedule in Figure 4.2 earlier in the chapter. Analyze this schedule to understand the nature of a fast-track project. Notice the following:

The construction of the retaining wall began while the ATLC building design was in the schematic design phase and the garage was about half designed. The garage construction began after the retaining wall was complete and about a half a year before the ATLC building foundation began. The garage was half complete when the ATLC building foundation started and opened just in time for the academic year in September of 2003, a full year before the building was to open. This would not have been possible without fast-tracking the job.

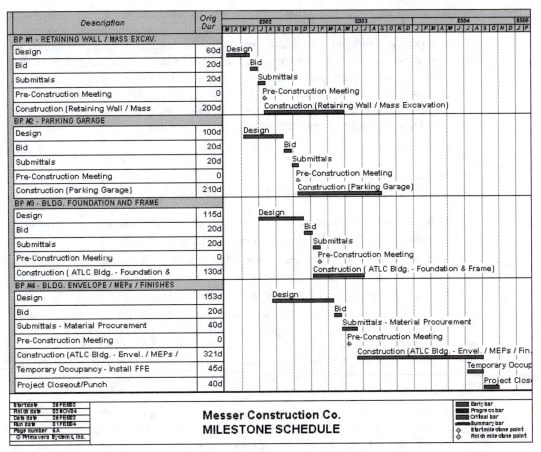

Description	Orig Dur	2002	2003	2004	2005
		M A M J J A S O N D	J F M A M J J A S O N D	J F M A M J J A S O N D	J F
BP #1 - RETAINING WALL / MASS EXCAV.					
Design	60d	Design			
Bid	20d	Bid			
Submittals	20d	Submittals			
Pre-Construction Meeting	0	Pre-Construction Meeting			
Construction (Retaining Wall / Mass	200d	Construction (Retaining Wall / Mass Excavation)			
BP #2 - PARKING GARAGE					
Design	100d	Design			
Bid	20d	Bid			
Submittals	20d	Submittals			
Pre-Construction Meeting	0	Pre-Construction Meeting			
Construction (Parking Garage)	210d	Construction (Parking Garage)			
BP #3 - BLDG. FOUNDATION AND FRAME					
Design	115d	Design			
Bid	20d	Bid			
Submittals	20d	Submittals			
Pre-Construction Meeting	0	Pre-Construction Meeting			
Construction (ATLC Bldg. - Foundation &	130d	Construction (ATLC Bldg. - Foundation & Frame)			
BP #4 - BLDG. ENVELOPE / MEPs / FINISHES					
Design	153d		Design		
Bid	20d		Bid		
Submittals - Material Procurement	40d		Submittals - Material Procurement		
Pre-Construction Meeting	0		Pre-Construction Meeting		
Construction (ATLC Bldg. - Envel. / MEPs /	321d		Construction (ATLC Bldg. - Envel. / MEPs / Fin.		
Temporary Occupancy - Install FFE	45d			Temporary Occup	
Project Closeout/Punch	40d			Project Clos	

Start date	28 FEB 2
Finish date	02 NOV 04
Data date	28 FEB 2
Run date	01 FEB 04
Page number	6A
© Primavera Systems, Inc.	

Messer Construction Co.
MILESTONE SCHEDULE

◼ Early bar
◼ Progress bar
◼ Critical bar
◼ Summary bar
◇ Start milestone point
◇ Finish milestone point

FIGURE 4.12

A fast-track schedule for the Advanced Technology and Learning Center at Cincinnati State. The project was fast-tracked with four phases, saving nine months on the project schedule and opening a full school year earlier. (Messer Construction)

Had the project been built under the traditional design-bid-build timing method, the design would have been completed in March of 2003, with the construction starting later that spring instead of the previous July—nine months earlier than when it actually started. What's more, the project would have finished in July of 2005—nine months later, thereby completely missing the 2004 school year for the college.

Fast-tracking calls for special contracting situations. For example, fast-tracking does not lend itself to the general contracting project delivery system or to single lump sum contracts. General contractors are typically hired under lump sum contracts to build the entire project. This is a problem since the construction begins long before the design is complete. The general contractor would never commit to the locked-in price of a lump sum contract when the design is incomplete. As a result, two choices surface: Don't build the project using general contracting *or* the general contractor will have to work under a type of contract that does not lock in the price, such as a cost plus a fee or a time and material contract. Both types of contracts shift the budget risk of the project to the owner and therefore are rarely used with fast-tracking. Another contracting situation particular to fast-tracking is the use of multiple contractors for the multiple phases. This results in a need for added coordination of these numerous contractors and, more importantly, creates a leadership void.

All the previously detailed problems can be solved by the use of agency construction management as the project delivery system. Agency construction management calls for the use of multiple prime contractors in contract with the owner and coordinated and supervised by the construction manager. Under this system these prime contractors can competitively bid on the various phases of the fast-tracking. The owner will be able to award lump sum contracts for the phases and the construction manager will be there to coordinate and supervise the entire project. The use of the design/build project delivery system would, in a similar fashion, alleviate these problems.

Beyond the issues previously addressed, the following lists detail additional advantages and disadvantages of fast-tracking.

ADVANTAGES OF FAST-TRACKING

The following are advantages of fast-tracking a project:

- *Saves time.* This is the obvious and most substantial advantage of fast-tracking. However, embedded in this advantage are other advantages.

- *Saves money.* The old adage is true, "time is money." There are numerous ways that saving time will save money.

- *Saves on indirect costs.* Indirect costs are costs that do not go directly in to the building, such as project management costs, the cost of the job trailer, security, temporary facilities, project insurance, and many others. These costs are sometimes referred to as general condition costs and can make up to 15 percent of the total project cost. Most of these costs are incurred as long as the project is continuing, therefore, substantial savings can be realized if the total project duration is reduced significantly.

- *Save on financing costs.* The owner pays interest on a construction loan while the project is under construction and pays off the construction loan with permanent financing when the project is complete. The construction loan interest is usually 2 percent to 5 percent higher, or more in certain situations, than the permanent financing. Therefore, the sooner the project is completed, the sooner the owner can close the construction loan with the permanent financing.

- *Disruption of business.* If the project is on the site of a business or is renovating a building that houses a business, disruption to the business can be significant. The quicker the work is performed, the better. Additionally, a business may have to move temporarily while waiting for a new building to be completed.

- *Convenience.* Anyone who has sat in a traffic jam due to road construction appreciates the advantage of completing the project ahead of schedule.

- *Safety concerns.* Projects under construction are inherently unsafe, not only for the construction workers, but also for the public that interface with the job.

- *Getting to the market.* It is important for owners to be able to sell their product faster, gain more market share, and beat out the competition.

- *Advantage to the contractor.* The primary reason to fast-track a job is to benefit the owner. Contractors typically do not make more or less money on a job that is fast-tracked. However, they might be able to make more profit from the job by reducing their overhead with a shorter schedule.

DISADVANTAGES OF FAST-TRACKING

Fast-tracking a project creates the potential for numerous problems. However, most if not all of these problems can be avoided or successfully administered with careful project management by the project team. It should also be noted that many of the problems detailed below also occur on projects that are built using the traditional design-bid-build timing method. The following are disadvantages that may occur due to fast-tracking a project:

- *Design problems.* Since the building is being designed in phases and the phases are released for construction, the project team never has the opportunity to view the entire design as a whole. Without this review, the designers may not see areas of conflict, overlap, or omission. This may lead to potential design problems, some of which are described below.

- *Owner's needs not met.* The project team may proceed into construction without having thoroughly considered all the elements of design or been able to perform a review of the whole project discussed above. As a consequence, the end product may not fully meet the needs of the owner as well as it might have with more consideration. This is often not detected until the owner occupies and experiences the project.

- *Potential for overdesign.* The following is an example of how fast-tracking can lead to overdesign. Early in the design of the project it is decided to place large components of the HVAC system on the roof of the building. This decision was made early in the design because the design of the foundation and structural frame had to be finalized so their construction could begin. To accommodate the HVAC loads, the foundation and structural frame were beefed-up. Later, as the design proceeded, that decision was reversed based on further information that had come to light about the project. However, it was too late to beef-down the foundation and structural frame since they were already built. Sometimes, this type of problem resulting from fast-tracking cannot be avoided.

- *Potential design conflicts.* Design conflicts occur on all projects and cannot be completely eliminated. However, fast-tracking potentially leads to more conflicts due to the disjointed nature of the design. For example, if the structural drawings were completed before the MEP design is complete, there is the potential for numerous interferences to occur between the building's structure and the HVAC duct runs, electrical cable tray and conduits, and plumbing penetrations in the floors and walls of the building. These types of interferences often are not detected until they occur out in the field, regardless of how the project is being built. However, more of them might be detected during the design if it was not phased.

- *Incomplete design and documents.* Incomplete design and documents can be a potential problem for any project. However, it may be argued that under fast-tracking this potential is magnified. As discussed and illustrated in Chapter 3, it is much cheaper to avoid a problem or detect it on the documents than to have to fix it in the field. This was shown in Figure 3.6 in Chapter 3.

- *Need for greater design coordination.* The potential design problems detailed above call for a greater need for design coordination. This would be the responsibility of the architect to closely coordinate the various design firms working for them as subconsultants.

- *Increased changes.* Design conflicts, omissions, interferences, and so on normally result in some type of change. These changes often cost the owner additional dollars because they usually are not covered in the contract.

- *Numerous contracts and contractors.* Another potential disadvantage not related to design problems is the need for multiple prime contractors to perform each phase of the project. Most owners would prefer to be in contract with one contractor, rather than several, which creates more risk and exposure to the owner. Rather than dealing with one problem contract, or potential overrun, or claim, the owner may have to deal with ten—or whatever the number may be.

■ *Interface of scope of work.* With multiple prime contractors performing the phases of the project, there is the potential problem of confusion over the scope of each contractor's work. In addition to confusion over the scope, there is always the possibility that the scope of each contract was not divided properly, and that one or more of the following three dilemmas may exist:

1. Item of work is left out of all contracts.
2. Item of work is put into more than one contract.
3. Item of work is put into the wrong contractor's contract.

All three situations will involve a change to one or more contracts. These types of contract modifications are usually made at a premium cost to the owner.

■ *Need for greater construction coordination.* The use of multiple prime contractors and other issues previously discussed result in a greater need for coordination throughout the construction of the project. Construction managers normally run jobs with multiple prime contractors and, therefore, have extensive experience addressing these concerns.

■ *Disadvantage to the contractor.* Because there may be more pressure and the need for more coordination and administration on the part of the contractor on a fast-track job, given the choice, most contractors would probably rather work a design-bid-build job than a fast-track project.

The potential disadvantages and problems listed above are not trivial. They make you appreciate how great the benefits of fast-tracking must be in the minds of some owners. These problems have the potential of wiping out any savings the owner would realize from completing the project sooner and may reduce other benefits as well. However, with diligent oversight, most of these disadvantages and problems can be avoided or lessened; therefore, owners decide to take the risk of fast-tracking their projects.

CHAPTER 5

Activities, Logic, and Duration

The first four chapters of the text were intended to provide the necessary framework and background for you to learn the terminology of scheduling and to gain an understanding of the environment and landscape that exists when the construction project schedule is created.

In the next four chapters, you will learn how to create accurate and realistic detailed construction schedules. The Delhi Medical Building shown in Figures 5.1a and 5.1b will be used as a sample project throughout the next four chapters. Selected sheets from the building drawings were bundled with the text and selected pages from the building's specifications are included in various sections throughout the next four chapters. Additionally, a partial set of plans for the USA Volleyball Centers was also bundled with the text. They will be used for the Student Scheduling Assignment at the end of Chapter 8.

FIGURE 5.1A
The Delhi Medical Building (south elevation), which will be used as the sample project over the next four chapters.

FIGURE 5.1B
The Delhi Medical Building (north elevation), which will be used as the
sample project over the next four chapters.

Every construction schedule includes the activities of the project laid out in a logical sequence with assigned durations. In this chapter, you will learn about *activities,
logic,* and *duration* in preparation for the next three chapters.

In Chapter 6, you will learn to draw, by hand, network diagrams of the schedule. A
network diagram is a rough, hand-drawn draft of the schedule showing the breakdown
of the project work into its activities in their logical sequence. To successfully create an
accurate schedule, it is imperative that the network diagram be prepared first.

In Chapter 7, you will learn how to manually calculate the schedule using the CPM
method. The calculations will determine the early start, early finish, late start, late finish, total float, and free float of each activity, as well as the total project duration and critical path(s) of the project.

In Chapter 8, the process all comes together. You will be taken step-by-step through
the creation of the construction project schedule of the Delhi Medical Building and then
will be assigned to create a schedule on your own for the USA Volleyball Centers.

The creation of a construction schedule starts with identifying the following schedule information:

- Identifying activities
- Logical sequencing of the activities
- Activity duration

IDENTIFYING ACTIVITIES

One definition of a project is that the project is the sum of its activities. The first step in
creating a schedule is to identify the activities that are needed to accomplish the project.
This is an important step in the process of creating the schedule because the activities
that are selected must encompass all the required project work. Additionally, these selected activities are important because they become the basis for tracking and controlling the progress of the work throughout the project.

The following topics are intended to provide a framework for identifying various
factors that need to be considered when identifying schedule activities:

- What is an activity?
- Types of activities
- Activity detail
- Activity guidelines
- Work breakdown structure (WBS)
- Activity categories
- Activity descriptions
- Activity IDs
- Additional activity information

WHAT IS AN ACTIVITY?

Construction projects, no matter how big or how small, are made up of a number of individual work items or tasks that must be completed in order to finish the project. These individual work items are usually referred to as activities.

While patterns often exist within similar types of projects yielding similar schedules, every construction project is unique and every project has a unique set of goals and objectives. Even if two identical buildings were to be built, they would be different due to differing site conditions. Therefore, every project will have a unique set of activities. These activities must be accomplished in order to achieve these goals and objectives.

Activities have the following characteristics:

- Activities usually consume time
- Activities usually consume resources
- Activities have a definable scope of work
- Activities have a definable start, finish, and sequence
- Activities are assignable
- Activities are measurable

Activities Usually Consume Time

The length of time consumed by an activity to complete its work is called the *duration*. The majority of construction activities consume time. The activity duration can be measured in different units, the most common being days. Activity duration will be discussed later in this chapter.

Activities that do not consume time are usually referred to as milestones. Milestones are significant events that highlight a turning point in the project. A milestone may be marked for the start of an event, its finish, or both.

Activities Usually Consume Resources

A resource is anything necessary to complete an activity. Some examples of resources include labor, material, equipment, money, management, and other contractors. Activities may require one or more resources to work. Activities do not have to use a resource to still be considered an activity. The best example of this is an activity placed into the schedule to allow cure time for concrete. This activity uses no resources.

Activities Have a Definable Scope of Work

By definition, an activity is an individual work item or task. The item of work that is to be accomplished by the activity must be definable by a specific scope of work to be performed. An example would be Hang Drywall—1st Floor. It is very clear what work is to be performed. However, an activity such as Clean-Up does not have a definable scope of work. While this is an important activity to perform, it is not clear who is to clean-up, where, and for how long. Since clean-up is an ongoing activity, it would be better to be left off the schedule and communicated in a different venue.

The work of the activity is usually performed at the project site, but does not have to be. One of the more recent developments in the construction industry is a practice entitled modularization. This was successfully used on the Northridge road project discussed at the beginning of Chapter 4. Modularization is the process of prefabricating large components of a structure, usually off-site, then shipping the components to the site and placing them in their final resting place. This process can save tremendous amounts of time on the construction schedule.

Activities Have a Definable Start, Finish, and Sequence

Each activity must have a definable start and finish point. The start of the activity will begin when work on the activity begins. The finish of the activity occurs when the scope of work defined for that activity is completed. The activity *Form Concrete Wall*, for instance, starts when the first piece of formwork is placed and finishes when the wall is completely formed and the activities that follow it are able to begin.

It should be noted that a *definable start and finish* does not mean an exact calendar date or positioned ordinal date in the project (e.g., day 17). Both of those dates will be computed for the scheduler when the schedule is eventually calculated using CPM.

In addition to a definable start and finish, each activity must have a sequenced spot in the schedule. This sequencing is often referred to as the *logic* of the schedule and will be discussed later in this chapter.

Activities Are Assignable

Each activity entails a specific item of work that must be accomplished for the project to be completed, and therefore must have a responsible party assigned to it that states who is going to perform the work. This is imperative to the project because it helps divide the project into manageable pieces and assigns those pieces to the party best suited to perform the work. This assignment is also very important when the project is underway and each activity is tracked and controlled for progress. Therefore, in addition to deciding what the activity is and how long it should take, the assignment tells who is responsible.

Activities Are Measurable

To be able to track the progress of the project, the progress of each activity must be tracked. In order to track the progress of the activities, they must be measurable. Activities can be measured in a few ways. The most common method is to measure the progress of the activity in terms of actual quantities of materials installed. Most activities include the installation of materials, and the quantity of the materials is usually known. These activities are measured in terms of actual quantities of materials put in place. For example, the installation of 50,000 square feet of metal stud partitions has an original duration of twenty-five days to install, which is 2,000 square feet per day. If 34,000 square feet were installed, to date, eight days would remain for this activity.

A second way is to approximate the percent complete of the activity based on a gut feeling for what has been accomplished compared to what is left to do. This method is very quick and easy and is accurate enough for most updates.

A third way to measure the progress of an activity is to simply measure the time that has elapsed on the activity compared to its original duration. This is the least accurate of the three methods because it assumes that the work is progressing at its expected pace, which can be a dangerous assumption in construction. Later in this chapter, there is a section entitled *Actual Duration and Productivity* that discusses reasons why actual durations and productivity might not be realized.

TYPES OF ACTIVITIES

The term *activity* can be applied to any of the three items listed below:

- Activity
- Milestone
- Hammock

Activity

The most common type of activity is the standard work item activity that was previously defined. It is easily the most common type of activity, probably making up about 99 percent of all activities found on project schedules.

Milestone

Milestones are significant events that highlight a turning point in the project. A milestone may be marked for the start of an event, its finish, or both; in other words, there are *start milestones* and *finish milestones*. Milestone activities do not have duration and do not have resources. However, it might be better to think of them as activities with *zero* duration. That is how they are handled when placed in a schedule and computed with CPM. That way they can exist and function as any other activity, but they do not add to the project's total duration.

Listed below are a few examples of milestones that are commonly used in construction schedules:

Notice to proceed. A notice to proceed is sent to the contractor from the owner and serves as the official notice to start the project. Any work performed by the contractor prior to receiving this notice is performed at the contractor's risk. The receipt of this notice also marks the official start date of construction, against which completion bonuses and/or penalties are measured.

Topping out. Topping out signifies the completion of the building's structural frame. There is often some type of ceremony with the last piece of steel, maybe a beam that has been signed by interested members of the project, being lifted into place.

Building enclosed. Building enclosed signifies that the skin and roof of the building is complete enough to begin to heat the building and begin interior finishes such as drywall. This is an important milestone since interior finishes are usually on the critical path.

Substantial completion. Substantial completion is the milestone that marks the completion of the project's construction. It is expected that there will still exist minor punchlist items and corrections to be completed before its final completion. The exact requirements defining substantial completion are identified in the agreements between the owner and the contractor(s).

Project complete. This is often the very last activity on the schedule and signifies the absolute completion of the project.

There are many different milestone activities that may be used on project schedules. Different contractors have certain ones that they prefer to use and different projects will dictate the use of different milestones.

Hammock

A hammock activity is a very useful type of activity, made popular by its use in scheduling software, that is rarely mentioned in textbooks. The hammock activity borrows its name from the hammock you might string up between two trees in the backyard. Like that hammock, the hammock activity is hooked between two activities on the schedule. Hammock activities do not have their own duration, but rather take on the longest duration of the paths between the two activities that they are hooked between.

A hammock activity commonly runs the entire length of the project from the network's first activity to its last. In this case the hammock will take on the duration of the total project. The use of this hammock is particularly helpful when a schedule has resources assigned to the activities, because all the general condition resources and indirect costs of the project that occur throughout the entire length of the project, such as project field staff, job trailer, and so forth, can reside there. This will be exemplified in much detail in the SureTrak Module 19 on resources.

Both milestone and hammock activities will be included in the Delhi Medical Building schedule and other schedules that you will create and work with in the coming chapters and modules.

ACTIVITY DETAIL

The activities of a schedule can be very general or very detailed. There is no rule of thumb to determine the correct level of detail for a project schedule—each project may be different based on various factors. Additionally, one project may require multiple schedules with differing levels of activity detail to be used in different ways, probably by different people. For example, the schedule that is given to the owner may have much less activity detail than the schedule used in the field to build the project.

While construction projects are unique and the level of activity detail can vary from one project to the next, projects do have their common elements. By using these common elements in the schedule, valuable historical data can be gathered and used on the current project to evaluate performance and develop labor productivity rates for future projects. Most construction projects, for instance, include flat concrete work such as sidewalks, driveways, or interior slabs. This flat concrete work, or *flatwork* as it is often called, is very much the same from job to job. Suppose that a slab crew placed 97,500 square feet of slab in eleven working days on a previous job. The daily rate would be almost 9,000 (8,863) square feet per day. If the next job had 70,000 square feet of slab to place, based on this historical data, it should take eight days to complete.

The following are various factors that may be considered when determining the level of detail for the schedule activities.

- *What is the purpose of the schedule?* Different schedules may be developed for the same project. As an example, the construction of a research building might require a separate, specific detailed schedule for the installation of a special piece of equipment.

- *Who is going to use the schedule?* As discussed earlier, different parties involved in the construction project will need schedules with varying levels of detail. Some scheduling softwares, including SureTrak, have the ability to create different summary levels of the detailed construction schedule without recreating the schedule. In Module 17, the student will learn how to create these summary schedules.

- *How complex is the project?* Generally, complex projects require more detailed activities than those that are less complex. The complexity of a project can be measured in a couple of ways. A power plant is a complex project due to the nature of what's being constructed. The construction of a runway at an existing airport is a complex project due to the logistics of construction at a functioning airport.

- *What is the management philosophy of the project?* The owner sets the tone of the management philosophy of the project in many ways, including scheduling. If the owner asks for a construction schedule in the RFP (request for proposal), there's a good indication that the project will, at least, require schedules to be used and updated periodically. The construction manager's philosophy is even more telling. Some managers like to use just summary schedules and are more hands-on, while others are more detail oriented and prefer to see the details of the construction laid out on paper.

  Regardless, most construction projects today require a detailed construction schedule. They are not always required to be updated periodically, but that is changing with updates being required more often as the overall use of computer-generated CPM schedules increases.

- *What information about the project was known when the schedule was prepared?* The previous chapter presented the evolution of the schedule. As discussed there, the schedule becomes more detailed as more information becomes known about the project. This is a particularly important factor when dealing with a fast-track job.

- *Who is performing the work?* Individual schedules with more detail are frequently provided to the trade contractors who are performing the work. These usually take the form of a *look-ahead schedule*. A look-ahead schedule graphically highlights and expands the timescale of a fixed period, like the next six weeks. This type of schedule allows the contractors to focus on the immediate work at hand. These types of schedules are often handed out at the weekly progress meetings that all the contractors attend. Figure 5.2a shows an example of a look-ahead schedule that was created using spreadsheet software.

  SureTrak allows you to create and customize many types of schedule layouts including look-ahead schedules. In Module 10, the student will create a two-week look-ahead schedule. Figure 5.2b shows an example of the two-week look-ahead schedule that the student will create later in Module 10.

ACTIVITY GUIDELINES
There are certain guidelines that should be followed when creating schedule activities to ensure the proper level of detail. These guidelines are listed as follows:

- *The activity should have a defined starting and stopping point.* Activities cannot be open ended on either end or the network will not work. Every activity needs to have a defined starting point and a defined stopping point. The starting point might be triggered when a preceding activity finishes, might be locked into a specific date, or might be at the beginning of the project. Similarly, an activity's stopping point is usually when its duration ends, or could be locked into a specific date, or it might be tied into the start or finish of another activity. This will be discussed in more detail later in this chapter in the discussion of activity logic.

- *Make sure the work of the activity is continuous.* If the work of the activity has a natural pause in it, it probably should be broken up into two activities. For example, if the installation of a piping system is waiting for a pressure test before being complete, it is better to break it up into two, or even three, distinct activities: Install Pipe, Test Pipe, and Complete Pipe.

- *The progress of the activity should be observable and measurable.* It is important to observe and measure progress in order to monitor and control the project schedule. Very broad activities have the type of progress that often is not measurable and sometimes not observable. A broad activity such as Design Project

SIX WEEK LOOK AHEAD SCHEDULE

CONTRACTOR	MESSER CONSTRUCTION
PROJECT NAME	Cincinnati State ATLC
PROJECT LOCATION	Cincinnati, Ohio
JOB NUMBER	361-2001-066 / 002-7620
PLANNER NAME	Thomas A. Bell

SIX WEEK EVALUATION PERIOD STARTING ON 6-Oct-03

STATUS	ACTIVITY	RESPONSIBLE PARTY	6-Oct	13-Oct	20-Oct	27-Oct	3-Nov	10-Nov	CONTRACTS / CO's	ENGINEERING	SUBMITTALS	SAFETY	RFI's	MATERIALS	LABOR	EQUIPMENT	PREREQUSITE	SPACE	COMMENTS / OTHER
	ATLC Raised Area Level 3																		
3	Ramp along Risers	Baker	X																Schedule start date 9/10/03
3	Slab on Metal Deck (Stage)	Baker	X																Schedule start date 9/10/03
3	Seating 3rd to 4th level	Baker	X																Schedule start date 9/22/03
	ATLC Frame SOMD																		
2	Topping Slab Area B Pour	Baker	X																Schedule start date 9/10/03
2	Slab on Metal Deck	Baker	X																Schedule start date 9/17/03
	ATLC Frame SOG																		
2	Pour 3 & 4	Baker	X																Schedule start date 9/25/03
	ATLC Building Skin																		
	Perimeter Studs																		
2	Perm studs Lv 4	Valley	X																Schedule Perm studs date 8/20/03
	Perm studs Lv 5	Valley	X																Schedule Perm studs date 9/15/03
	Perm studs Lv 6	Valley		X	X	X	X												Schedule Perm studs date 10/13/03
	Demo Kitchen Skin																		
	Steel over Demo Kitchen (SEQ 7)	OHIOSTEEL				X													Schedule start date 10/13/03
	Kitchen Roof	Beischel						X											Schedule start date 11/03/03/11/17/03 **Revised**
	Column Line A-E																		
	Sheathing West CL B-A (cr2)	Valley	S																Schedule start date 8/19/03/complete
1	Sheathing East CL A-E (cr1)	Valley	X																Schedule start date 8/25/03
	Flr 2&3 Curtainwall CL 4-3, B-E (cr-1)	Waltek	X	X	X														Schedule start date 9/15/03?Started 10/6/03
	Stair C Curtain Wall (Cr1)	Waltek		X	X														Schedule start date 9/23/03/Started 10/6/03
	Steel @ Stair C (Seq 3)	OHIOSTEEL	X	X	X														Schedule start date 9/10/03// 10/8/03 Revised
	Stair C Roof	Beischel																	Schedule start date 11/03/03// 11/28/03 Revised
	Column Line 1-8																		
	Sheathing South CL 1-3.6 (Cr1)	Valley	S																Schedule start date 9/08/03
1	Level 3 & 4 Auditorium Steel (Seq 1)	OHIOSTEEL	X																Schedule start date 9/08/03
	Steel Over Auditorium (Seq 2)	OHIOSTEEL	X																Schedule start date 9/11/03
	Sheathing South CL 4-8 (Cr 1)	Valley	X	X	X														Schedule start date 10/08/03

Page 1 of 3

10/8/2003

FIGURE 5.2A

Six-week look-ahead schedule created with a spreadsheet program.
(Messer Construction)

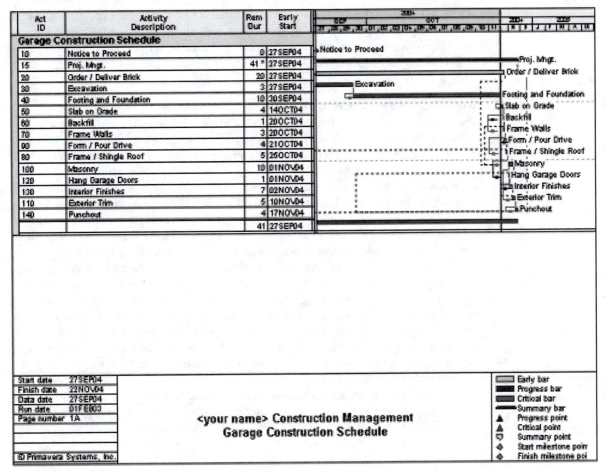

FIGURE 5.2B
Two-week look-ahead schedule that will be created by the students in Module 10.

probably has a start and end date on the milestone schedule, but it is difficult to measure. Its progress is observable only when the architect submits updated drawings and is roughly measurable by determining approximately where the design is in the overall process. Activities on the construction schedule should be detailed enough to allow the activity's progress to be measured.

■ *The resources should not change significantly over the duration of the activity.* If the project schedule reflects the use of the resources of each activity, it is best to keep the activities detailed enough to avoid significant resource changes as the activity proceeds. For example, if a tower crane was being used to raise the precast curtain wall for the upper half of a building and a mobile crane was being used for the lower half, it would be better to break that work into two activities, rather than one. If left at one, the resource reporting would be inaccurate.

■ *Ensure that reporting requirements are met.* The owner may want to keep track of the project using certain types of reports. Suppose the owner will receive a tax credit for the cost of installing certain pollution-control equipment on their manufacturing facility and the installation of this equipment is tied to a much larger renovation project. The construction manager will have to break out that information from the reports. This might affect how the construction scheduling activities are laid out. There are many other situations that call for different reporting requirements; therefore, it is important for the construction manager to solicit the views of the owner relative to project reporting early in the project process.

When determining the level of activity detail that is best suited for a project, one other consideration to examine is the project's work breakdown structure (WBS), if one exists. The work breakdown structure could also be used to help develop the appropriate level of detail for the schedule.

WORK BREAKDOWN STRUCTURE (WBS)

The term *work breakdown structure,* (WBS) is used in the industry to describe a framework for organizing and dividing the project into manageable sections using a hierarchical structure, with each section taking on an increasingly greater level of detail.

The WBS is not a schedule, and it does not sequence activities; rather, it merely lists, in increasing levels of detail, items of work from the project. The WBS usually includes multiple levels—five or more. The first, and broadest, level is the project itself containing just that one single item, whereas the last, and most detailed, level might include an item as detailed as a work crew or even an individual from the crew. Figure 5.3 shows an example of a typical work breakdown structure from a project with the associated WBS code numbers.

The contractor may use the WBS across many management areas of the company including estimating, purchasing, accounting, scheduling, budgeting, and project management. A cost code numbering system is often incorporated into the WBS allowing it to be used for cross-indexing of data between systems. For example, estimating items organized by the WBS codes can be cross-referenced and integrated into the contractor's accounting system. The WBS is often developed by the accounting department to help keep track of project costs. The WBS code numbers often tie directly into the accounting cost code numbering system.

There is often a WBS level entitled *Activity* and it is usually the one closest to the level of detail found on the typical construction schedule. Therefore, it is usually the one used to help develop the appropriate level of schedule detail.

WBS Code	Project	Work Division	System	Component	Item	Activity	Sub-Activity
Project							
CS	Building						
Work Division							
CS.03		Concrete					
System							
CS.03.01			Foundation				
Component							
CS.03.01.01				Footing			
CS.03.01.02				Wall			
Item							
CS.03.01.01.01					Spread Footing		
CS.03.01.01.02					Wall Footing		
CS.03.01.01.03					Drilled Piers		
Activity							
CS.03.01.01.01.01						Excavate Spread Footing	
CS.03.01.01.01.02						Form Spread Footing	
CS.03.01.01.01.03						Reinforcement	
CS.03.01.01.01.04						Pour and Finish	
CS.03.01.01.01.05						Strip Forms	
CS.03.01.01.01.06						Backfill	
Sub-Activity							
CS.03.01.01.01.02.01							Labor
CS.03.01.01.01.02.02							Material
CS.03.01.01.01.02.03							Equipment

FIGURE 5.3
Work breakdown structure (WBS) with associated WBS code numbers.

ACTIVITY CATEGORIES

Once the work of the project is divided up into its activities, there is sometimes a desire to group or sort the activities into categories. There are many categories that can be used for breaking up the work of the project; some of the more common are listed below:

- Component of the building
- Phase of the project
- Location of work
- Trade contractors performing the work
- Supervisors responsible for the work
- Work crews

Each category would have specific groups that the activities would be sorted into. For example, the component of the building category might have for its groups the following: sitework, foundation, structure, skin, MEPs, and finishes.

Multiple categories are sometimes used together. For instance, a component of the work is the skin of the building, usually referred to as the curtain wall. But rather than having one curtain wall activity for the entire project, the curtain wall might be broken down into several activities for each story of the building, giving the schedule more detail and making this work easier to monitor, measure, and control. A third category might even be added to this. Suppose the work is to be supervised by two individuals, Smith and Jones, and Jones is in charge of the curtain walls. Considering all three categories, an activity for this work might read: Curtain Wall—3rd Floor (Jones).

ACTIVITY DESCRIPTIONS

The descriptions assigned to the schedule activities are very important if the schedule is to serve as an effective communication tool. The activity descriptions must be both precise and concise. Long activity descriptions on networks generated by scheduling softwares will cause the network to spill onto multiple pages or, if forced to fit onto one page, will cause the network to be scaled down to a point where it might not be readable. This will become evident to students when they create and print various schedules using the SureTrak scheduling software in the modules later in the text.

Short descriptions are advantageous, but still must be able to effectively communicate the scope of the activity's work, and possibly other information such as location or responsibility. Additionally, the description has to mean the same thing to all who read it, including the owners who may not be as familiar with construction industry terms.

The best plan for creating effective activity descriptions is to use a two-word, verb-subject format, for example, Install Footing. The word *install* is the verb and *footing* is the subject. Rarely do articles, such as *of, the, a, to,* and so forth, serve a purpose in the description, other than taking up valuable space. Therefore, the description Install the Footing is not correct. Abbreviations and initializations are acceptable, but make sure they are consistent—do not abbreviate Footing, Ftg on one activity and Foot. on another. Use standard industry abbreviations and initializations whenever possible.

ACTIVITY IDs

The activity identification (ID) is the number or letter given to the activity. It is best to draw out the network diagram completely and revise it, if need be, before assigning activity IDs to the activities on the network.

There is a natural tendency for people to think that the activity ID number or letter must be in the proper alphabetic or numeric order. This is not true. The order of the activity number or letter is unimportant.

When converting the hand-drawn network into a scheduling software, it is imperative that each activity be given an ID. There are two reasons for this. It makes the transfer of activity information easier and helps avoid mistakes when making the transfer. Secondly, most softwares, including SureTrak, require an ID for all activities because it is used as the primary identifier of the scheduling software.

ADDITIONAL ACTIVITY INFORMATION

There are many other types of data and information that can be gathered and assigned to activities. Listed below are some of the more common types that are frequently incorporated into the schedule:

- *Budget.* By assigning a budgeted amount to each activity on the schedule, the project team will be able to effectively monitor the cash flow of the project. When a budgeted amount is assigned to an activity, it is expected that the money is spread evenly across the duration of the activity. For example, if an activity has a budgeted amount of $12,000 assigned to it and the activity is eight days in duration, the daily budgeted amount will be $1,500 per day. From this information the project cash flow can be determined for the entire project.

- *Resources.* A resource is anything it takes to get the job done such as labor, materials, equipment, management, and so on—really anything that is needed to accomplish the work. These different resources can be assigned to the appropriate activities on a daily basis. By summing the daily resource requirement for each activity, the total requirement for each day can be determined. This allows the construction manager to view a single activity or look at the project as a whole, thereby providing an effective method for monitoring and measuring project progress. The total resource requirement can be compared to available resources to predict and avoid resource shortfalls. A resource profile for the project can be developed and used to level resource requirements. Historical data can also be gathered about the use of resources on this job to be used for scheduling on future projects.

- *Value.* When budget and resources are assigned to activities, their value can be measured and variances can be forecasted. Actual expenditures of money and/or resources can be recorded and compared to the planned expenditures based on the schedule. Using *earned value* concepts, variances can be forecasted. Here is an example.

> Suppose the erection of a granite curtain wall on a building is scheduled to take 160 hours of crane time and the crane was assigned as a resource to the granite erection activity. The erection of the granite has been proceeding and is 40 percent complete. This is easily measured by simply counting the square feet of granite erected and comparing it to the total. Since 40 percent of the granite is installed, it would be expected that 40 percent, or 64 hours (40 percent of 160 hours), of the crane time would be used up. But suppose further that the actual crane time recorded for granite erection so far has been only 50 hours. Based on this scenario, the current (positive) variance is 14 hours (64 − 50 hours). If the use of the crane continues at this positive rate for the remainder of the activity, the total forecasted use of the crane would be 125 (50 hours ÷ 40%) hours, with a total forecasted variance of a positive 35 hours—thereby providing additional profit to the contractor.

This scenario demonstrates the power of scheduling and is just one example of the many types of additional activity information that can be incorporated into the project schedule.

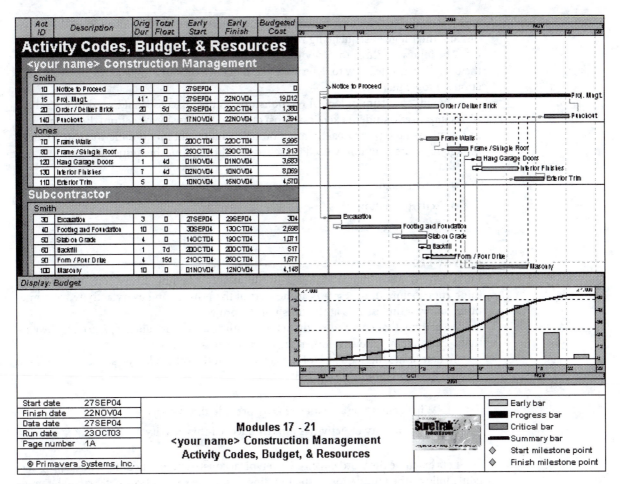

FIGURE 5.4
Construction schedule showing other types of activity information including responsibility, budget for each activity, and the project cash flow.

Figure 5.4 shows the garage construction schedule that the students will create using SureTrak later in the modules. This project schedule shows the following additional activity information:

- Two levels of responsibility are listed for the activities: the first is a contractor responsibility—either <your name> construction management or subcontractor, and the second is by individual—either *Smith* or *Jones*.

- Budget information for each activity is shown in a column in the data area of the schedule.

- The total project cash flow is shown directly beneath the activity bars on the same timescale, indicating that the cash flow is generated from the activities above.

This information is the topic of Modules 17, 18, and 20 and was added to the project schedule in those modules as part of the exercises performed by the students.

LOGICAL SEQUENCING OF THE ACTIVITIES

As the scheduler or project manager lays out the activities on the network diagram, they are building the project in their mind, and at the same time are actually developing the logical sequence of the activities. As the activities are being laid out and connected to each other, the connections denote the logic. Therefore, the identification of the activities and their logical sequencing really happens together.

The following three topics will help you understand the relationship of the logic to the overall schedule, how to determine the sequence of activities, and the different variations of logic that exist.

The full spectrum of logical relationships will be discussed and used in the schedule examples and student exercises. Most other textbooks shy away from these other logical relationship types by barely mentioning them, or not mentioning them at all, even though most are commonly used on schedules throughout the industry.

- Activity logic
- Activity relationships
- Activity lag

ACTIVITY LOGIC

Every activity has a logical sequence in the project schedule. Every activity has something come before it, unless it is at the start of the project; and every activity has something follow it, unless it is at the finish of the project.

An activity that comes directly before another activity is called a *predecessor.* An activity that directly follows another activity is called a *successor.*

To determine the sequence of the activities on the schedule, the scheduler needs to ask two questions about *each* activity:

1. What activity or activities *directly* precede this activity ?
2. What activity or activities *directly* succeed this activity ?

Let's examine the word *directly.* On a typical construction schedule, landscaping certainly follows the foundation of the building, but it does not follow it *directly.* The predecessors and successors of an activity are only those that are directly connected to the activity. Here are two examples. (1) What activity directly precedes Foundation Walls?—Footings. Therefore, the activity Footings is the predecessor to Foundation Walls. (2) What activity directly succeeds (follows) Foundation Walls?—Slab-on-Grade. Therefore, the activity Slab-on-Grade is the successor to Foundation Walls.

It is also important to note that there is *no need* to determine what activities are running concurrently with the activity in question. This information will be displayed when the schedule network diagram is drawn.

So what really determines the logical sequencing of activities? Most activities follow each other because of a physical connection. A physical connection exists between two activities when one activity cannot start until the other activity is either partially or totally complete. For example, foundation walls are physically built on top of their footings; therefore, the foundation walls cannot begin until the footings are complete.

There are other connections that must be considered when sequencing activities. Some of the more common are detailed as follows:

1. *Safety.* A safety connection exists between two activities when performing the two activities simultaneously will result in a safety hazard for the project. There are times, for instance, during the construction of a multistory building when it is hazardous for one crew to be working below another crew due to the possibility of falling materials, equipment, or debris. Outside of this connection, the two activities may have nothing in common.
2. *Equipment resources.* Two activities are connected through resources when both activities need the same resource at the same time and there is only

enough of the resource available for one activity at a time. A typical example of this is when there is a tower crane on a project. Numerous activities often share the crane and have to be staggered to compensate for this.

3. *Materials.* Some materials take longer to be delivered or the delivery might be delayed. For instance, windows with special glass such as color tinted or *lowe* glass take much longer to get in. These materials are referred to as long lead items and measures are often taken to expedite their procurement. The logic of the schedule must reflect these conditions.

4. *Preference.* A preferential connection exists when a contractor prefers to sequence an activity a certain way. For example, when placing the gravel for the slab-on-grade and running the underground plumbing, which do you do first? Different contractors will schedule this differently. Usually the construction manager will get the plumbing contractor and the slab contractor together to decide. If the area is large enough, they both might be able to work at the same time.

5. *Working area.* As referenced in the previous example, the size of the working area will determine how much work can be performed at the same time in one area.

These connections and others will be demonstrated in Chapter 8 when the Delhi Medical Building schedule is developed and revised.

ACTIVITY RELATIONSHIPS

There are four types of activity relationships that can exist between two sequenced activities. An *activity relationship* describes the exact way that one activity follows another. For example, when most people think about one activity following another, let's say A and B, they normally think that when activity A is finished, activity B can start. This is the default relationship in most people's minds. However, there are three other types of activity relationships. The one just described is the most often used and is called finish-to-start. The four activity relationship types are:

- Finish-to-start (FS)
- Start-to-start (SS)
- Finish-to-finish (FF)
- Start-to-finish (SF)

Finish-to-Start (FS)

As previously discussed, finish-to-start (FS) is the traditional activity relationship type and is surely the most commonly used type. It can be described this way:

> When activity A finishes, activity B will start.

Finish-to-Start is the default relationship in the SureTrak software. Figure 5.5 graphically shows the finish-to-start relationship type in both precedence diagramming notation and in a bar graph format.

Start-to-Start (SS)

The start-to-start (SS) relationship type is the next most commonly used type. It can be described this way:

> When activity A starts, activity B will start.

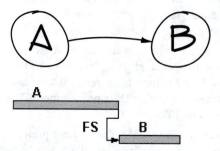

FIGURE 5.5
The finish-to-start (FS) relationship type shown in both precedence diagramming notation and in a bar graph format.

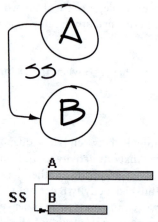

FIGURE 5.6
The start-to-start (SS) relationship type shown in both precedence diagramming notation and in a bar graph format.

As an example, let activity A be Start Project and let activity B be Project Management. The project management should begin as soon as the project starts, so using the start-to-start relationship, project management will start as soon as the project starts. Figure 5.6 graphically shows the start-to-start relationship type in both precedence diagramming notation and in a bar graph format.

Finish-to-Finish (FF)

The finish-to-finish (FF) relationship type can be described this way:

> When activity A finishes, activity B will finish.

To explain finish-to-finish, let's use the same project management activity, but on the back end of the project this time. The project management of the project should end as soon as the project ends, so let activity A be Project Complete and let activity B be Project Management. Using the finish-to-finish relationship, project management will finish as soon as the project is complete. Figure 5.7 graphically shows the finish-to-finish relationship type in both precedence diagramming notation and in a bar graph format.

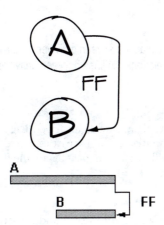

FIGURE 5.7
The finish-to-finish (FF) relationship type shown in both precedence diagramming notation and in a bar graph format.

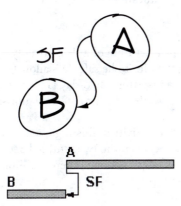

FIGURE 5.8
The start-to-finish (SF) relationship type shown in both precedence diagramming notation and in a bar graph format.

Start-to-Finish (SF)

The start-to-finish relationship type is rarely ever used in construction. It can be described this way:

> When activity A starts, activity B will finish.

It is difficult to come up with a scenario that would use the start-to-finish relationship type, but here's one that might help explain it. Suppose that a project is approaching its grand opening and, as part of the project schedule, there is an activity advertising the grand opening of the project, but the actual date of the grand opening is not set. The owner wants the advertising to continue all the way up to the day of the grand opening. Therefore, the advertising would finish right as the grand opening would start. Using the start-to-finish relationship, the Grand Opening would be activity A and the Advertising would be activity B. So when activity A (Grand Opening) starts, activity B (Advertising) will finish.

Figure 5.8 shows the start-to-finish relationship type both in precedence diagramming notation and in a bar graph format.

ACTIVITY LAG

Lag is the name given to the extra time purposefully placed between activities by the scheduler. Lag is associated with the connecting (relationship) lines between activities.

> **Note:**
> Lag is sometimes referred to, or confused with, activity float. This is incorrect. Lag and float are completely different. Activity float occurs naturally between activities when the project schedule is calculated using CPM. Chapter 7 will discuss, in great detail, the float that naturally occurs when the schedule is calculated.

The purposeful placement of lag in the schedule will be discussed and illustrated using the four previously listed relationship types. The placement of lag by the project scheduler into the schedule is a powerful tool allowing further refinement of the schedule and additional control. The following examples show how the scheduler might use lag to refine the schedule and to more closely reflect the real relationship that exists between two activities. When lag is added between activities, it is a good practice to draw the relationship line for two as a dashed line to help indicate that a lag exists.

Finish-to-Start (FS) with Lag

When installing ceramic tile, there needs to be a set time of at least twenty-four hours between laying the ceramic tile and grouting the tile. To be safe, let's allow two (2) days for the tile to set. This can be accomplished by inserting a two-day lag between the two activities, Lay Tile and Grout Tile. Figure 5.9 shows the finish-to-start relationship of Lay Tile and Grout Tile with a two-day lag.

Rather than using a lag in-between the two activities, this logic could also be accomplished by inserting an additional activity between the two, entitled *Set Time,* with a two-day duration. More often than not, this is how it is done. Therefore, finish-to-start activities do not use lags as much as the other types.

Start-to-Start (SS) with Lag

The most common use of lag in scheduling is with start-to-start activities. A very common occurrence in construction is for one activity to begin, progress for a while, then be followed by another. For example, HVAC rough-in usually precedes the plumbing and electrical rough-ins. However, the HVAC does not have to be completed before the other two begin; it just has to get started first and get out in front. This allows the HVAC contractor to get the main duct runs started in the building before the plumbing and electrical start and allows the HVAC to stay in front of the plumbing and electrical. Figure 5.10 shows *HVAC Rough-In* with a start-to-start relationship with the Plumbing Rough-In and Electrical Rough-In with a ten (10)-day lag.

Finish-to-Finish (FF)

Project closeout is the name given to the exercise of completing all the paperwork at the end of the project. It starts as the work begins to wind down and usually continues on for a few weeks (and sometimes much longer) after the project is punched out. To show this logic on the schedule, Project Closeout would have to finish fifteen (15) days after Punchout finishes. This relationship is shown in Figure 5.11.

Start-to-Finish (SF)

Using the previous grand opening and advertisement example, suppose that the advertisement was to continue two (2) days into a four-day grand opening before stopping.

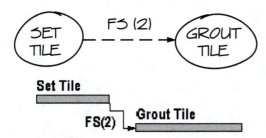

FIGURE 5.9
A finish-to-start (FS) relationship type shown in both precedence diagramming notation and in a bar graph format with a two (2)-day lag placed between the two activities.

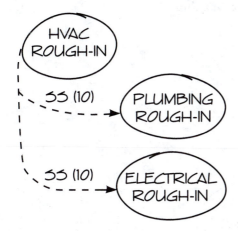

FIGURE 5.10
A start-to-start (SS) relationship shown in both precedence diagramming notation and in a bar graph format with a ten (10)-day lag.

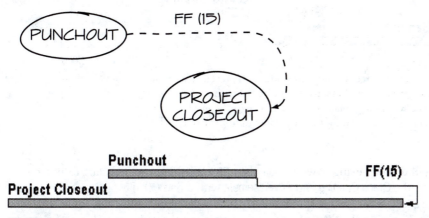

FIGURE 5.11
A finish-to-finish (FF) relationship shown in both precedence diagramming notation and in a bar graph format with a fifteen (15)-day lag placed between the end of *Punchout* and *Project Closeout*.

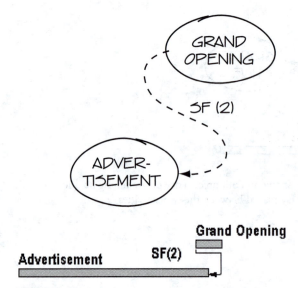

FIGURE 5.12
A start-to-finish (SF) relationship shown in both
precedence diagramming notation and in a bar graph
format with a two (2)-day positive lag placed between
the *grand opening* and the *advertisement*.

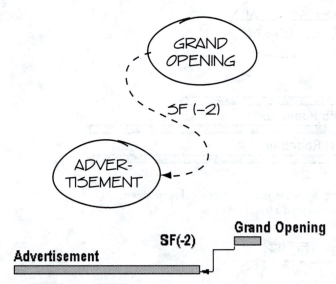

FIGURE 5.13
A start-to-finish (SF) relationship shown in both precedence
diagramming notation and in a bar graph format with a (−2) day
lag placed between the *grand opening* and the *advertisement*.
Notice that the successor (*advertisement*) moves to the left.

This would be done using a two (2)-day lag. Figure 5.12 shows the start-to-finish relationship of the Grand Opening and Advertisement with a two (2)-day lag.

Notice in the bar graphs (precedence diagrams are not time-scaled) that the lag, if
a positive number, will shift the successor activity to the right, regardless of the relationship type. If a negative float is used, the successor activity shifts to the left. Figure
5.13 shows the same relationship from Figure 5.12, except with a (−2) day float. This

is the logic that would be needed if the owner wanted the Advertisement to stop two (2)-days *before* the Grand Opening.

The ability to use lag is a unique feature of the precedence diagramming method (PDM) that does not exist with the other diagramming methods. As will be seen, activity lag is a necessary ingredient of PDM. Without it, the overlapping of concurrent activities without splitting the activities is impossible. This is one of the major features of PDM that will be demonstrated in the next chapter.

ACTIVITY DURATION

The duration of an activity is the amount of time that is required to complete the activity. When assigning the duration of an activity, the following topics should be considered:

- Planning unit
- Factors to consider when determining duration
- Calculating/assigning activity duration
- Factors affecting actual duration and productivity

PLANNING UNIT

The planning unit is the time unit used to measure the duration of the activities on the schedule. Most construction project schedules use a *day* as the planning unit.

Be careful not to confuse the *planning unit* with the *timescale* that is used to space the activity bars shown on the schedule. The two are completely independent of each other. For example, a project may use the day as the planning unit but show the activities laid out on a monthly timescale. Figure 5.14 shows a schedule with activities using a *daily* planning unit laid out on a *weekly* timescale. Notice the original duration, listed in days, compared to the length of the bars on the timescale.

Projects are sometimes scheduled in different planning units as described below:

- Years
- Months
- Weeks
- Days
- Hours
- Minutes, seconds, and fractions of seconds

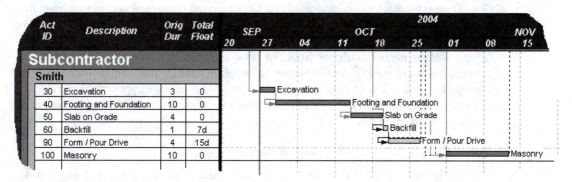

FIGURE 5.14
Activities using a *daily* planning unit laid out on a *weekly* timescale.

Years

Projects that use years as their planning unit are not that common. Large projects that span over many years might be general enough not to require a smaller unit. For example, a city council might adopt an urban revitalization program that spans twenty years or a state department of transportation may have a long multiyear plan to rebuild highway bridges throughout the state.

The preliminary plan of a large project in the early stages of formation might also initially use years as the planning unit when limited project information exists, then change to a smaller planning unit when the schedule is refined and updated with more information.

Months

Projects using months as the planning unit are also not that common. However, milestone schedules sometimes utilize the monthly planning unit since the activities on milestone schedules are quite broad with long durations. Like the yearly planning unit, the monthly planning unit also allows for the display of long periods of time in shorter spaces. However, once the bid package schedule and construction schedule are developed, a daily planning unit is usually used.

Weeks

The weekly planning unit might be used for milestone, bid package, and construction schedules when the total project duration is multiyear on very long duration projects, such as a power plant or paper mill.

Days

The day is the predominant planning unit used in construction project scheduling. The work performed on most construction activities fits this time unit best. Construction activities are too broad to conveniently fit into hour time units and too small for weeks. That is, there are many activities that are less than a week long and very few that are less than a day. Because of its frequent use, time stipulations used in most contracts, specifications, purchase agreements, and other documents used by the construction industry are expressed in days.

Hours

The timing of some projects is so critical that the day is too broad of a planning unit. Short-duration, complex projects will use the hour as the planning unit so the projects can be scheduled with much greater precision. These precise schedules are vital on projects where systems, or entire processes, are shut down—a typical occurrence of industrial facilities. Often the shutdown is only a few days long with the work scheduled around the clock.

Power plants, for instance, normally have planned outages to perform maintenance and repair work in the spring and fall, when electric power demand is at its lowest. The outage schedule runs twenty-four hours per day for usually two weeks, with two, ten-hour shifts separated with two hours in-between each shift. The two-hour periods between shifts are used to deliver materials, supplies, tools, water, and anything else that might be needed for the next shift. If orchestrated and managed properly, a tremendous amount of work can be accomplished. This is a typical schedule when a system or process is taken off line.

Minutes, Seconds, and Fractions of Seconds

Even the most critical construction projects would not require schedules that are planned by the minute, second, or the fraction of a second. However, CPM project scheduling and computerized project scheduling are not limited only to the construction industry. There are projects where the total project duration is less than a second. In electronics, for instance, the operation of a circuit or even computer operation is scheduled. And in the mechanical world, a manufacturing process that might take only minutes is often scheduled out during the planning and design of the process to help illustrate the flow of the process.

FACTORS TO CONSIDER WHEN DETERMINING DURATION

The duration of an activity is determined by two main factors: owners want their projects built on time and contractors want to maximize profits. When a contractor determines the duration of an activity, they look at how much time they have been given to perform the work and, from there, how they can resource the work to maximize their profits. Additionally, there may be other factors they may have to consider. The following discussion analyzes these factors:

- Available time
- Resourcing to maximize profits
- Other factors

Available Time

Projects today rarely have the luxury of time. While most projects may not actually be fast-tracked, most seem to be on the fast track. More and more often, owners are asking to have their projects built in hurried time frames and contractors are agreeing to these aggressive time frames.

A new scheduling philosophy sometimes called *reverse-phase scheduling* or *lean construction* starts with the project end date and schedules the project backwards, removing any fat (extra time) that might be in the schedule.

The advantage of these aggressive schedules and new philosophies to the construction process, and specifically the scheduling process, is that it requires greater communication up front between all parties involved in the project and it fosters a greater sense of teamwork and partnering, eventually leading to buy-in and commitment to the schedule of all parties involved in the project.

Out of this, contractors develop or may be given windows of available time within which they agree to complete their activities; thus, the activity duration is determined. This is the single most common way that activity durations are determined. It often starts with a single provision for the completion of the entire project, which in turn is divided into individual windows for each phase of the construction such as foundation, drywall, masonry, HVAC, and so on. Eventually this leads to individual windows of available time for each activity.

This method may seem unnatural for determining activity duration. It may seem that the work of the activity is forced into the duration. In some cases that is true, and hopefully with revisions to the schedule before it is made final, these will be identified and reworked. However, the overall goal is for the activities to have the appropriate durations assigned and for the contractor to have the ability to perform the work efficiently and profitably. Additionally, not all projects are scheduled this way, or not all components of a project may be scheduled this way.

Resourcing to Maximize Profit

The second most influential factor for determining the duration of an activity is the contractor's profitability. Whether the activity duration is given to the contractor or the contractor determines the duration, the contractor will assign the appropriate resources to the activity that will maximize profit. A resource is anything needed to complete an activity: labor, equipment, tools, material, and so on. The contractor will want to assign the most efficient resources to the work. For example, the contractor would not want to have too many or too few workers on a job. Too many could cause a problem where workers are getting in each other's way and becoming less productive. Too few workers could result in inefficient installation of materials—think of a bricklayer waiting around for more mortar.

Equipment and tools also are important resources that can greatly affect productivity and profits. Not having enough tools or the right tools or equipment can drastically affect profits. Similarly, having equipment and tools sit idle is a direct drain on profits.

The contractor will plan for the best mix of resources to accommodate a given window of available time to perform the work. However, if the duration was not preset, the contractor would assign the resources and calculate the duration based on those resources. Later in this chapter, we will demonstrate how to calculate activity durations based on resources assigned by calculating the duration of the masonry, interior and exterior metal stud walls, and the drywall of the Delhi Medical Building.

Other Factors

Other factors to consider when determining the duration of an activity are listed below. Depending on their severity, they may or may not override the duration already established based on the available window of time or on the assigned resources.

- *Safety concerns.* Safety on the project cannot be compromised. If there is a safety concern that affects the duration of an activity, the activity duration will be changed or the safety concern mitigated.

- *Availability of materials.* A few years back there was a shortage of gypsum board throughout the country. Drywall durations slowed because contractors simply could not get the board.

- *Availability of equipment and tools.* A three-yard bucket versus a one-yard bucket on a backhoe may significantly speed up excavation for something like spread footings; however, one wouldn't want to use that to excavate for the underground plumbing in the Delhi Medical Building.

- *Overcrowded work area.* Contractors always have to be careful how many workers they put in one area. Likewise, the construction manager has to be careful how many contractors, with their crews, to put in one work area. Durations may have to be adjusted accordingly.

- *Special techniques.* Special construction techniques such as modularization and fabrication may speed up activity durations considerably. These techniques were highlighted in the Northridge highway project referenced at the beginning of Chapter 4.

- *Special conditions.* Special conditions may exist such as renovations, or building in or near existing businesses that require duration adjustments. For example, building in and around an airport raises numerous safety and security considerations that will affect the project.

- *Shift work.* Durations can be significantly reduced with multiple shifts on the projects. This was used on the Northridge project also. Construction work may have to be moved to a second or third shift to avoid conflicts with an operating business or institution.

- *Overtime.* Construction activities often work overtime to make up lost time or slower-than-expected productivity. Occasionally activities are planned to be performed using overtime; their durations will reflect this.

CALCULATING / ASSIGNING DURATION

Activity durations are determined based on the various factors previously discussed. Once the factors are considered, the actual duration needs to be calculated or assigned. This next section discusses how durations are calculated using examples from the Delhi Medical Building and how they are assigned.

Regardless of whether they are calculated or assigned, there are certain attributes that apply to most durations. Activity durations are estimates, intuitive and subjective in nature, and despite what care may have been taken to develop the duration, in the end it is still an estimate. Activity durations are subject to numerous factors that could affect the accuracy of the duration. Some of those factors are discussed in the next section.

Additionally, there are certain assumptions that should be made when calculating / assigning activity durations. The durations are made using the planning unit of time. Durations are based on normal workdays and normal workhours, not overtime. Normal crews and equipment are used for the activities unless otherwise noted. Extra duration time should not be added to the activity unless noted with the reason stated.

Activity durations may be calculated and/or assigned based on the following:

- Quantity and productivity
- Gut feeling
- Past projects
- Locked-in durations / dates
- Input from trade contractors
- Combination

Quantity and Productivity

Most activity durations for construction schedules are calculated using the quantity of work that must be accomplished and the productivity rate for the work. The duration is equal to the quantity of work divided by the productivity rate, as stated in the following formula:

$$\text{Activity Duration } = \frac{\text{Quantity of Work}}{\text{Productivity Rate}}$$

For example, the curtain wall shown in Figure 5.15 can be installed at the rate of fifty linear feet per day. The total quantity of curtain wall for that level of the building is 233 feet; therefore, the activity duration is 233 ÷ 50 = 4.6 days. Therefore, use a five-day duration for that level of the building.

This is the most common way to calculate activity durations. This method is explained in the following list and examples from the Delhi Medical Building will be used as examples of the method.

- *Quantity of work.* The quantity of work includes all work necessary to complete the activity. It is described in some measurable unit that may or may not be the unit of material being installed. For example, drywall is installed by the sheet or board. The estimating and scheduling unit normally used for hanging drywall is the board, but the unit for finishing is the square foot. These will be the same units used for tracking the progress of the activities.
  The quantity of work can be generated a number of different ways:
  - *Quantity take-off.* The most common source for the quantity of work is through the quantity take-off, the compilation of materials and equipment

FIGURE 5.15
Curtain wall installation at fifty linear feet per day.

necessary to build the project. It is normally taken-off (compiled) by system at differing levels of detail depending on what is being taken off. It must be noted that the breakdown of the estimate does not always match the breakdown of scheduling activities. For example, structural steel is taken off one piece at a time using pounds as the take-off unit, but the erection activity for structural steel is probably much more broad with a different breakdown such as *third floor steel erection*. The unit is floor instead of pounds, and the entire floor is included instead of one piece at a time.

- *Bid documents.* The bidding documents sometimes list estimated quantities of materials for the project. This is particularly true on public projects using a unit price contract, such as roadway, utility, and other large civil projects.

- *Bid estimate.* The quantity of work used to calculate the duration of some activities is not based on the installation of materials, but rather some other criteria, such as the number of months planned to have a tower crane on the job. This information would be found in the bid estimate prepared by the contractor. Other information found in the bid estimate, relevant to establishing activity durations from quantities of work, are crew size and make-up, equipment types expected to be used, and construction methods.

- *Past experience.* Some quantities are difficult to measure, such as the tons of gravel ultimately used on a project or how long a certain piece of equipment might be needed on the job. Information from past projects or past experiences can be used as a parameter to develop these quantities, provided that the two projects are similar enough.

■ *Productivity rates.* A productivity rate is the quantity of work that can be accomplished in one hour or one day. The rate is based on an expectation of normal conditions including crew size, equipment usage, general working conditions, and others. This will be the rate against which actual productivity is measured.

Productivity rates can be generated a number of different ways:

- *Past experience.* The most common source, as well as the *most reliable* source for productivity rates for various construction activities, is from the past experiences of the contractor. While every project is different, most construction activities are quite repetitive from one job to the next. Take, for instance, the worker in Figure 5.15 again. There is a good chance that that worker has installed the same, or a very similar, curtain wall system, using the same piece of lifting equipment, the same tools, in roughly the same working conditions. Therefore, the productivity rate of fifty linear feet per day is probably a very solid number.

- *Trade contractors.* If you do not know how long it will take to install an item or how long a particular piece of equipment will be needed, ask someone who does. Trade contractors have tremendous expertise in their field. Their knowledge should be drawn upon whenever there is a need.

- *Other outside sources.* Numerous outside sources exist that can be used to gather information about the installation rates of materials or the use of equipment. Some examples are suppliers, manufacturers, and fabricators of materials, public agencies, industry and trade organizations, and owners.

- *Estimating guides.* Estimating guides are useful for general purposes. Even though they are published nationally, they have conversion indexes that can be used to convert the cost and productivity to the contractor's local area. The bigger problem with estimating guides is that the productivity rates, labor expenses, and material prices are not the same as those from the contractor's company and are very difficult to match up. It is difficult to know what is included in the guide's productivity rate.

At the end of the chapter there are *In-Class Exercises* and *Student Exercises* to perform that teach the student how to determine activity durations based on quantities and productivity rates.

Gut Feeling

As stated earlier, estimating activity durations is intuitive and subjective by nature. Contractors build a tremendous amount of experience up over the years. Therefore, when they analyze an activity for duration, the gut feeling they get is their intuition kicking in and drawing upon those many years of experience. As unscientific as this may sound, the many years of project experience provide an overall feel for the accuracy of the duration.

Contractors will often combine the calculated duration with their gut feeling; that is, they will calculate the duration using the quantity and productivity rate for the activity, then see if they feel good about the answer. The fact that they will often adjust the calculated duration based on their gut feeling is a testament to their confidence in their gut feeling. However, there is good reason for this confidence. In addition to the years of experience, the contractor will analyze the activity duration in the context of the project as well. There are many factors that can affect a productivity rate (they will be reviewed in the next section). The contractor can see how the duration might be affected, but the productivity rate is blind.

Past Projects

Historical data is the name given to the data that contractors collect and compile about estimating and scheduling information from past projects such as material costs, installation costs, productivity rates, equipment needs, conversion factors, and others. This data is drawn from the actual performance of their crews or subcontractors on past jobs.

It is as good as gold to them because it is based on their work crews, using their equipment, supervised by their foremen and managers, on their jobsites with materials furnished by their suppliers, or using their subcontractors. The more items that can be fixed as in previous jobs, the better the historical data is and the less chance there is for a variance.

This data can vary widely in appearance. It might be the number of scaffolding units needed to brick a building, the correct crew mix and size to place and finish a garage slab, or the amount of welding rods consumed while installing a process pipe system. While none of these data items are actual productivity rates, they all can affect productivity and therefore need to be considered when determining the duration of an activity.

At the end of the chapter, In-Class Exercise #4 and Student Exercise #4 teach the student to calculate activity durations based on information from past projects.

Locked-In Durations / Dates

As discussed in the previous section, contractors often develop or are given a finite duration to perform an activity. Sometimes, in addition to the specified duration, the contractor is given locked-in start and finish dates to perform the activity. In this case, not only is the duration already determined, but the time frame of the activity is also set. This is more common in construction than one might expect. In a sense, this is what the construction manager or general contractor does to the trade contractors on every job. They tell the trade contractor, "This is the window that you have to do your work." The trade contractor then has to find a way to get it done—or find a way to convince the CM or GC to expand/move the window.

Although the contractor does not have to determine the duration of the activity, he or she does have to determine how to accomplish the activity within the duration and will still need to use the previously discussed information. But in this case, the duration will drive the data, rather than the data determining the duration.

For example, suppose 175,000 bricks needed to be laid and the rate for laying brick on a similar past job was 2,800 bricks per day. Dividing 175,000 bricks by 2,800 bricks per day results in a sixty-three (62.5)-day duration. In this case, however, the bricks have to be laid between October 1st and November 11th, which is only thirty days. Based on this, the productivity rate (driven by the duration) must be 5,833 bricks per day (175,000 brick ÷ 30 days). The contractor is left with the task of figuring out how to get it done. Information from the previous discussion will be helpful to figure it out.

Input from Trade Contractors

Trade contractors are the experts in their field and are often used to help determine the duration of activities and even whole phases of work. This may happen in a formal setting when the general contractor or construction manager calls a meeting of all trade contractors to develop the project schedule, or more informally uses a phone call or visit to seek out the advice of just a few trades.

Some trades are more difficult to estimate and schedule than others. Take electrical, for instance. The electrical trade does not have one single overriding material or unit to estimate and schedule with. Masonry has brick or block and the finishing trades have square feet of finish surface to develop an all-encompassing rate to use for scheduling. However, the electrical trade has numerous and differing materials measured by different units. It has wire, fixtures, cable tray, switchgear, conduit, circuit panels, control systems, and so on running and placed throughout the entire building. It is tough to get a handle on all of this. In addition, this trade often also installs security and telecommunications systems, and it becomes even more confusing. Complicating the picture even more is the fact that these installations are performed in three separate periods of time throughout the project. The electrical contractor arrives early on the job to run utilities and underground wiring, then comes back to do the rough-in work which is the longest of the three, and finally returns to do the finish work.

The GC or CM should have a pretty good idea how long these phases, as well as those of other trades, should take, but will often consult with the trades to develop the durations for this work.

Combination

In the end, the determination of an activity duration is probably more often than not some combination of the above. Considering the importance of the accuracy of the schedule durations to the overall end date of the project, the contractor, construction manager, and project team will want to use any and all data to help determine the most accurate durations possible.

FACTORS AFFECTING ACTUAL DURATION AND PRODUCTIVITY

Construction is an inexact technology. While great care is taken to develop accurate activity duration, many factors may affect that duration once the project is underway. Many of the characteristics that make construction a risky business (see Chapter 1) also become factors that can affect activity duration. The following are factors that may affect the duration of an activity once the project has begun:

- *Experience of manager.* The ability of the construction manager to plan, organize, and orchestrate the project is an extremely important factor in the overall progress of all the activities. It may well be the most important of all factors.

   A well-managed job runs smoothly, or at least as smoothly as can be expected. Problems are resolved and the work proceeds. A job that is not run well will negatively affect many aspects of the job in a subtle way, ultimately leading to numerous squabbles and claims, probable cost overruns, and missed activity durations and dates.

- *Built outdoors.* Maybe the greatest single factor that affects construction productivity is that the project is built outdoors in the weather. This is most crucial to durations when the project is coming out of the ground. Once past that phase, the second most crucial phase directly follows the first when the building is still unenclosed. After the building is enclosed, the effect of the weather on the construction is greatly diminished.

- *Labor productivity.* Another important factor that affects productivity and, in turn, activity duration is the productivity of the labor force. Labor productivity is not constant and can vary significantly from project to project or even from location to location on the same project. Even if the many other factors listed here do not affect labor productivity, the laborers themselves may simply not work at the pace anticipated in the duration.

- *Equipment productivity.* Equipment productivity is a function of operator skill and the equipment itself. It is very important to practice periodic maintenance of all equipment to keep it running effectively. When equipment breaks down and workers are standing idle, the productivity plummets.

- *Material availability.* When talking about material availability with respect to productivity, one initially envisions an activity running out of materials before it is completed and work crew standing idle. While that is certainly a problem, it is less common than other, more subtle problems. Materials need to be located in a convenient area close to where they are to be installed. They must also be left unobstructed by other materials, equipment, and workers. If the materials have to be lifted, a staging area must be established with the material within reach of the crane. Large inventories of materials at the site can also congest the site and lower productivity. The construction manager must be able to carefully schedule the delivery of materials to balance the production needs with available laydown and storage space. Consumable materials such as welding rods, nails, staples, and so on do not take up much space, but they nonetheless must also be carefully inventoried. Any and all of these factors can greatly affect activity duration.

- *Safety practices.* Jobsite safety is everyone's responsibility. While there are more important reasons to keep a jobsite safe, studies have shown that jobsites that exhibit a safe work environment experience higher productivity rates than sites with lower safety records.

- *Modularization.* Modularization in construction is the method of building some parts of the project in components, usually off-site, and delivering them to the project to be lifted into place. This method saves significant amounts of construction time. If modularization is used, the time savings will positively affect many other durations.

- *Uniqueness of projects.* When a project is built, it most likely has never been built before. Contractors have to learn as they go. Normally, productivity will improve as experience is gained through repetitive tasks on the project. For instance, multistory buildings are normally similar from floor to floor, so there is a learning curve that would help the productivity to improve as the job progresses.

- *Misinterpretation of documents.* The end product of the activity is a three-dimensional object built from a two-dimensional set of documents. This is an underlying reason for the workers misinterpreting the plans and specifications. Another reason is the accuracy of the plans and specifications. Both will reduce productivity.

- *Numerous parties.* It is not uncommon for a small- to medium-size project to have hundreds of different companies involved in the construction—although not all at one time, of course. However, without the careful orchestration of these many parties, even two or three in one area can affect productivity and therefore activity duration.

- *Enormity of size.* There are numerous potential issues related to the enormous size of construction projects that can affect duration. The fact that most of the work is performed above the ground can create many difficulties. Add to that the usual tightness of most project sites and limited room for staging and laydown of materials, and the potential for problems can mount.

- *Work restrictions.* Work restrictions are often imposed when the construction activities are adjacent to or within an existing functioning facility. An addition to a hospital, for example, might require the workers to adhere to noise, dust, vibration, odor, hygiene, and even dress code restrictions. These many restrictions will require the construction manager to reevaluate all activity durations.

- *Labor agreement restrictions.* The local craft labor union agreements sometimes have clauses related to production guidelines, jurisdictional boundaries, limits on piecework, limits on time studies, and limits on prefabrication that may have a negative effect on productivity.

- *Congested work area.* In addition to materials, workers can also congest the work area. Multiple activities taking place in the same area can reduce productivity and in turn affect activity duration.

- *Continuous overtime.* Numerous studies have shown that continuous overtime leads to lower productivity and eventually results in less work being performed per day with the overtime than was being performed without it. The business roundtable conducted a study in 1980 entitled, "Cost Effectiveness Study C–3." It demonstrated that workers working sixty hours per week, in the ninth straight week, were accomplishing the same amount of work that they were accomplishing in a normal forty-hour workweek without the overtime.

IN-CLASS EXERCISE #1
DELHI MEDICAL BUILDING
Duration Calculation—Masonry

Based on the drawings from the Delhi Medical Building, the partial specification provided in Appendix A, and the information that follows, calculate the duration of laying the brick on the north and west elevations of the building. This duration will be added to the duration for the other two elevations and used in Chapter 8 for the activity entitled *Masonry*.

The student will calculate the south and east elevations in *Student Exercise #1*.

The calculations for the take-off and duration of the north and west elevations are provided on the take-off sheets shown on the pages after the specification sheet.

Given:
1. Expected crew for a job this size would be four (4) brick masons and two (2) laborers.
2. Productivity rate per brick mason for different size brick:
   - Standard = 400 brick/day
   - King = 385 brick/day
   - Jumbo = 360 brick/day
3. Brick quantities per square foot of wall surface area (includes factor for waste):
   - Standard = 7.4/SF
   - King = 5.7/SF
   - Jumbo = 3.3/SF

Instructions:
Based on the partial specification provided in Appendix A, determine what size brick is to be used on the building. Perform the quantity take-off of the area of brick on the north and west elevations. Determine the total number of bricks on both elevations. Based on the total number of bricks, the productivity rate for the appropriate brick size, and crew size, determine the total duration (in days) for the two elevations.

Construction Project Scheduling
with Computer Integration *using SureTrak*

Division MASONRY
Phase BRICK VENEER
Location NORTH & WEST ELEV.
Notes IN-CLASS EXERCISE #1

Project DELHI MEDICAL BLDG.
Job No. _____ Page 1 of 6
Estimated By _____
Approved By _____

Description	Quantity	Unit
BRICK VENEER TAKE-OFF		
NORTH ELEVATION: (DIMENSIONS)		
— HEIGHT OF BRICK (MIDDLE PART)		
• FROM SECTION 1 ON PAGE A8		
10'-0" (2ND FLOOR TO TRUSS BRG.)		
⟨10"⟩ (MEASURE DOWN TO SOFFIT)		
⟨2"⟩ " ESTIMATED TO TOP OF BRICK		
+ 8" (ADD FOR BRICK LEDGE — SEE SECT. 2 ON PG. A8)		
9'-8"		
— HEIGHT OF BRICK (GABLE END — FROM BRICK LEDGE TO RIDGE)		
• FROM SECTION 1 ON PAGE A8 AND NORTH ELEV. ON PAGE A6		
(8" + 3'-3" + 4'-1") = 8'-0" (FROM BRICK LEDGE TO UNDERSIDE OF SOLDIER COURSE)		
+ 9'-0" (SCALED OFF: FROM UNDERSIDE OF SOLDIER COURSE TO RIDGE)		
17'-0" TOTAL GABLE END HEIGHT FROM BRICK LEDGE TO RIDGE		
(SEE DIMENSION ILLUSTRATION ON NEXT PAGE)		

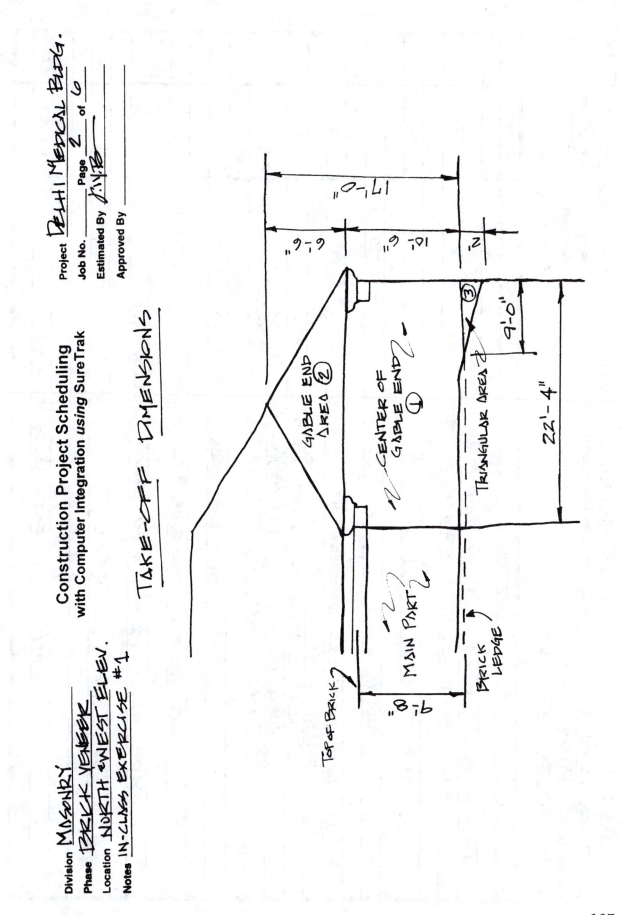

Construction Project Scheduling
with Computer Integration *using* SureTrak

Division **MASONRY**
Phase **BRICK VENEER**
Location **NORTH & WEST ELEV.**
Notes **IN-CLASS EXERCISE #1**

Project **DELHI MEDICAL BLDG.**
Job No. _____ Page **2** of **6**
Estimated By _____
Approved By _____

TAKE-OFF DIMENSIONS

GABLE END AREA ②

CENTER OF GABLE END ①

TRIANGULAR AREA

MAIN PART

TOP OF BRICK

BRICK LEDGE

17'-0"
6'-6"
10'-6"
2"
9'-0"
22'-4"
9'-8"

Construction Project Scheduling
with Computer Integration *using SureTrak*

Project DELHI MEDICAL BLDG
Job No. _____ Page 3 of 6
Estimated By _____
Approved By _____

Division MASONRY
Phase BRICK VENEER
Location NORTH & WEST ELEV.
Notes IN-CLASS EXERCISE #1

Description	Quantity	Unit
NORTH ELEVATION: (TAKE-OFF)		
• DO NOT SUBTRACT FOR OPENINGS YET		
1. MAIN PART (59'-0" × 9'-8")		
— (59.0')(9.66') = 570 SF		
2. GABLE ENDS (2 ON NORTH ELEV.)		
AREAS:		
① CENTER AREA = (22.33')(10.5') = 234 SF		
② GABLE END AREA = (½)(22.33')(6.5') = 73 SF		
③ TRIANGULAR AREA = (½)(9.0')(2.0') = 9 SF		
TOTAL GABLE END AREA 316 SF		
TOTAL FOR BOTH GABLE ENDS = (2)(316 SF) = 632 SF		
3. SIDE WALLS (2' WIDE × 9'-8" TALL — (1) ON EACH SIDE)		
— (2 SIDES)(2.0')(9.66') = 39 SF		
TOTAL AREA NORTH ELEVATION	1241	SF

Division MASONRY

Phase BRICK VENEER

Location NORTH & WEST ELEV.

Notes IN-CLASS EXERCISE #1

Project DELHI MEDICAL BLDG.

Job No. _____ **Page** 4 of 6

Estimated By JNB

Approved By _____

Description	Quantity	Unit
WEST ELEVATION : (DIMENSIONS AND TAKE-OFF)		
— FULL HEIGHT OF WEST ELEV. BRICK :		
9'-8" (HEIGHT OF NORTH ELEV. BRICK)		
12'-0" (FLOOR-TO-FLOOR HEIGHT. NOTE: DO NOT ADD IN 8" BRICK LEDGE, IT WAS ALREADY ADDED TO 9'-8" DIM.)		
TOTAL HGHT. 21'-8"		
— AREA BENEATH STEPPED BRICK LEDGE :		
• ASSUME A TRIANGULAR AREA WITH SCALED-OFF DIMENSIONS :		
— BASE = 29'-0" HEIGHT = 9'-6"		
TAKE-OFF :		
1. FULL HEIGHT × ENTIRE WIDTH (21'-8" × 51'-4")		
(21.66')(51.33') = 1112 SF		
2. LESS TRIANGULAR AREA BENEATH BRICK LEDGE = (138) SF		
(1/2)(29.0')(9.5')		
TOTAL AREA WEST ELEVATION	974	SF

109

Description	Quantity	Unit
__NORTH & WEST ELEVATIONS:__ (OPENINGS)		
1. DOUBLE WINDOWS (5'-0" × 4'-0")		
— (5.0')(4.0') (10 WINDOWS) = ⟨200⟩		SF
2. SINGLE WINDOWS (2'-6" × 4'-0")		
— (2.5')(4.0') (4 WINDOWS) = ⟨40⟩		SF
3. SINGLE DOORS — WITH FRAME (3'-4" × 7'-4")		
— (3.33')(7.33')(2 DOORS) = ⟨49⟩		SF
4. GABLE END VENTS (2'-8" φ -SCALED)		
— π(2.66/2)²(2 VENTS) = ⟨11⟩		SF
5. NORTH ELEV. MAIN ENTRANCE (7'-4" × 7'-4" - SCALED)		
— (7.33')(7.33') = ⟨54⟩		SF
TOTAL OPENINGS — NORTH & WEST ELEV.	⟨354⟩	SF

110

Division MASONRY

Phase BRICK VENEER

Location NORTH & WEST ELEV.

Notes IN-CLASS EXERCISE #1

Project DELHI MEDICAL BLDG.

Job No. _____ Page 6 of 6

Estimated By JWB

Approved By _____

Description	Quantity	Unit
DURATION CALCULATION OF BRICK (NORTH & WEST) ELEV.		
1. TOTAL BRICK		
— NORTH ELEVATION 1241 SF		
— WEST ELEVATION 974 SF		
— (LESS) OPENINGS (354) SF		
TOTAL BRICK AREA 1861 SF		
2. TOTAL BRICK:		
• STANDARD SIZE BRICK IS SPEC'D OUT		
• USE (7.4 BRICK / SF) FOR MATERIAL		
— (7.4 BRICK/SF)(1861 SF) = 13,771 BRICK QTY	13.8	M
3. CALCULATE DURATION		
— PRODUCTIVITY RATE = 400 BRICK PER MASON PER DAY		
— CREW SIZE = (4) BRICK MASONS WITH (2) LABORERS		
— CREW PRODUCTIVITY RATE:		
(4 BRICK MASONS)(400 BRICK PER MASON PER DAY) =	1600 BRICK/DAY	
DURATION = $\dfrac{13,771 \text{ BRICK}}{1600 \text{ BRICK/DAY}}$ = 8.6 DAYS ∴ USE	9	DAYS

111

IN-CLASS EXERCISE #2
DELHI MEDICAL BUILDING
Duration Calculation—First Floor Exterior Studs/Sheathing

Based on the drawings from the Delhi Medical Building and the information below, calculate the duration of framing, sheathing, and wrapping in building paper and the first floor exterior metal stud walls of the building (see number 4 below). This duration will be used in Chapter 8 for the activity entitled 1st Floor Exterior Studs/Sheathing.

The student will calculate the second floor exterior metal stud walls in Student Exercise #2.

The calculations for the take-off and duration of the first floor exterior metal stud walls are provided on the take-off sheets on the following pages.

Given:

1. Expected crew for a job this size would be two (2) carpenters and one (1) laborer to install the metal studs, to hang the sheathing, and to wrap the building.

2. Sheathing board size is $4' \times 10'$ sheets.

3. Productivity rate per carpenter for:
   - Metal stud exterior wall framing = 32 LF/day
   - Hanging exterior sheathing per board = 16 board/day
   - Install building paper = 3,000 SF/day

4. Addendum #1 shows the addition of building paper to the exterior wall system of the entire building, thereby completely eliminating the need to finish the exterior wall sheathing.

Instructions:

Perform the quantity take-off of the first floor exterior stud walls. Determine the total linear feet of wall, the total number of boards of sheathing, and the total square footage of exterior wall. Based on these take-offs, the productivity rates listed, and crew size, determine the total duration (in days) for the first floor exterior stud walls/sheathing.

Division FINISHES
Phase GYPSUM WALL SYSTEMS
Location 1ST FLR. EXT. STUDS / SHEATHING
Notes IN-CLASS EXERCISE #2

Project DELHI MEDICAL BLDG.
Job No. _____
Page 1 of 2
Estimated By J.11PTS
Approved By _____

Description	Quantity	Unit
TAKEOFF: 1ST FLOOR EXTERIOR WALLS (STUDS, SHEATHING, WRAP)		
1. TOTAL LENGTH OF 1ST FLOOR EXTERIOR STUD WALL:		
20'-4" WEST ELEVATION (SEE DIMENSIONS PG. A2)		
22'-4" GABLE END		
3'-4" SIDE WALL		
59'-0" CENTER		
3'-4" SIDE WALL		
22'-4" GABLE END		
20'-4" EAST ELEVATION		
151'-0" TOTAL LF 1ST FLR. EXT. STUD WALL	151	LF
2. TOTAL AREA OF 1ST FLR. EXT. STUD WALL:		
WALL HEIGHT = 12'-0"		
TOTAL AREA = (151 LF)(12') = 1812 SF (DO NOT SUBTRACT FOR OPNG)	1812	SF
3. TOTAL NUMBER BOARD (USE 4'x10' SHEETS = 40 SF/BOARD)		
- 1812 SF / 40 SF/BOARD = 45.3 BOARDS ∴ USE	46	BOARD

113

Division FINISHES   **Construction Project Scheduling**
with Computer Integration *using* SureTrak

Phase GYPSUM WALL SYSTEMS

Location 1ST FLR. EXT. STUDS/SHEATHING

Notes IN-CLASS EXERCISE #2

Project DELHI MEDICAL BLDG.

Job No. _____ Page 2 of 2

Estimated By _____

Approved By _____

Description	Quantity	Unit
DURATION CALCULATION: 1ST FLR. EXT. STUDS/SHEATHING		
1. STUDS:		
• BASED ON: 32 LF/DAY PER CARPENTER		
CREW SIZE = (2) CARP. AND (1) LABORER		
CREW PRODUCTIVITY = (32 LF/DAY)(2) CARP. = 64 LF/DAY		
— 151 LF / 64 LF/DAY =	2.4	DAYS
2. SHEATHING: (4'x10' BOARDS)		
• BASED ON: 16 BOARD/DAY PER CARPENTER		
CREW SIZE = (2) CARP. AND (1) LABORER		
CREW PRODUCTIVITY = (16 BOARD/DAY)(2) CARP. = 32 BOARD/DAY		
— 46 BOARD / 32 BOARD/DAY =	1.4	DAYS
3. BUILDING WRAP: (TYRM WRAP)		
• BASED ON: 3000 SF/DAY PER CARPENTER		
CREW SIZE = (2) CARP. AND (1) LABORER		
CREW PRODUCTIVITY = (3000 SF/DAY)(2) CARP. = 6000 SF/DAY		
— 1812 SF / 6000 SF/DAY =	.3	DAYS
TOTAL DURATION = 2.4 + 1.4 + .3 = 4.1 DAYS ∴ USE	5	DAYS

114

IN-CLASS EXERCISE #3 DELHI MEDICAL BUILDING
Duration Calculation—First Floor Interior Partitions

Based on the drawings from the Delhi Medical Building and the information below, calculate the duration of framing the first floor interior metal stud partitions and furring channels. The student will calculate the second floor interior metal stud partitions and furring channels in *Student Exercise #3*.

The installation of interior metal studs is often a two-step process. The first step is to layout the partitions and install the top tracks of the stud partitions. After that is complete, the HVAC contractor comes in to install the main duct runs. The partitions will be completed after the duct runs are installed. Depending on the size of the job, the interior partitions might be built in one step alongside the HVAC duct runs.

On the Delhi Medical Building, we'll install the partitions in two steps, creating two activities: 1st Floor Layout and Top Track and 1st Floor Interior Studs. The furring channels along the back and side foundation walls and around the elevator shaft will be included in the duration with the interior studs. The durations we calculate will be used in Chapter 8 for these two activities on the *revised* schedule.

The calculations for the take-off and duration of the first floor interior metal stud partitions are provided on the take-off sheets on the following pages.

Given:

1. Expected crew for a job this size for the layout and top track would be two (2) carpenters and the crew to install metal studs would be two (2) carpenters and one (1) laborer.

2. Productivity rates per carpenter for:
   - Layout = 200 LF of partition/day
   - Install top track = 200 LF of partition/day
   - Install metal studs = 56 LF of partition/day
   - Install furring channels = 56 LF of partition/day

Instructions:

Perform the quantity take-off of the first floor interior partitions and furred out walls. Based on these take-offs, the productivity rates listed, and crew size, determine the total duration (in days) for the first floor layout and top track and the partitions and furred out walls.

Division FINISHES
Phase INTERIOR PARTITIONS
Location 1ST FLOOR
Notes IN-CLASS EXERCISE #3

Construction Project Scheduling
with Computer Integration *using* SureTrak

Project DELHI MEDICAL BUILDING
Job No. ______ Page 1 of 2
Estimated By J.V.B.
Approved By ______

Description	Quantity	Unit
TAKE-OFF: 1ST FLR. INTERIOR PARTITIONS (AND FURRED WALLS)		
NOTE: LAYOUT & TOP TRACK NOT NEEDED FOR FURRED OUT WALLS		
1. TOTAL LF OF 1ST FLR. PARTITIONS		
– TYPE A PARTITION = 117 LF (SCALED OFF)		
– TYPE A1 " = 474 LF		
– TYPE B " = 45 LF		
– TYPE C " = 11 LF		
TOTAL 1ST FLR. INT. PART.	647	LF
2. TOTAL FURRING CHANNEL WALL		
– TYPE D WALL = 23 LF		
– BACK AND SIDE FOUNDATION WALLS = 168 LF		
TOTAL 1ST FLR. FURRED WALLS	191	LF

Division **FINISHES**

Phase **INTERIOR PARTITIONS**

Location **1ST FLOOR**

Notes **IN-CLASS EXERCISE #3**

Project **DELHI MEDICAL BUILDING**

Job No. _____

Estimated By _____ Page **2** of **2**

Approved By _____

Description	Quantity	Unit
DURATION CALCULATIONS: 1ST FLOOR LAYOUT AND TOP TRACK		
1ST FLOOR INTERIOR STUDS		
1. 1ST FLOOR LAYOUT AND TOP TRACK		
• LAYOUT - BASED ON: (200 LF/DAY PER CARP.) (2) CARP. CREW = 400 LF/DAY		
= 647 LF / 400 LF/DAY = 1.6 DAYS		
• TOP TRACK - BASED ON: (200 LF/DAY PER CARP.) (2) CARP. CREW = 400 LF/DAY		
= 647 LF / 400 LF/DAY = 1.6 DAYS		
TOTAL 1ST FLR. LAYOUT AND TOP TRACK = 3.2 DAYS ∴ USE	4	DAYS
2. 1ST FLOOR INTERIOR STUDS (CALCULATE STUDS AND FURRING TOGETHER		
SINCE THEIR PRODUCTIVITY RATES		
ARE THE SAME		
— TOTAL STUDS AND FURRING CHANNELS = 647 LF + 191 LF = 838 LF		
• TOTAL DURATION - BASED ON: (56 LF/DAY) (2) CARP. CREW = 112 LF/DAY		
NOTE: (1) LABORER IN CREW ALSO BUT NOT PART OF CALCULATION - SUPPORT ONLY		
= 838 LF / 112 LF/DAY = 7.48 DAYS ∴ USE	8	DAYS

IN-CLASS EXERCISE #4
DELHI MEDICAL BUILDING
Duration Calculation—First Floor Interior Doors and Hardware

Based on the drawings from the Delhi Medical Building and the information below, calculate the duration of installing the first floor interior doors and hardware. This duration will be used in Chapter 8 on the *revised* schedule for the activity entitled 1st Floor Doors and Hardware.

The student will calculate the second floor interior doors and hardware in *Student Exercise #4*.

The calculations for the take-off and duration of the first floor interior doors and hardware are provided on the take-off sheet on the next page.

Given:

　　1. On a similar job, your interior finishes contractor installed 118 similar type interior doors with similar hardware in seventeen days.

Instructions:

Based on the information provided above from your interior finishes trade contractor, determine the total duration (in days) for the first floor interior doors and hardware.

Division DOORS & WINDOWS

Phase INTERIOR DOORS & HDWD.

Location 1ST FLOOR

Notes IN-CLASS EXERCISE #4

Project DELHI MEDICAL BLDG.

Job No. _____ Page 1 of 1

Estimated By /M.B—

Approved By _____

Description	Quantity	Unit
(1ST FLOOR INTERIOR DOORS & HARDWARE		
TAKE-OFF		
1. TOTAL INTERIOR DOORS (FROM COUNT)	34	EA
DURATION		
• BASED ON INFORMATION FROM TRADE CONTRACTOR ON PAST JOB		
— PREVIOUS JOB: 118 DOORS WERE INSTALLED IN 17 DAYS		
RATE = 118 DOORS / 17 DAY'S = 6.9 DOORS/DAY ∴ USE 7		
— DELHI MEDICAL BUILDING:		
34 DOORS / 7 DOORS/DAY = 4.85 DAYS ∴ USE	5	DAYS

STUDENT EXERCISE #1 DELHI MEDICAL BUILDING
Duration Calculation—Masonry

Based on the drawings from the Delhi Medical Building, the partial specification provided in Appendix A, and the information below, calculate the duration of laying the brick on the south and east elevations. This duration will be added to the duration for north and west elevations and used in Chapter 8 for the activity entitled *Masonry*.

The calculations for the take-off and duration of the south and east elevations will be provided by your instructor.

1. Expected crew for a job this size would be four (4) brick masons and two (2) laborers.
2. Productivity rate per brick mason for different size brick:
   - Standard = 400 brick/day
   - King = 385 brick/day
   - Jumbo = 360 brick/day
3. Brick quantities per square foot of wall surface area (includes factor for waste):
   - Standard = 7.4/SF
   - King = 5.7/SF
   - Jumbo = 3.3/SF

Instructions:

Based on the partial specification provided in Appendix A, determine what size brick is to be used on the building. Perform the quantity take-off of the area of brick on the south and east elevations. Determine the total number of bricks on both elevations. Based on the total number of bricks, the productivity rate for the appropriate brick size, and crew size, determine the total duration (in days) for the two elevations.

STUDENT EXERCISE #2 DELHI MEDICAL BUILDING
Duration Calculation—Second Floor Exterior Studs/Sheathing

Based on the drawings from the Delhi Medical Building and the information below, calculate the duration of framing, sheathing, and wrapping (see number 4) the second floor exterior metal stud walls. This duration will be used in Chapter 8 for the activity entitled 2nd Floor Exterior Studs/Sheathing.

Given:
1. Expected crew for a job this size would be two (2) carpenters and one (1) laborer to install the metal studs, to hang the sheathing, and to wrap the building. However, to help speed up the job, (3) carpenters will be used to erect the studs.
2. Sheathing board size is 4′ × 10′ sheets.

3. Productivity rate per (1) carpenter for:
   - Metal stud exterior wall framing = 32 LF/day
   - Hanging exterior sheathing per board = 16 board/day
   - Install building paper = 3,000 SF/day
4. Addendum #1 shows the addition of building paper to the exterior wall system of the entire building, thereby completely eliminating the need to finish the exterior wall sheathing.

Instructions:
Perform the quantity take-off of the second floor exterior stud walls. Determine the total linear feet of wall, the total number of boards of sheathing, and the total square footage of exterior wall. Based on these take-offs, the productivity rates listed, and crew size, determine the total duration (in days) for the second floor exterior stud walls/sheathing.

STUDENT EXERCISE #3 DELHI MEDICAL BUILDING
Duration Calculation—Second Floor Interior Partitions

Based on the drawings from the Delhi Medical Building and the information below, calculate the duration of framing the second floor interior metal stud partitions and furring channels.

The installation of interior metal studs is often a two-step process. The first step is to layout the partitions and install the top tracks of the stud partitions. After that is complete, the HVAC contractor comes in to install the main duct runs. The partitions will be completed after the duct runs are installed. Depending on the size of the job, the interior partitions might be built in one step alongside the HVAC duct runs.

On the Delhi Medical Building, we'll install the partitions in two steps, creating two activities: 2nd Floor Layout and Top Track and 2nd Floor Interior Studs. The furring channels around the elevator shaft will be included in the duration with the interior studs. The durations we calculate will be used in Chapter 8 for these two activities on the *revised* schedule.

The calculations for the take-off and duration of the second floor interior metal stud partitions will be provided to you by your instructor.

Given:
1. Expected crew for a job this size for the layout and top track would be two (2) carpenters and the crew to install metal studs would be two (2) carpenters and one (1) laborer.

2. Productivity rates per (1) carpenter for:
   - Layout = 200 LF of partition/day
   - Install top track = 200 LF of partition/day
   - Install metal studs = 56 LF of partition/day
   - Install furring channels = 56 LF of partition/day

Instructions:
Perform the quantity take-off of the second floor interior partitions and furred out walls. Based on these take-offs, the productivity rates listed, and crew size, determine the total duration (in days) for the second floor layout and top track and the partitions and furred out walls.

STUDENT EXERCISE #4 DELHI MEDICAL BUILDING
Duration Calculation—Second Floor Interior Doors and Hardware

Based on the drawings from the Delhi Medical Building and the information below, calculate the duration of installing the second floor interior doors and hardware. This duration will be used in Chapter 8 on the *revised* schedule for the activity entitled 2nd Floor Doors and Hardware.

Given:

    1. On a similar job, your interior finishes contractor installed 118 similar type interior doors with similar hardware in seventeen days.

Instructions:

Based on the information provided above from your interior finishes trade contractor, determine the total duration (in days) for the second floor interior doors and hardware.

CHAPTER 6
Network Diagrams

IMPORTANCE OF DRAWING THE NETWORK

Generally, schedulers and project managers follow one of two processes to develop a schedule. One way is right and one way is wrong.

1. They sit down at a computer and start typing activities into the software.

or

2. They begin by *hand*-drawing a rough network diagram on a big piece of paper. This is the right way.

Hand-drawing a rough network diagram on a big piece of paper is still the best way to develop the proper schedule logic. As you build the project in your head, handwriting down the project activities in their logical sequence, missing or improper logic is much easier to spot as the diagram takes shape before your eyes.

After the activities and logic are set, durations can be assigned to each activity, thereby providing a second full review of the schedule. Necessary adjustments can easily be made on the hand-drawn diagram. Having the full schedule visible in a single view allows for accurate, efficient, and reliable reviews until the scheduler or project manager feels the schedule is accurate. At this point the schedule is ready to be input into the computer.

So much is riding on the quality of the logic that you cannot skip hand-drawing the rough diagram. Starting the schedule with the keyboard and mouse before the logic is developed is a recipe for disaster. Logic tends to get lost once a program swallows it up. In addition, scrolling around a computer screen can never be as "all-seeing" as viewing the entire schedule in a single view. A schedule with *bad logic* is dangerous. Once the schedule is input into the computer, it is very difficult (and very time-consuming) to find bad logic, if it can even be found at all. While it may be tempting to skip the hand-drawn network diagram to save time, the price paid in time and money for bad logic, missing activities, or other inaccuracies could be devastating.

Drawing a rough diagram of the project schedule as it is developed has other advantages and is strongly recommended for the following reasons:

- *It helps you lay out the job in your mind.* The single best way to ensure that an activity is not forgotten or logically misplaced is to "build the job in your head" as you draw the network diagram. By doing this, you will visualize each step of the project and sequence the activities accordingly. Additionally, it may help you remember an activity that you otherwise would have forgotten or think of a different process/method that may save money.

- *It makes your computerized schedule much more accurate and reliable.* The computer will not correct your bad logic. The most accurate way to input the logic into the computer with the least mistakes is to do it directly from the hand-drawn network. Inputting the logic this way enhances the computerized schedule's accuracy and reliability.

123

This will become evident to the students when they add the logic to the garage construction schedule in Module 4. They will add the logic to the activities in SureTrak from a hand-drawn network diagram.

- *It saves time.* Many schedulers and project managers will skip the step of hand-drawing the schedule to save time. We've already mentioned how it can save time in the long run if bad logic is detected; but beyond that, drawing the network first can save time in the overall schedule development.

The hand-drawn networks do not have to be pretty—they are rarely, if ever, used as a presentation document. Rather, their sole intent is to be used as a tool for the scheduler or project manager to help create the most accurate and reliable project schedule possible. Therefore, they can be drawn quickly and without pretense. The only people who will ever see them are those involved with the development of the schedule.

WHAT IS A NETWORK DIAGRAM?

A network diagram, the name given to the graphical representation of a project schedule, allows the users to see interrelations and dependencies of the activities and, with it, the flow of the project.

Network diagrams were developed in the 1950s to facilitate the network planning and scheduling methods that originated when the U.S. Navy Special Projects Office set out to create a new method of planning for weapons systems, specifically the Polaris Missile System. The result of this effort was the *Program Evaluation Review Technique,* now called PERT by most. PERT did not apply that well to the construction industry, so further development took place, which resulted in the *Critical Path Method,* known to most as CPM. Both PERT and CPM required projects to be represented graphically, so network diagramming methods were developed to do this.

BAR CHARTS VERSUS NETWORK DIAGRAMMING

Although bar charts had been around for many years when network diagramming methods were developed in the late 1950s, they were not capable of effectively monitoring and controlling projects. Their shortcoming was the result of one major deficiency: they were not able to predict the effect of changes and delays on the schedule.

Network diagrams are built around the concept of precedence, which links all the activities together with logic. Precedence assumes that one activity has to finish before the activity that follows it, or its successor, can begin. Bar charts do not have this logical relationship built into their activities. Therefore, any change made to the sequence or duration of an activity in the bar chart will affect only that activity. In order to determine the impact of any change, the entire bar chart would have to be reworked.

Network diagrams have the logical ties between activities built into their activities. A change in the sequence or duration to any activity in the network schedule will carry forward throughout the entire project. The concept of precedence is necessary to effectively monitor and control a project. It is this concept that makes network diagrams so effective in monitoring and controlling project schedules.

NETWORK DIAGRAMMING METHODS

The three types of network diagramming methods will be summarized in the following sections with listed advantages and disadvantages:

- Activity-On-Arrow (AOA)
- Activity-On-Node (AON)
- Precedence Diagramming Method (PDM)

FIGURE 6.1
An activity drawn using the Activity-On-Arrow (AOA) diagramming method.

Activity-On-Arrow (AOA)

The Activity-On-Arrow (AOA) is sometimes referred to as the Arrow Diagramming Method (ADM) or the *i-j* Diagramming method. Regardless of the name, it consists of representing the activity with a horizontal arrow placed between two nodes. As the arrow moves from right to left, it is intended to represent the progression of the activity's work. The use of the nodes is intended to show the start and finish of the activity. The node on the left of the activity is referred to as the *i* node and the node to the right of the activity is referred to as the *j* node. The *i-j* nodes are numbered, which allows each activity to be identified by a unique *i-j* number set. An example of an activity drawn using the AOA network is shown in Figure 6.1.

The AOA method was the first diagramming method used to represent the critical path method in early publications. As a consequence, it caught on and was used for years to represent project schedules. Additionally, it was the method used initially when CPM and PERT networks were first analyzed and solved by the use of computers. This helped solidify the use of the arrow method in the early days.

A negative characteristic of AOA is the need for *dummy* activities due to logical constraints natural to the arrow diagramming method. A dummy activity is an activity that has to be added to the schedule network to show the proper logical sequence of the schedule activities. Dummy activities have zero duration; therefore, they add no extra time to the project schedule. This is a significant disadvantage of the arrow method because it adds additional activities to the network and makes the network considerably more difficult to draw.

Additionally, manual CPM calculations are more difficult with AOA, although all calculations performed on all three methods will yield the exact same result. The arrow method is limited to the Finish-to-Start relationship type.

Advantages of AOA
- Activities can be time-scaled.
- Horizontal nature of the arrow communicates progress of the activity.
- Schedule communicates the flow of the work well.

Disadvantages of AOA
- Need for dummy activities make the networks very difficult to draw.
- Confusing nature may lead to incorrect networks.
- No longer supported by most scheduling softwares.
- Dummy activities add extra activities to the schedule.
- More difficult to manually calculate CPM.
- Limited to Finish-to-Start activity relationships.

For the reasons listed above, the Activity-On-Arrow method has lost favor with most of the construction industry and its use has declined sharply since the 1990s.

Activity-On-Node (AON)

The Activity-On-Node (AON) diagramming method consists of a single node representing the activity. The node can be shaped in any form (circle, square, bar, diamond, etc.) and is connected by a line or arrow to the other activities that it is logically tied to. This method has no logical constraints and, therefore, does not require dummy activities. The AON diagrams are considerably less confusing and considerably easier to draw than arrow diagrams. An example of a single activity drawn using the AON network is shown in Figure 6.2.

The AON method requires a unique identifier for each activity, which is usually a letter or number. Additionally, since more than one node can start and/or end the project, the AON networks may need a *Start* and/or *End* node to tie the schedule together at the beginning and end of the network. Manual CPM calculations are easier with the AON method, although all calculations performed on all three methods will yield the exact same result. The AON method is also limited to the finish-to-start relationship type.

Advantages of AON
- Method is very easy to learn.
- Network diagrams are very easy to draw.
- There is no need for dummy activities.
- Diagrams are simple to read and follow.
- Flow of the project is clearly illustrated.
- Method is supported by most scheduling softwares.
- Easy to manually calculate CPM.

Disadvantages of AON
- Limited to Finish-to-Start activity relationships.
- Does not easily display the progress of its activities or the project.
- Activities cannot be time-scaled.
- May need to use a start and/or end node(s).

The AON method is taught in most textbooks. However, it is inadequate for most construction industry schedules due to the fact that it is limited to only Finish-to-Start activities. Only very simple or straightforward schedules would benefit from its use.

Precedence Diagramming Method (PDM)

The Precedence Diagramming Method is an extension of the Activity-On-Node (AON) method and is nearly identical to it with one difference: it allows for the use of all four activity relationship types. Like the AON method, it consists of a single node representing the activity. The node can be shaped in any form (circle, square, bar, diamond, etc.)

FIGURE 6.2
A single activity drawn using the Activity-On-Node (AON) diagramming method.

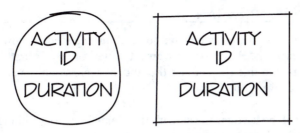

FIGURE 6.3
Two common ways to draw a single activity using the Precedence Diagramming Method (PDM).

and is connected by a line or arrow to the other activities that it is logically tied to. This method has no logical constraints and, therefore, does not require dummy activities. Precedence diagrams are considerably less confusing and considerably easier to draw than arrow diagrams. An example of a single activity drawn two different ways using the precedence method is shown in Figure 6.3.

The precedence method requires a unique identifier for each activity, which is usually a letter or number. Additionally, since more than one node can start and/or end the project, the precedence networks may need a *start* and/or *end* node to tie the schedule together at the beginning and end of the network.

Manual CPM calculations are much easier with both the precedence and AON methods than the AOA method. However, since the precedence method is not limited to just the finish-to-start relationship type, the calculations for the three other relationship types can be complicated, as different calculation methods may be used, yielding multiple results for dates, total float, and project duration. This will be discussed in more detail in the next chapter.

Advantages of PDM
- Method is very easy to learn.
- Can use all four relationship types.
- Network diagrams better represent the actual workflow of the project.
- Network diagrams are very easy to draw.
- There is no need for dummy activities.
- Diagrams are simple to read and follow.
- Method is supported by most scheduling softwares.

Disadvantages of PDM
- Calculation of the non-finish-to-start activities can be complicated and can yield multiple results for dates, total float, and project duration.
- Does not easily display the progress of its activities or the project.
- Activities cannot be time-scaled.
- May need to use a Start and/or End node(s).

The precedence method, the most popular diagramming method used in the construction industry today, is the most flexible and powerful of the three methods due to its use of the four relationship types. Additionally, the use of the four relationship types allows the network to better represent the actual project workflow. Nearly every scheduling software on the market uses the PDM method.

Based on the compelling reasons previously discussed, the Precedence Diagramming Method will be used exclusively throughout the remainder of this text.

DRAWING THE PRECEDENCE NETWORK DIAGRAM

The remainder of this chapter is devoted to teaching the student how to draw precedence network diagrams. However, there are a few items to cover first. For ease of simplicity, the examples in this chapter and the student exercises at the end of the chapter will follow these conventions:

1. Letters will be used for the activity IDs. Some networks will include activity descriptions for informational purposes.
2. The logical sequencing of the activities will be provided for each example. Durations will also be provided but will not be used until the next chapter.
3. Networks that have more than one activity starting and/or finishing the network will use a *Start* node before the first activities and an *End* node after the last activities.

Drawing a precedence network diagram using the PDM method is quite easy. The following topics will take the student through the process of learning how to draw a precedence network diagram. That is followed by three in-class practice exercises, which are followed by six student exercises at the end of the chapter.

- Drawing activities and connecting activities
- Drawing the different relationship types (review from Chapter 5)
- Step-by-step example of drawing a network

DRAWING ACTIVITIES AND CONNECTING ACTIVITIES

As stated earlier, there are many different and acceptable ways to draw the activity nodes such as circles, squares, bars, diamonds, and so forth. There are also different ways to draw the connecting lines that connect one activity to the next. There is not a right or wrong way. What is most important is that the network diagram communicates with the individual(s) who need to use it.

As stated earlier, with the extensive and widespread use of scheduling softwares, rough, hand-drawn networks are rarely, if ever, used as a presentation document. Rather, their sole intent is to be used as a tool for the scheduler or project manager to help create the most accurate and reliable project schedule possible. Therefore, they should be drawn quickly and without pretense. The only people who will ever see them are those involved with the development of the schedule.

Figures 6.4A through 6.4E demonstrate some of the more common methods used to draw activity nodes and connecting lines. The logic shown in the illustrations is: activity B follows activity A.

Notice that the last example combines a square activity node with a diamond-shaped node (often used for milestone activities), connected with an arrow line. This is a good way to separate normal activities from milestones. In the next section, dashed connecting lines will be used when there is a lag between activities. Again, this is a good way to visually highlight a different condition.

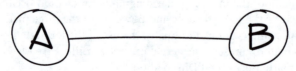

FIGURE 6.4A
Circle activity nodes with a connecting line without an arrowhead.

FIGURE 6.4B
Circle activity nodes with an arrow connecting line.

FIGURE 6.4C
Square activity nodes with an arrow connecting line.

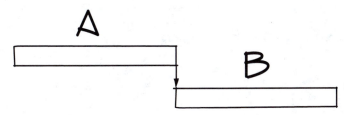

FIGURE 6.4D
Bar activity nodes with an arrow connecting line.

FIGURE 6.4E
Diamond activity node (often used for milestone activities) combined with a square activity node with an arrow connecting line.

For this text, different shapes will be used for different schedules to allow the student to see variation; however, the diamond shape will always be used for milestones and dashed lines will always be used for connecting lines *with lag*.

DRAWING THE DIFFERENT RELATIONSHIP TYPES
Refer back to Figures 5.5 through 5.13 in Chapter 5 for individual examples of how to draw the four relationship types. These examples demonstrate how the four different relationship types should be drawn and are shown with and without lag.

STEP-BY-STEP EXAMPLE OF DRAWING A NETWORK
The following is a step-by-step example of how to draft a network diagram. Many of the common activity sequences in a typical network are illustrated in this example. The schedule activities with their logical sequence are listed in total below, followed by Figure 6.5, which shows the network diagram of the schedule activities and their logical sequence drawn in stages.

Activities and their logical sequence step-by-step:

- Activity A starts the project.
- B follows A.
- C, D follow B.
- E follows C.
- F follows C, D.
- G, H follow E, F.
- I follows F with a start-to-start relationship with a (4)-day lag.
- J follows G, H, and I.
- K (hammock activity) follows A with a start-to-start relationship and a (0)-day lag. Activity J follows activity K with a finish-to-finish relationship and a (0)-day lag.
- J ends the project.

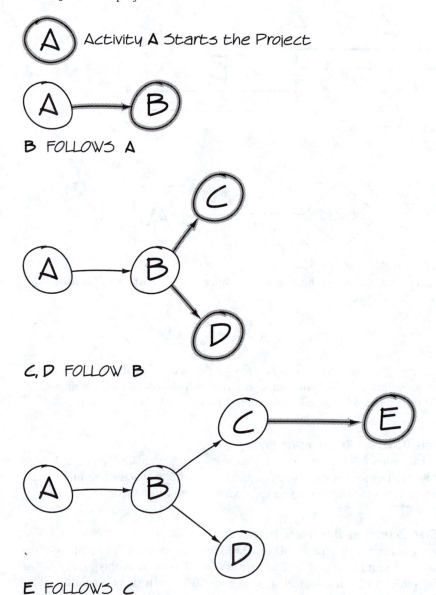

FIGURE 6.5
Step-by-step example of drawing a network diagram using PDM.

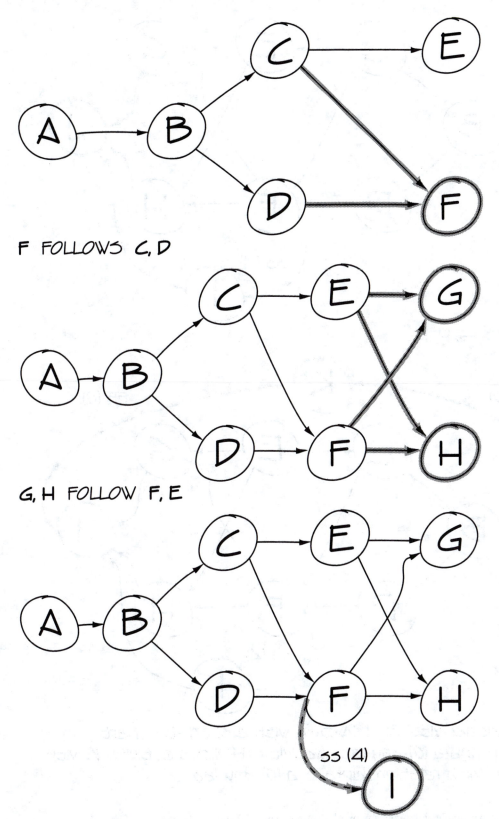

F FOLLOWS C, D

G, H FOLLOW F, E

I FOLLOWS F with a start-to-start relationship with a (4)-day lag

FIGURE 6.5
Continuation of Step-by-Step example of drawing a network diagram using PDM.

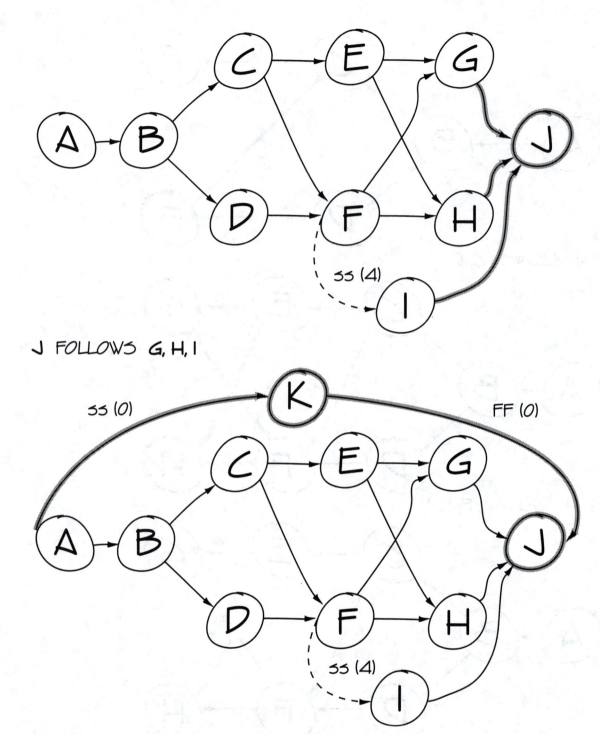

J FOLLOWS G, H, I

K (hammock activity) FOLLOWS **A** with a start-to start relationship and a (0)-day lag. Activity **J** follows activity **K** with a finish-to-finish relationship and a (0)-day lag.

FIGURE 6.5
Continuation of Step-by-Step example of drawing a network diagram using PDM.

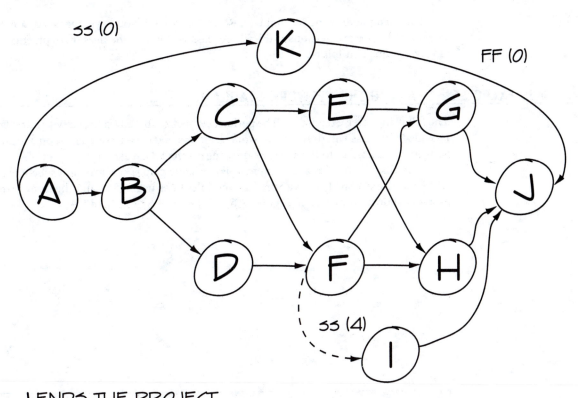

ss (0)

FF (0)

ss (4)

J ENDS THE PROJECT.

FIGURE 6.5
Conclusion of Step-by-Step example of drawing a network diagram using PDM.

The example drawing is complete. Review it to see if you have questions. Your instructor will answer questions and lead the class as it works the next three practice network diagrams that follow.

IN-CLASS EXERCISES: DRAWING THE NETWORK DIAGRAMS

The following three exercises will be performed in class. Based on the activities and logic provided, the class will draw the network diagrams. Each exercise is listed on a separate page with the answer to the network drawing on the following page.

Note that the third practice exercise is the same garage construction schedule that will be used extensively in the SureTrak modules later in the text and the same project that was shown previously in Figures 4.6, 4.7a, 4.7b, 4.8, 5.2b, and 5.4.

IN-CLASS EXERCISE
Practice Exercise #1

Based on the activities and logic provided below, draw the network diagram for this project. The activity durations are shown, but will not be used until the next chapter. The network drawing is shown in Figure 6.6 on the following page.

Activity(s)	Logical Sequence	Activity(s)	Activity	Duration
A	Starts the project		A	4
B	Follow(s)	A	B	2
C, D	Follow	B	C	6
E	Follow(s)	C	D	1
F	Follow(s)	D	E	7
G	Follow(s)	E	F	6
H, I	Follow	F	G	5
J	Follow(s)	G, H	H	3
K	Follow(s)	H	I	8
L	Follow(s)	I	J	9
M	Follow(s)	J, K, L	K	2
N, O	Follow	M	L	1
P	Follow(s)	N, O	M	6
P	Ends the project		N	1
			O	9
			P	7

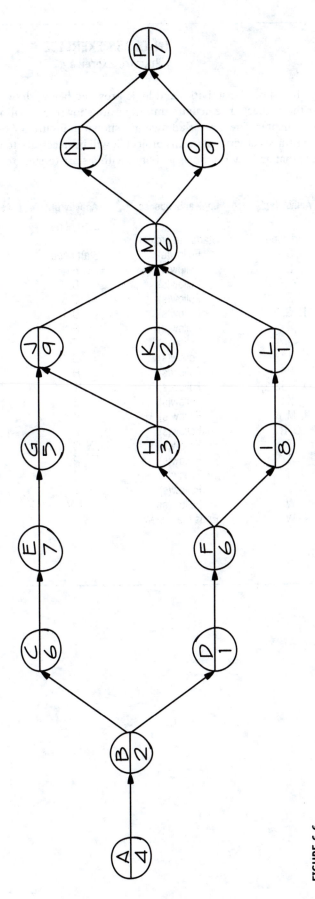

FIGURE 6.6
Practice Exercise #1 network diagram.

135

IN-CLASS EXERCISE
Practice Exercise #2

Based on the activities and logic provided below, draw the network diagram for this project. The activity durations are shown, but will not be used until the next chapter. The network drawing is shown in Figure 6.7 on the following page. Since three activities start this project, it will be necessary to use a *Start* node. Also note that activity P follows activity I with a start-to-start relationship with a (2)-day lag.

Activity(s)	Logical Sequence	Activity(s)	Activity	Duration
		Start node		0
Start node	Starts the project		A	4
A, B, C	Follow(s)	Start node	B	3
D	Follow(s)	A	C	2
G, F	Follow(s)	B	D	2
E	Follow(s)	C	E	5
H, G, F	Follow(s)	D	F	1
F	Follow(s)	E	G	6
J	Follow(s)	F	H	5
I	Follow(s)	G	I	7
P	Follow(s)	H	J	7
L, O, P(SS(2))	Follow(s)	I	K	6
K	Follow(s)	J	L	5
L, M, N	Follow(s)	K	M	1
Q, R	Follow(s)	L	N	4
T	Follow(s)	M, N, O, Q, R	O	6
S	Follow(s)	P	P	9
U	Follow(s)	S	Q	2
V	Follow(s)	T	R	3
W	Follow(s)	U, V	V	9
W	Ends the project		T	6
			U	4
			V	1
			W	2

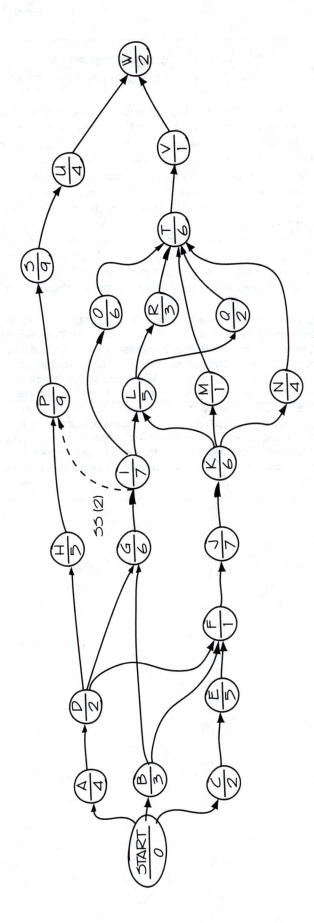

FIGURE 6.7

Practice Exercise #2 network diagram.

137

IN-CLASS EXERCISE
Practice Exercise #3

The notes below detail the activities necessary to build a garage. This is the same garage construction schedule that will be used extensively in the SureTrak modules later in the text and the same project that was shown previously in Figures 4.6, 4.7a, 4.7b, 4.8, 5.2b, and 5.4. From these notes, create the network diagram for the garage. The activity ID and descriptions are shown in *bold italic*, and the durations are shown in parentheses and italic. The activity durations are shown, but will not be used until the next chapter. You *do not* need to include the description of the activity.

The network drawing is shown in Figure 6.8. Additionally, the same network is shown in Figure 6.9, but drawn using different nodes and with some additional activity information shown. Compare the two to verify that they are the same. What is different about them? What additional information is shown?

Once you've received the *A–notice to proceed* (milestone activity–0 days), begin *B–excavation* (3) and *C–order / deliver* the *brick* (20) so it comes in on time. The *D–footing and foundation* (10) will follow the excavation and precede *E–slab-on-grade* (4). When the slab is done, both the *F–exterior wall framing* (3) and *G–backfill* (1) can begin. After the backfill is complete, you can *H–form and pour the drive* (4). Your framing crew will begin to *I–frame and shingle the roof* (5) after they finish framing the exterior walls. The *J–masonry* (10) can begin after the roof and backfill is complete and the brick has been delivered. The *K–exterior trim* (5) can begin seven days SS(7) after the masonry begins.

On the inside of the garage, you can *L–hang the garage door* (1) after the roof is complete. After the door is hung, you can begin the *M–interior finishes* (7). The project can be *N–punched out* (4) after the masonry, exterior trim, the drive, and interior finishes are completed. The *O–Project management* (hammock activity–?? days) will start when notice to proceed starts and finish when punchout finishes.

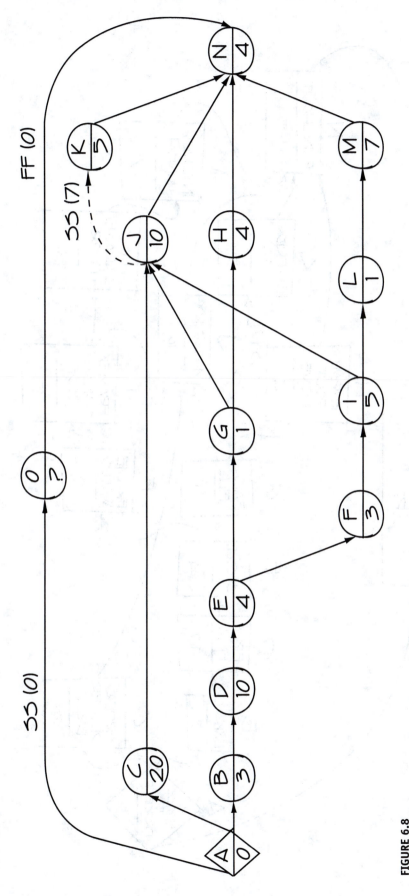

FIGURE 6.8
Practice Exercise #3 network diagram.

139

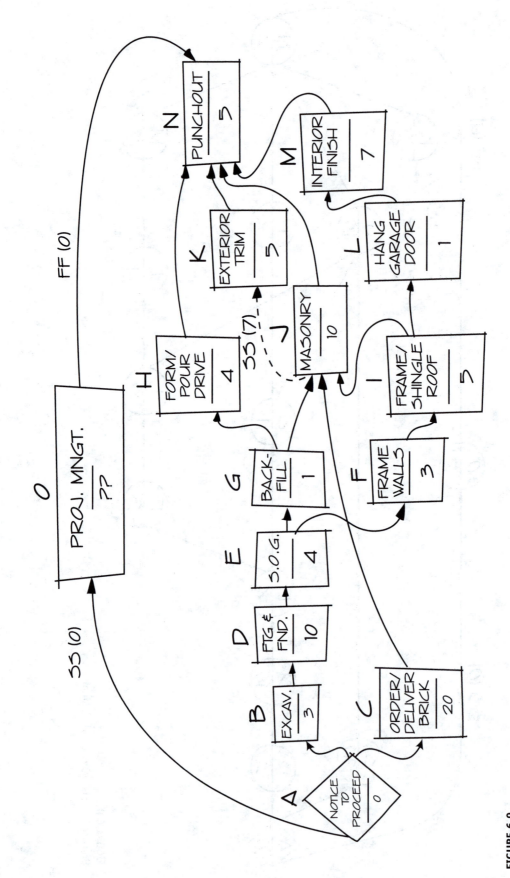

FIGURE 6.9
Practice Exercise #3 network diagram drawn a bit differently and shown with activity IDs and descriptions.

STUDENT EXERCISES: DRAWING THE NETWORK DIAGRAMS

The student exercises on the following pages describe the activities, in various ways, of six project schedules. The student is to draw a network diagram for each project based on the information provided. Activity durations and some descriptions have also been provided. The activity durations are shown, but will not be used until the next chapter. If the description is provided, include an abbreviated description in the node. You may want to draw these on 11 × 17-inch paper.

The students will also need to include *Start* and *End* nodes if a network starts and/or ends with more than one activity. Milestone activities should be drawn using a diamond as the node. Connecting lines that have lag should be dashed.

STUDENT EXERCISE
Exercise #1

Based on the activities and logic provided below, draw the network diagram for this project. The activity durations are shown, but will not be used until the next chapter.

Activity(s)	Logical Sequence	Activity(s)	Activity	Duration
A, B	Starts the project		A	3
C, D	Follow(s)	A	B	1
E, F	Follow(s)	B	C	2
G	Follow(s)	C	D	6
H	Follow(s)	D	E	4
I, O	Follow(s)	F	F	9
J, K	Follow(s)	G, D	G	2
L	Follow(s)	H	H	3
M, N	Follow(s)	I	I	8
O	Follow(s)	F	J	7
P, Q	Follow(s)	J	K	6
R	Follow(s)	K, L	L	6
S, T	Follow(s)	M	M	1
U	Follow(s)	T, N	N	2
V	Follow(s)	P, Q	O	4
W	Follow(s)	E, R, S	P	3
X	Follow(s)	W	Q	6
Y	Follow(s)	U	R	7
Z	Follow(s)	X, U	S	1
O, V, Y, Z	End the project		T	6
			U	2
			V	5
			W	4
			X	5
			Y	3
			Z	1

STUDENT EXERCISE
Exercise #2

Based on the activities and logic provided below, draw the network diagram for this project. The activity durations are shown, but will not be used until the next chapter.

Activity(s) and their logical sequence	Activity	Duration
B and E start project.	A	2
A and D follow B.	B	3
A precedes C.	C	4
Both C and D must be complete before F starts.	D	5
F and E precede G.	E	6
H follows F.	F	2
I follows both G and H and precedes J.	G	2
J must be complete before L and K start.	H	3
N follows L which follows J.	I	14
P follows N and precedes R.	J	5
P precedes Q.	K	3
M follows K.	L	2
Q and R cannot start until M is complete.	M	1
O follows M.	N	3
S and T follow Q and O and precede V.	O	4
U follows R and precedes V.	P	5
V is the last activity.	Q	6
	R	1
	S	2
	T	1
	U	7
	V	2

STUDENT EXERCISE
Exercise #3

Based on the activities and logic provided in the notes below, draw the network diagram for this project. The activity durations are shown, but will not be used until the next chapter. Since the activities do not have IDs, include an abbreviated description in the node. However, if you were going to input this schedule into a scheduling software, you would have to ID the activities.

Once you have received the **notice to proceed** *(milestone activity–0 days)*, begin **excavation** *(3)* and **order / deliver** the **brick** *(20)* so it comes in on time. The **footing and foundation** *(13)* will follow the excavation and precede **slab-on-grade** *(4)*. When the slab is done, both the **exterior wall framing** *(7)* and **backfill** *(2)* can begin. You will start running the **site utilities** *(10)* with the backhoe when you are done backfilling. Your framing crew will begin to **frame and shingle the roof** *(6)* and frame the **interior partitions** *(9)* after they finish framing the exterior walls. Your electrical contractor doesn't want to do the **electrical work** *(5)* until after the interior walls are up and the site utilities have been run to the building. This way they can save an extra trip. When they are done with the electrical work, they can install the **space heaters** *(6)*.

The **masonry** *(10)* can begin after the roof and backfill is complete and the brick has been delivered. The **exterior trim** *(4)* can start after the masonry is complete. **Landscaping** *(4)* will follow both masonry and the site utility runs. The project can be **punched out** *(3)* after the exterior trim, landscaping, and space heaters are done. **Project management** *(hammock activity)* will start when notice to proceed starts and will finish when punchout finishes.

STUDENT EXERCISE
Exercise #4

Based on the activities and logic provided in the notes below, draw the network diagram for this project. Since the activities do not have IDs, include an abbreviated description in the node. The activity durations are shown, but will not be used until the next chapter. However, if you were going to input this schedule into a scheduling software, you would have to ID the activities.

The following network illustrates the sequence involved in building one house:

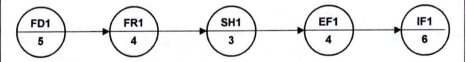

Where:

(FD1 = Foundation of house 1)
(FR1 = Framing of house 1)
(SH1 = Sheathing of house 1)
(EF1 = Exterior finish of house 1)
(FD1 = Interior finish of house 1)

Suppose you are a homebuilder and want to build five (5) homes as soon as possible but you have only one crew per each activity (i.e., one foundation crew, one framing crew, etc.).

Design the network diagram that would sequence the activities of the five crews to minimize total project (all five homes) duration.

STUDENT EXERCISE #5

Based on the activities and logic provided in the notes below, draw the network diagram for this project. The activity durations are shown, but will not be used until the next chapter. Since the activities do not have IDs, include an abbreviated description in the node. However, if you were going to input this schedule into a scheduling software, you would have to ID the activities.

Once you have received the **notice to proceed** (milestone activity–0), begin **excavation** (20), **order / deliver** the **steel** (60), and **order / deliver** the **brick** (40) so they come in on time. The **footing and foundation** (20) and the **underslab utilities** (12) will follow the excavation and precede **slab-on-grade** (5). When the slab is done and the steel is on site, you can begin to **erect** the **steel** (20).

When the steel is erected you can begin framing the **exterior walls** (13) with your framing crew. When the exterior walls are done and the brick has been delivered to the site, start the **masonry** (10). After your framing crew is done with the exterior walls, they can begin framing the **interior partitions** (25). Ten days after the interior partitions begin, you can begin **HVAC rough-in** (25) and five days after that begins, you can begin the **electrical rough-in** (17). The **plumbing rough-in** (12) will begin seven days after the electrical rough-in begins.

When the masonry is done, you can begin to **roof** (10) the building. When the roof is done, install the **exterior doors and windows** (13); however, you can't do this until your crew is done with the interior partitions.

Interior finishes (40) can begin after the exterior doors and windows are installed and the HVAC, electrical, and plumbing rough-ins are complete. **Project management** (hammock activity–??) will start when notice to proceed starts and finish when interior finishes ends. Interior finishes is the last activity.

STUDENT EXERCISE
Exercise #6

The Delhi Medical Building will be used as the sample project in Chapter 8 when a construction schedule is created and revised. In this exercise, you will be creating a bid package schedule of the Delhi Medical Building. A bid package schedule is the schedule that comes between the very broad milestone schedule and the very detailed construction schedule. It is divided into activities roughly equal to the different trade contracts that will be bid out. It is typically added to the bidding documents, so the bidders will have an idea when their portion of the work will take place. You will also create this same schedule in SureTrak in Module 8.

Based on the activities and logic provided in the notes below, draw the network diagram for the bid package schedule of the Delhi Medical Building. Since the activities do not have IDs, include an abbreviated description in the node. There are thirty-nine activities (*shown in bold italics*) below with their duration, logic, and activity type (if it is other than a task).

Once you have received the ***notice to proceed*** *(milestone activity–0),* begin to ***mobilize / site layout*** *(5)* and begin the ***submittals and approvals*** *(20)* process. Once you are mobilized, begin the ***excavation*** *(10),* which will be followed by the ***site utility runs*** *(15).* After the submittals are approved you can ***order / deliver long lead materials*** *(30),* and begin to review ***coordination drawings*** *(40).* The ***footings*** *(7)* will start two days after the excavation *starts* and will precede the ***foundation walls*** *(20).* The ***underslab rough-ins*** *(13)* will start ten days after the foundation walls *start.* The ***slab-on-grade*** *(4)* will follow both the underslab rough-ins and the foundation walls. The ***1st floor exterior studs*** *(5)* will follow slab-on-grade.

When the 1st floor exterior studs are complete and the steel, as part of the long lead materials, has arrived, you can ***erect steel and slab-on-deck*** *(14).* When this is finished and the slab has cured you can ***backfill*** *(8),* begin the ***2nd floor exterior studs*** *(6),* and the ***1st floor interior studs*** *(12).* The 2nd floor exterior studs will be followed by ***frame and shingle the roof*** *(19).* The ***1st floor rough-ins*** *(27)* will start four days after the 1st floor interior studs *start* and after the coordination drawings are complete. The ***1st floor drywall*** *(11)* will follow the rough-ins. The ***2nd floor interior studs*** *(11)* will start nine days after the roof framing *starts*—by then the sheathing will be down on the roof, but not until the stud crew is done with the 1st floor interior studs. You can install the ***exterior doors and windows*** *(5)* after the roof is framed and shingled.

The ***masonry*** *(25)* can begin after the foundation is backfilled and the exterior doors and windows are installed. The brick is already on site as part of the long lead materials. The ***exterior trim, painting, and finishes*** *(31)* will start when the masonry is complete. The ***storm retention*** *(7)* work will start after the site utility runs and the backfill is completed, followed by the remainder of the ***site improvements*** *(52).*

The ***2nd floor rough-ins*** *(28)* will start four days after the 2nd floor interior studs *start.* The ***2nd floor drywall*** *(14)* will follow the 2nd floor rough-ins, the 2nd floor interior studs, and the 1st floor drywall. The ***1st floor prime coat*** *(5)* will follow the 1st floor drywall. When the painters are complete on the 1st floor, they will move up to paint the ***2nd floor prime coat*** *(5),* provided the 2nd floor drywall is complete. The ***1st floor ceiling grids, doors & hardware, and casework*** *(8)* will follow the 1st floor prime coat. When the carpenters are complete on the 1st floor, they will move up to begin the ***2nd floor ceiling grids, doors & hardware, and casework*** *(7),* provided the 2nd floor prime coat is complete.

When ceiling grids, doors & hardware, and casework are complete on both floors, the ***interior trim*** *(7)* can begin. When the trim is complete, the ***finish paint*** *(5)* will begin, followed by the ***flooring*** *(15).* The ***finish plumbing*** *(10),* ***finish electric*** *(8),* and ***finish HVAC*** *(8)* for the entire building will follow the 2nd floor ceiling grids, doors and hardware, and casework.

Punchlist *(5)* will follow site improvements, exterior trim, painting, and finishes, flooring, and the finish plumbing, electric, and HVAC. ***Project management*** *(hammock activity–??)* will start when notice to proceed starts and finish when punchlist finishes. Punchlist is the last activity of the project.

CHAPTER 7
CPM Calculations

The most powerful development in scheduling is the Critical Path Method (CPM). It has become the universal scheduling method in the construction industry as well as just about every other industry that has to plan, schedule, monitor, and coordinate any type of complex project. For example, when Boeing designed and built its 777 jetliner, it utilized CPM to plan and coordinate that multiyear effort. Drug companies will use CPM to plan and schedule the long process of researching and testing new drugs. Any type of project or process that is complex and/or drawn out will benefit from CPM's many capabilities.

Among the most important capabilities of CPM are the following two:

1. With very little project information (activities, durations, and logic), the CPM calculation will yield the following project and activity information: early start and finish dates, late start and finish dates, the minimum total project duration, total float of all activities, free float of all activities, and the critical path, or paths, of the project.

2. The CPM schedule is able to reflect the effect of changes that occur as the project proceeds and the schedule is updated. CPM predicts the effect of changes that the project team applies to the schedule. Since all the activities of the CPM schedule are linked together, changes made to the schedule carry forward throughout the entire schedule.

Some might argue that with the advent of powerful scheduling software programs, it is not necessary for students to learn how to manually calculate a CPM schedule. The problem with that reasoning is that the students would not know how to determine the validity of the schedule. There is a tendency for students, and many others, to believe that whatever comes out of a computer has to be right. If students do not know where the CPM data came from or how it is generated, they cannot fully understand the schedule.

There are other reasons students learn to manually calculate CPM schedules. By doing so they gain an intuitive feel for what the calculation actually does to the schedule and how the various dates, floats, and critical activities are generated. They will be able to better gauge the effects of change on the schedule. They will be able to use the full capabilities of the schedule and scheduling software. Additionally, they will better understand and be able to detect when the computer is outputting a bad schedule. The computer is a dumb tool. It only knows what you tell it. So when you accidentally say that Landscaping directly follows the Foundation in a schedule, it won't catch that obvious logic mistake.

In this chapter, the student will learn how to fully calculate PDM network schedules, including schedules that have start-to-start and finish-to-finish relationship types with lag.

CPM CALCULATIONS

Once the project network has been diagrammed and durations are assigned to the activities, the schedule is ready to be calculated. The schedule can be calculated using any time unit as long as all the activities are using that same unit. For the schedules created in this text, the time unit used is the *day*. When the schedule is calculated, the calculations do not yield calendar dates, but rather *ordinal* time increments. An ordinal time increment is a time period not tied to a calendar date, but to a unit of time—in our case, a day. Therefore, one working day is one ordinal day. And seven ordinal days is not one week, but rather, one week and two working days.

Once the schedule is calculated, the ordinal days can be converted to calendar dates. Care must be taken to not show work occurring on *off days* or holidays. Making this conversion by hand is very time-consuming and quite tedious, but happened often in the early days of scheduling. Today, scheduling software performs this task instantly.

As the schedule is calculated, the following information will be generated about each activity: early start (ES), early finish (EF), late start (LS), late finish (LF), and total float (TF). Additionally, the free float of the connecting lines will be calculated. This information builds upon itself, and therefore needs to be displayed on the network. Just as there are many ways to draw the activity nodes, there are also many different ways to display this information on the node. In this text, the information will be displayed as shown in Figure 7.1.

The following is a step-by-step example of how to calculate a precedence network diagram using CPM. The schedule that will be calculated is the same schedule that was used in the previous chapter for the network diagramming example, and is shown in Figure 7.2. Notice that the durations have been added to this schedule.

The next few sections will display the CPM calculation method step-by-step, starting with the forward pass.

FORWARD PASS

Calculating the forward pass will yield the following information:

- The early start and early finish of each activity in the network schedule.
- The minimum total project duration.

When performing the forward pass, it is assumed that all activities in the network will start as soon as possible, finish as soon as possible, and, when complete, the activities that follow it will start immediately.

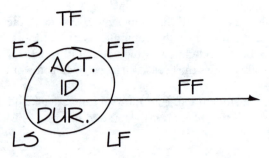

FIGURE 7.1
Activity node displayed with CPM calculation information.

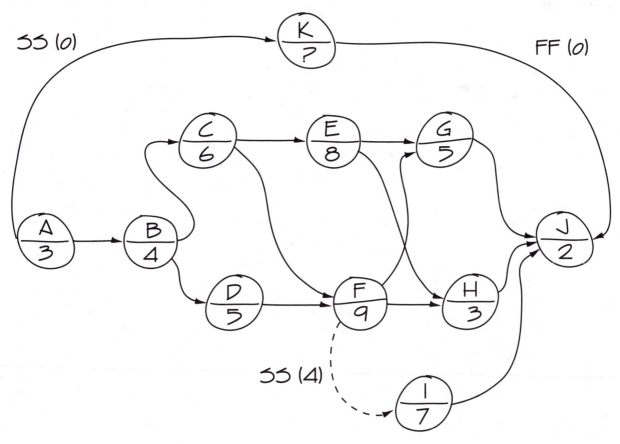

FIGURE 7.2
PDM network diagram to be used for CPM calculations.

GETTING STARTED

The starting point of the forward pass is the first activity in the network. The early start time for the first activity of any network is day zero. This follows what is called the *end of day convention* which says that the early start of an activity starts at the end of the previous workday. Using this convention keeps the schedule from picking up an extra day that has no work. For that reason, the early start of activity A, and therefore the project, is 0 and is marked as shown in Figure 7.3.

The next step is to calculate the early finish of activity A, but first let's define the early finish of an activity.

EARLY FINISH (EF)

The early finish of an activity can be defined as follows:

$$\text{Early Finish (EF)} = \text{Early Start (ES)} + \text{Duration.}$$

The early finish of an activity is simply the early start of that activity plus the duration of that activity. Therefore, since activity A has an early start of 0 and a duration of 3, its early finish is 3 (EF = 0 + 3), as shown in Figure 7.4.

Activity A is complete. We next have to calculate the early start of activity B, but first let's define the early start of an activity.

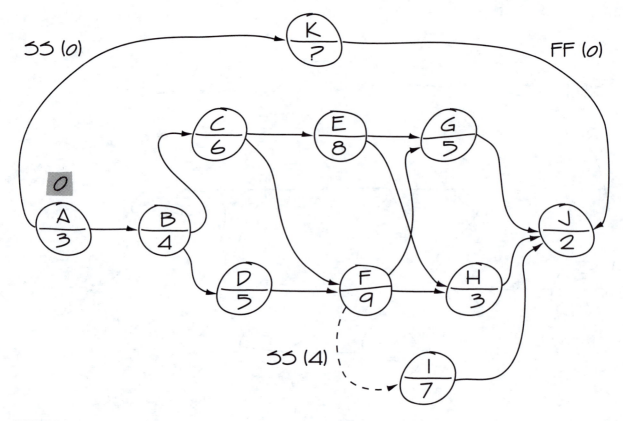

FIGURE 7.3
The start of the CPM calculation shown with the early start of activity A using the end of day convention.

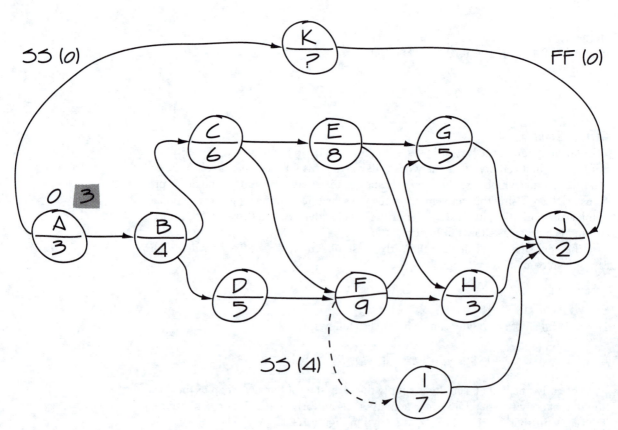

FIGURE 7.4
Early finish of activity A shown on the node.

150

EARLY START (ES)

The early start of an activity can be defined as follows:

> The early start (ES) of an activity is the earliest an activity can start based on the earliest the activity, or activities, preceding it finished.

From this we can see that since the early finish of activity A is 3, the early start of activity B is also 3. And from the early finish definition, we know that the early finish of activity B is 7 (EF = 3 + 4). The early start and early finish of activity B are shown in Figure 7.5.

To calculate the early start of an activity when *more than one* activity precedes the activity, the early start of the activity is taken from the preceding activity with the **highest** early finish. This is an important concept to grasp. We will need to consider this a little bit down the road when we are calculating the early start of activity F. Notice that it has two activities preceding it (C and D).

With this knowledge in hand, continue to calculate the early starts and early finishes of the remainder of the activities.

Early Start and Finish of Activities C and D

Since the early finish of activity B is 7, the early start of both activities C and D is 7. Therefore, the early finish of activity C is 13 (EF = 7 + 6) and the early finish of activity D is 12 (EF = 7 + 5), as shown in Figure 7.6.

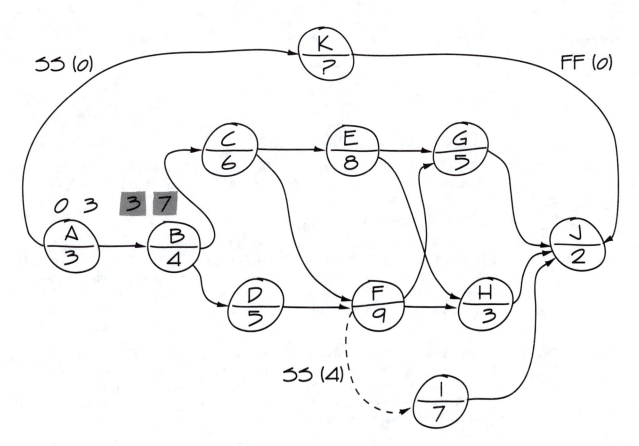

FIGURE 7.5
Early start and finish of activity B.

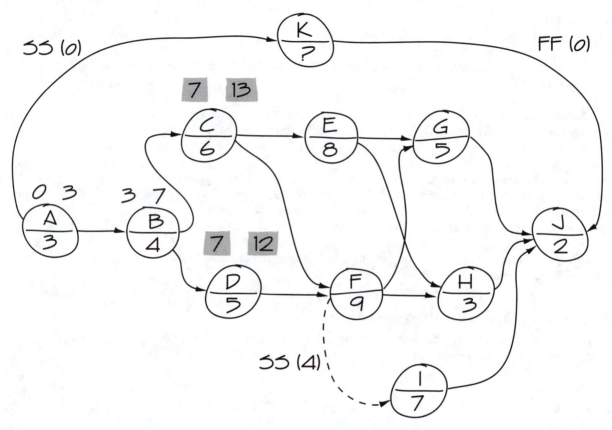

FIGURE 7.6
Early start and finish of activities C and D.

Early Start and Finish of Activity E

Since the early finish of activity C is 13, the early start of activity E is also 13. Therefore, the early finish of activity E is 21 (EF = 13 + 8), as shown in Figure 7.7.

Early Start and Finish of Activity F

Activity F has two activities preceding it, C and D. Activity F cannot start until *both* of these activities are complete. Activity D will be complete on day 12; however, activity C will not be complete until day 13. Therefore, activity F cannot begin until day 13—the early finish of C. Consequently, the early start of activity F is day 13. Since the early start of activity F is 13, the early finish is 22 (EF = 13 + 9), as shown in Figure 7.8.

EARLY START AND EARLY FINISH OF ACTIVITIES WITH START-TO-START RELATIONSHIPS

The power of the precedence diagramming method is the use of all four relationship types. However, be careful because the CPM calculation is a bit different for these various relationship types. The early start of an activity that has a start-to-start relationship with its predecessor can be defined and calculated as follows:

> The early start (ES) of an activity that has a start-to-start relationship with its predecessor is equal to the early start of the predecessor plus the lag, if a lag exists.

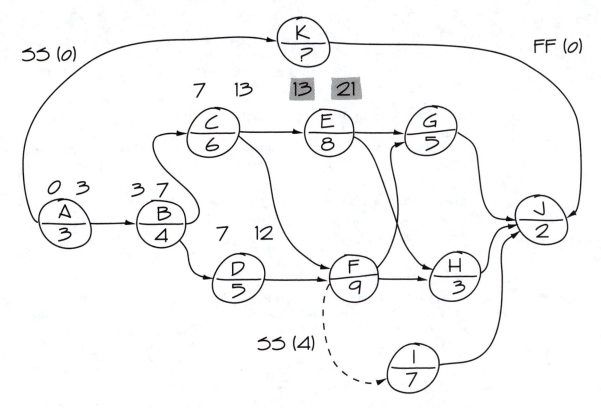

FIGURE 7.7
Early start and finish of activity E.

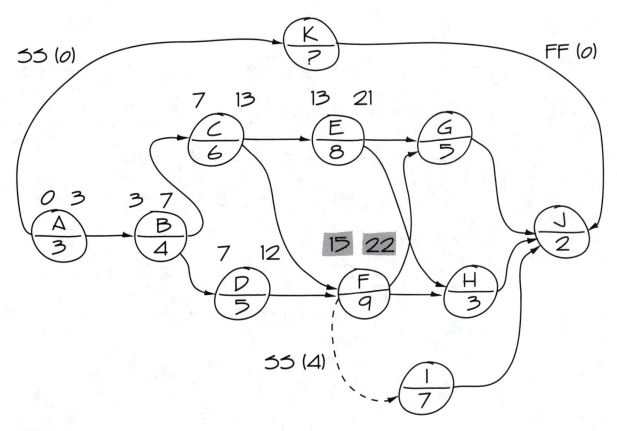

FIGURE 7.8
Early start and finish of activity F.

The early start of an activity that has a start-to-start relationship with its predecessor is determined using the following formula:

$$\text{Early Start (ES)}_{\text{of start-to-start activity}} = \text{Early Start (ES)}_{\text{of predecessor}} + \text{Lag.}$$

The early finish of an activity that has a start-to-start relationship with its predecessor is calculated no differently than other activities.

Early Start and Finish of Activity I

Based on the previous definition and formula, the early start of activity I is 17 (ES = 13 + 4). The early finish of activity I is 24 (EF = 17 + 7), as shown in Figure 7.9.

Early Start and Finish of Activities G and H

Both activities G and H follow activities E and F. The early finish of activity E is day 21 and the early finish of activity F is day 22. From that, we choose day 22 to be the early start of activities G and H. Therefore, the early finish of activity G is 27 (EF = 22 + 5) and the early finish of activity H is 25 (EF = 22 + 3), as shown in Figure 7.10.

Early Start and Finish of Activity J

Activity J follows activities G, H, and I. The highest early finish of those three activities is 27, from G. Therefore, the early start of activity J is 27. The early finish of J is 29 (EF = 27 + 2), as shown in Figure 7.11.

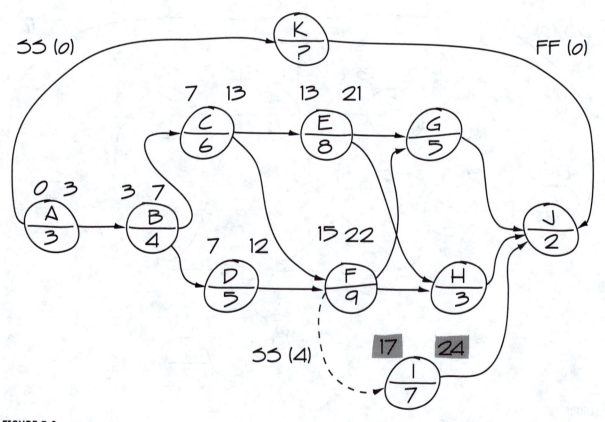

FIGURE 7.9
Early start and finish of activity I (notice the start-to-start relationship).

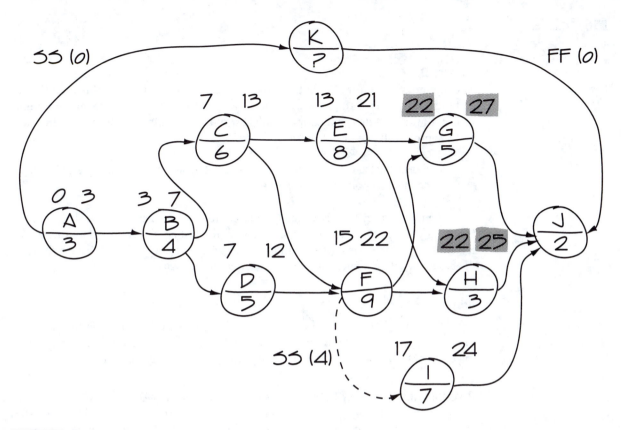

FIGURE 7.10
Early start and finish of activities G and H.

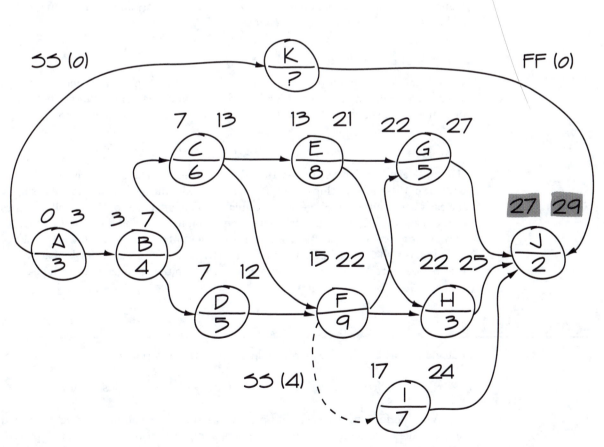

FIGURE 7.11
Early start and finish of activity J.

PROJECT DURATION

The minimum total duration of the project is determined by the early finish of the last activity of the project. If the project has more than one last activity, the minimum total project duration is determined by the *highest* of the early finishes of the activities that end the project. It can be defined as follows:

> Project Duration = Early finish of the last activity of the project or the highest of the early finishes of the activities that end the project.

As mentioned in the last chapter, when more than one activity ends the project, it is a good practice to create an *end node* that all the last activities can go to, thereby establishing the end node as the singular last activity. The end node will have a duration of zero and is often a milestone activity such as Project Complete.

Project Duration

Activity J is the last activity of the project and has an early finish of 29; therefore, the minimum total project duration for the schedule is 29 days. Remember, that is 29 working days, not calendar days; therefore, the project is about six weeks long.

DURATION AND THE EARLY START AND EARLY FINISH OF A HAMMOCK ACTIVITY

Now that the total project duration has been determined, the duration and the early start and finish of the hammock activity can be determined. A hammock activity is a special type of activity that stretches between two or more activities. It does not have a duration assigned to it initially because it takes on the duration of the chain of activities that it spans. Hammock activities cannot have lag and are completely dependent upon the start and finish of the activities they are connected to.

Duration of a Hammock Activity (Activity K)

The hammock activity for the sample network spans from beginning to end. Therefore, since the total project duration is 29 days, that becomes the duration of the hammock (activity K) and should be handwritten into the duration field of the hammock.

Early Start and Finish of a Hammock Activity (Activity K)

Hammock activities have start-to-start and finish-to-finish relationships as their default. Because of these relationships, the early start and early finish of the hammock is simply the early start and finish of the activities that they are attached to. Hammock activities cannot have lag and are completely dependent upon the start and finish of the activities they are connected to. Therefore, since the early start of activity A is 0, the early start of activity K is also 0. Since the early finish of activity J is 29, the early finish of activity K is also 29. Figure 7.12 shows the sample network with the completed forward pass.

BACKWARD PASS

Calculating the backward pass will yield the following information:

■ The late finish and late start of each activity in the network schedule.

When performing the backward pass, it is assumed that all network activities will finish as late as possible and start as late as possible. It is also assumed that all preceding activities will finish as late as possible.

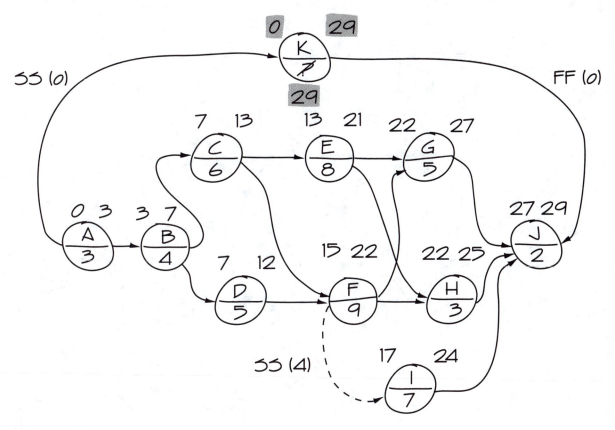

FIGURE 7.12
The completed forward pass, including the duration, early start, and early finish of activity K, the hammock activity.

GETTING STARTED
The starting point of performing the backward pass is the last activity in the network. The minimum total project duration has been determined from the forward pass. This duration must be maintained; therefore, the latest the last activity of the project can finish is equal to the early finish of the last activity. Therefore, the late finish of the project is determined from the early finish of the last activity of the project—activity J in our case, which is day 29, as shown in Figure 7.13.

The next step is to calculate the late start of activity J, but first let's define the late start of an activity.

LATE START (LS)
The late start of an activity can be defined as follows:

> The late start (LS) of an activity is the latest the activity can start without affecting the total project duration.

The late start can be determined as follows:

$$\text{Late start (LS)} = \text{late finish (LF)} - \text{duration.}$$

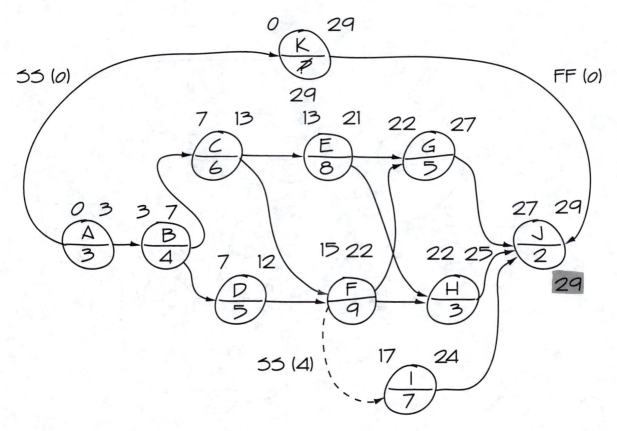

FIGURE 7.13
The late finish of J and the beginning of the backward pass.

The late start of an activity is simply the late finish of that activity minus the duration of that activity. Therefore, since activity J has a late finish of 29 and a duration of 2, its late start is 27 (LS = 29 − 2), as shown in Figure 7.14.

Activity J is complete. Next, we need to begin to move back through the network (the backward pass) calculating the remainder of the activities' late finishes and late starts. Let's move next to activity G, but first, we'll define the late finish of an activity.

LATE FINISH (LF)

The late finish of an activity can be defined as follows:

> The late finish (LF) of an activity is the latest the activity can finish without affecting the total project duration.

It is determined as follows:

> The late finish (LF) of an activity is the latest an activity can finish based on the latest the activity, or activities, succeeding it started.

From this we can see that since the late start of activity J is 27, the late finish of activity G is also 27. And from the late start definition, we know that the late start of activity G is 22 (LS = 27 − 5). The late finish and late start of activity G are shown in Figure 7.15.

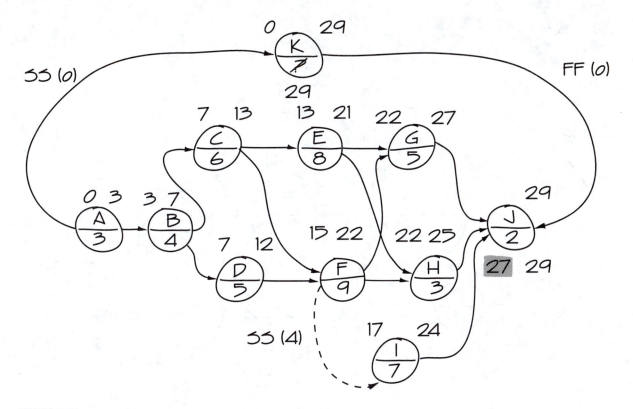

FIGURE 7.14
Late start of activity J.

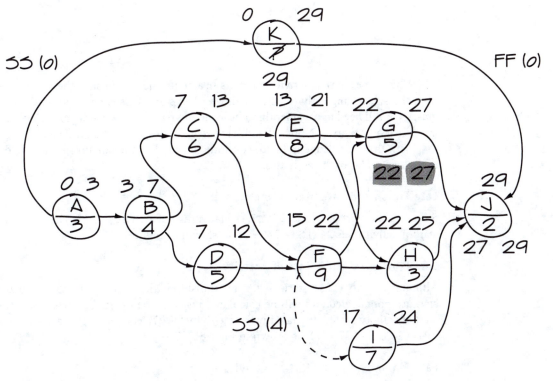

FIGURE 7.15
Late finish and late start of activity G.

159

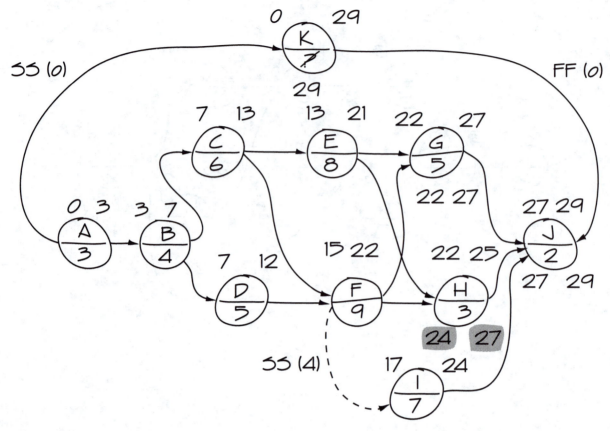

FIGURE 7.16
Late finish and late start of activity H.

When *more than one* activity succeeds an activity, the late finish of the activity is taken from the succeeding activity with the *lowest* late start. This is an important concept to grasp. We will need to consider this a little bit down the road when we are calculating the late finish of activity E. Notice that it has two activities succeeding it (G and H).

With this knowledge in hand, continue to calculate the late finishes and late starts of the remainder of the activities.

Late Finish and Late Start of Activity H

Since the late start of activity J is 27, the late finish of activity H is 27. Therefore, the late start of activity H is 24 (LS = 27 − 3), as shown in Figure 7.16.

Late Finish and Late Start of Activity I

Although activity I has a start-to-start relationship with activity F, its late finish and late start are not affected and will be calculated just like the other activities. Since the late start of activity J is 27, the late finish of activity I is 27. Therefore, the late start of activity I is 20 (LS = 27 − 7), as shown in Figure 7.17.

Late Finish and Late Start of Activity E

Activity E has two successors, activity G and activity H. Activity E has to be complete before *both* activities G and H begin. Activity H has a late start of day 24, but activity G has

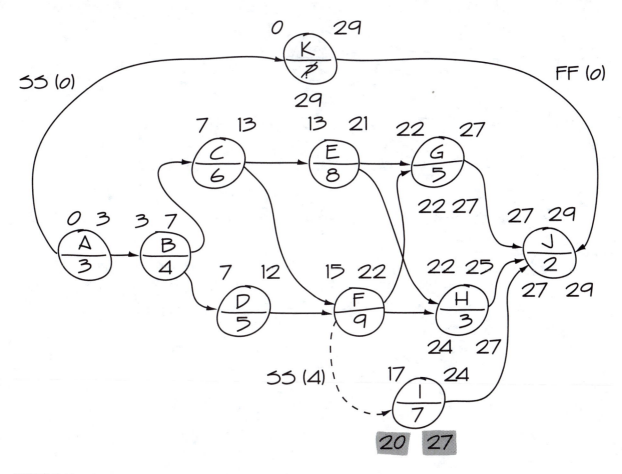

FIGURE 7.17
Late finish and late start of activity I.

a late start of day 22. Therefore, if activity E has to be finished in time for both to begin, it has to be finished by day 22—the late start of G. Consequently, the late finish of activity E is day 22. Since the late finish of activity E is 22, the late start of activity E is 14 (LS = 22 − 8), as shown in Figure 7.18.

Late Finish and Late Start of Activities with Successors That Have Start-to-Start Relationships

When an activity's successor has a start-to-start relationship with the activity, like activity F and its successor, activity I, the late start of the activity has to be calculated with multiple considerations. The late finish is calculated no differently.

For example, examine activity F. Activity F has three successors, G, H, and I. Activities G and H have the normal finish-to-start relationship with activity F. Activity I has a start-to-start relationship with activity F. Activity I could be called activity F's start-to-start successor.

The late *finish* of activity F will be calculated no differently than any other activity. It will use the lowest late start of G or H, independent of activity I.

> The start-to-start successors of an activity do not figure into the late finish calculation of the activity.

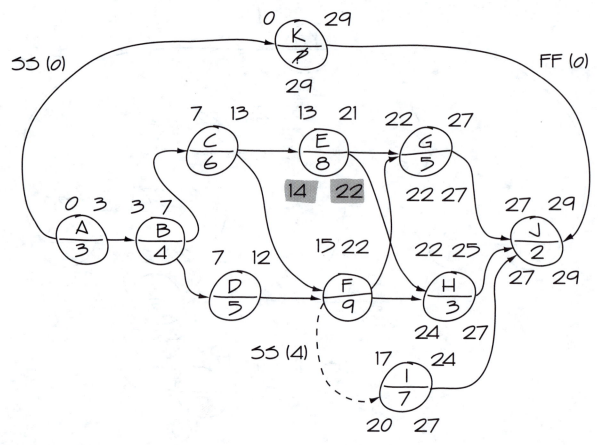

FIGURE 7.18
Late finish and late start of activity E.

However, the late *start* of activity F is determined based on two considerations, choosing the lowest value they yield: Activity F will generate a late start using the normal calculation based on its late finish minus its duration *and* activity F will generate a late start based on the late start of its start-to-start successors minus the lag time in-between the two. Both of these late starts must be considered and the lowest value they yield must be chosen.

These two considerations would need to be examined for any activity that has a start-to-start successor. Also note that if an activity has more than one start-to-start successor, a late start would have to be determined for each, then compared for the lowest value. The definition and formulas below address the two conditions discussed:

The late start (LS) of an activity that has a start-to-start successor(s) is determined by choosing the lowest value from either of the two following calculations:

1. Late Start $(LS)_{of\ activity}$ = Late Finish $(LF)_{of\ activity}$ − Duration$_{of\ activity}$.
2. Late Start $(LS)_{of\ activity}$ = Late Start $(LS)_{of\ start-to-start\ successor(s)}$ − Lag.

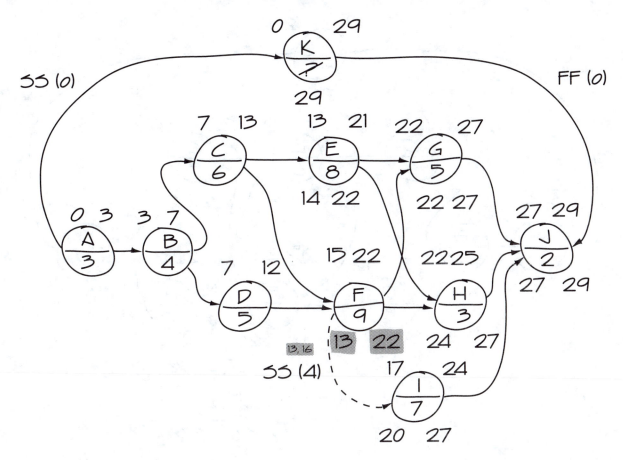

FIGURE 7.19
Late finish and late start of activity F.

Late Finish and Late Start of Activity F

The late finish for activity F is calculated no differently than the previous late finishes. It is the lower value of the late start of G (22) and the late start of H (24). Choose 22 for the late finish of F.

As previously mentioned, the late start of activity F is determined based on two considerations, choosing the lowest value they yield. The first late start is calculated from the first formula; it is simply the late finish of activity F minus its duration (LS = 22 − 9), which equals 13. The second late start is calculated from the second formula; it is the late *start* of activity I minus the lag (LS = 20 − 4), which equals 16. Notice that they are both written as little numbers (13, 16) on the network. Sometimes students like to write the choices down on the network as they perform the passes; however, it is not necessary. Comparing them, choose the lower of the two—13 for the late start of activity F, as shown in Figure 7.19.

Late Finish and Late Start of Activity D

Since the late start of activity F is 13, the late finish of activity D is 13. Therefore, the late start of activity D is 8 (LS = 13 − 5), as shown in Figure 7.20.

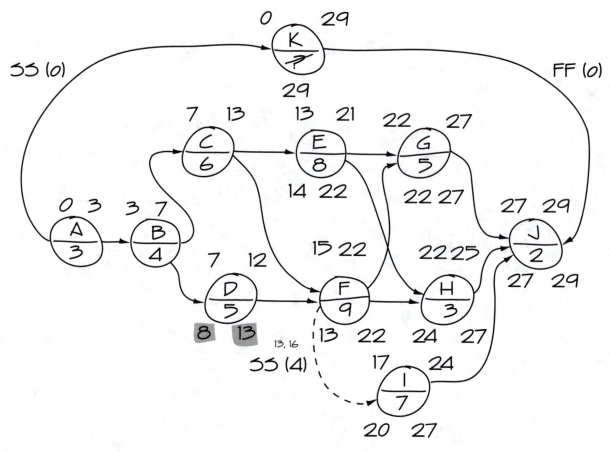

FIGURE 7.20
Late finish and late start of activity D.

Late Finish and Late Start of Activity C

Activity C has two successors, activity E and activity F. Activity C has to be complete before both activities E and F begin. Activity E has a late start of day 14 and activity F has a late start of day 13; therefore, activity C must be finished by day 13. Since the late finish of activity C is 13, the late start of activity C is 7 (LS = 13 − 6), as shown in Figure 7.21.

Late Finish and Late Start of Activity B

Activity B has two successors, activity C and activity D. Activity B has to be complete before both activities C and D begin. Activity C has a late start of day 7 and activity D has a late start of day 8; therefore, choose day 7 for the late finish of activity B. Since the late finish of activity B is 7, the late start of activity B is 3 (LS = 7 − 4), as shown in Figure 7.22.

Late Finish and Late Start of Activity A

Since the late start of activity B is 3, the late finish of activity A is 3. Therefore, the late start of activity A is 0 (LS = 3 − 3), as shown in Figure 7.23.

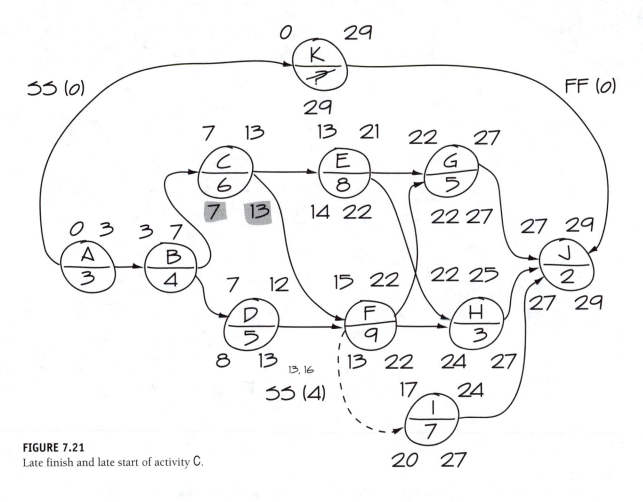

FIGURE 7.21
Late finish and late start of activity C.

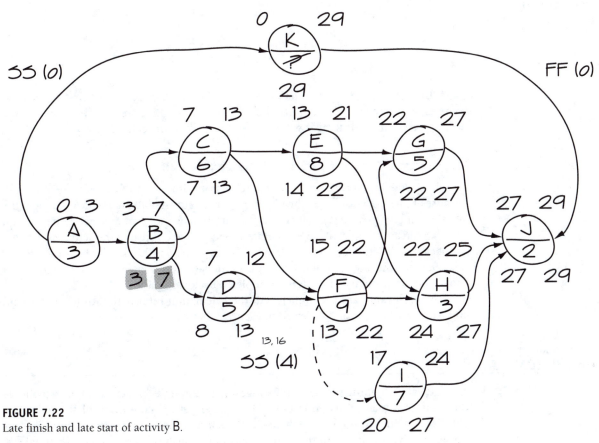

FIGURE 7.22
Late finish and late start of activity B.

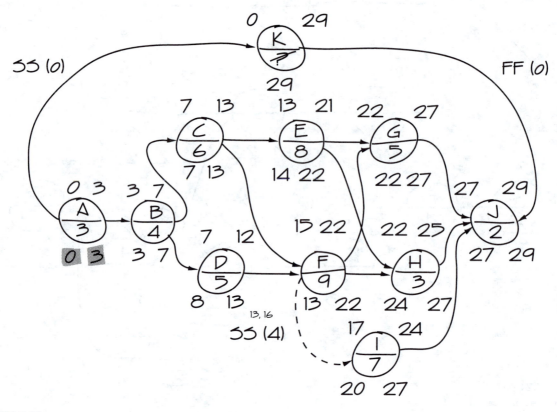

FIGURE 7.23
Late finish and late start of activity A in addition to all the other calculation information from both the forward and backward passes.

If the network does not come back to zero for the late start of the first activity (or come back to zero for at least one of the first activities if there are more than one) of the network, a mathematical error was made somewhere in the calculations.

Late Start and Finish of a Hammock Activity (Activity K)

Hammock activities have start-to-start and finish-to-finish relationships as their default. Because of these relationships, the late start and late finish of the hammock is simply the late start and finish of the activities that they are attached to. Hammock activities cannot have lag and are completely dependent upon the start and finish of the activities they are connected to. Therefore, since the late finish of activity J is 29, the late finish of activity K is 29. Since the late start of activity A is 0, the late start of activity K is 0. Figure 7.24 shows the sample network with the completed backward pass.

The backward pass is complete. All the calculation information from the forward and backward passes can be viewed in Figure 7.24.

THE CRITICAL PATH

The critical path of the project is the longest path through the network that establishes the minimum total project duration. The critical path is comprised of the unbroken chain of activities through the network with zero total float. There can be multiple critical paths. Every activity on the critical path must finish on time; otherwise, it will re-

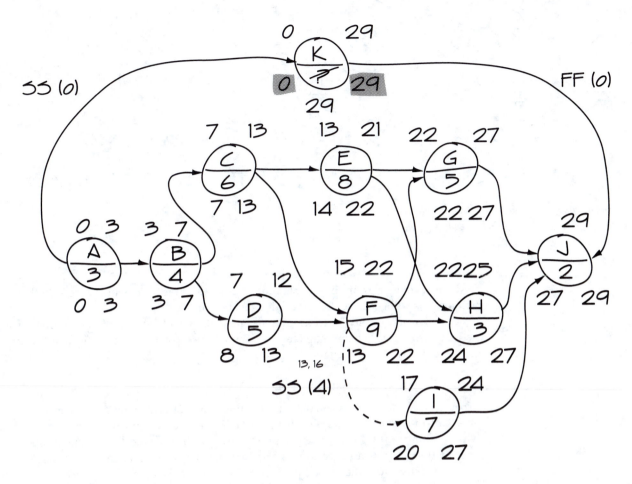

FIGURE 7.24
The completed backward pass, including the late finish and late start of activity K, the hammock activity.

sult in the project end date being delayed. If a critical activity goes two days late, for example, then the project end date will go two days late.

Activities that are not on the critical path are said to have float. There are two types of float that an activity can have: total float and free float. Both are discussed next.

TOTAL FLOAT

The total float of an activity can be defined as follows:

> The total float (TF) of an activity is the amount of time an activity's duration can be lengthened without affecting the total project duration.

Total float is a *shared float;* that is, the total float along a partial path or subchain of the network *must be shared* with all the activities in that subchain and does not belong to one particular activity. This will become evident as the total floats are calculated for the in-class practice exercises.

The total float of an activity can be calculated using any one of the following three formulas:

1. Total Float (TF) = Late Finish (LF) − Early Finish (EF).
2. Total Float (TF) = Late Start (LS) − Early Start (ES).
3. Total Float (TF) = Late Finish (LF) − Early Start (ES) − Duration.

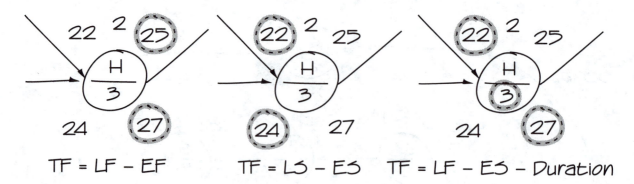

FIGURE 7.25
The total float of activity H using all three formulas.

Using activity H from the sample project as an example, notice in Figure 7.25 that each formula will generate the same value for the total float.

Choosing any of the three formulas, calculate the total floats for all the activities of the sample project. When complete, the sample project with the activity total floats added should appear as in Figure 7.26.

Calculating the Total Float with Start-to-Start Activities

A special condition exists when determining the total float of an activity that has one or more start-to-start successors. This happens later in the second practice exercise on activity I and in the third practice exercise on activity J. If the critical path runs through the activity's start-to-start successor, the activity may have two different total floats. We will use activity I from the second practice exercise as an example.

Figure 7.27 shows a partial drawing of the second practice exercise network showing activity I. Notice that the critical path runs through activity G, then *through only the start* of activity I, through activity P (activity I's start-to-start successor), and on from there. Because the critical path runs through only the start of activity I, only the start of activity I is critical, with zero days of total float. The finish of activity I is not critical, since it has two days of float.

So, which total float do you use when calculating the schedule? You should list both, since they both have value and meaning. Since activity P is critical, it has to start on time. Since its start is dependent upon activity I starting on time, the *start* of activity I cannot be delayed—and therefore is critical. However, once activity I gets started, it shares two extra days of total float to finish. Therefore, activity I has two values for its total float, a start float of zero days and a finish float of two days. Most scheduling softwares, including SureTrak, will list only one total float for each activity, usually choosing the lowest float. This will be demonstrated again with activity J in the third practice exercise, the garage construction schedule, which will be used extensively in the SureTrak modules later in the text.

CRITICAL PATH

The critical path of the project can be defined as follows:

> The critical path(s) of the project is the unbroken chain, or chains, of activities with zero total float.

The sample exercise has two critical paths, the path going through the activities (A, B, C, F, G, and J) and the critical path going through the hammock activity K. Hammock activities that span from start to finish are always critical. In addition to the hammock,

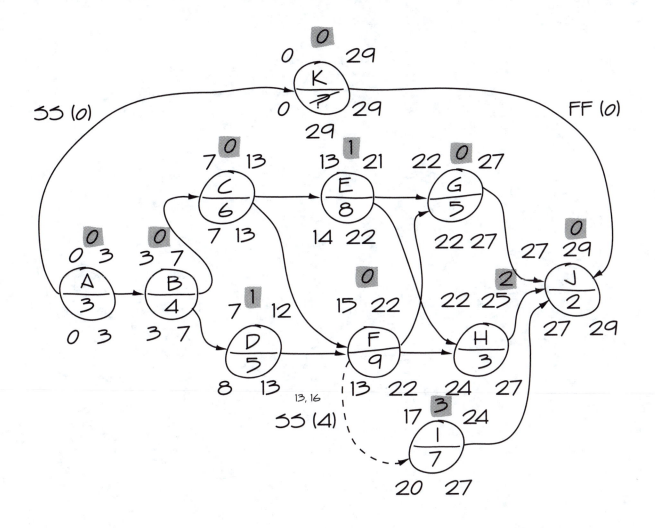

FIGURE 7.26
Sample project with the total floats of the activities added to the calculation information.

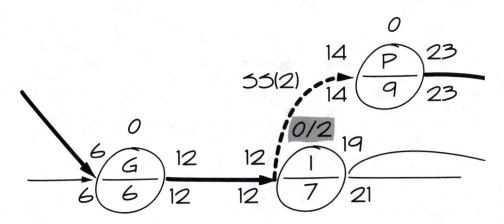

FIGURE 7.27
Partial drawing of the second practice exercise highlighting activity I.

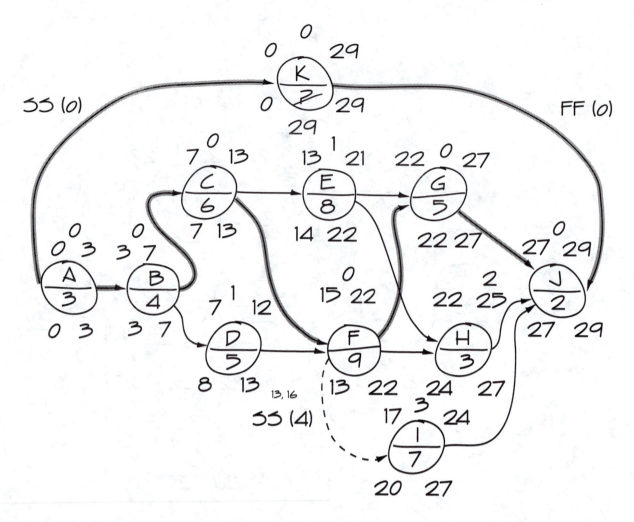

FIGURE 7.28
Sample project with the critical paths highlighted.

there will always be at least one other critical path. The critical paths of the sample project are highlighted and can be seen in Figure 7.28.

FREE FLOAT

The free float of an activity can be defined as the amount of time an activity's start or duration can be extended without affecting the start of its successor(s). In some texts, free float is sometimes referred to or confused with **lag.** This is incorrect. Lag and free float are different. Lag is the extra time *purposefully* placed between activities to better reflect the reality of the project schedule. Free float is the extra time between activities that *naturally occur* in project schedules that is identified through the CPM calculations.

An activity will have a separate free float for every successor it has. Free float is defined and calculated differently depending on the relationship between the two activities.

Free Float Between Finish-to-Start Activities

The free float of an activity with a finish-to-start successor(s) can be defined as follows:

The free float $(FF)_{FS}$ of an activity with a finish-to-start successor(s) is the amount of time that the start or duration of the activity can be lengthened without affecting the start of successor activity(s) that directly follows it.

If an activity has more than one successor, a free float will be calculated for each successor of that activity. Since the connecting line between an activity and its successor is unique to that pair of activities, it is a good practice to write the free float there on the connecting line when manually calculating the schedule.

The free float of an activity with a finish-to-start successor(s) can be calculated using the following formula:

$$\text{Free Float (FF)}_{\text{of activity w/FS}} = \text{Early Start (ES)}_{\text{of successor}} - \text{Early Finish (EF)}_{\text{of the activity}}.$$

Using activity H again from the sample project as an example, the free float of activity H equals the early start of activity J minus the early finish of activity H, which equals 2 (FF = 27 − 25).

Free Float Between Start-to-Start Activities

Free float can also exist between an activity and its start-to-start successor. The free float of an activity with a start-to-start successor can be defined as follows:

The free float $(FF)_{SS}$ of an activity with a start-to-start successor(s) is the amount of time that the start of the activity can be delayed without affecting the start of its start-to-start successor(s).

If an activity has more than one start-to-start successor, a free float must be calculated for each start-to-start successor of that activity.

The free float of an activity with a start-to-start successor(s) can be calculated using the following formula:

$$\text{Free float (FF)}_{\text{of activity w/SS}} = \text{Early Start (ES)}_{\text{of SS successor}} - \text{Early Start (ES)}_{\text{of activity}} - \text{Lag}.$$

Using activity F from the sample project as an example, the free float of activity F relative to activity I, its start-to-start successor, equals 0, from the calculation: early start of activity I minus the early start of activity F minus the lag (FF = 17 − 13 − 4).

Free Float Between Finish-to-Finish Activities

Free float can also exist between an activity and its finish-to-finish successor. The free float of an activity with a finish-to-finish successor can be defined as follows:

The free float $(FF)_{FF}$ of an activity with a finish-to-finish successor(s) is the amount of time that the finish of that activity can be delayed without affecting the finish of its finish-to-finish successor(s).

If an activity has more than one finish-to-finish successor, a free float must be calculated for each finish-to-finish successor of that activity.

The free float of an activity with a finish-to-finish successor(s) can be calculated using the following formula:

$$\text{Free Float (FF)}_{\text{of activity w/FF}} = \text{Early Finish (EF)}_{\text{of FF successor}} - \text{Early Finish (EF)}_{\text{of activity}} - \text{Lag}.$$

Using activity K from the sample project as an example, the free float of activity K relative to activity J, its finish-to-finish successor, equals 0, from the calculation: early finish of activity K minus the early finish of activity J minus the lag (FF = 29 − 29 − 0).

Free Float Between Start-to-Finish Activities

Free float that exists between activities that have a start-to-finish relationship can be calculated but is almost always equal to zero. In fact, it is difficult to imagine a situation when there would exist a free float between these activities; therefore, these calculations will not be discussed.

Complete the CPM calculations by calculating the remainder of the free floats for all the activities of the sample project, writing the free float on the common connector lines between the two. When complete, the sample project with the activity free floats as well as all the rest of the calculation information is as shown in Figure 7.29.

The CPM calculations are complete. All the calculation information can be viewed in Figure 7.29.

The CPM calculation information is often displayed in a tabular form as well. This may be seen in schedule reports or other types of network reports. Table 7.1 shows the early start, early finish, late start, late finish, total float, and free float of the sample project.

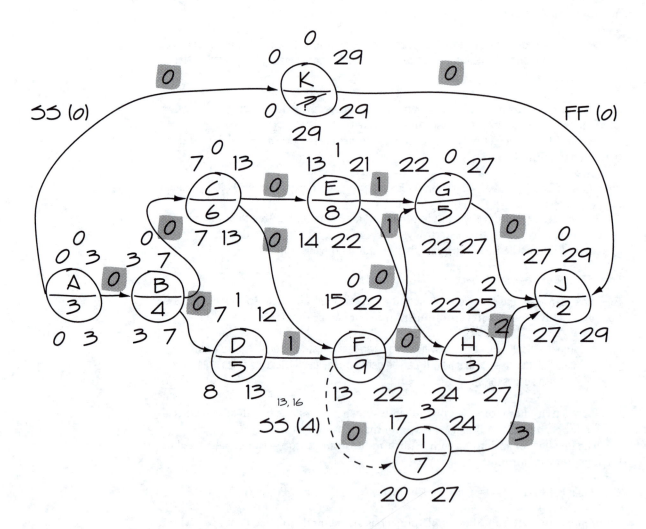

FIGURE 7.29
Sample project with all the calculated activity information shown, including the activity free floats.

TABLE 7.1   Activity information from the CPM calculation displayed in a tabular form.

SAMPLE PROJECT

CPM Activity Information

ACT	DUR	ES	EF	LS	LF	TF	FF	REL. LINES
A	3	0	3	0	3	0	0	A-B
B	4	3	7	3	7	0	0	B-C
C	6	7	13	7	13	0	0	B-D
D	5	7	12	8	13	1	0	C-E
E	8	13	21	14	22	1	0	C-F
F	9	13	22	13	22	0	1	D-F
G	5	22	27	22	27	0	1	E-G
H	3	22	25	24	27	2	1	E-H
I	7	17	24	20	27	3	0	F-G
J	2	27	29	27	29	0	0	F-H
K	29*	0	29	0	29	0	0	F-I
							0	G-J
							2	H-J
							3	I-J
							0	A-K
							0	J-K

* Hammock duration is set by the project duration.

IN-CLASS EXERCISES: CALCULATING THE CPM NETWORK

The following three practice exercises were used in the previous chapter to practice drawing the network diagrams. They will be used here to perform the manual CPM calculations in class. The third practice exercise is the same garage construction schedule that will be used extensively in the SureTrak modules later in the text and the same project that was shown previously in Figures 4.4, 4.5a, 4.5b, 4.6, and 5.3.

Calculate the early start, early finish, project duration, late start, late finish, total float, critical path, and free float, writing the calculated information for each activity directly onto the practice network diagrams provided. The answers to the network calculations can be seen on the illustrations following each practice exercise.

Next, fill in the blank tabular forms provided with all the activity information that you just calculated and wrote down onto the practice exercise networks. Care must be taken to ensure that the correct information is filled into the appropriate cells of the blank tabular forms. The answers to the filled-in tabular forms will follow each blank form.

Turn to the next page to begin the in-class exercises.

IN-CLASS EXERCISE
Practice Exercise #1

1. Calculate the ES, EF, LS, LF, TF, FF, project duration, and critical path on the network diagram below. The answers are provided in Figure 7.30.

2. Then, fill in all calculated activity information onto the blank tabular form provided. The answers to the tabular forms follow each blank form.

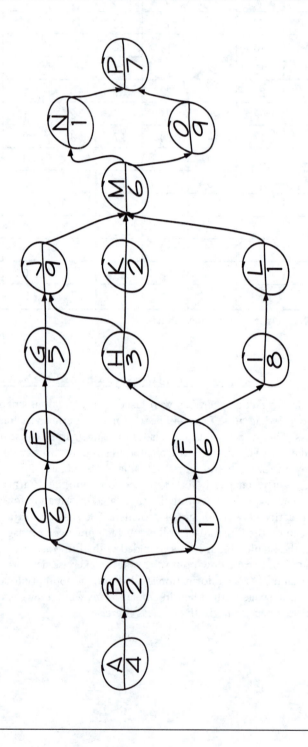

IN-CLASS EXERCISE
Practice Exercise #1

Act	Dur	ES	EF	LS	LF	TF	FF	Rel. Lines
A	4							A-B
B	2							B-C
C	6							B-D
D	1							C-E
E	7							D-F
F	6							E-G
G	5							F-H
H	3							F-I
I	8							G-J
J	9							H-J
K	2							H-K
L	1							I-L
M	6							J-M
N	1							K-M
O	9							L-M
P	7							M-N
								M-O
								N-P
								O-P

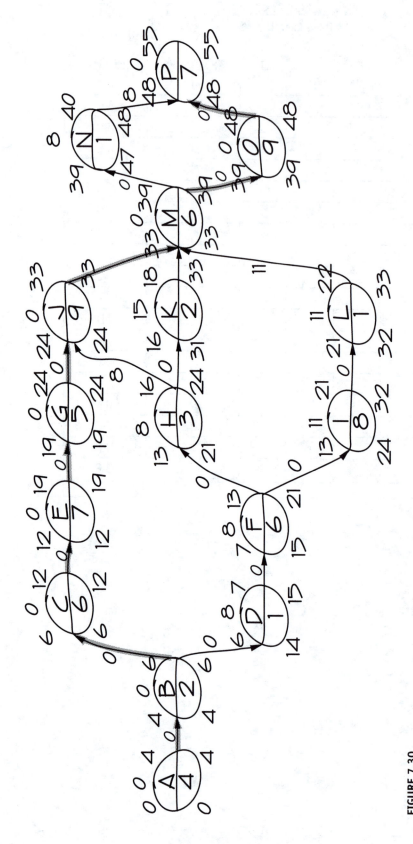

FIGURE 7.30
Practice Exercise #1 with calculated CPM activity information and highlighted critical path.

IN-CLASS EXERCISE
Practice Exercise #1

Act	Dur	ES	EF	LS	LF	TF	FF	Rel. Lines
A	4	0	4	0	4	0	0	A-B
B	2	4	6	4	6	0	0	B-C
C	6	6	12	6	12	0	0	B-D
D	1	6	7	14	15	8	0	C-E
E	7	12	19	12	19	0	0	D-F
F	6	7	13	15	21	8	0	E-G
G	5	19	24	19	24	0	0	F-H
H	3	13	16	21	24	8	0	F-I
I	8	13	21	24	32	11	0	G-J
J	9	24	33	24	33	0	8	H-J
K	2	16	18	31	33	15	0	H-K
L	1	21	22	32	33	11	0	I-L
M	6	33	39	33	39	0	0	J-M
N	1	39	40	47	48	8	15	K-M
O	9	39	48	39	48	0	11	L-M
P	7	48	55	48	55	0	0	M-N
							0	M-O
							8	N-P
							0	O-P

IN-CLASS EXERCISE
Practice Exercise #2

1. Calculate the ES, EF, LS, LF, TF, FF, project duration, and critical path on the network diagram below. The answers are provided in Figure 7.31.

2. Then, fill in all calculated activity information onto the blank tabular form provided. The answers to the tabular forms follow each blank form.

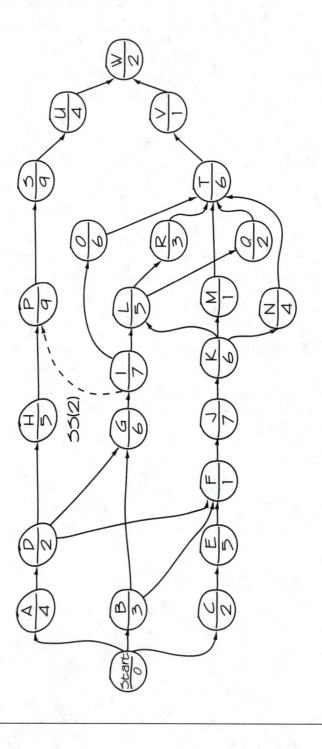

IN-CLASS EXERCISE
Practice Exercise #2

Act	Dur	ES	EF	LS	LF	TF	FF	Rel. Lines
A	4							A-D
B	3							B-G
C	2							B-F
D	2							C-E
E	5							D-H
F	1							D-G
G	6							D-F
H	5							E-F
I	7							F-J
J	7							G-I
K	6							H-P
L	5							I-P
M	1							I-O
N	4							I-L
O	6							J-K
P	9							K-L
Q	2							K-M
R	3							K-N
S	9							L-R
T	6							L-Q
U	4							M-T
V	1							N-T
W	2							O-T
								P-S
								Q-T
								R-T
								S-U
								T-V
								U-W
								V-W

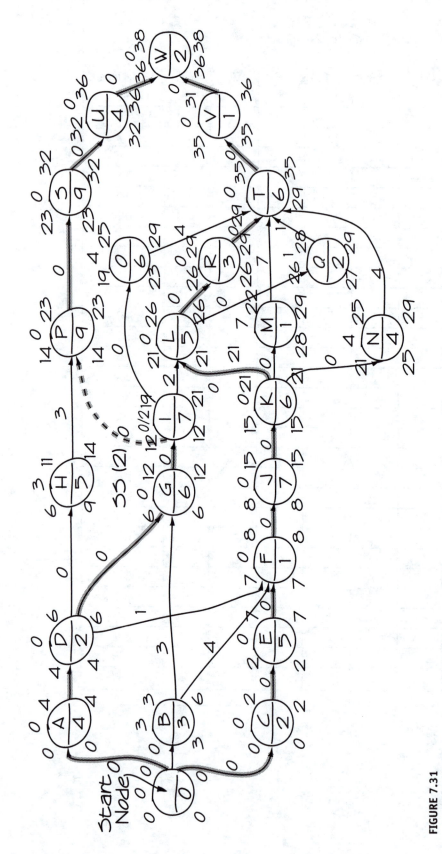

FIGURE 7.31
Practice Exercise #2 with calculated CPM activity information and both highlighted critical paths.

IN-CLASS EXERCISE
Practice Exercise #2

Act	Dur	ES	EF	LS	LF	TF	FF	Rel. Lines
A	4	0	4	0	4	0	0	A-D
B	3	0	3	3	6	3	3	B-G
C	2	0	2	0	2	0	4	B-F
D	2	4	6	4	6	0	0	C-E
E	5	2	7	2	7	C	0	D-H
F	1	7	8	7	8	0	0	D-G
G	6	6	12	6	12	0	1	D-F
H	5	6	11	9	14	3	0	E-F
I	7	12	19	12	21	0 / 2	0	F-J
J	7	8	15	8	15	0	0	G-I
K	6	15	21	15	21	0	3	H-P
L	5	21	26	21	26	0	0	I-P
M	1	21	22	28	29	7	0	I-O
N	4	21	25	25	29	4	2	I-L
O	6	19	25	23	29	4	0	J-K
P	9	14	23	14	23	0	0	K-L
Q	2	26	28	27	29	1	0	K-M
R	3	26	29	26	29	0	0	K-N
S	9	23	32	23	32	0	0	L-R
T	6	29	35	29	35	0	0	L-Q
U	4	32	36	32	36	0	7	M-T
V	1	35	36	35	36	0	4	N-T
W	2	36	38	36	38	0	4	O-T
							0	P-S
							1	Q-T
							0	R-T
							0	S-U
							0	T-V
							0	U-W
							0	V-W

IN-CLASS EXERCISE
Practice Exercise #3

1. Calculate the ES, EF, LS, LF, TF, FF, project duration, and critical path on the network diagram below. The answers are provided in Figure 7.32.

2. Then, fill in all calculated activity information onto the blank tabular form provided. The answers to the tabular forms follow each blank form.

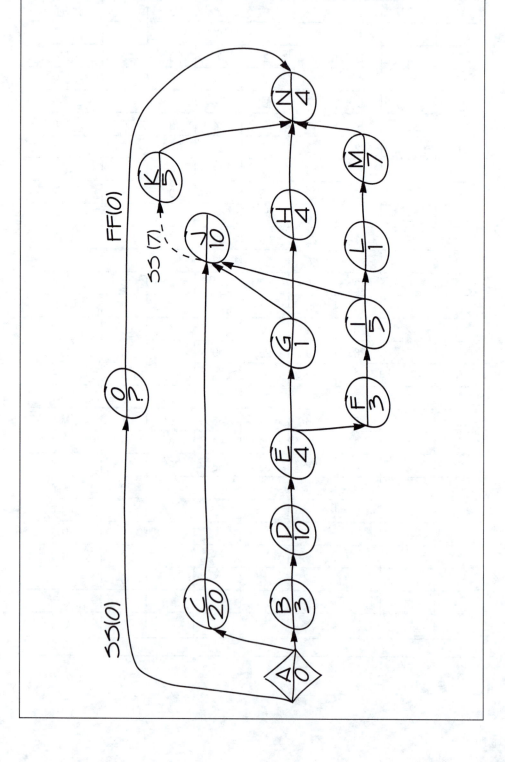

IN-CLASS EXERCISE
Practice Exercise #3

Act	Dur	ES	EF	LS	LF	TF	FF	Rel. Lines
A	0							A-C
B	3							A-B
C	20							A-O
D	10							B-D
E	4							C-J
F	3							D-E
G	1							E-G
H	4							E-F
I	5							F-I
J	10							G-J
K	5							G-H
L	1							H-N
M	7							I-J
N	4							I-L
O	?							J-K
								J-N
								K-N
								L-M
								M-N
								O-N

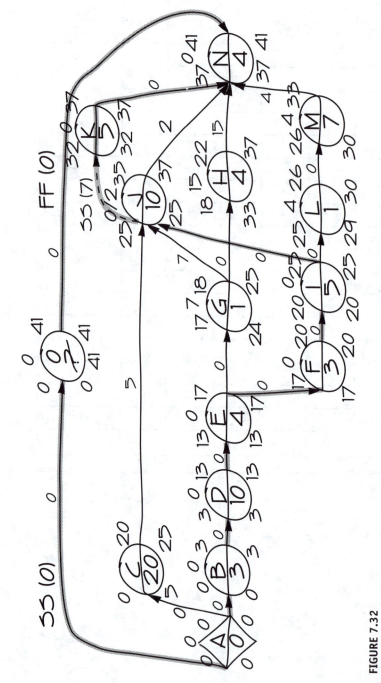

FIGURE 7.32
Practice Exercise #3 with calculated CPM activity information and both highlighted critical paths.

IN-CLASS EXERCISE
Practice Exercise #3

Act	Dur	ES	EF	LS	LF	TF	FF	Rel. Lines
A	0	0	0	0	0	0	0	A-C
B	3	0	3	0	3	0	0	A-B
C	20	0	20	5	25	5	0	A-O
D	10	3	13	3	13	0	0	B-D
E	4	13	17	13	17	0	5	C-J
F	3	17	20	17	20	0	0	D-E
G	1	17	18	24	25	7	0	E-G
H	4	18	22	33	37	15	0	E-F
I	5	20	25	20	25	0	0	F-I
J	10	25	35	25	37	0 / 2	7	G-J
K	5	32	37	32	37	0	0	G-H
L	1	25	26	29	30	4	15	H-N
M	7	26	33	30	37	4	0	I-J
N	4	37	41	37	41	0	0	I-L
O	?	0	41	0	41	0	0	J-K
							2	J-N
							0	K-N
							0	L-M
							4	M-N
							0	O-N

STUDENT EXERCISES: CALCULATING THE CPM NETWORK

In the following student exercises, the network diagrams provided will be used to perform manual CPM calculations. The student will calculate the early start, early finish, project duration, late start, late finish, total float, critical path, and free float, writing the calculated information for each activity directly onto the network diagrams. Tear out the network diagrams to turn in to your instructor. The answers to the network calculations will be provided by your instructor.

Next, students will fill in the blank tabular forms provided with all the activity information that they just calculated on the networks. Care must be taken to ensure that the correct information is filled into the appropriate cells on the blank tabular forms. Tear out the tabular forms to turn in to your instructor. The answers to the filled-in tabular forms will be provided by your instructor.

Each exercise is listed on a separate page. Turn to the next page to begin the student exercises.

STUDENT EXERCISE
Exercise #1

1. Calculate the ES, EF, LS, LF, TF, FF, project duration, and critical path on the network diagram below. Your instructor will provide the answers.

2. Then, fill in all calculated activity information onto the blank tabular form provided. Your instructor will provide the answers.

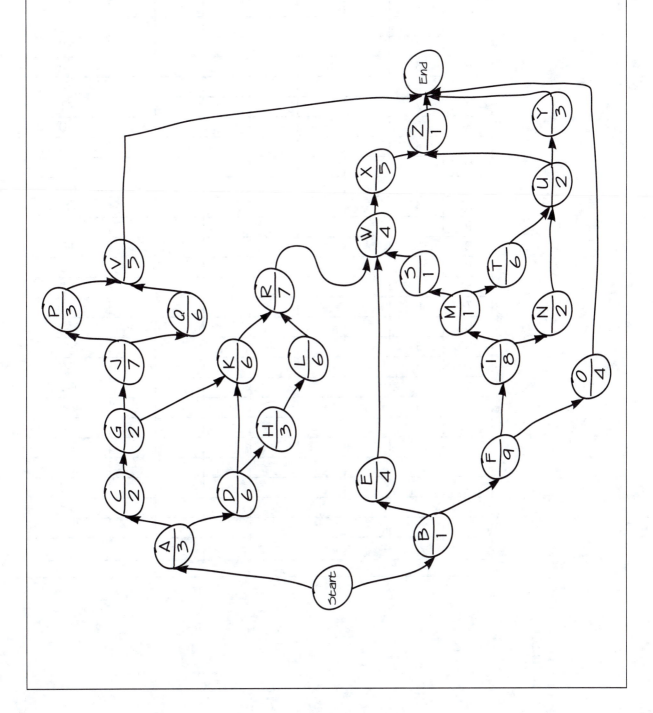

STUDENT EXERCISE
Exercise #1

Act	Dur	ES	EF	LS	LF	TF	FF	Rel. Lines
A	3							A-C
B	1							A-D
C	2							B-E
D	6							B-F
E	4							C-G
F	9							D-J
G	2							D-K
H	3							D-H
I	8							E-W
J	7							F-I
K	6							F-O
L	6							G-J
M	1							G-K
N	2							H-L
O	4							I-M
P	3							I-N
Q	6							J-P
R	7							J-Q
S	1							K-R
T	6							L-R
U	2							M-S
V	5							M-T
W	4							N-U
X	5							P-V
Y	3							Q-V
Z	1							R-W
								S-W
								T-U
								U-Z
								U-Y
								W-X
								X-Z

1. Calculate the ES, EF, LS, LF, TF, FF, project duration, and critical path on the network diagram below. Your instructor will provide the answers.

2. Then, fill in all calculated activity information onto the blank tabular form provided. Your instructor will provide the answers.

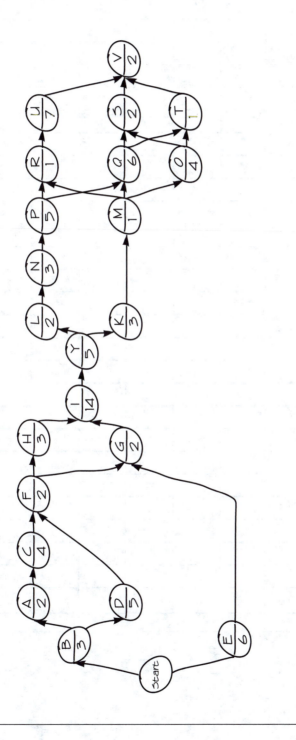

STUDENT EXERCISE
Exercise #2

Act	Dur	ES	EF	LS	LF	TF	FF	Rel. Lines
A	2							B-A
B	3							B-D
C	4							E-G
D	5							A-C
E	6							D-F
F	2							C-F
G	2							F-H
H	3							F-G
I	14							H-I
J	5							G-I
K	3							I-J
L	2							J-L
M	1							J-K
N	3							L-N
O	4							K-M
P	5							N-P
Q	6							P-R
R	1							P-Q
S	2							M-R
T	1							M-Q
U	7							M-O
V	2							R-U
								Q-S
								Q-T
								O-S
								O-T
								U-V
								S-V
								T-V

STUDENT EXERCISE
Exercise #3

1. Calculate the ES, EF, LS, LF, TF, FF, project duration, and critical path on the network diagram below. Your instructor will provide the answers.

2. Then, fill in all calculated activity information onto the blank tabular form provided. Your instructor will provide the answers.

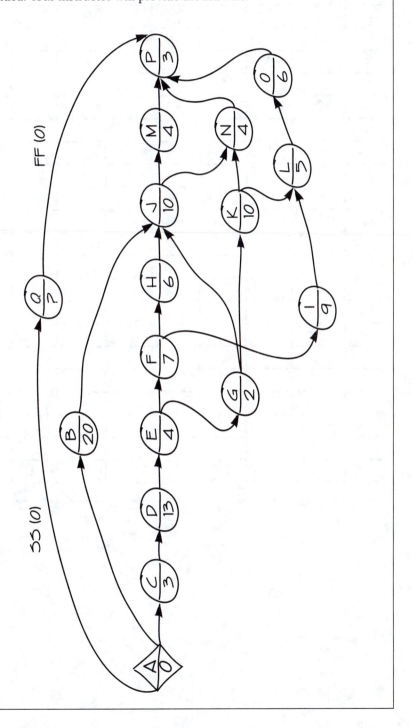

STUDENT EXERCISE
Exercise #3

Act	Dur	ES	EF	LS	LF	TF	FF	Rel. Lines
A	0							A-B
B	20							A-C
C	3							A-Q
D	13							B-J
E	4							C-D
F	7							D-E
G	2							E-F
H	6							E-G
I	9							F-H
J	10							F-I
K	10							G-J
L	5							G-K
M	4							H-J
N	4							I-L
O	6							J-M
P	3							J-N
Q	?							K-N
								K-L
								L-O
								M-P
								N-P
								O-P
								Q-P

STUDENT EXERCISE
Exercise #4

1. Calculate the ES, EF, LS, LF, TF, FF, project duration, and critical path on the network diagram below. Your instructor will provide the answers.

2. Then, fill in all calculated activity information onto the blank tabular form provided. Your instructor will provide the answers.

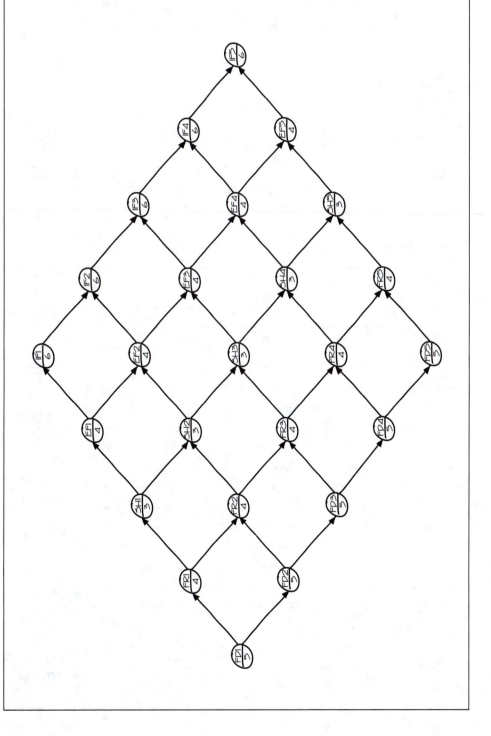

STUDENT EXERCISE
Exercise #4

Act	Dur	ES	EF	LS	LF	TF	FF	Rel. Lines
FD1	5							FD1-FD2
FD2	5							FD2-FD3
FD3	5							FD3-FD4
FD4	5							FD4-FD5
FD5	5							FR1-FR2
FR1	4							FR2-FR3
FR2	4							FR3 -FR4
FR3	4							FR4-FR5
FR4	4							SH1-SH2
FR5	4							SH2-SH3
SH1	3							SH3-SH4
SH2	3							SH4-SH5
SH3	3							EF1-EF2
SH4	3							EF2-EF3
SH5	3							EF3-EF4
EF1	4							EF4-EF5
EF2	4							IF1-IF2
EF3	4							IF2-IF3
EF4	4							IF3-IF4
EF5	4							IF4-IF5
IF1	6							FD1- FR1
IF2	6							FR1-SH1
IF3	6							SH1-EF1
IF4	6							EF1-IF1
IF5	6							FD2 -FR2
								FR2-SH2
								SH2-EF2
								EF2-IF2
								FD3-FR3
								FR3-SH3
								SH3-EF3
								EF3-IF3
								FD4-FR4
								FR4-SH4
								SH4-EF4
								EF4-IF4
								FD5-FR5
								FR5-SH5
								SH5-EF5
								EF5-IF5

STUDENT EXERCISE
Exercise #5

STUDENT EXERCISE
Exercise #5

1. Calculate the ES, EF, LS, LF, TF, FF, project duration, and critical path on the network diagram below. Your instructor will provide the answers.

2. Then, fill in all calculated activity information onto the blank tabular form provided. Your instructor will provide the answers.

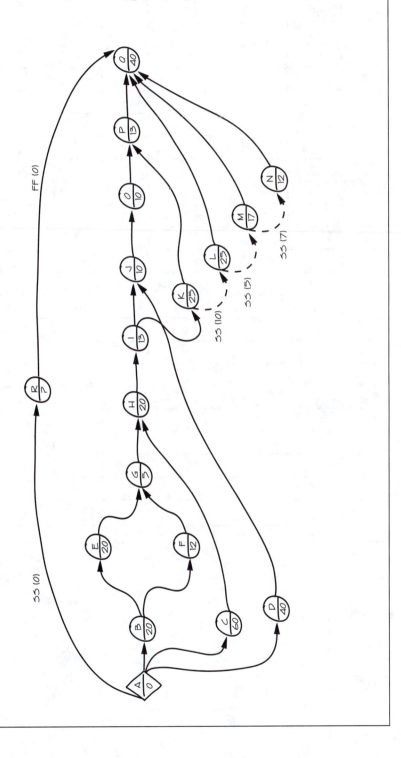

STUDENT EXERCISE
Exercise #5

Act	Dur	ES	EF	LS	LF	TF	FF	Rel. Lines
A	0							A-B
B	20							A-C
C	60							A-D
D	40							A-R
E	20							B-E
F	12							B-F
G	5							C-H
H	20							D-J
I	13							E-G
J	10							F-G
K	25							G-H
L	25							H-I
M	17							I-J
N	12							I-K
O	10							J-O
P	13							K-L
Q	40							K-P
R	?							L-M
								L-Q
								M-N
								M-Q
								N-Q
								O-P
								P-Q
								R-Q

STUDENT EXERCISE
Exercise #6

   Below is the bid package schedule of the Delhi Medical Building. You will create this schedule in Sure-Trak in Module 8. The schedule is on two pages. It may be easier to tear out the pages to work on them. Notice that the activity nodes are rectangles with numbers for the activity IDs.

1. Calculate the ES, EF, LS, LF, TF, FF, project duration, and critical path on the network diagram below. Your instructor will provide the answers.

2. Then, fill in all calculated activity information onto the blank tabular form provided. Your instructor will provide the answers.

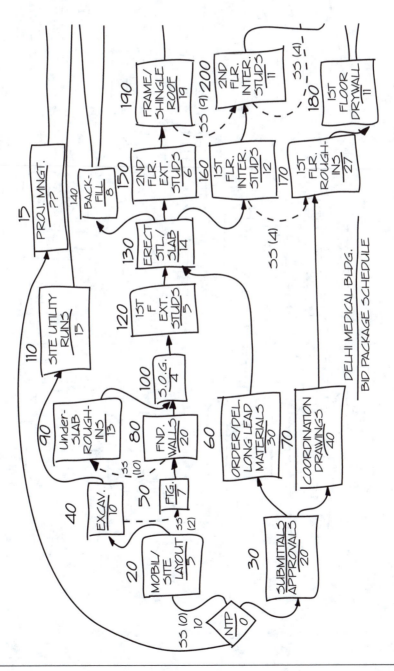

DELHI MEDICAL BLDG.
BID PACKAGE SCHEDULE

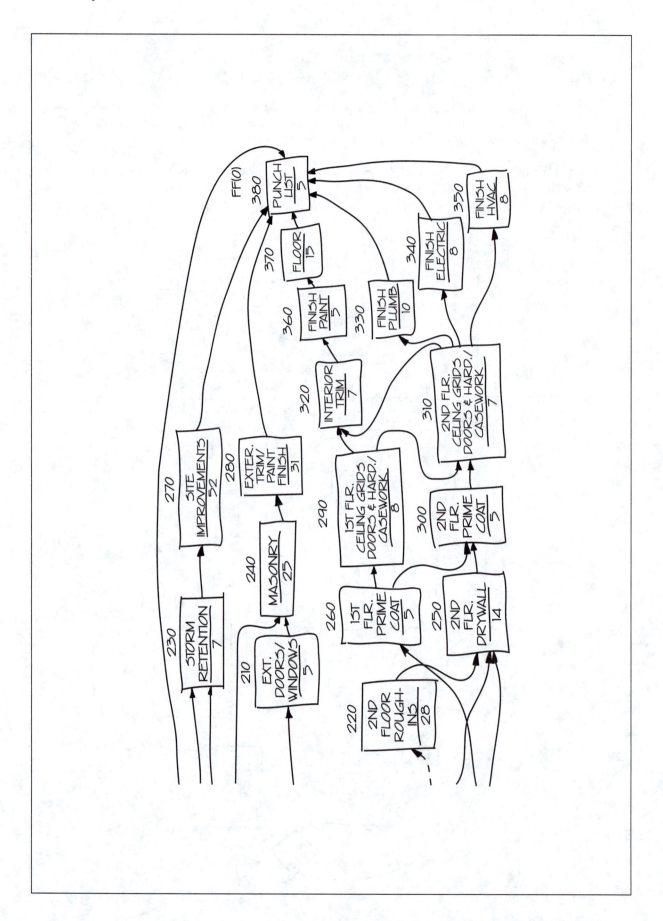

STUDENT EXERCISE
Exercise #6

Act	Dur	ES	EF	LS	LF	TF	FF	Rel. Lines
10	0							10–15
15	?							10–20
20	5							10–30
30	20							15–380
40	10							20–40
50	7							30–60
60	30							30–70
70	40							40–50
80	20							40–110
90	13							50–80
100	4							60–130
110	15							70–170
120	5							80–90
130	14							80–100
140	8							90–100
150	6							100–120
160	12							110–230
170	27							120–130
180	11							130–140
190	19							130–150
200	11							130–160
210	5							140–230
220	28							140–240
230	7							150–190
240	25							160–170
250	14							160–200
260	5							170–180
270	52							180–250
280	31							180–260
290	8							190–210
300	5							200–220
310	7							200–250
320	7							210–240

STUDENT EXERCISE
Exercise #6—*Continued*

Act	Dur	ES	EF	LS	LF	TF	FF	Rel. Lines
330	10							220–250
340	8							230–270
350	8							240–280
360	5							250–300
370	15							260–290
380	5							260–300
								270–380
								280–380
								290–310
								290–320
								300–310
								310–320
								310–330
								310–340
								310–350
								320–360
								330–380
								340–380
								350–380
								360–370
								370–380

CHAPTER 8
Creating Construction Schedules

In this chapter the student will learn how to create a detailed construction schedule. Students will be taken, step-by-step, through the typical process of developing and creating a schedule. After the schedule is created, it will then be analyzed for areas of improvement and compression. From that analysis, a revised construction schedule will be generated. Next, each student will manually calculate the critical path and floats of the revised schedule and evaluate the benefits of the revision. Finally, as part of the *capstone project* for the text, the student will prepare a detailed construction schedule for a different project.

The project used as the sample for how to create a schedule, the Delhi Medical Building, was used for examples in Chapter 5 to calculate durations. It was also used as an example of a bid package schedule throughout the text. It was drawn as a network diagram in Chapter 6 and manually calculated in Chapter 7, then created in SureTrak in Module 10. The building used for the capstone project is the USA Volleyball Centers. The Delhi Medical Building can be seen in Figures 8.1A and 8.1B. Partial sets of plans for both buildings were bundled with the text. The original and revised construction schedules of the Delhi Medical Building, which are the topics of this chapter, were also included with the text.

DOCUMENT REVIEW

The starting point in the process of creating a construction schedule is learning about the project. The scheduler has to completely understand how the building goes together to create a detailed, accurate, and reliable construction schedule. This is accomplished through reviewing the documents that are available, visiting the site, and talking with the architect and owner, among other things. The documents will include, at a minimum, the drawings and specifications. Some project managers and schedulers will begin to review the specs first, while others will initially open the drawings. Regardless, eventually both have to be examined thoroughly. As the review begins, the task unfolds to identify the *knowns* and *unknowns* of the project.

DRAWING REVIEW
Reviewing the drawings of the Delhi building will help the student get a feel for the project and understand how the building is being put together. It is obviously helpful for any scheduler to have a working knowledge of building construction methods and materials. The presumption here is that the student has, at least, some knowledge of

FIGURE 8.1A
The Delhi Medical Building (south elevation), which will be the sample project used to develop a construction schedule.
With permission from Champlin/Haupt Architects, Cincinnati, OH

FIGURE 8.1B
The Delhi Medical Building (north elevation), which will be the sample project used to develop a construction schedule.
With permission from Champlin/Haupt Architects, Cincinnati, OH

these things. However, we will perform a rather exhaustive review of the drawings, just in case they do not.

Spread out the partial set of plans from the Delhi Medical Building. They should include sheets A1, A2, A3, A6, A7, A8, A9, S1, S2, and ME1. Let's look at each sheet individually to see what can be learned.

Sheet A6—Elevations

Elevations can provide a tremendous amount of information very quickly. They are usually the closest thing to a *picture* of the finished building that exists.

At first glance, at the Delhi Medical Building there may be some confusion, such as "Is this a one-story or two-story building?" However, if you look at the side elevations, you can see that the building is sloped down from north to south. Therefore, it is a two-story building, with the first floor (lower level) being a slab-on-grade. Because of this, the foundation wall located along the north elevation and partially along the two sides elevations not only supports the building, but must also retain the earth. The wall will contain plenty of steel and may take a bit longer to build.

Looking at the side elevations, notice that the brick is stepped down along the sides and sits on a rather intricate brick ledge that is cast into the side of the foundation wall—adding even more time to the construction of the foundation. The side elevations also reveal that the footing is stepped down once. This is very common when building on a sloped lot.

The building's skin is brick with a little bit of exterior insulation finish system (EIFS), a synthetic (oil-based) form of stucco. It is also sometimes referred to as Dryvit®, which is the name of one of the first companies to sell that product.

The building has a hip roof with numerous gables framed into it. It is covered with fiberglass shingles. This will take longer to build than a conventional flat roof that you often see used on commercial buildings. The floor-to-floor heights indicate a 12'-0" height from the first floor to the second and a 10'-0" height from the second floor to the truss bearing. It is not clear on this sheet why there is a difference. We'll probably see why on one of the section sheets. Finally, the east elevation shows a set of concrete steps descending from the high side down to the lower level.

Sheet A2—First Floor Plan

Floor plans display a tremendous amount of information. It is the best place to go to get a look at what's inside the building. They show the layout of each space as well as what is in each space, the footprint of the building, overall dimensions, and the placement of doors and windows. If the elevations are the closest thing to a picture of the finished building, the floor plans are the best way to *take a walk* through the building.

As you look at the plan, the first thing to notice is that the building is *built-out*. Buildings are sometimes built as a shell with the interior left bare until a tenant leases the space, at which point the space is designed and built-out to suit the tenant. In this case the first floor is built-out as a single medical office. What comes to view immediately are the numerous examination rooms. Each one of these rooms will have a sink and, therefore, plumbing. Since this office is on a slab, a significant amount of underground plumbing will be required, which will impact the schedule. In addition to the plumbing in the exam rooms, there are four bathrooms, a mechanical room, and a janitor's closet—all requiring plumbing.

The other significant piece of information shown on this plan is the overall dimensions of the building. The building is approximately 100 feet by 50 feet—making each floor 5,000 square feet and the total building 10,000 square feet. The building is bumped out on all four corners, necessitating the four gable roofs previously noticed on the north and south elevations.

This plan also shows a hydraulic elevator and a set of steps going up to the second floor. Because of the open steps, this lobby will be open to the lobby above and therefore will be part of that fire-separated space. This will be an issue with respect to the wall that separates this space from the rest of the building.

The bottom of the sheet contains the schedule for the partition types. It shows the various types of interior partitions to be built. Most of the walls are simply metal stud with drywall on each side; however, some are filled with sound attenuation (insulation) batting. Because this is a doctor's office with side-by-side examination rooms, most of the walls will be built with this sound insulation. The exterior walls are not shown on the partition key. It appears that the front of the building and half of the two side walls are different from the back wall and the two back halves of the side walls. We will learn later from other drawings why they are different.

Sheet A3—Second Floor Plan

Looking at the second floor plan reveals that this space is also built-out; in this case, with two separate offices separated by a common lobby. Each office is a medical office and, therefore, will require similar amounts of plumbing as described on the first floor. Because the upper lobby is open to the lobby below, this entire space will be treated as one single, fire-separated area. The second floor also has a mechanical room, which is obviously where most of the mechanical equipment will be placed. Room 214 is an X-ray room and therefore will require lead-lined drywall and other special construction requirements to protect the rest of the building from X-ray radiation.

Sheet A1—Site Plan

The best way to think of the site plan is that it is a view of the entire site as if you were looking down on the site from about 150 feet in the air. The site plan shows the building as it is placed on the site and all of the other improvements made to the site outside the building's footprint. They include all paving, drives, walkways, and out-buildings or structures such as fences built to hide dumpsters. Additionally, the topography is usually shown with existing and proposed grades along with the storm water retention system. Utility runs are sometimes also shown on the site plan, but in this case, they are shown separately on sheet ME1.

The most significant feature of the site plan is the topography. The site slopes down rather steeply from back to front, 36 feet over approximately 280 feet. Notice the elevation of 856 feet at the top of the site to 820 feet down in the street (Rapid Run). Sloped lots are always a bit more difficult to build on than flat lots. There may be less laydown area for materials and consideration must be made to provide parking for equipment and trucks. Moreover, a concrete truck will have to be able to get around the entire building to pour the wall and slab. A temporary road may have to be built to accommodate this. Otherwise the concrete will have to be pumped. This will be an added cost to the job and may also add time to these activities.

There are two parking lots shown on the north and south sides of the building that are to be paved in asphalt. The typical asphalt detail is shown in the center of the sheet. Also shown are the walkways around the building including the steps on the east side that we saw earlier on the elevation sheet. Notice the condenser pads with surrounding wood fence on each side of the building. This is an example of an item that would not be critical.

In general, it is a rather tight site. There will definitely not be room for a dry retention basin to be built on the site; therefore, a significant underground storm water retention system is shown. Notice the 36- and 42-inch corrugated metal pipe (CMP) running between two A-type catch basins on the low side of each parking lot. These catch basins are connected to two other catch basins out in the yard and are eventually connected to an existing catch basin on the site. What's significant about this system from a scheduling point of view is that the construction of the system will have to be scheduled in such a way as to not interfere with the site utility runs and the construction near and around the building.

Sheet ME1—MEP Site Plan

MEP stands for mechanical, electrical, and plumbing. Therefore, the MEP site plan will show the layout and location of the different utility runs to the building. The sanitary sewer runs along the west side of the building and connects to an existing sanitary line there. The gas line also runs along this side from the street to the meters. These two runs should be relatively free of scheduling conflicts since they stay alongside of the building.

However, the electric and water lines run through the south parking lot and into the building, passing beneath, presumably, the storm water retention CMP pipes and beneath the front walk. Add to this that there is an alternate (Alternate FP-1) to place fire protection throughout the building. If that alternate is taken, a meter pit will have to be placed in the south parking lot and two separate lines will be run from there into the building. All of these activities will have to be carefully coordinated with other site activities.

Other information shown on this sheet is the placement and circuit runs for the site lighting, details of the poles, and the placement of the air conditioning condensers. The fact that there are numerous condensing units (see all the CU units) shown on this plan tells us that smaller individual units will be used for the HVAC system rather than one large chiller unit.

Sheet A7—Building Sections

A building section is a full cut through the building. Normally two sections are shown illustrating a cut in each direction. The view is as if someone cut through the entire building and took away half of it, exposing the other half. These views are important to see how the building goes together.

First look at building section 1/A7. It is the cut through the shorter dimension of the building. We can see details of the two entrances and, in their background, we see elevation views of the two sidewalls. This is the only place on the drawings where this is shown. The two-story entrance is shown in even more detail in section 1 on sheet A9.

With the view from this section, we begin to see some of the structural details of the building. Notice the full height foundation wall to the right supporting open-web bar joists. We presume that this is how the second floor is framed. It is not yet clear what supports the walls on the south elevation, but it appears to be some type of stud wall. We can see that the roof is constructed using wood trusses. This type of roof construction is typical for residential buildings and is a bit unusual for a commercial building. It will definitely have to be fire separated from the rest of the building.

We can see details of the round-top dormer and see that the elevator shaft extends up into the truss space. This will require scheduling coordination between the construction of these two objects. In addition, there is a view through the stairs, various rooms, and two of the lobby entrances into the offices.

The long cut through the building shows many of these same features and confirms wood trusses throughout the building for the roof and bar joists for the second floor. We see the elevator pit with the hydraulic piston and the shaft wall that shows a masonry potéa.

> *Potéa,* pronounced (pō-shaý), is the drafting term used to describe the cross-hatching and symbolization used on architectural plans to represent materials. Potéa is sometime spelled potché.

Notice the 45° angle lines on the walls of the elevator shaft. That is the potéa for masonry. Look at the first floor walls on this section. It is still unclear what the structure is; however, it appears to be concrete. The wall to the right is shown in section 1 on sheet A8. We'll go there next.

Sheet A8—Wall Sections

A wall section is similar to a building section in that it is a cut through a section of wall of the building exposing the inside of the wall, its components, and how the wall goes together. Sheet A8 shows three different wall sections. Section 1 is taken from the east elevation, section 2 is taken from the north elevation, and section 3 is taken from the south elevation. We'll analyze section 1 first.

Notice that the first floor wall consists of the foundation wall with furring channels, with one inch of insulation and gypsum wallboard (drywall). The second floor wall is built using six-inch metal studs, on top of which sit the wood trusses. The second floor is built with steel bar joists. This explains the difference in floor-to-floor heights from the first floor to the second. The first floor is two feet higher to allow room for the steel joists. Notice also on this section the very deep brick ledge. The dimension from the bottom of the brick ledge to the first floor slab says Varies because the brick ledge on both elevations steps down. Look at the trusses to notice that the underside of the trusses has one-half inch gyp (short for gypsum wallboard). This confirms the suspicion that the trusses are fire separated from the rest of the building.

Section 2 shows the full height foundation wall with full twelve-inch thickness nearly up to the top. There is a small brick ledge. The steel bar joists support a metal deck that, in turn, supports a concrete deck. Notice the note about the waterproofing. The system calls for a rubber membrane to be used in conjunction with a protective board wherever the finish grade line is above the finish floor. This will include quite a bit of area, including the entire foundation on the north side and all the area on the east and west sides beneath the step-down brick ledge. A quick take-off of this area puts it at approximately 1,700 square feet. This will probably take a couple of weeks rather than the conventional spray on dampproofing that takes only a couple of hours. This is a good example of how missing a note like that might cause a real problem in the schedule down the road.

Section 3 shows a six-inch metal stud wall on the first and second floors. Acoustical drop-in ceiling seems to be used throughout the building as it appears on all floors of all sections. The windows are listed as wood-clad double-hung windows. This type of window will probably not be that difficult to get in; however, until we read the specification, we won't know for sure. Limestone sills are shown. They will have to be ordered with enough lead time so they come in on time.

Sheet A9—Entry Elevation and Wall Section

This section provides a detailed view of how the entry of the building on the south side is built. Considering the width of the glass opening that is on both floors at the entry, the structure is weakened. Therefore, this section and elevation display what additional framing has been provided to compensate for the openings. Note that only the left side of the framing is shown on the elevation and therefore it is presumed that the right side is a mirror image of the left. This is done to save room on the paper, allowing the section and elevation to be placed, in horizontal line, on the same sheet at the largest scale possible. Both the section and elevation are drawn at 3/4" = 1'−0" scale. If the full elevation was drawn, they would have to be drawn at 1/2" = 1'−0", or less, to both fit on one sheet.

These two views do a good job describing how this area will be built. Notice the pier and wall footings and foundations on the section. The framing detail of the canopy roof is laid out but not dimensioned. This allows leeway for the builder. Notice also that the canopy roof framing is anchored in brick. This brick is not shown anywhere else on the drawings. The framing for the opening is done in tube steel. Most tube steel is square. It is called tube steel because it is hollow on the inside. The elevation gives some detail of the members to be used and the finish of the members, calling out vinyl clad Pella® windows, standing seam metal roof on the canopy of zinc plated steel which is then painted, stained doors, and pre-fab wood columns with a steel support bolted to the footing inside.

Sheet S1—Foundation Plan and Second Floor Framing Plan

This is the first of two structural sheets. It shows the foundation plan along with the numerous sections of the different walls that comprise the foundation. The second floor framing plan details the steel framing that supports the second floor.

Reviewing the various sections of the foundation plan, start on the north elevation wall. The wall type is that of section 4/S1. Looking at that section on this same page, you see the full height, full 12" thickness wall with the shallow 8" brick ledge on top. Notice the significant amount of steel in the wall to help support it as a retaining wall. Foundation walls on low-story buildings typically have to resist a greater load from the weight of the earth than they do from the weight above. Moving to the side walls, look at section 1/S1. This is the foundation wall on the east and west sides that is full height with the stepped-down brick ledge. The full height and length of this wall can be seen by the dark dashed line on both elevations on sheet A6. The length of this wall is dimensioned on the first floor plan on page A2.

Section 3/S1 illustrates the short frost wall, so called because the foundation and footing have to extend below the frost depth specified by the local building code. In the area where this building is built, the code specifies that the bottom of the footing must be placed 30" below the grade line. Section 7/S1 details the wall along the front of the building. It is a frost wall also and is similar to the other frost wall, except it is not as tall and has a wider footing, 3' wide, rather than 2'. The footing is wider because this wall carries more load than the side wall. The north and south walls are carrying nearly half the weight of the second floor load and nearly all of the roof weight. Consequently, you would expect the footings to be wider than those side walls.

The second floor framing plan shows the open web bar joists that span the second floor. Notice the special framing around the opening in the second floor to accommodate the elevator and stairs. There are numerous special pieces to be fabricated. Between this steel and the framing steel around the front entrance, the delivery time for all the steel may easily become critical. Delivery of structural steel is very often on the critical path. The remainder of the sections on this sheet show various other framing, connection, and construction details.

Sheet S2—Roof Framing Plan and South Wall Structural Elevation

The roof framing plan is the basic layout of the roof framing members. Since this building has a conventional prefabricated wood truss roof frame, the roof framing plan is not very detailed. The truss manufacturer will design the roof trusses in accordance with their own design practices and will submit shop drawings of their design. The shop drawings will be reviewed and approved by the engineer. At that point the trusses can be manufactured. Trusses are considered a material with a long lead time; however, since they are not needed until after the structure is in place, their fabrication and delivery is normally not critical.

Look at the south wall structural elevation and section 4/S2. Both show different views of the framing of the building. The walls are framed from heavy gauge metal studs topped with a continuous tube steel member. The second floor bar joists rest on the tube steel and support the metal deck and concrete slab. The second floor walls are framed in the same way—metal studs, topped with a continuous tube steel member supporting the roof trusses.

Section 5/S2 details the columns inside the building showing the footing, column, and beam. The remainder of the page is filled with other sections and general notes.

SPECIFICATION REVIEW

Project drawings are intended to show *quantity and configuration,* that is, how much, what size, and how is it arranged and put together. Project specifications are intended to show *quality and workmanship.* Notes on drawings are considered specifications. When there is a conflict between the drawings and specifications, the specifications prevail. We will see an example of that later on in this review.

Specifications can be long winded. Someone once said, "One out of every one-thousand words in a spec is important, but if you miss it, you may have just lost the ranch." It is much easier to learn how to read drawings than specifications. Part of the reason is that most everything on the drawing has some meaning to someone building the project. Specifications are wordier and are written in *quasi-legalize*. Many things that you already know, or that are obvious, or that might not pertain to your project are written down. Specifications start out generic in form and are customized for each project. Much of the generic information remains in the spec.

The real challenge is to sift through this stuff to find the important and *extremely* important item(s) that may cost or save your company thousands of dollars. For instance, there may be just one line in the spec that says that your company is responsible for paying sales tax on all materials. If you don't catch that, that miss could cost your company over 5 percent. With that one miss, you might have lost half of your company's profit.

The best way to attack a specification is to read it one section at a time. As an example, if you are about to perform a quantity take-off on masonry, read that section of the specification.

A project this size would typically have a specification that is several hundred pages long. Several pages were selected from the specification for the Delhi Medical Building and are included in Appendix A. They are listed below with their topic:

- Table of contents
- Section 00012—Description of work
- Section 00300—Bid form
- Section 01400—Allowances
- Section 01500—Alternates
- Section 04200—Unit masonry
- Section 06192—Prefabricated wood trusses
- Section 07110—Sheet membrane waterproofing
- Section 08610—Wood windows
- Section 14240—Hydraulic elevators

Table of Contents

The table of contents is the best place to get a quick review of what is in the project. As you scan through the topics of the table of contents you will see what is included in the project. Look through the table of contents for the Delhi Medical Building and read the topics there. What jumps out at you? Some buildings will have special equipment or construction requirements. For instance, Figure 2.2 in Chapter 2 shows a demonstration kitchen under construction at the Midwest Culinary Institute. As you review the index you want to look for items that will require special consideration.

The Delhi building is rather straightforward. An example of an item that will require special consideration is the hydraulic elevator. We will review that section of the spec later.

Section 00012—Description of Work

This section describes the project's scope including a delineation of the contract documents. Included in this list of documents is the schedule of drawings. Check the schedule and determine which drawings were not included with the text.

You may have noticed on this section that the bidders are required to break out the cost of each tenant improvement and alternate. The immediate question that comes to mind relative to the schedule is whether each tenant finish package might be awarded to a different contractor. If so, the schedule might not include work on the interior of the building after all. This section goes on to say that the entire contract for construction will be awarded to a single contractor.

Section 00300—Bid Form

It is very common for all the contractors who are bidding on a job to use the same bid form. It makes comparing the bids much easier. Section 00300 is the bid form used on the Delhi building. There is always important information on the bid form, including the single most important piece of information, relative to the schedule. The last line of the first page of this section lists the date for substantial completion: April 1, 2003. Listed further up on this same page is the bid due date of June 21, 2002. That leaves only nine months and ten days from the time of the bid opening and the substantial completion of the building.

Many other items of interest are included on the bid form. It asks for individual pricing on the different alternates, including the fire protection alternate. Additional sections on the bid form address changes to the contract, the provision for a performance bond, and substitutions.

Section 01400—Allowances

An allowance is an amount of money to be included in the contractor's base bid that is set aside for a particular item of construction. They are established to defer selection of an item until more information is available.

It is always good to review the list of allowances relative to the schedule to get an idea of the scope of these items. For example, if a project this size has a landscape allowance of $100,000, the logical placement and duration of the landscaping activity might need to be carefully considered.

In this case the landscaping allowance was only $10,000, which is a nominal amount. The signage allowance for interior signs is $1,000 and exterior is $2,000. These are minimal amounts, particularly the exterior allowance. Two thousand dollars is barely enough for a spotlight, or a lit, professionally painted wood sign. This surely will not impact the schedule.

Section 01500—Alternates

An alternate is an option to change to an alternative material, system, method, and so forth. The change is priced with the bid, giving the owner the cost of the change while still allowing the owner to delay the decision to make the change. An alternate may eliminate an item, add an item, or change an item.

It is always good to review the list of alternates relative to the schedule to get an idea of the scope of these items. For example, if this project takes the fire protection alternate, the sprinkler rough-in and finish will have to be fit into the schedule considering the logical placement and duration of these activities.

Section 04200—Unit Masonry

When reviewing the masonry specification relative to its potential impact on the schedule, there are a number of things to look for. The first and foremost is the size of the brick to be used on the project. For example, a standard size brick can be laid at a rate of about 400 brick per day per brick mason. A jumbo size brick can be laid at a rate of about 360. However, the jumbo size brick covers over twice as much area as a standard size brick, so the brick duration for the masonry activity using jumbo brick will be half that of a standard brick.

Notice the spec calls for a standard size brick. Other specifications will affect the productivity of the masonry. Some jobs have significant amounts of brick trim work, use colored mortar, or call for special brick shapes or different patterns to be used. The Delhi project calls for rowlocks around the four round vents on the four gable ends. Other than that, there is not very much that will detract from the brick productivity.

Section 06192—Prefabricated Wood Trusses

This section of the spec spells out the submittal and approval process that was explained earlier in this chapter relative to the prefabricated wood trusses. It refers to the standards to which they have to be designed and the submittal process.

Section 07110—Sheet Membrane Waterproofing

The wall section on sheet A8 called for a rubber membrane waterproofing. This section of the specification describes this work. Remember, specifications describe quality and workmanship. Read this section of the spec, paying particular attention to the section entitled *Execution*. Try to determine, based on the process, how many square feet of waterproofing a two-person crew would install per day.

This multistep process includes cleaning and preparing the surface, applying a prime coat, applying adhesive to the membrane, flashing and sealing joints, installing the protective board, and cleaning up. Based on this, one might expect to complete about 105 to 200 square feet per day. This is equal to fifteen to twenty linear feet per day of a twelve-foot-tall foundation wall that is covered to within two feet of the top of the wall. Based on this productivity the Delhi foundation would need about ten days to complete the waterproofing.

There is one line in this spec section that warrants further investigating. Under the installation section it says, *Schedule installation to minimize period of exposure of sheet waterproofing materials.* This could mean many things; for instance, that workers can only work with the material for a half-day at a time. Who knows? The prudent thing to do is to contact the manufacturer to see what this might mean.

Section 08610—Wood Windows

This section specifies the wood windows to be used on the project including the double-hung units and the fixed unit. You might recall from sheet A9 that the plans called for Pella® fixed windows. However, the spec calls out for either Anderson® or Marvin® windows. So which is right? Can any of the three be used?

Since the specification overrides the drawings, the selection should come from Anderson® or Marvin®. However, approved equal substitutions are allowed (see section 00300—bid form, 00300-5, IV, item 1). Since windows are typically a long lead item, the decision on which window to use might be based on which window can be delivered first.

Section 14240—Hydraulic Elevators

Based on the submittal process outline in the specification, a duration to submit, approve, order, and deliver the hydraulic elevator will be set at sixty working days, which is twelve weeks.

The specification review would be even more extensive had we included the entire specification. However, between the review of the drawings and the review of the specifications, we have identified the major problem areas for the Delhi Medical Building that need special consideration.

IDENTIFY THE UP-FRONTS

At the same time that you are reviewing and analyzing the project drawings and specifications, you must also begin the process of carrying out the *up-front* activities.

> *Up-fronts* is a term given to the many activities that have to be performed before and during the early stages of construction that do not consist of physical construction work.

A clear example of an up-front is a building permit. Without it, the work obviously does not begin. Many up-front activities have to do with the procurement of the material for the project.

When a project is bid out, the bidding documents often specify multiple (often three) materials for the same purpose that the bidder may choose from. Additionally, bidders are usually allowed to suggest substitutions of materials of equal quality that they are familiar with. The hope is that the best material will be selected at the lowest price for the project.

After the contract is awarded, there is the long process of the various contractors submitting for approval the materials they actually had included in their bid. The submittal is made to the construction manager or general contractor and passed on to the architect or engineer for approval.

As part of the submittal, material samples, shop drawings, manufacturer catalogs, and instructions, as well as other paperwork, is generated and approved, at which point it becomes part of the contract.

Once the submittals are approved the materials can be ordered. This phase of the process is called *buyout,* where the construction manager and the trade contractors begin to buyout the project. While most materials might be ordered right away, they may not be delivered right away if they are not needed yet—they would only get in the way. However, there are some materials that must be ordered immediately because they will be needed soon and may take a long time to fabricate. These are commonly referred to as long lead items. Two good examples are steel and glass. The fabrication and delivery of steel for the building's structure is sometimes a critical activity due to its long lead and its early need; that is, it takes a long time to get in and it is needed early in the life of the project—right after the foundations are completed. Glass can take a while to get in also, but it is not needed quite as early since the windows are installed with the skin of the building after the structural frame is erected. However, if you need a special type of glass, such as color tinted or low-e, it may become critical.

There are a number of long lead items that are typical of most building construction projects:

- Steel
- Glass
- Brick
- Stone
- Doors
- Trusses
- Electrical equipment
- HVAC equipment
- Elevators
- Casework
- Hardware
- Other equipment

Once the submittals are made and approved, materials have been ordered, and it is clear what is going to be put into the building, the coordination drawings can begin.

> Coordination drawings are used to help organize and communicate the placement of the mechanical, electrical, plumbing, fire protection, telecommunication, security, and other utilities throughout the building.

The coordination drawing usually begins with the HVAC contractor since their ductwork is the largest of all the utilities and the least flexible to change. They will layout the route they plan to take on the drawings, then pass them on. The plumbing contractor goes next since they are the next least flexible at working around difficulties. If the job has fire protection, it would go next. From there, electrical takes over, followed by security, telecommunication, and others. When complete, there is a plan developed to coordinate the placement of these many utilities.

The project isn't really completely designed until all the up-front activities are complete.

CREATING CONSTRUCTION SCHEDULES

The textbook has taken the student through the various topics and exercises that are required to prepare them with the skills and knowledge that are necessary to create a construction schedule. They have learned about the three components common to every schedule: activities, logic, and duration. They have learned to draw precedence network diagrams. They have learned how to manually calculate the critical path of the schedule, and with that, the nuances and interactions between activities that occur within the schedule. And they have learned how to analyze the project and its documents in preparation for creating the project schedule. What's left is to go, step-by-step, through how a construction schedule is created. We will do that next, using the Delhi Medical Building.

The first draft and revised draft of the construction schedule for the Delhi Medical Building are included with this text. The first draft of any schedule usually has a little bit of fat in it. However, it serves to get the job down on paper where it can be analyzed more closely for areas of improvement and compression. The first draft came in at 10 1/4 months (231 days). The bidding documents call for a 9 1/4 month window from bid opening to substantial completion; therefore, a substantial challenge awaits in the revision.

Spread out the first draft construction schedule along with the plans for the building. **You should follow along on the schedule as the creation of it is discussed.** As you follow along, take note of areas for improvement and compression that can be applied to the schedule in the revision.

FIRST DRAFT CONSTRUCTION SCHEDULE (DELHI MEDICAL BUILDING)

When scheduling a construction project, all projects are different and at the same time all projects are the same. If you are creating a schedule for a highway bridge versus a power plant versus a commercial building, all three project schedules will be very different. But there will also be characteristics of all three that are the same. For example, all three will start with some type of site preparation, all three will have some type of foundation and structure, and all three will have some level of finishes.

The schedule we will create for the Delhi Medical Building will be very typical of any building being constructed. The principles we discuss can be applied to the construction of most any type of building and the flow of the work is similar on most building projects. For example, the inside of the building is usually critical. There is usually a race between the foundation and slab activities with the order and delivery of the steel to see which one gets done first. If one is not critical, the other one is. An important milestone is to get the building enclosed and watertight *and* to get your rough-ins roughed in, because you can't start hanging drywall until both happen—and drywall is almost always critical.

The schedule for the Delhi job addresses construction activities only. It is presumed that the design is complete, the project has been bid out, and that all the building permits have been obtained.

The schedule we are about to create will be created one activity at a time. When going through this process it might be easier to talk about the schedule in sections rather than from start to finish as a whole. Therefore, we will divide the project up into the following main areas or phases (how we breakdown the project is not important; the phases won't even show up on the schedule):

- Getting started
- Up-fronts
- Sitework
- Foundation
- Structural frame
- Roof
- Skin
- Interior studs and MEP rough-ins
- Drywall
- Interior finishes
- Exterior finishes
- Getting finished

Getting Started

The hardest parts of any construction project are getting started and getting finished. Once the project is underway and all the contractors are oriented to the site and know what's in front of them, the project will flow on its own energy. However, getting it to that point takes a lot of work. For different reasons discussed later, getting the project finished is also difficult. The first 10 percent and the last 10 percent of the project are the most difficult.

Network schedules should always start at a single node and end at a single node. For this reason, it is a good practice to always start the project with the start milestone activity, notice to proceed. Start milestones have zero days duration and are drawn on the network diagram as diamond-shaped nodes. Some of the very first activities to occur on a project are site clearing, demolition, site layout, and mobilization. The Delhi site had nothing to demolish or clear. Mobilization is the act of establishing a presence on the site and might include setting a job trailer or tool trailer on-site, providing for temporary electrical and putting up the project sign. A minimum of five days is needed for this duration, or longer in some cases. The duration of the site layout is dependent upon the size if the building and parking is to be laid out. Added to that could be the layout of streets, retention basins, fences, or other objects on the site. A survey crew should be able to layout this project in three days.

Up-Fronts

The up-front activities were discussed in some detail earlier. Deciding what activities to include on the schedule to track really depends on the scope of the items. Long lead items and special items that are hard to get are normally included. The majority of the materials that go into a project are off-the-shelf. Off-the-shelf items are normally *not* tracked by the schedule, but are equally important.

On this job, seven items were identified: steel, trusses, elevator, brick, doors and windows, HVAC, and the casework. On the Delhi schedule, each activity will have its own submit and approve activity with a twenty-day turnaround duration. Some schedules will use just one activity for all the job submittals. In this time the submittal must be made, reviewed, commented upon if needed, and approved.

After the material is approved, it will be ordered. The Order / Deliver activity is one way to show two events in just one activity. In this case it only takes a day to actually order the material; the rest of the time is used to fabricate (if needed) and deliver it to the site. The durations of each order / deliver activity will vary for each material depending on many different factors. The durations shown on the schedule are average for those materials on a building this size. Some schedules may combine the entire procurement process of submittal, approval, order, and delivery into one activity and use an activity such as Procure Steel to represent the entire process.

After the submittals are approved and materials ordered, the coordination drawings and meetings can begin. Since the HVAC contractor will begin the rough-ins first, they will also have the first shot at the coordination drawings, followed by plumbing, electrical, and then the other trades that may be required. Two weeks (10 days) with each trade is usually enough time to layout the runs. Throughout this time there are usually coordination meetings with all the involved trades to hash out issues that arise as this review takes place.

Sitework

Sitework can be divided into two distinct areas: work to be done before the building begins and work that will be performed after the structure of the building is complete. The first site work activity after the site is cleared is to prepare the building pad. The building pad is almost always critical. The building pad is the name given to the flat area left after excavation is complete and the foundation work is ready to begin. Other sitework outside the building's footprint includes earthwork (cut and fill) that may have to be done, utility runs from the street to the building, leveling and grading of the eventual parking areas, and storm water retention.

Since the excavation of the building pad is most critical, it will follow mobilization and the site layout. It will take ten days to excavate the pad, level the two areas for parking, build a temporary access road around the building for the concrete trucks, and ready the rest of the site for the utility runs. Once the excavation is complete, the meter pit begins and the elevator shaft can be drilled. Since the elevator is hydraulic, it has a shaft that has to go into the ground. The hole is drilled and the sleeve is placed inside the hole. The shaft will move up and down within the sleeve.

After the meter pit is dropped into the ground, the utilities can begin to be run. The utilities that need to be run from the street to the building include gas, water, electric, sanitary sewer, phone line, and cable. If all of these utilities were run back-to-back it might only take a week to run them all, but it is more likely that they will all be run over a three to four week period. It may not be known if the fire protection alternate was taken by the owner, so it is best to go ahead and schedule this work. That means that a meter pit, referred to above, will have to be installed. This pit is where the domestic line is separated from the sprinkler line.

Foundation

It is day 17 of the project and the chain of activities that go through the foundation are critical. Once the shaft is drilled and sleeve placed, the footing crew can arrive. The building is large enough that the footing crew can build the continuous wall footing, column footings, and elevator pit slab all at the same time. They will take three to four days to firm these up and a day to pour. The foundation can begin after the footings are poured and the elevator pit walls will be built by the same crew at the same time.

When the foundation walls are complete, the underground plumbing can begin. The plumbing goes first before the electric simply because their pipes are deeper than the electrical conduit. The plumbing will take a while since there are so many examination rooms, all of which have plumbing. The plumbing contractor will have two plumbers and one operator doing this work. All of this underground will have to be trenched in, which the operator will do with a backhoe. They will run lines from one side to the other and will take fourteen days. This really can't be speeded up. If you put more plumbers in there, they will be waiting around for the operator and, therefore, won't be efficient or save much time. There would never be enough room to add one more operator and another piece of equipment.

The electrical contractor will follow the plumber and faces a similar problem in taking all the electric underground to those rooms. Most of their runs will not require trenching, so although three or four electricians might be put on this work, it will still take ten days. When the electric is complete, the slab can begin and will take four days.

On the outside of the building the draintile piping and waterproofing can begin after the slab is complete. The special waterproofing system called out for this building was reviewed earlier in this chapter. Both of these activities will be performed by the same crew and will take fifteen days total.

After the slab is complete both the first floor exterior studs can begin and the 6" concrete block elevator shaft wall can begin to be built (it will only be built up to the second floor for now). These two activities can go on at the same time. The elevator shaft wall supports part of the second floor steel framing and the first floor exterior studs support the second floor bar joists. Both of these activities need to be accomplished before the steel can be erected.

As previously mentioned, it is always a close race to see which is critical, the arrival of the structural steel or the group of activities through the foundation that precede the steel's erection. In this case, it wasn't a very close race. The early finish of the arrival of the steel is day 50. The early finish of the first floor exterior studs and sheathing is day 75. The path through the foundation is twenty-five days (50%) longer. That's quite a difference. Twenty-five days is five weeks, or over a month, on a project that is supposed to be only a bit over nine months long. Why do you think that the difference was so great on this job?

There is always more than one answer, but what seems to jump out right away is the twenty-four combined days of duration for the underground plumbing and electric. We expected this to be an issue based on the number of exam rooms in the first floor medical office. But we've already looked at ways of putting more plumbers and electricians in that area—so what's the solution? We'll have to revisit that part of the schedule in the revision and take a hard look.

Structural Frame

It is now day 75 of the project and the building is ready for the erection of the structural steel. Based on the schedule, the steel has been ready for over a month. The structural steel will be erected in eight days followed by the bar joists, decking, and pour stops, which will take another four days. The pour stops are the steel angles welded around the perimeter of the decking that act as formwork for the concrete slab poured onto the deck. The slab will take two days to pour. The second floor exterior stud walls can begin after the slab is poured and will take six days to build. The remainder of the 6" block elevator shaft wall can continue after the slab has cured for three days. When the shaft and second floor walls are complete, the roof can begin.

Roof

The roof trusses and sheathing will start on day 95 after the second floor exterior studs and sheathing are built and the masons are complete with the elevator shaft wall. The trusses were complete and ready to be delivered much earlier, but were shipped just in time to be erected so they didn't take up needed room on the site. Since the trusses will be lifted into place with a crane, you cannot have any other trades working in this area for reasons of safety. Once the roof is sheathed, the dormer metal, shingles, and flashing can proceed.

Skin

Once the roofing is complete, work on the building's exterior can begin. The logical tie between the roof shingle activity and other exterior work is not a physical sequence, but one of safety. Work cannot occur on or around the exterior of the building when other work is going on above it. The first activity will be to install the exterior doors and windows, which can begin on day 114. They have to be installed before the brick begins.

The other activity that has to be completed before the brick begins is the backfill and compaction. Brick masons need to work right up against the building and cannot if it is not backfilled. Here's the problem: The building cannot be backfilled and compacted until the slab-on-deck is cured, which will be on day 92. This logical relationship between the backfill of the building and the curing of the slab is not a physical sequence, but one of structural integrity. The cured slab supports the wall by resisting the lateral forces created from the pressure of the earth. By the time the slab is cured, the second floor exterior walls have begun. This creates a safety issue since the walls are being installed directly above the backfilling. This safety issue continues after the walls are completed as the roof trusses are installed and the roof sheathed and shingled. At this point it is day 114, the backfill has still not begun, and the exterior doors and windows have begun to be installed. The doors and windows can be installed while the building is being backfilled and compacted as long as they work in different areas, so the backfill will start when the installation of the doors and windows start. This will be a start-to-start relationship with a zero (0)-day lag.

Once the backfill and compaction is complete and the doors and windows are installed, the brickwork can begin. Both activities are five days long, so they should end at the same time.

Sitework (cont'd)

Now that the structure is complete and the building is backfilled, sitework activities will start up again. The storm retention piping can begin and should take a little over a week (7 days) to complete. When complete, the electrical runs for the parking lot light poles can be run, followed by forming and pouring the concrete light pole bases. The exterior flatwork will also follow the storm retention piping as well as the brickwork. The exterior flatwork includes all the sidewalks around the building and the steps on the east side. The walk along the street was taken out of the contract in the first addendum. The walkways around the building are too close to the brick and the retention piping on the north side to work on at the same time. When the exterior flatwork is done and the light pole bases have been poured, the parking lot sub base and binder course can be laid down.

Interior Studs and MEP Rough-Ins

Moving back inside the building, once the roof is trussed and sheathed, workers can move back into the building to start laying out the interior walls and installing the top track of the stud walls. With the layout on the floor and the top track above, the location of interior walls can easily be seen. This will allow the first of many succeeding rough-ins to begin.

This is a schedule area that is perfectly suited for the use of the start-to-start relationship with lags, because normally one contractor simply has to get out in front of another.

The HVAC contractor will start the main duct runs first since they are the largest and least flexible. It is much easier for them to install the duct when the walls are not built and no other trades are in the same space. They will start five days after the layout and top track starts. Five days after the HVAC starts, the interior studs can begin. This will give the HVAC contractor enough time to get all the main trunk lines installed before the stud walls catch up with them. At this point the HVAC contractor will be working with the secondary duct lines.

The plumbing and sprinkler contractor(s) can start five days after the studs begin. The same contractor may do the plumbing and fire protection piping. They go before the electrical contractor because their piping is less flexible. Both will start with their overhead lines, which are not typically laid out inside walls. By the time the plumber moves down into the walls, many will be built. The electrical contractor and others such as security and telecommunications will start five days after the plumbing contractor starts. When all the rough-ins are complete and inspected, the drywall can begin.

Drywall

Drywall is an important milestone in the construction process since there are so many things that have to happen before it begins. As just stated, everything that runs inside the walls has to be complete and tested. The building has to be watertight to hang the board, and when the finishing begins, the space must be heated with either temporary or permanent heat. The drywall contractor usually installs the insulation as they hang the board. The drywall activity will follow the completion of all the rough-ins, the interior studs, and the installation of the doors and windows.

Interior Finishes

Once the drywall is complete the interior finishes can begin. The first thing to do is paint the walls with a prime coat and first coat of paint. This should take ten days to do the entire building. Five days after the painting starts you can start the grids for the drop ceilings and start to install the interior doors with their hardware. Five days after you begin the doors, you can start to install the casework and countertops. When the doors, painting, and casework are complete, you can begin the interior trim.

When the ceiling grids are complete you can begin to finish the electric and HVAC since the lighting fixtures, HVAC diffusers, and return duct grills lay into the grids. When those activities are complete, the ceiling pads for the drop ceiling can be laid. After they are laid, the sprinkler heads can be installed. The finish plumbing can begin after the countertops are installed. The plumbers will drop the sinks into the tops and install the fixtures. The finish paint will follow the interior trim and the flooring will follow the painters.

Exterior Finishes

The EIFS (exterior insulation finish system) is located above the brick on the second floor of the south elevation. Since the brickwork always starts at the lowest point and moves up from there, the EIFS might as well wait until the brick masonry is complete. Neither activity is critical, and the brick masons might leave their scaffolding up long enough for this work to be completed. When the EIFS is complete, the exterior trim will follow; however, it can't start until the exterior flatwork is complete. These two activities are too close together to go on at the same time. This is another example of a logical tie between two activities that is not due to physical sequencing. Once the trim is done, the exterior of the building can be painted and, after that, the gutters and downspouts can be installed. However, there still might be a conflict. The exterior steps on the east side of the building will begin when the flatwork begins but will take five more days to complete. Concrete steps are difficult to form and place, particularly steps with a carriage (side) to them. Therefore, these steps will be finishing up the first five days that the exterior trim is proceeding, necessitating the trim crew to stay off the east side until the steps are done. The construction manager will have to coordinate this with the two contractors.

The parking lot can be completed by installing the light posts, then paving the lot with the wearing course of asphalt, striping the spaces, and placing the wheel blocks. When this is complete, the site can be finished, graded, and landscaped.

Getting Finished

Finishing the project is always a challenge. It entails numerous inspections of the various systems, the development and resolution of punchlist items, and the closeout of the trade contracts. The building has to be turned over to the owner, which includes training on the systems and functions of the building and coordinating their move-in, not to mention the turnover of instruction manuals and warranty information.

A finish milestone was added to the end of the project in addition to a project management hammock activity that runs from start to finish. You'll see how effective project management hammocks are in the SureTrak modules.

The project is complete and came in at 10 1/4 months (231 days). The bidding documents call for a 9 1/4 month window from bid opening to substantial completion. As stated earlier, the first draft of any schedule usually has a little bit of fat in it. However, it serves to get the job down on paper where it can be analyzed more closely for areas of improvement and compression. So the question is, how much can this schedule be compressed? We'll see in the revision.

Answer the questions on the Schedule Analysis—First Draft Construction Schedule on the next page. Tear it out and turn it in to your instructor, then move on to the revision of the schedule.

SCHEDULE ANALYSIS
First Draft Construction Schedule
Delhi Medical Building

Name _____

Instructions: Answer the following questions. Type answers on a separate sheet of paper in 14 point font. Tear this page out and staple it to your answer sheet.

1. How would you compress the chain of activities that move through the *Foundation* activity to save time?

2. If the *Storm Retention* activity is proceeding at the same time as the *Brick Masonry* activity. How would you coordinate this work to avoid interferences?

3. Will the activities that follow the *Storm Retention* activity interfere with the activities that follow the *Brick Masonry* activity?

4. Based on your review of the first draft schedule, what other areas might become tight (or critical) if the excavation and foundation were compressed?

5. List areas of improvement or compression that you have detected while reviewing the first draft schedule that were not already addressed in the revised schedule or the text (must list at least one).

REVISING THE SCHEDULE

The first draft of the construction schedule came in at 10 1/4 months (231 days). We don't know what the exact end date will be because we have not put this schedule on a calendar yet, since we know that it still has to be compressed. However, we do know that the bidding documents call for the project to be complete on April 1st, 2003, and that the bid date is June 21st, 2002. That allows nine months and ten days from the time of the bid to substantial completion. However, you have to allow at least a month from the time of the bid to the start of construction for signing the contract, securing permits (if not secured), and taking care of other paperwork. The realistic start date for the construction of the building is probably August 1st, 2002. Add the current 10 1/4 month schedule to that, and the end date of the project lands sometime in June of 2004.

Subtracting the time for signing the contract and such leaves only eight months for the construction. That does not even provide float time for unknowns. Preferably we want the schedule to be 7 1/2 months long.

Let's begin the analysis of the first draft to see if there are enough areas of improvement to compress nearly three months out of that 10 1/4 month schedule. The revised draft construction schedule was also included with the text. It has the revised activities, logic, and durations, but has yet to be calculated. We'll do that after we review the revisions that were made.

Spread out the revised draft construction schedule to be viewed along with the first draft construction schedule and the plans for the building. **You will follow along on both schedules to see the changes that were made from the first draft to the revised draft as discussed below.**

REVISED DRAFT CONSTRUCTION SCHEDULE (DELHI MEDICAL BUILDING)

There are four main areas where the schedule was revised:

- Excavation
- Underground plumbing and electric
- Interior rough-ins
- Interior finishes

Excavation

On the first draft the excavation activity is ten days long. This includes excavating the building pad as well as leveling the two areas for parking, building a temporary access road around the building for the concrete trucks, and readying the rest of the site for the utility runs. Notice that the next activity is to drill the elevator shaft, which is followed by the footing work. Both of these activities are critical. Why couldn't the shaft be drilled right after the building pad is excavated? This would proceed while the remainder of the mass excavation is being done. After the shaft is drilled, the footing work can follow and should not interfere with the mass excavation, which will still be going on.

To make these changes, the Excavation activity from the first draft has to be split into two activities: Excavate Pad with a two day duration and Mass Excavation with an eight-day duration. The logic will be changed so the Drill & Sleeve Elevator Shaft activity will directly follow Excavate Pad. Mass Excavation will also follow Excavate Pad and precede Meter Pit.

Look at the revised draft to see these changes, which will save eight days—almost two weeks—and didn't require the addition of more resources, but nonetheless resulted in refining the logic of the schedule.

Underground Plumbing and Electric

In the first draft of the schedule we saw how the underground plumbing and electrical took twenty-four days combined and could not start until after the foundation was complete due to limited space. This resulted in a schedule with the foundation chain of activities finishing significantly longer (25 days) than the delivery of the structural steel.

The construction manager asked the plumbing, electrical, and foundation contractors to meet to discuss what might be done to compress this time.

The electrical contractor immediately came up with an idea to save seven days out of her activity. She suggested running all the first floor electric overhead rather than underground. This would require a few minor changes to the drawings, but was not expected to be a problem. She thought they could do this later when the first floor was being roughed in. She would then add another crew to do these runs, so the rough-in duration would not have to change. She would still need three days to run the main feeds underground into and throughout the building. She planned to do this when the plumbers finished with their work.

The plumbers were looking for a way to reduce their duration and also start sooner. They mentioned that their company had a mini-excavator that they used in tight areas and wondered, if they used that rather than a backhoe, if they would be able to start when the foundation was half complete. They thought that if the foundation could start in one side and progress to the other, there might be enough room for them to begin. In addition to that, they also looked at the manpower loading on the underground work and decided that they could add a third plumber with just the one operator on the mini-excavator. Although it's not as large, they thought that they would be able to work faster with the mini-excavator due to its small size and mobility. In the end they reduced their work duration from fourteen to ten days with the extra plumber and also moved the start of this work up ten days using a start-to-start relationship with a ten-day lag with the foundation activity. Based on these changes, the plumber will catch up with the foundation contractor and should be finishing at the same time. This may still cause a problem down the road, but both parties agreed that it's worth a try.

The following *microschedules* show the chain of the foundation activities from both the first draft of the construction schedule and the revised draft. The first draft shows a total duration for this chain of activities at 53 days ($70 - 17 = 53$). The revised draft, which includes the schedule improvements just detailed, shows a total duration for this chain, now at 32 days ($49 - 17 = 32$). This is a savings of twenty-one workdays—nearly a month off the schedule. See Figures 8.2 and 8.3.

Look at the revised draft to see these changes. These changes will save twenty-one days—almost an entire month off the first draft of the schedule. They were the result of changing an equipment resource, a minor redesign of the electrical runs, changing the start time of an activity, adding crews, and reevaluating the logistics of the space.

Interior Rough-Ins

Look at the start of the interior walls' layout on the first draft and notice that they begin after the building is under roof. On the surface, that seems to be the appropriate logic to use. However, why couldn't the walls on the first floor begin after the second floor slab had been poured? Work would be taking place on the floor above, but the workers on the first floor would be protected. Along with the walls the MEP rough-ins could begin also. By the time the walls are complete on the first floor, the second exterior walls and roof might be complete, allowing the interior wall crew to move up to the second floor and begin there. The MEP rough-ins could follow the walls up to the second floor.

This practice of phasing the interior walls and rough-ins from floor to floor is very common on larger, multistory buildings. Since the tenant spaces on the first and second floors are very much the same, the durations can simply be cut in half for most activities. The sequence of the activities of each phase would be almost the same as that on the first draft schedule using the same start-to-start relationship types with the same lags. There are only two differences. The relationship types between the Layout and Top Track activities and their successors, HVAC Rough-In, were changed to finish-to-starts

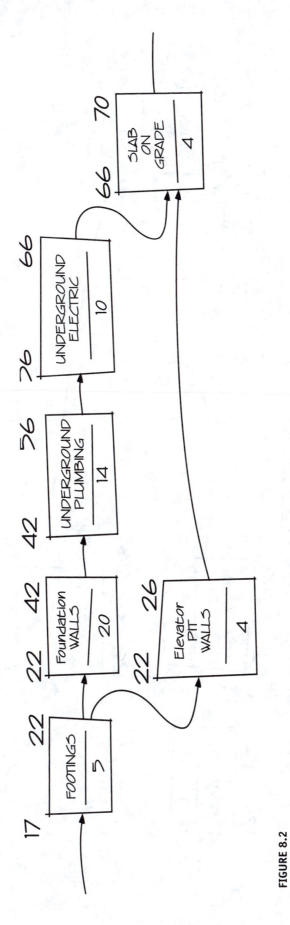

FIGURE 8.2
Microschedule of the foundation chain of activities from the first draft construction schedule of the Delhi Medical Building showing a fifty-three-day duration.

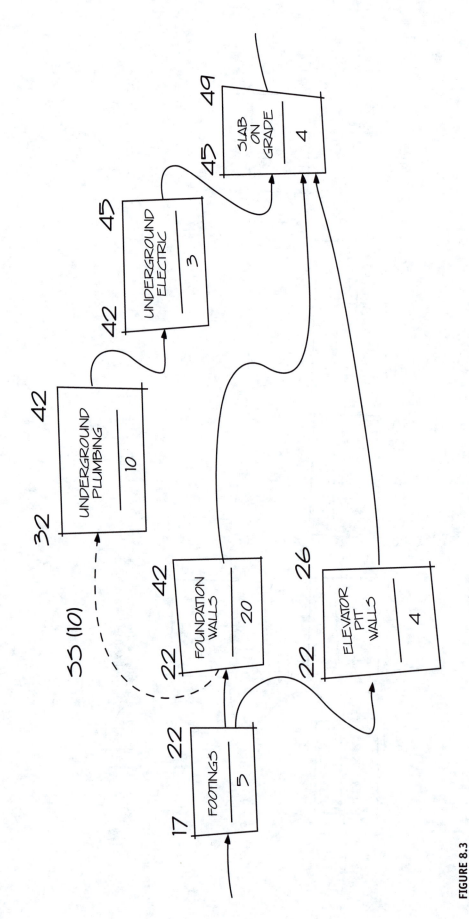

FIGURE 8.3

Microschedule of the foundation chain of activities from the revised draft construction schedule of the Delhi Medical Building showing a thirty-two-day duration for the same work as above.

from start-to-starts for simplicity sake. The second difference was with the duration of the Plumbing Rough-In activity. Three days were added to it because the plumbing contractor thought that their productivity would be slowed by phasing the work.

Look at the revised draft. The first floor phase starts with 1st Floor Layout and Top Track following Slab-on-Deck and continues through to 1st Floor Insulate, Hang, and Finish Drywall. The second floor phase starts with 2nd Floor Layout and Top Track following the Roof Trusses and Sheathing activity *and* it also follows the 1st Floor Layout and Top Track activity since the second floor layout can't begin until the crew is finished with the first floor. This phase ends with 2nd Floor Insulate, Hang, and Finish Drywall. Each activity in the second floor phase should also follow their counterpart from the first floor phase, thereby ensuring that two crews won't be needed.

When work is phased in this fashion it is completed sooner because it starts sooner. In addition, the additional breakdown of activities may schedule the work more efficiently. For example, on the revised draft schedule, the drywall on the first floor is started sooner; therefore, when the plumbing rough-in on the second floor (which is carrying the critical path) is complete, there are only fourteen days of drywall remaining, rather than twenty-five days, at this same point on the first draft schedule. That is an eleven-day savings.

Interior Finishes

Since the first floor drywall will finish before the second floor, the interior finishes on that floor were also phased like they were on the interior rough-ins. Look at the revised draft schedule and notice that the activities from 1st Floor Prime Coat through 1st Floor Casework have been phased.

In conclusion, we can't tell the results of the revised schedule until it is calculated. If the schedule isn't compressed enough, more revisions may have to be made. In the schedule analysis for the revised construction schedule, you will first calculate the revised draft, then answer questions about the draft. Move on to the Schedule Analysis—Revised Construction Schedule on the next page. Tear it out and turn it in to your instructor.

SCHEDULE ANALYSIS
Revised Construction Schedule
Delhi Medical Building

Name _____

Preface: Start by calculating the revised construction schedule. Use the schedule that came with the text. *Note:* **Use pencil so mistakes can be erased.** After calculating the schedule, answer the questions below. Turn the schedule analysis in to your instructor along with the calculated schedule.

1. What is the total project duration? (in days) _____

   In weeks (divide the number of days by 5) _____

   In months (divide the number of weeks by 4.5) _____

2. How many days were saved by compressing the following areas?

   Excavation _____ Foundation _____ Interior Finishes _____

3. What activity(s) is (are) critical on the revised draft that were not critical before?

   _____

4. Since the two steel procurement activities are now critical on the revised schedule, how many days can those activities be compressed before the foundation area of the schedule becomes critical again? _____

5. What would happen to the revised schedule if the *Final Grading* activity also followed *Gutters and Downspouts*?

   _____

   _____

6. How long lead item is the next most critical item? _____

7. The critical path goes through both the *1st Floor Plumbing Rough-In* and the *2nd Floor Plumbing Rough-In* activities. Why would this be expected on this particular project?

   _____

   _____

   _____

   _____

CAPSTONE PROJECT
USA Volleyball Centers
Creating the Construction Schedule

The capstone project for the textbook is intended to bring together the many topics presented in the text into one single student project. In addition to the work that follows, complete Module 27 in the SureTrak section of the text.

Included with the textbook were five sheets of drawings from the USA Volleyball Centers project. The drawings from the project are from the design development phase and were created as a prototype center to be built through the country.

You will create a first draft construction schedule for the USA Volleyball Centers, then analyze and create a revised construction schedule with the goal of identifying areas of improvement and compressing the schedule. The instructions listed below will be used to create *each* schedule.

Given: The project will be built on a relatively flat lot with all utilities at the street.

First Draft Construction Schedule

1. Based on the drawings provided of the USA Volleyball Centers, and the information below, draw a precedence network diagram of the USA Volleyball Centers.
2. Calculate the ES, EF, LS, LF, TF, FF, project duration, and critical path on the network diagram (use pencil).
3. Then, fill in all calculated activity information onto the blank tabular forms provided.
4. See Module 27 in the SureTrak section of the text for instructions to create this same schedule in SureTrak.

Revised Construction Schedule

1. Analyze the first draft of the schedule for areas of improvement and opportunities for compression.
2. Based on this analysis, draw a revised precedence network diagram of the USA Volleyball Centers including your revisions.
3. Calculate the ES, EF, LS, LF, TF, FF, project duration, and critical path on the network diagram (use pencil).
4. Then, fill in all calculated activity information onto the blank tabular forms provided.
5. See Module 27 in the SureTrak section of the text for instructions to create this same revised schedule in SureTrak.

CAPSTONE PROJECT
USA Volleyball Centers

ACT	DUR	ES	EF	LS	LF	TF	FF	REL. LINES

CAPSTONE PROJECT
USA Volleyball Centers

ACT	DUR	ES	EF	LS	LF	TF	FF	REL. LINES

CAPSTONE PROJECT
USA Volleyball Centers

ACT	DUR	ES	EF	LS	LF	TF	FF	REL. LINES

CAPSTONE PROJECT
USA Volleyball Centers

ACT	DUR	ES	EF	LS	LF	TF	FF	REL. LINES

CAPSTONE PROJECT
USA Volleyball Centers

ACT	DUR	ES	EF	LS	LF	TF	FF	REL. LINES

CAPSTONE PROJECT
USA Volleyball Centers

ACT	DUR	ES	EF	LS	LF	TF	FF	REL. LINES

CAPSTONE PROJECT
USA Volleyball Centers

ACT	DUR	ES	EF	LS	LF	TF	FF	REL. LINES

CAPSTONE PROJECT
USA Volleyball Centers

ACT	DUR	ES	EF	LS	LF	TF	FF	REL. LINES

MODULE 1
Drawing the Schedule by Hand

Preface: In Module 1, you will hand-draw the schedule that you will using throughout the SureTrak modules. When creating a schedule on the computer, it is imperative to draw the schedule out first, rather than to just start typing in activities and their relationships. A computerized schedule is only as good as the information it is based on. Drawing the schedule by hand helps ensure an accurate and reliable schedule.

DRAWING THE NETWORK SCHEDULE

1. Based on the notes below, draw by hand the garage construction schedule. However, this time include on the schedule all the information that is in the spreadsheet in Table M1.1. Notice that for this schedule, and all the rest of the SureTrak schedules, we will be using numbers for the activity IDs rather than letters. In the notes below, the numbered activity IDs are in front of the activity descriptions and the durations are behind in parentheses—all in italics. You may want to abbreviate information to help make it fit on the paper. When complete, compare your hand-drawn schedule with the one shown in Figure M1.1.

    Once you've received the *10–notice to proceed* (milestone activity–0 days), *20–order/deliver the brick* (20) so it comes in on time and begin the *30–excavation* (3). The *40–footing and foundation* (10) will follow the excavation and precede *50–slab-on-grade* (4). When the slab is done, both the *60–backfill* (1) and *70–exterior wall framing* (3) can begin. After the backfill is complete, you can *90–form and pour the drive* (4). Your framing crew will begin to *80–frame and shingle the roof* (5) after they finish framing the exterior walls. The *100–masonry* (10) can begin after the roof and backfill is complete and the brick has been delivered. The *110–exterior trim* (5) can begin seven days (SS7) after the masonry begins.

    On the inside of the garage, you can *120–hang the garage door* (1) after the roof is complete. After the door is hung, you can begin the *130–interior finishes* (7). The project can be *140–punched out* (4) after the masonry, exterior trim, the drive, and interior finishes are completed. The *15–project management* (hammock activity–?? days) will start when notice to proceed starts and finish when punchout finishes.

2. Module 1 is complete. Turn a photocopy of your hand-drawn schedule in to your instructor. Move on to Module 2 and begin to use the SureTrak software.

TABLE M1.1   Garage construction schedule

	Activity Information				
Act Id	Activity Description	Dur	Budget	Contract	Resp
10	Notice to Proceed (Start Milestone)	0	0.00	<your co.>	Smith
15	Proj. Mngt. (Hammock)	??	0.00	<your co.>	Smith
20	Order / Deliver Brick	20	1380.00	<your co.>	Smith
30	Excavation	3	304.00	Sub	Smith
40	Footing and Foundation	10	2698.00	Sub	Smith
50	Slab-on-Grade	4	1071.00	Sub	Smith
60	Backfill	1	517.00	Sub	Smith
70	Frame Walls	3	2766.00	<your co.>	Jones
80	Frame / Shingle Roof	5	3603.00	<your co.>	Jones
90	Form / Pour Drive	4	1677.00	Sub	Smith
100	Masonry	10	4148.00	Sub	Smith
110	Exterior Trim	5	323.00	<your co.>	Jones
120	Hang Garage Doors	1	3000.00	<your co.>	Jones
130	Interior Finishes	7	1435.00	<your co.>	Jones
140	Punch Out	4	0.00	<your co.>	Smith

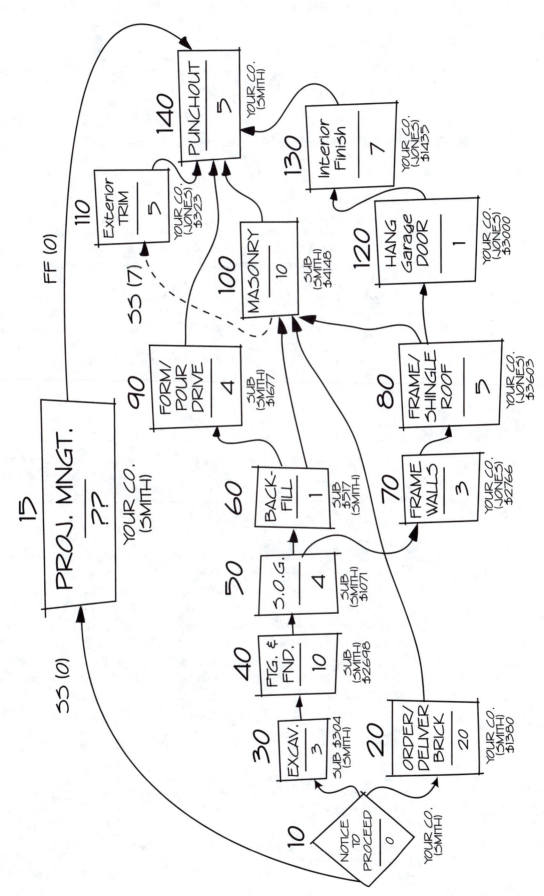

FIGURE M1.1

241

MODULE 2
Creating a Project

Preface: At this point, you should have drawn the project schedule out by hand on a big piece of paper. It might look ugly, but that's OK—you are the only one who is going to see it. It is important to draw the schedule out first. Some people will skip that step, but that can be dangerous, because it is very difficult to lay out a schedule straight from your head and into the computer without making mistakes that might doom the schedule.

In this module, you will learn how to open SureTrak, create a project schedule, fill out the project information, and save the project to the hard drive. You will use the Garage Construction Schedule project that you drew by hand in Module 1.

The garage project will be the subject project you will be working with throughout most of the SureTrak portion of the text.

OPENING THE SOFTWARE

1. To start SureTrak, double-click the icon on the desktop (if it is there); otherwise,

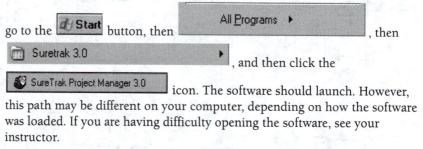

go to the [Start] button, then [All Programs ▶], then [Suretrak 3.0 ▶], and then click the [SureTrak Project Manager 3.0] icon. The software should launch. However, this path may be different on your computer, depending on how the software was loaded. If you are having difficulty opening the software, see your instructor.

2. After you enter the software, the Welcome screen appears. Close the Welcome screen. What's left is the Entrance screen, as shown in Figure M2.1.

3. *A note of caution.* Be aware that, in this software, to get from one field to another—use the *Tab* key or click from field to field. *Do not* use the *Enter* key to go from field to field.

4. Before you begin, there are a few settings to check. Go to Tools, then Options . . . . In the [Project] tab, select the following default settings as shown in Figure M2.2.

5. Next go to the [Defaults] tab of the same window (Tools, then Options . . .). In the Resource defaults area, uncheck the

Controls <u>d</u>uration (driving) setting as shown in Figure M2.3. Click OK.

FIGURE M2.1

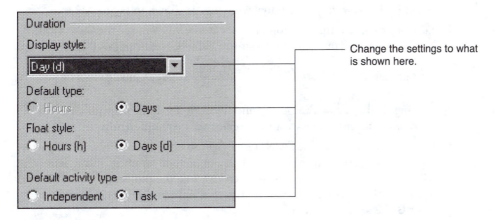

FIGURE M2.2

FIGURE M2.3

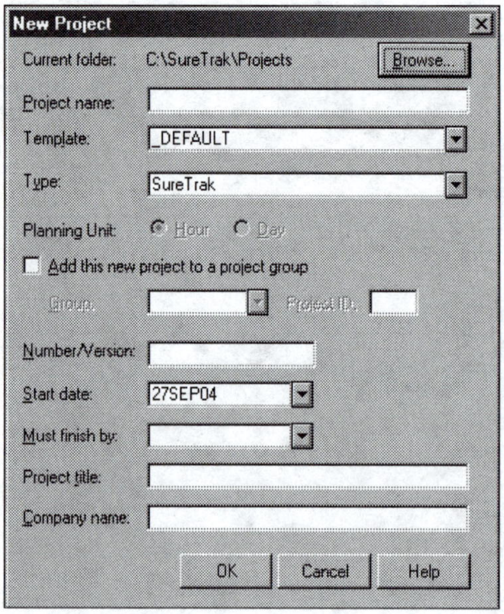

FIGURE M2.4

CREATING THE PROJECT

6. To create a new project, go to the File command, and click New . . . , or simply click the ▢ icon. If it appears, click [No] to the Project KickStart Wizard. The New Project window will open as shown in Figure M2.4.

7. *Current folder:* On the very top of this window you will see the Current folder: listed. Schedules you create will automatically be stored in this folder. The path probably reads [C:\...\SureTrak\Projects] . You can change this by clicking the [Browse...] button and selecting the folder of your choice. *Do not change the path,* unless your instructor tells you differently.

8. *Project name:* Click in the Project name: field to enter an *exactly* four-character project name. The project name, which can include numbers and/or letters, will appear at the top of the project screen when the project is open. Since we will be working with the garage project that was hand-drawn in Module 1, enter **GARG** as the project name.

9. *Template:* Use the _DEFAULT template for this project, so *tab past this field.* The Template: field allows you to use an existing (template) project as the starting point for your project.

10. *Type:* Select **Project Groups** as the Type: if it is not already selected. As a general rule, I would suggest always using project groups as the project type. Making this selection as the project type allows this project to be merged and become part of a larger schedule, and also allows its dictionaries, calendars, resources, activity codes, and WBS codes to be transferred to other projects that you may create later. We'll be transferring project resources later in Module 24.

11. *Planning unit:* Click **Day** for the Planning Unit: as shown [Planning Unit:　○ Hour　● Day] . Do not Add this new project to a project group, so tab past that field.

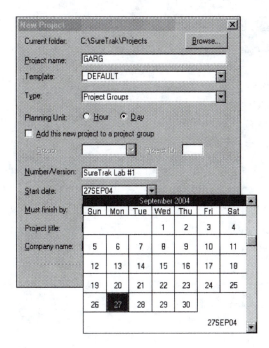

FIGURE M2.5

12. *Number/version:* The Number/Version: field is an optional field that allows you to describe different versions of the same project. As an example, when creating monthly updates of the schedule, you might call the update "April Update" and enter that in the Number/Version: field. You can enter up to sixteen alphanumeric (letters and/or numbers) characters. Enter **SureTrak Lab #1** in the Number/Version: field. Your instructor may want you to enter something different.

13. *Start date:* The project **Start date:** is a required entry that identifies the date that the project will start. The start date of the project can be changed at any time. To enter the date, click the pull-down calendar, scroll to the appropriate date, and double-click on the date as shown in Figure M2.5. Enter **27SEP04** for the start date for this project.

14. *Must finish by:* **Do not click in this field.** Do not enter a Must finish by: date. *Tab past* this field. By entering a date in this field, you will force a finish date for the project rather than letting the software calculate the finish date. This may result in negative float for some or all of the activities. The date is entered using the pull-down calendar, the same way the start date is entered. A scheduler might use this field to create "what if" scenarios with a given end date. However, for this project, make sure this field is blank. If a date appears in this field, highlight it and delete it.

15. *Project title:* The Project title: field allows for a thirty-six-character project title. Spaces, punctuation characters, and any other characters are acceptable. By default, the project title is printed on the hard copy of the schedule and tabular reports. Enter **Garage Construction Schedule** for the project title.

16. *Company name:* The Company name: field allows for a thirty-six-character company name, client name, customer, or anything else you might choose to enter. Spaces, punctuation characters, and any other characters are acceptable. By default, the company name is printed on the hard copy of the schedule and tabular reports. Enter ***<your name>* Construction Management** for the company name.

New Project

Current folder:	C:\SureTrak\Projects	Browse...
Project name:	GARG
Template:	_DEFAULT
Type:	Project Groups
Planning Unit:	○ Hour ● Day
☐ Add this new project to a project group
Group:		Project ID:
Number/Version:	SureTrak Lab #1
Start date:	27SEP04
Must finish by:	
Project title:	Garage Construction Schedule
Company name:	<your name> Construction Management

OK   Cancel   Help

FIGURE M2.6

17. At this point the project information has been entered. Verify that your entries match those shown in Figure M2.6. After verifying your entries, click **OK** to create the project.

18. The main screen in SureTrak, called the Project window, will display next. It contains activity columns on the left and an empty bar chart on the right. It is the screen that you will work from most of the time in SureTrak. See Figure M2.7 for a detailed view of this screen and descriptions of its components. Review all the different areas of the screen, then move on to the next instruction.

19. If you need to get back to the previous screen where you filled in all the project information, go to File, then Project Overview. . . . Go back there once, just to see the screen (Figure M2.8). Notice that the screen is laid out a bit differently and that some fields that are now grayed-out and can no longer be changed. When you are finished looking at this window click to return to the project window.

SAVING THE PROJECT

20. Save the garage construction schedule project to the hard drive. To save the project, go to File, then Save, or simply click the ▣ button. This will save the project and changes you have made up to that point to the hard drive. It will be saved under the same filename and to the same file folder and will overwrite previously saved information.

21. Module 2 is complete. Move on to Module 3.

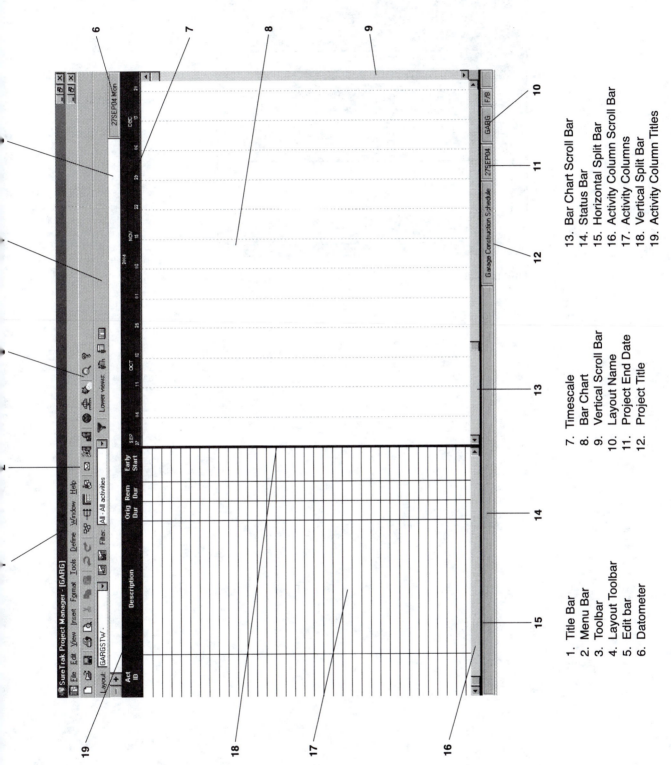

1. Title Bar
2. Menu Bar
3. Toolbar
4. Layout Toolbar
5. Edit bar
6. Datometer

7. Timescale
8. Bar Chart
9. Vertical Scroll Bar
10. Layout Name
11. Project End Date
12. Project Title

13. Bar Chart Scroll Bar
14. Status Bar
15. Horizontal Split Bar
16. Activity Column Scroll Bar
17. Activity Columns
18. Vertical Split Bar
19. Activity Column Titles

FIGURE M2.7

247

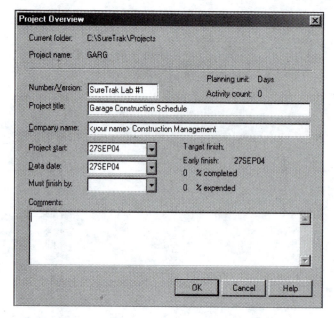

FIGURE M2.8

MODULE **3**

Adding Activities

Preface: At this point, you have created and saved the project.

In this module, you will learn how to input the project activities in various ways, change activity IDs, use the spellcheck feature of the software, and change activity types.

You will continue with GARG project, the garage construction schedule. The project window should be visible on your screen if you are continuing from Module 2.

1. The project window is the main screen of the software (see Figure M2.7 for a description of the various components of this window). This is where nearly all your work in the software will occur. The spreadsheet on the left is where the activities and other data go and the open field on the right is where the activity bars will appear. You will input the activities of the project into the spreadsheet section on the left.

2. Using the hand-drawn schedule you drew in Module 1, input the activities for the garage construction schedule project. For the exact activity descriptions, refer back to Table M1.1 in Module 1. Type the descriptions exactly how they are shown in the Table M1.1. Pay close attention to caps, abbreviations, and spaces.

   Activities can be entered a couple of different ways, including directly onto the spreadsheet, which seems to be the quickest way to enter activities.

   This is how we will do it. Start by clicking the [+] button in the upper left-hand corner. The first activity ID will appear (1000). Change the activity ID to **10** by highlighting it as shown in Figure M3.1 and deleting the two zeros.

   Then click [✔] to accept this ID. Activity IDs can be up to ten alphanumeric characters. Each activity in the schedule must have a unique activity ID.

   Next click in the description cell and type in the activity description, **Notice to Proceed.** Activity descriptions can be up to forty-eight characters long. How you type the description here is how it will appear on the

   schedule—so be careful with spelling and capitalizations. Click [✔] to

Act ID	Description	Orig Dur	Rem Dur	Early Start	SEP 27
1000		1	1	27SEP04	

FIGURE M3.1

249

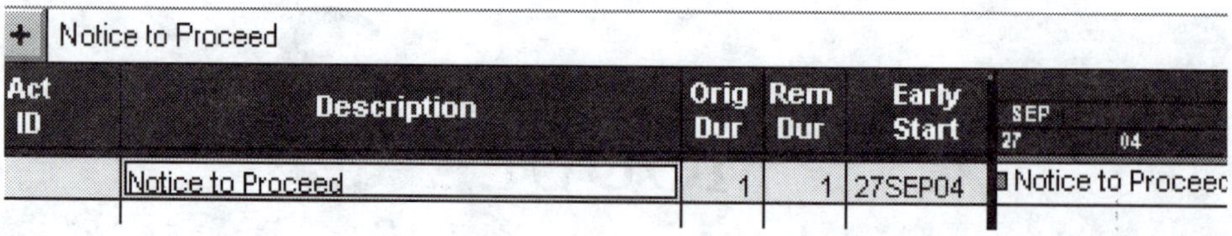

+	Notice to Proceed					
Act ID	Description	Orig Dur	Rem Dur	Early Start	SEP 27	04
	Notice to Proceed	1	1	27SEP04	▫ Notice to Proceec	

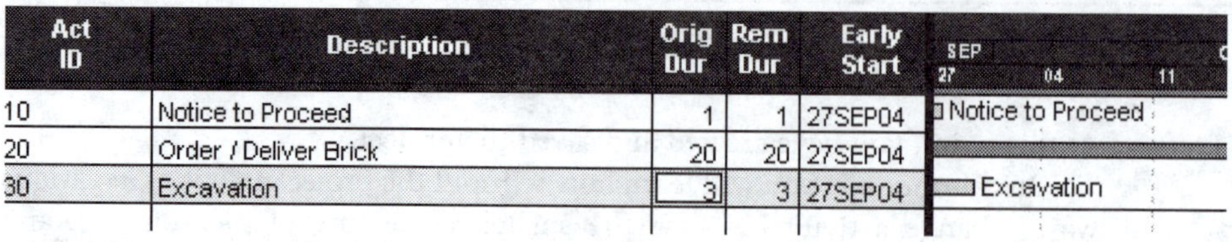

FIGURE M3.2

Act ID	Description	Orig Dur	Rem Dur	Early Start	SEP 27	04	11
10	Notice to Proceed	1	1	27SEP04	▫ Notice to Proceed		
20	Order / Deliver Brick	20	20	27SEP04			
30	Excavation	3	3	27SEP04	▫ Excavation		

FIGURE M3.3

accept this description. For now leave the original duration as is. This first activity should look like Figure M3.2.

3. Click the ➕ button to bring up the next activity ID. Notice activity ID 20 automatically comes up. SureTrak automatically generates activity IDs in increments of 10. Type in the description **Order / Deliver Brick** into the description cell. Click into the Orig Dur (original duration) cell and input the duration of 20 for this activity. Click ✔ to accept this duration.

4. Enter the next activity, activity ID 30, **Excavation**, 3 day duration. The first three activities will look like those in Figure M3.3.

(F.Y.I.)   SureTrak automatically generates activity IDs in increments of 10:

- You can change the activity increment by going to Tools, Options . . . then to the Default tab.

- The increment can be changed in this field   Increase activity ID by: [10] .

- You can also overwrite the activity ID by simply typing over it.

Enter the remainder of the activities of the garage schedule with the exception of #15—Project Management, which we will enter last in the next step. You might find it quicker to first enter all the activity IDs, then all their descriptions, and then all their durations. To do this, click in activity #30's ID cell, then hit the down arrow (⬇) on your keyboard (or click the ➕ button) until all the IDs come up through activity ID #140, as shown in Figure M3.4. If you happen to click too many times and accidentally add an extra activity, simply highlight the unwanted activity and click the ➖ button (or the Delete key on the keyboard), then say [Yes] to delete the activity.

Go back up to the description cell next to activity ID #40 and type in the description (Footing and Foundation). You can just hit the down arrow on your keyboard to get to the next description cell so you *don't* have to keep clicking

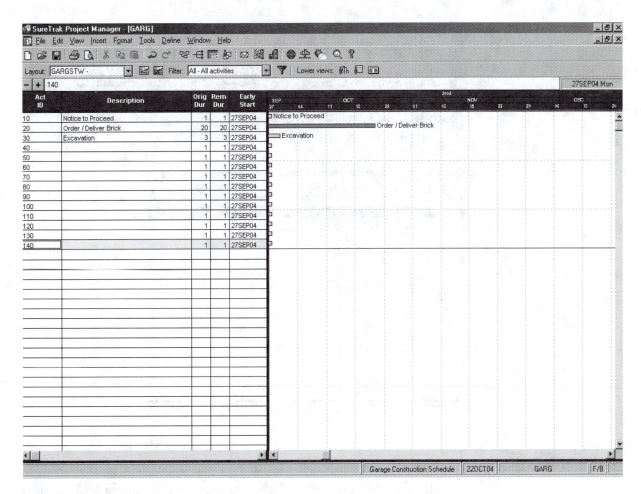

FIGURE M3.4

the button after each entry. Enter the remainder of the descriptions, and then the durations in a similar manner after that.

5. The last activity to enter is #15—Project Management. Click the ⊞ button to add another activity. Notice activity #150 comes up. Click in the activity ID cell (150) and change the activity ID from 150 to 15. Notice that the software automatically places this activity numerically between 10 and 20. Enter **Proj. Mngt.** as the activity description—you'll see later why we abbreviated it. Leave the duration as is. All the activities for the garage schedule are now entered as shown in Figure M3.5. However, the schedule is not complete, as it currently shows all the activities starting at the same time. Since the computer does not know what activities follow what (called the logic of the schedule), it still has to be input. You will add the logic to the schedule in Module 4, but first there are a few more things to do.

(F.Y.I.) Activity information can also be entered in other ways:

■ Activity information can be entered in the activity form, the place where most other data relating to the activities is input. There are many ways to turn it on. Go to View, Activity Form *or* hit the F7 key, which acts as a toggle switch, *or* click the 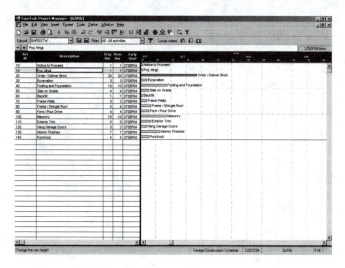 button, *or* double-click on any activity. Once it's turned on, you can click the **More >>** button to see additional fields.

■ Activity information can also be copied and pasted from other projects (we'll do this later in Module 24) or from an Excel spreadsheet—provided the column headings match up and are in the proper order.

FIGURE M3.5

USING SPELLCHECK

6. After the activities are entered, check your spelling by going to Tools, Custom Tools, then Excel Spellcheck. The item Activity Descriptions should already be highlighted. If not, highlight it and then click the **>>** button to select it, as shown in Figure M3.6. Click OK to run the spellcheck until it is complete. You may want to add certain words like Punchout to the dictionary.

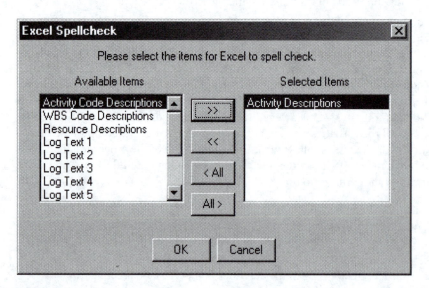

FIGURE M3.6

7. SureTrak has seven different activity types that serve different purposes. We will use many of them as we go through the various exercises in this text. The default activity type is either *task* or *independent*, depending on what was selected when the software was loaded. We set the default to *task* early on, in Module 2. Two other activity types that we will use on the Garage Schedule are Start Milestone and Hammock. A start milestone is an activity with zero duration that simply signifies the start of a major event or phase, or any other important point in your project. We will make the Notice to Proceed activity a start milestone. A hammock is an activity that is strung between the beginning and end of a group of activities. The duration of the hammock depends on the duration of the group. We will make the Proj. Mngt. activity a hammock activity that goes from start to finish on the project; that is, it will start when Notice to Proceed starts and finish when Punchout finishes.

   Change the Activity Type for activity 10 and 15. We'll do this in the Activity Form.

   ■ Turn on the Activity Form by going to Ⅴiew, then Ạctivity Form, hit the F7 key, or click the 🖾 button.

   ■ We will need to view the additional fields of the Activity Form to get to the Act. Type field, so click the **More >>** button.

   ■ Highlight the Notice to Proceed activity by clicking on its description. Click in the Act. Type *field,* then click the pull-down menu to see the seven activity types as shown in Figure M3.7.

   ■ Select Start milestone, then click the OK button in the activity form. Notice that the duration turned to "0" and the bar on the chart turned to an orange diamond, as shown in Figure M3.8.

   ■ Using the same process, change Proj. Mngt. to a **Hammock** activity. Notice, as shown in Figure M3.8, that the Proj. Mngt. bar turned to a blue line equal to the longest activity on the project and its duration went to 20* with an asterisk. The asterisk indicates that the duration is controlled by the project's duration.

8. Module 3 is now complete. It is a good idea to periodically save the project to the hard drive, particularly after you have completed a particular project task like adding activities. So, save the garage schedule project to the hard drive. Remember, to save the project to the hard drive (under the same filename and to the same file folder), go to Ḟile, then Ṣave, or simply click the 💾 button. This will save the project and changes you have made up to that point and overwrite previously saved information. For more specific information on saving, see Module 6.

Currently the computer thinks that all the activities start on the first day of the project (look at the bars on the schedule), so you will have to tell the computer what follows what—that is, the logic of the schedule—covered next in Module 4.

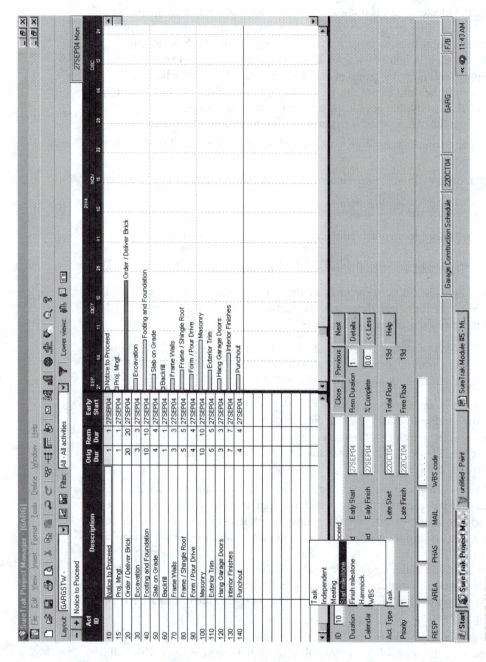

FIGURE M3.7

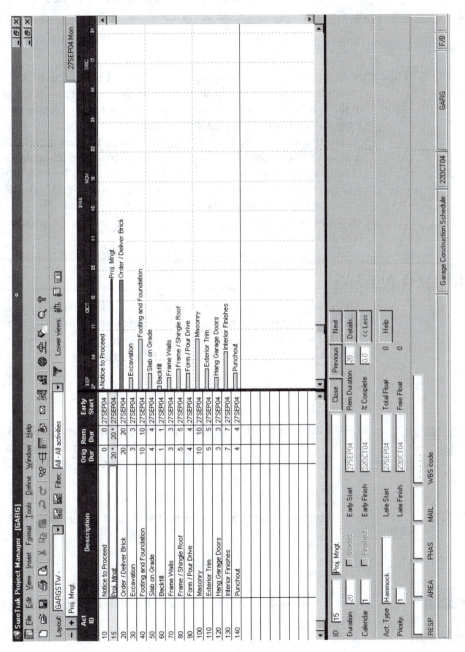

FIGURE M3.8

MODULE 4

Adding Logic (Successors)

Preface: At this point, you have entered in all of the schedule activities. Currently the computer thinks that all the activities start on the first day of the project (look at the bars on the schedule), so you will have to tell the computer what follows what—that is, input the logic of the schedule.

In this module, you will learn about the four different relationship types and something called lag, how to input the logic of the schedule using the successors window, and how to turn on the relationship lines. Additionally, you will learn how to add buttons (icons) to the toolbar and learn how to create *screen-captures* of screens that you might want to keep as a way of taking notes on the software. You will continue using **GARG project**, the garage construction schedule.

RELATIONSHIP TYPES AND LAG

1. Before we add the logic to the schedule, we need to review the four types of activity relationships. The four types of logical relationships that activities can have are shown and briefly explained in Figure M4.1. A full explanation of the relationship types can be found in Chapter 5.

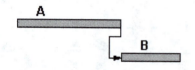

Finish-to-Start (FS) - When activty A finishes, activty B will start. This is the traditional relationship type and is the default type in SureTrak.

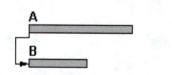

Start-to-Start (SS) - Activity B will start when activity A starts.

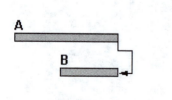

Finish-to-Finish (FF) - Activity B finishes when activity A finishes.

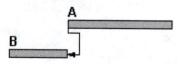

Start-to-Finish (SF) - Activty B cannot finish until activity A starts. This relationship type is very rarely used.

FIGURE M4.1

256

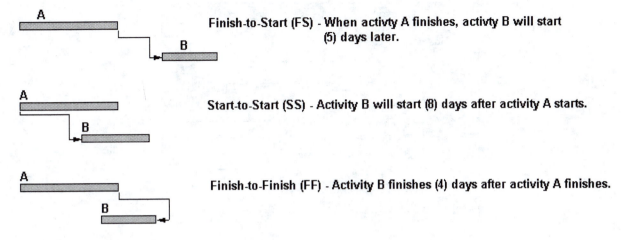

FIGURE M4.2

Activities normally follow each other immediately. As an example, in the Finish-to-Start relationship in Figure M4.1, when activity A finishes, activity B can begin immediately. There is no extra time or *lag* time in-between each activity. Figure M4.2 shows the three most common relationship types, but now with a lag time in each.

ADDING LOGIC

2. The logic of the garage schedule is shown on the hand-drawn schedule created in Module 1 (see Figure M1.1). Inputting logic must be done very carefully. If the logic is input incorrectly, the schedule will be inaccurate and unreliable *and* it may be difficult to find the reason why. That is why it is important to draw the schedule freehand first on a big piece of paper and input the logic from that into the SureTrak schedule. Remember the computer does not know if the logic of the schedule is wrong and therefore can't tell you where a mistake might be located. Using the hand-drawn schedule from Module 1 (Figure M1.1), prepare to input the logic into the SureTrak schedule.

3. There are a couple different ways to input logic in SureTrak. We will use the Successors window. I think it is the best method to use to avoid mistakes. Go to Underline{V}iew, Activity Underline{D}etail, and then to Underline{S}uccessors to open this window (Figure M4.3). Highlight the first activity (Notice to Proceed). Notice that that activity appears in the Successors window. Click the ⊞ button to input the first successor, and then click the pull-down button ▾, to see all the activities. The activities seem to be out of order, but they are actually in numeric order. Select activity 15—Proj. Mngt., as shown in Figure M4.3. Notice that the relationship type defaulted to SS—Start to Start. Hammock activities normally have Start-to-Start and Finish-to-Finish relationships on their front and back; therefore, SureTrak sets those as the default relationship types on each side for hammock activities.

4. Using the same process, add activity 20—Order / Deliver Brick and activity 30—Excavation as successors to Notice to Proceed. It does not matter which one gets added first. When complete, the Successors window for Notice to Proceed should look like the one in Figure M4.4.

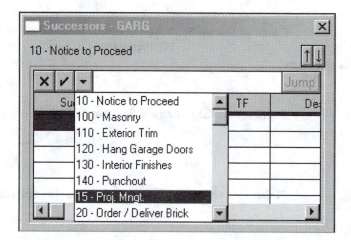

FIGURE M4.3

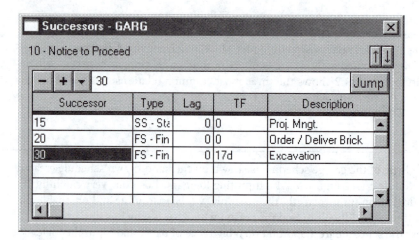

FIGURE M4.4

5. Click the ↓ button in the successors window to move down to the next activity, 15—Proj. Mngt. It is always best to input logic in the order that the activities are laid out—from top to bottom, rather than jumping around. This will help make sure that you do not miss an activity. Therefore, always use the

   ↓ button to move down through the activities. The successor of Proj. Mngt. is the last activity of the project, 140— Punchout, so add Punchout as its successor. Notice that the relationship type defaulted to Finish-to-Finish.

6. Click the ↓ button to move down to the next activity, 20—Order / Deliver Brick. Input its successor (Masonry). Using the hand-drawn schedule, input the successors to the remainder of the activities. Notice that as you enter the successors, the bars start to move around and the schedule changes. This is because the Automatic Schedule Calculation feature is turned on. You need not pay attention to this while entering the successors.

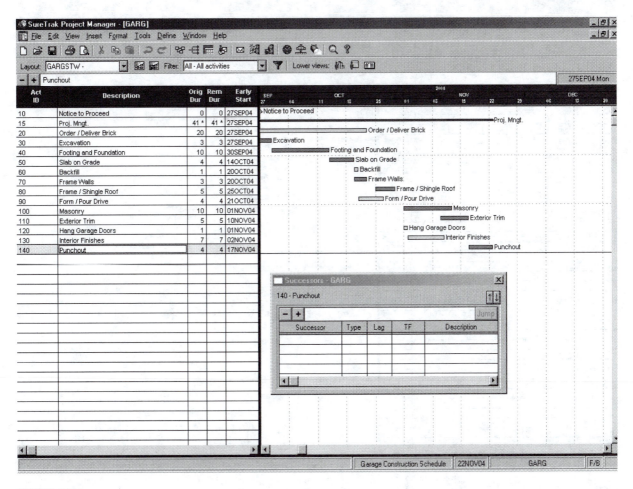

FIGURE M4.5

7. Note that one of the two successors of Masonry is 110—Exterior Trim and that it has a **SS—Start to Start** relationship with a **7**-day lag. Make sure you enter it that way. Also note that the last activity, 140 — Punchout, has no successors.

8. After you have entered all the successors of the schedule, it is a good idea to review all the activities' successors to make sure they are correct. The finish date for the project should be 22NOV04, which can be found on the bottom right-hand side of the schedule. Additionally, the duration of the Proj. Mngt. activity should be 41. If yours is different, check to make sure the durations are correct and recheck the successors. Your schedule should look like the one in Figure M4.5. If it does, move on to instruction #10. If all the activities are still lined up at the start date, go to instruction #9.

9. Your schedule should look like the one in Figure M4.5. If it does, move on to instruction #10. If all the activities are still lined up at the start date, continue with this instruction.

   As mentioned in step 6, the activity bars should automatically align themselves in the timescale according to the logic. If they didn't and they are still lined up at the start date, this automatic feature is not turned on.

   To calculate the schedule, click the Schedule icon ![icon]. The schedule now should look like Figure M4.5. To turn on this automatic feature for

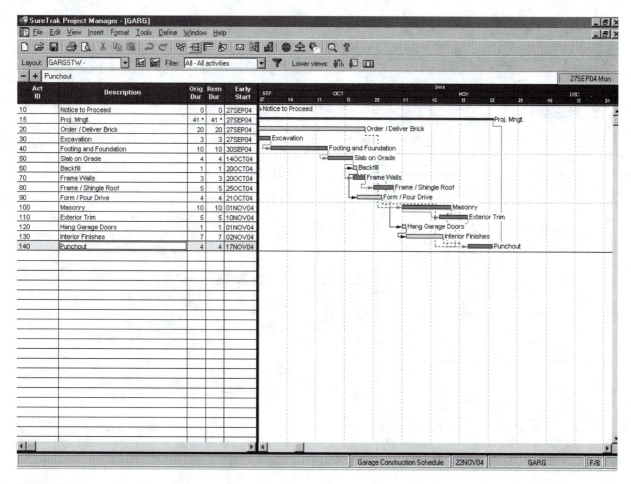

FIGURE M4.6

future schedules, go to Tools, then Schedule . . . , and in the bottom of the schedule window, turn On the Automatic Schedule Calculation. Click OK.

10. Close the Successors window.

11. Turn on the relationship lines by clicking the ⊞ button. These lines show the logical connection between activities. Some people think they clutter the schedule up too much. To turn them off, simply click the icon again. With the relationship lines turned on and the Successors window closed, the schedule should look like Figure M4.6.

The garage construction schedule is complete! Take a look at the screen and see if the schedule makes sense to you. Compare it to the hand-drawn schedule that it was based on. Which one communicates the construction information better?

Everything that you do to the schedule from this point on utilizes additional software features that make the schedule look different or reflect different information about the work. However, the three components that are necessary to schedule, *activities, duration,* and *logic,* are not changed or affected by these other features. Before you move on to the next module, add the Successors Detail button (icon) to the toolbar using the directions in the next section.

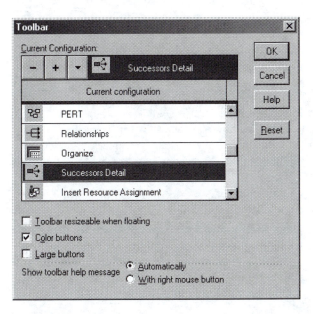

FIGURE M4.7

ADDING BUTTONS (ICONS) TO THE TOOLBAR

12. You may want to add buttons (icons) to the toolbar for frequently used menu-driven tasks. An example is the Successors Detail button which opens and closes the Successors window. It is currently *not* on the toolbar. To add it to the toolbar, go to Tools, Customize, then Toolbar . . . to open the Toolbar window. The current configuration of the toolbar is shown. Scroll down to

the 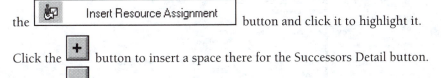 button and click it to highlight it.

Click the button to insert a space there for the Successors Detail button.

Click the to pull-down and select (click) the Successors Detail button

. The Toolbar window should look like Figure M4.7. Leave the other settings as is, and click OK. The Successors Detail button should now appear on the toolbar.

(F.Y.I.)

You may want to develop your own screen-capture or window-capture training documents to help you remember details about the software. They are easy to create. Follow the instructions below.

- Go to the screen *or* window you want to capture. Click on any particular items you want highlighted, as I've shown in the following examples. I have highlighted the menu path you need to take to open the Successors window in Figure M4.8 and highlighted the Proj. Mngt. activity in the Successors window in Figure M4.9.

- When highlighted, hit the *Print Screen* key on the keyboard to capture the entire screen *or* to capture just the active window on the screen, hold down the *Alt* key on your keyboard and hit the *Print Screen* key. This will capture whichever window is active.

- Next, open up 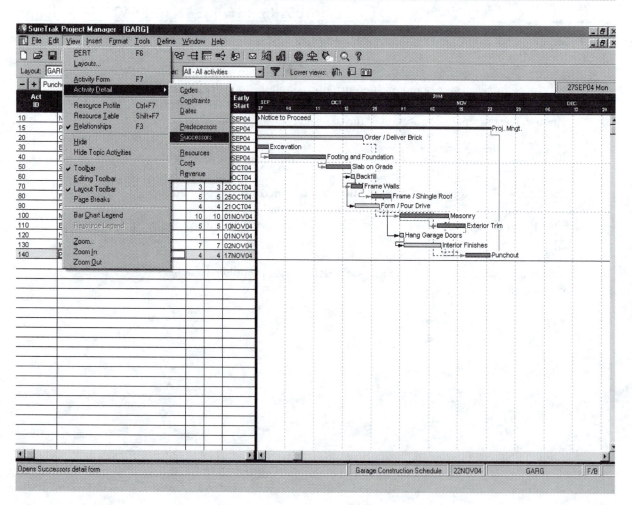 Microsoft Word and click the button to create a new document.

- Paste the capture onto the new document by clicking the button.

- Add any notes you may want to the document and you are done.

FIGURE M4.8

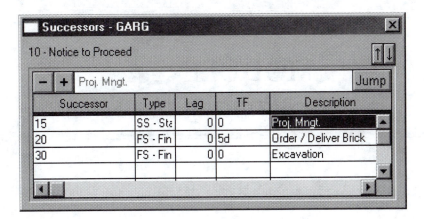

FIGURE M4.9

CREATING SCREEN-CAPTURES AND WINDOW-CAPTURES

13. Module 4 is complete. Save the garage schedule project to the hard drive by clicking the 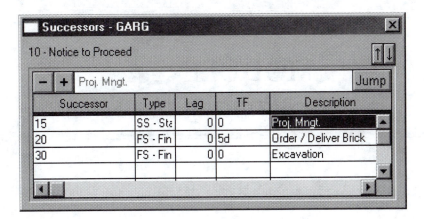 button.

MODULE 5
Printing the Schedule

Preface: At this point, the garage schedule is complete. The next step is to print the schedule.

In this module, you will learn how to print preview and print out a schedule. You will print out the garage construction schedule.

PRINTING THE SCHEDULE

1. You can print the schedule from the project window or from the Print Preview. However, it is always best to preview the schedule before printing because that is the only way to see the full schedule on the screen at one time. You will be able to verify that it looks the way you want it to look and that it is on the number of pages you prefer. To preview the schedule, click the ⬚ button, or go to File, Print Preview (Figure M5.1).

2. Zoom in on the schedule by clicking the ⬚ button, or going to View, Zoom In, *or* by clicking anywhere on the schedule (notice that the cursor turns into a magnifying glass when hovering over the schedule). To zoom back out to the original view, click the ⬚ *View single page* button or go to View, Single Page.

3. Look at the garage schedule in the print preview. Notice the titles, dates, and legend in the footer.

4. To print a schedule from the print preview, go to File Print . . ., or simply click the ⬚ button. To print a schedule from the project window, go to

---

(F.Y.I.)

■ Often schedules will appear on multiple pages. If the *View page* buttons are lit up as shown here ◄ ► ▲ ▼ , then you know there are multiple pages. To see all the pages at once, click the ⬚ *View all pages* button. To view individual pages click the ⬚ *View single page* button.

File, Print . . ., or simply click the 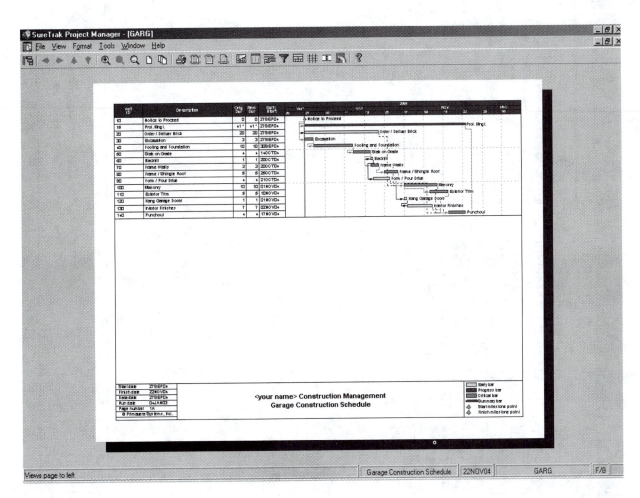 button. Print the garage schedule. The garage construction schedule printout is shown in Figure M5.2.

5. Click the (Bar Chart) button to get back to the Bar Chart view in the project window.

6. Module 5 is complete. Save the garage schedule project and answer the questions in the *Schedule Analysis—Modules 1–5* before moving on to Module 6. Turn the Schedule Analysis in to your instructor along with the schedule printout.

FIGURE M5.1

Act ID	Description	Orig Dur	Rem Dur	Early Start
10	Notice to Proceed	0	0	27SEP04
15	Proj. Mngt.	41 *	41 *	27SEP04
20	Order / Deliver Brick	20	20	27SEP04
30	Excavation	3	3	27SEP04
40	Footing and Foundation	10	10	30SEP04
50	Slab on Grade	4	4	14OCT04
60	Backfill	1	1	20OCT04
70	Frame Walls	3	3	20OCT04
80	Frame / Shingle Roof	5	5	25OCT04
90	Form / Pour Drive	4	4	21OCT04
100	Masonry	10	10	01NOV04
110	Exterior Trim	5	5	10NOV04
120	Hang Garage Doors	1	1	01NOV04
130	Interior Finishes	7	7	02NOV04
140	Punchout	4	4	17NOV04

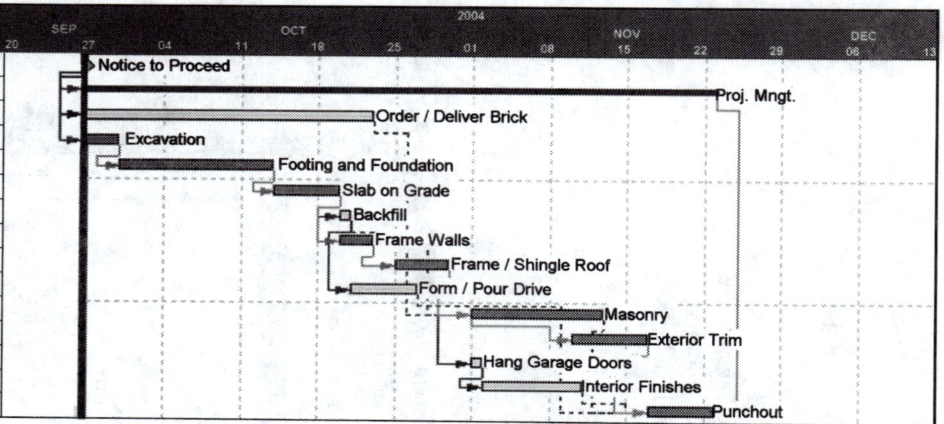

<your name> Construction Management
Garage Construction Schedule

Start date	27SEP04
Finish date	22NOV04
Data date	27SEP04
Run date	23FEB04
Page number	1A
© Primavera Systems, Inc.	

Legend:
- Early bar
- Progress bar
- Critical bar
- Summary bar
- ◇ Start milestone point
- ◇ Finish milestone point

FIGURE M5.2

SCHEDULE ANALYSIS
Garage Construction Schedule

Name _____

After completing Modules 1 through 5, answer the following questions from the schedule printout and Bar Chart view. Turn the Schedule Analysis in to your instructor along with the schedule printout.

1. What is the end date of the project? _____

   State where the end date is shown in the following three areas of the schedule:

   - *Bar Chart screen* _____
   - *Print preview* _____
   - *Within schedule data* _____

2. What is the total project duration? _____

   Where on the schedule did you find this? _____

   Is that in **workdays** *or* **calendar days** (circle one)?

3. Name the smallest timescale increment shown on the schedule:

   Days, Weeks, or **Months?**

4. What sightlines are shown on the schedule:

   Vertical or **Horizontal** or **Both?**

   If vertical, at what interval are they placed? _____

   If horizontal, at what interval are they placed? _____

5. Are the activities graphically connected to each other?

   Yes   No

6. What work is being performed on the fourth week of the project (*list by activity IDs*)?

   _____

7. How can you tell which activities are critical?

   _____

8. List all the critical activities of the schedule (*list by activity IDs*).

   _____

9. Where do you go to change the name and title that appear on the bottom of the schedule in the title box?

   _____

MODULE 6
Saving and Closing a Project

Preface: At this point, you have created and printed the project, and saved it to the hard drive. In this module, you will learn more about saving the project.

We will review how to save a project to the hard drive and learn two different ways to save it to a disk. Additionally, you will learn how to save the project under a different name and in a different file folder, how to activate the automatic save feature of the software (and why you might not want to use it!), and how to close a project. You will save the garage construction schedule project from the previous module.

SAVING THE PROJECT TO THE HARD DRIVE

1. Save the garage schedule project to the hard drive. To save the project to the hard drive under the same filename and to the same file folder, go to File, then Save, or simply click the ▢ button. This will save the project and changes you have made up to that point and overwrite previously saved information.

SAVING THE PROJECT TO A DISK

There are two ways to save the project to a disk. The first method is easier but may take several minutes to save (particularly to a floppy diskette). The second is more complicated, but saves in a matter of seconds.

2. *Method One:* To save the project to a disk, go to File, Save As . . . (see Figure M6.1), then click the ▢ Browse... button. Select the ⊞ 3½ Floppy (A:) directory for a floppy diskette *or* the ⊞ ZIP-100 (D:) directory for a zip disk. After selecting the directory, click ▢ OK . Verify that the Current folder: is correct, and then click ▢ OK to save the project. It may take *several minutes* for the schedule to save to the disk, particularly to a floppy diskette. See the next instruction (#3) for a much faster but more complicated way to save the project to a disk.

3. *Method Two:* The second method uses Explore—your computer's file manager. It is a bit more complicated but may *save* up to fifteen minutes. To do this, follow these instructions:

   ■ Open up Explore by right-clicking on the ▢ Start button and selecting ▢ Explore .

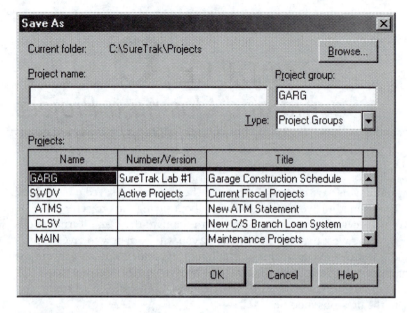

FIGURE M6.1

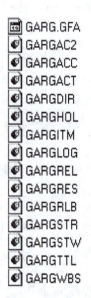

FIGURE M6.2

- Go to the directory folder that you set the project up in. There you should find fifteen (15) files (see Figure M6.2). If they are not arranged this way, go to <u>V</u>iew and click <u>L</u>ist with the project name (GARG) as the prefix.

- Highlight them by single-clicking the top file, then, while holding the *Shift* key on your keyboard down, single-click the bottom file. Release the *Shift* key and the mouse—they should remain highlighted.

- Drag-and-drop the files by single-clicking (and holding) the files anywhere in the highlighted area and dragging them over onto the diskette until it highlights as shown in Figure M6.3, then releasing (dropping) them.

FIGURE M6.3

- They should copy over in about one minute.

- After they copy, you can check the diskette to make sure the files are there by double-clicking on that directory.

- Your instructor can help you with this procedure, if need be.

(F.Y.I.)

This second method of saving the project through Explore can be used to save any type of file to a diskette.

SAVING THE PROJECT UNDER A DIFFERENT NAME

4. At some point, you may want to save the project under a different name. You can create a new project that is an exact copy of the active project as it exists at the moment. You may want to do this for the following reasons:

- To create a copy, with a different name, of the project so you can perform *what if* project scenarios. The different scenarios are performed on the copy and the original *uncontaminated* schedule is left intact.

- To create updates to the project such as monthly updates. In this case you will copy and rename the previous month's project and update it accordingly. *Note:* Since you are confined to a four-character project name for each update, you might want to adopt a naming convention such as using the same two letters to identify the project, followed by two numbers to identify the updates. As an example, GR01, GR02, GR03, and so on for garage schedule 01, garage schedule 02, garage schedule 03, and so on.

- To create a new schedule that is similar to the one you have created in the past, rather than starting from scratch, you could open and rename the project and make changes accordingly.

To save the project under a different name, go to File, Save As . . ., and enter the new filename in the Project name: field. Verify the Current folder: is correct and the Type field says

Project Groups. Click [OK] .

SAVING THE PROJECT TO A DIFFERENT FOLDER

5. To save the project into a different file folder, use the File, Save As . . .

command and simply [Browse...] to change the folder. Verify the project

name, then click [OK] .

AUTOMATIC SAVE FEATURE (AND A WORD ABOUT THE UNDO ↩ AND REDO ↪ BUTTONS)

SureTrak has an automatic save feature that will save the project at time intervals that you can set. I would strongly suggest that you *do not use* this feature—and here's why. Occasionally, when working with the schedule, you might make a mistake and not know how it happened or how to fix it. You cannot count on the *Undo* button to fix it. There are many ways to reverse errant clicks, typing, and other erroneous data. But if you need to undo numerous or deep changes to the schedule, it is sometimes easiest to close the project without saving the changes and then re-open it. While this may take extra time, at least you are back to the point before the mistake. If the automatic save feature is turned on, these changes might have been inadvertently saved.

The undo and redo features in the software are unpredictable and not reliable. They don't always undo the last thing you did and can cause trouble. For that reason, I would not suggest using these buttons.

CLOSING THE PROJECT

You should always save before you close the project unless you do not want the changes you made to be saved. When you close the project without saving, if you have made

changes, you will be prompted by the question in Figure M6.4. If you click [Yes] ,

the project will be saved, as is, to the default folder. If you answer [No] , the changes you made to the project since opening it or previously saving will not be saved.

6. Close the garage construction schedule and save changes, if necessary. Move on to Module 7.

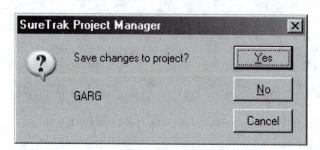

FIGURE M6.4

MODULE 7
Opening a Project

Preface: At this point, you have created and saved the project, then closed it.

In this module, you will learn how to open a project.

If you are continuing from Module 6, you will re-open the garage construction schedule project following the directions below. These directions will also apply to opening any other project you have created in SureTrak.

1. Whenever you open any project in SureTrak, *always* open it from the hard drive. This will ensure that you will be working from the hard drive and not the floppy. The software runs considerably faster when the project is opened from the hard drive.

2. Open the garage construction schedule project (GARG) by going to File, then

   Open . . . , or simply clicking the [icon] button. The Open Project window should appear as in Figure M7.1. Check the Current folder: at the top of the window to make sure you are opening the project from the hard drive.

   Browse... , if need be, to get to the correct folder.

3. Make sure that the project type is Project Groups. Since the garage schedule project was created as a project group, *it can only be found under this project type. Note: A common mistake made when students can't find their projects is that they don't have the correct project type selected in this window.* If project group is not selected as the project type, click the pull-down menu to select it, as shown in Figure M7.2.

4. With Project Groups selected as the project type, scroll down until you find the GARG project. To open it, either double-click it *or* single-click it and then click OK. The project will open and the bar chart view will be visible in the project window on your screen. If you have difficulties opening the project, ask your instructor for help.

5. Review the re-opened garage schedule. When you open an existing project, SureTrak displays the activities and other project information as they were last arranged, and saved, in the project window. This arrangement is known as a layout. Layouts control the project window contents and the appearance of each item. You will learn more about layouts in Module 10.

6. Close the garage schedule. Say "No" if prompted to save changes. Move on to Module 8 to start the next schedule—the Delhi Medical Building project.

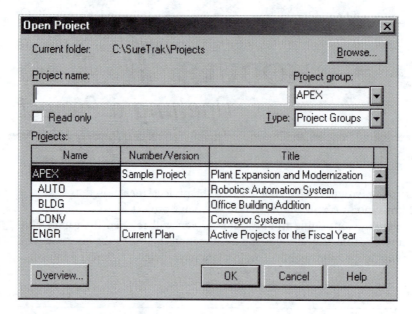

FIGURE M7.1

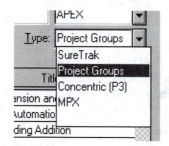

FIGURE M7.2

MODULE 8

Delhi Medical Building— Bid Package Schedule

Preface: At this point, you have created a hand-drawn and computerized CPM schedule with the help of Modules 1 through 7. In this module, you will review what you have learned in Modules 1 through 7 by creating a hand-drawn and computerized schedule for the Delhi Medical Building.

The Delhi Medical Building was the subject of Student Exercises #6 in Chapters 6 and 7 and was used as the sample project in Chapter 8 when the construction schedule was created and revised. The schedule you will be creating in SureTrak in this module is that same bid package schedule. A bid package schedule is the schedule that comes between the very broad milestone schedule and the very detailed construction schedule. It is divided into activities roughly equal to the different trade contracts that will be bid out. It is typically added to the bidding documents, so the bidders will have an idea when their portion of the work will take place.

If you already created the hand-drawn schedule in Chapter 6 of the Bid Package Schedule for the Delhi Medical Building (Student Exercise #6) you can skip instruction #1 below and move directly to #2 (you will need your hand-drawn schedule you created in Student Exercise #6).

DRAW THE SCHEDULE

1. Based on the information below, draw the project's bid package schedule for the Delhi Medical Building by hand. Remember, to create a schedule, you need only three things: *activities, duration,* and *logic*.

There are thirty-nine activities (shown in bold italics) below with their duration, logic, and activity type (if it is other than a task).

Once you have received the **notice to proceed** (milestone activity—0), begin to **mobilize / site layout** (5) and begin the **submittals and approvals** (20) process. Once you are mobilized, begin the **excavation** (10), which will be followed by the **site utility runs** (15). After the submittals are approved you can order / deliver long lead materials (30) and begin to review **coordination drawings** (40). The **footings** (7) will start two days after the excavation starts and will precede the **foundation walls** (20). The **underslab rough-ins** (13) will start ten days after the foundation walls start. The **slab-on-grade** (4) will follow both the underslab rough-ins and the foundation walls. The **1st floor exterior studs** (5) will follow slab-on-grade.

When the first floor exterior studs are complete and the steel, as part of the long lead materials, has arrived, you can **erect steel and slab-on-deck** (14). When this is finished and the slab has cured, you can **backfill** (8), begin the **2nd floor exterior studs** (6), and the **1st floor interior studs** (12). The second floor exterior studs will be followed by **frame and shingle the roof** (19). The **1st floor rough-ins** (27) will start four days after the first floor interior studs start, and after the coordination drawings are complete. The **2nd floor drywall** (11) will follow the rough-ins. The **1st floor interior studs** (11) will start nine days

275

after the roof framing *starts*—by then the sheathing will be down on the roof, but not until the stud crew is done with the first floor interior studs. You can install the **exterior doors and windows** *(5)* after the roof is framed and shingled.

The **masonry** *(25)* can begin after the foundation is backfilled and the exterior doors and windows are installed. The brick is already on site as part of the long lead materials. The **exterior trim, painting, and finishes** *(31)* will start when the masonry is complete. The **storm retention** *(7)* work was started after the site utility runs and the backfill were completed and was followed by the remainder of the **site improvements** *(52)*.

The **2nd floor rough-ins** *(28)* will start four days after the second floor interior studs start. The **2nd floor drywall** *(14)* will follow the second floor rough-ins, the second floor interior studs, and the first floor drywall. The **1st floor prime coat** *(5)* will follow the first floor drywall. When the painters are complete on the first floor, they will move up to paint the **2nd floor prime coat** *(5)* provided the second floor drywall is complete. The **1st floor ceiling grids, doors and hardware, and casework** *(8)* will follow the first floor prime coat. When the carpenters are complete on the first floor, they will move up to begin the **2nd floor ceiling grids, doors and hardware, and casework** *(7)*, provided the second floor prime coat is complete.

When ceiling grids, doors & hardware, and casework are complete on both floors, the **interior trim** *(7)* can begin. When the trim is complete, the **finish paint** *(5)* will begin, followed by the **flooring** *(15)*. The **finish plumbing** *(10)*, **finish electric** *(8)*, and finish HVAC *(8)* for the entire building will follow the second floor ceiling grids, doors & hardware, and casework.

Punchlist *(5)* will follow site improvements, exterior trim, painting, finishes, flooring, and the finish plumbing, electric, and HVAC. **Project management** (**hammock activity— ??**) will start when notice to proceed starts and finish when punchlist finishes. Punchlist is the last activity of the project.

2. When complete, compare your hand-drawn schedule to Figure M8.1a and M8.1b. Follow the logic through your hand-drawn schedule to verify that it is the same.

3. Transfer the activity IDs from Figure M8.1a and M8.1b onto *your* hand-drawn schedule, so the activities match-up when you create the SureTrak schedule.

CREATE THE SURETRAK SCHEDULE

4. Create the SureTrak schedule for the Delhi Medical Building. Make sure that the schedule is placed in the correct folder. To change folders, click the

   Browse... button. The Project name for the schedule should be DMBS. Tab past the Temp_late field. Make sure that Project Groups is selected as the Type. Click

   Day as the Planning unit as shown 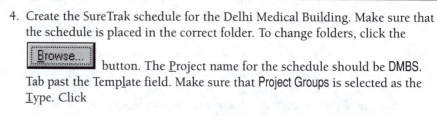 Enter in the Number/Version field Bid Package, and 13APR05 for the Start date, and tab past the Must finish by field. The Project title will be Delhi Medical Building Schedule, and the Company name will be <your name> Construction Management. Then click OK.

5. Input the schedule activities, activity type (if other than Task), durations, and logic from the hand-drawn schedule you created. If need be, refer back to the instructions from Modules 2 through 7. Remember to run spellcheck after you type in the activities. You may want to save the schedule periodically (rather than saving it at the very end) once you complete various stages of input and are sure that they are correct.

6. When complete, turn on the relationship lines and preview the

   schedule from the print preview 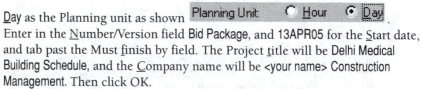. Notice that the schedule is on more than one page both horizontally and vertically. Click the View, All Pages

   button to see all the pages at once. Compare your schedule to Figure M8.2.

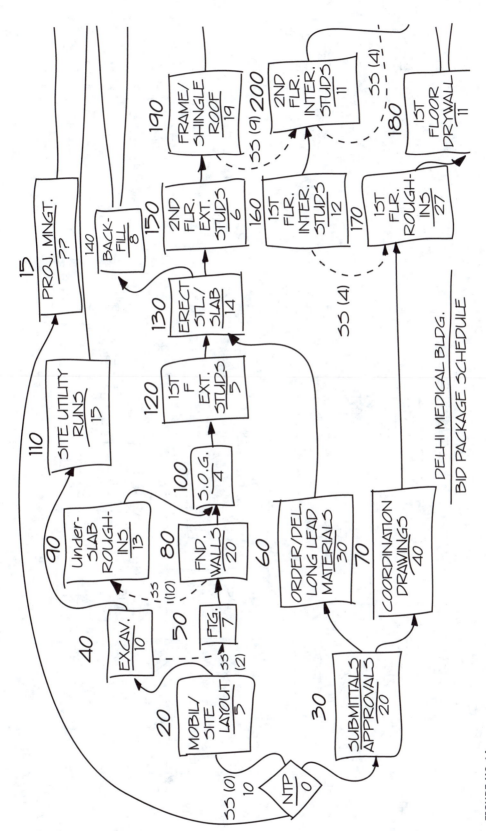

DELHI MEDICAL BLDG.

BID PACKAGE SCHEDULE

FIGURE M8.1A

277

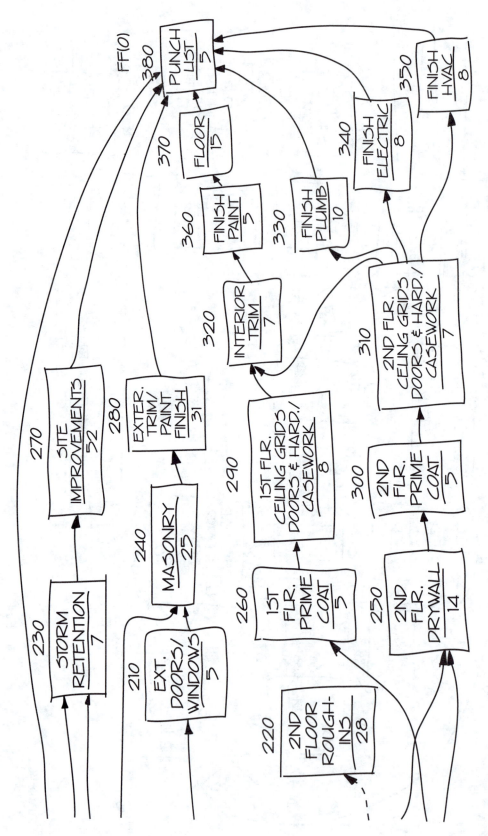

FF(0)

FIGURE M8.1B

278

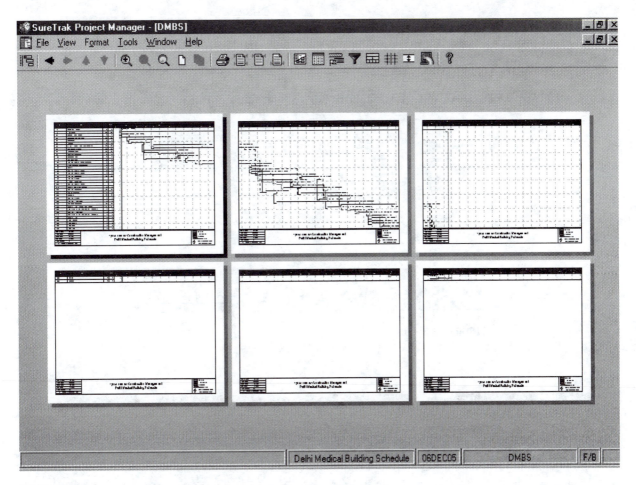

FIGURE M8.2

7. Let's format the schedule to fit on one page vertically, rather than two. We'll do this by changing the height of the footer from the default. Open the page setup window to the **Footer** tab by clicking the ![button] button, or going to File, Page Setup . . . , then clicking the **Footer** tab. See Figure M8.3.

8. In the upper right-hand corner, change the footer **Height:** to 0.50 inches, then click ![OK] .

9. The schedule should be on only one vertical page and still three pages horizontally, as shown in Figure M8.4.

10. Print out the schedule to see how SureTrak handles multipage schedules. The bid package schedule for the Delhi Medical Building is shown in Figures M8.5a through M8.5c. Compare the results of this schedule with the same schedule you manually calculated in Student Exercise 6 at the end of Chapter 7. Is the number of working days the same? Is the critical path the same?

11. Module 8 is complete. Save ![save] the DMBS bid package schedule and move on to Module 9.

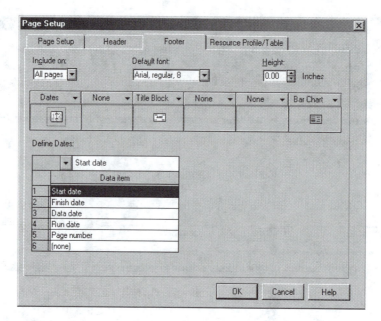

FIGURE M8.3

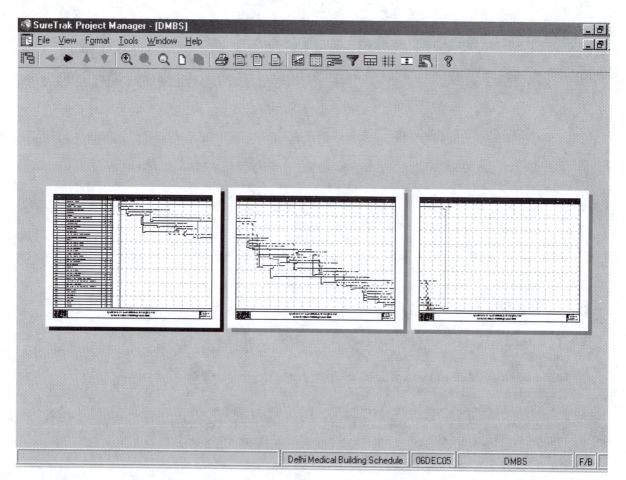

FIGURE M8.4

Act ID	Description	Orig Dur	Rem Dur
10	Notice to Proceed	0	0
15	Proj. Mngt.	169 *	169 *
20	Mobilize / Site Layout	5	5
30	Submittals and Approvals	20	20
40	Excavation	10	10
50	Footings	7	7
60	Order / Deliver Long Lead Materials	30	30
70	Coordination Drawings	40	40
80	Foundation Walls	20	20
90	Underslab Rough-Ins	13	13
100	Slab-on-Grade	4	4
110	Site Utility Runs	15	15
120	1st Floor Exterior Studs/Sheathing	5	5
130	Erect Steel and Slab-on-Deck	14	14
140	Backfill	8	8
150	2nd Floor Exterior Studs	6	6
160	1st Floor Interior Studs	12	12
170	1st Floor Rough-Ins	27	27
180	1st Floor Drywall	11	11
190	Frame / Shingle Roof	19	19
200	2nd Floor Interior Studs	11	11
210	Exterior Doors and Windows	5	5
220	2nd Floor Rough-Ins	28	28
230	Storm Retention	7	7
240	Masonry	25	25
250	2nd Floor Drywall	14	14
260	1st Floor Prime Coat	5	5
270	Site Improvements	52	52
280	Exterior Trim, Painting, and Finishes	31	31
290	1st Flr Clg. Grids, Doors&Hrdwr, Casework	8	8
300	2nd Floor Prime Coat	5	5
310	2nd Flr Clg. Grids, Doors&Hrdwr, Casework	7	7
320	Interior Trim	7	7
330	Finish Plumbing	10	10
340	Finish Electric	8	8
350	Finish HVAC	8	8
360	Finish Paint	5	5
370	Flooring	15	15
380	Punchlist	5	5

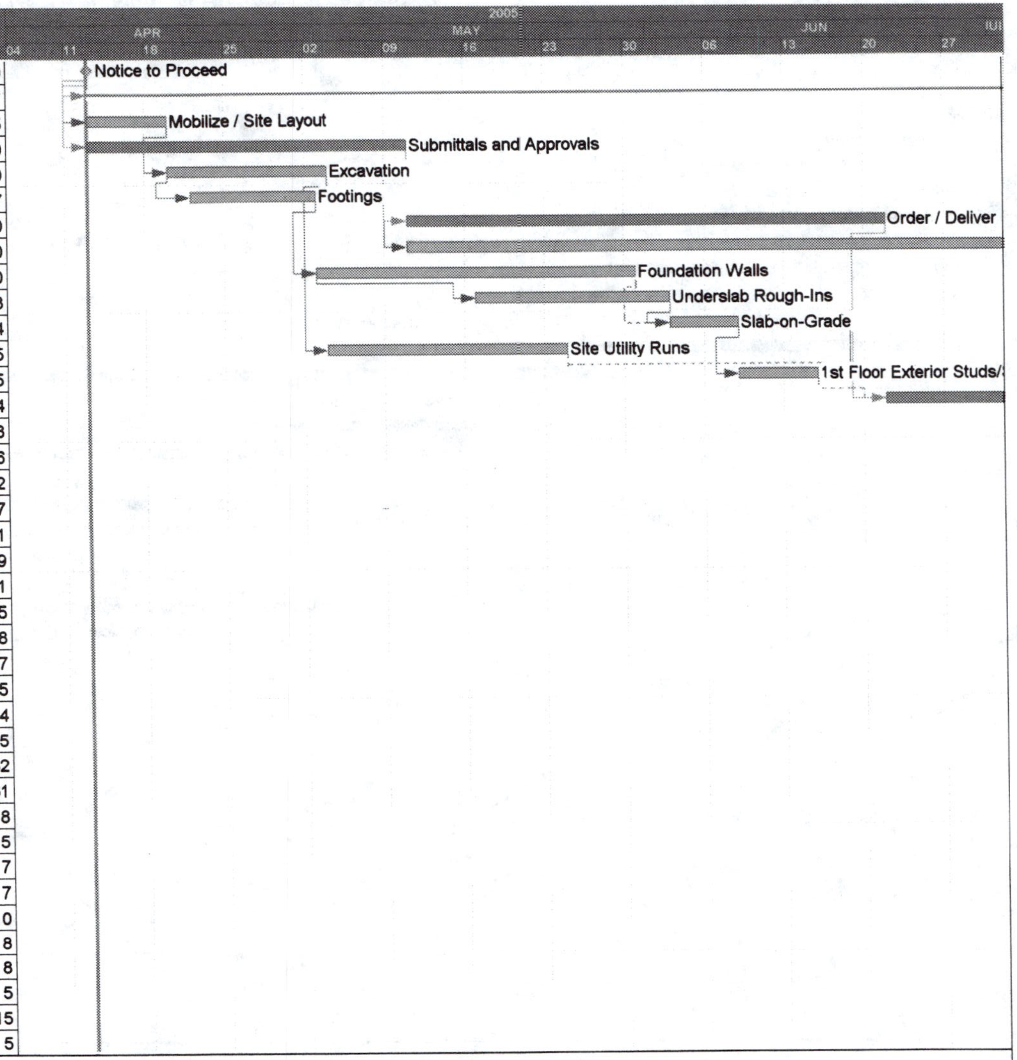

Start date 13APR05
Finish date 06DEC05
Data date 13APR05
Run date 05FEB04
Page number 1A
© Primavera Systems, Inc.

<your name> Construction Management
Delhi Medical Building Schedule

Legend:
- Early bar
- Progress bar
- Critical bar
- Summary bar
- Start milestone point
- Finish milestone point

FIGURE M8.5A

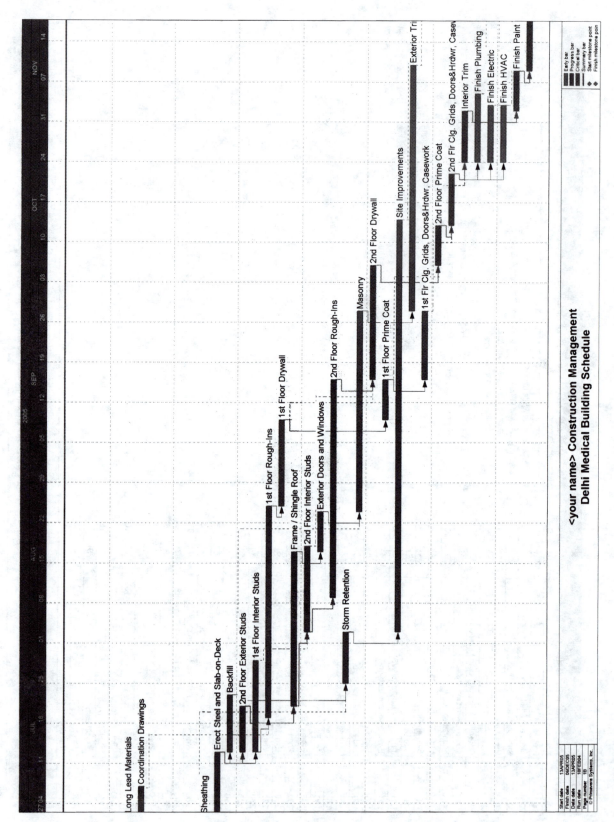

FIGURE M8.5B

<your name> **Construction Management**
Delhi Medical Building Schedule

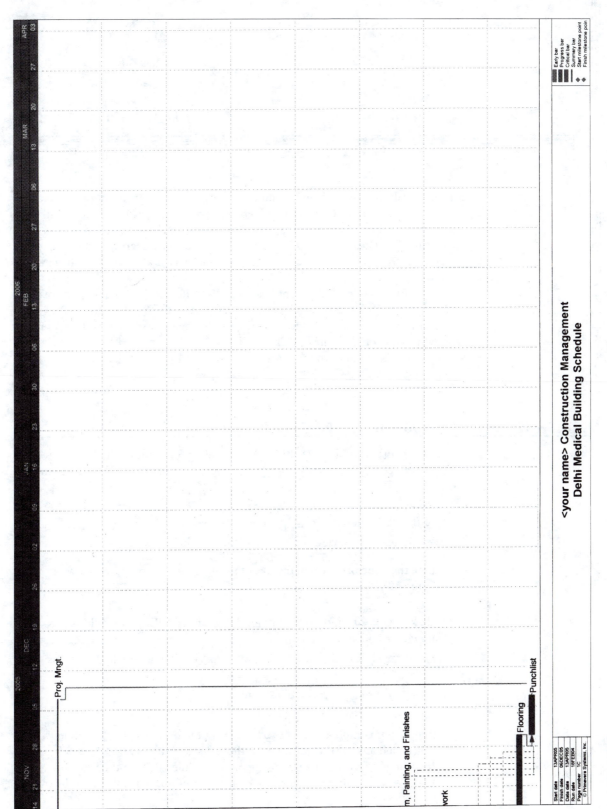

FIGURE M8.5C

283

MODULE 9

The PERT View

Preface: SureTrak can display the schedule two different ways in the project window. The first is the Bar Chart view, which we have been using up to this point. The other is called the PERT view. The PERT view displays the schedule as a diagram of activity boxes and relationship lines in a flowchart manner. This view of the schedule is very much like the hand-drawn schedules we have been working with.

PERT stands for Program Evaluation and Review Techniques and was developed by the Navy in the late 1950s as part of the Polaris Missile Program. PERT is used when you need to focus on the logical sequence of the activities, rather than on the schedule dates.

In this module, you will learn about the PERT view and analyze the Delhi Medical Building schedule in the PERT view.

CHANGING THE PROJECT WINDOW TO THE PERT VIEW

1. Change the view of the Delhi Medical Building Schedule to the PERT view. You can change the view in three ways. Go to View, then PERT, *or* press the

    F6 key on the keyboard, *or* simply click the [button] button. See Figure M9.1 for the PERT view.

2. Go to the print preview [button] to view the schedule. Notice the schedule is on more than one page. Click the [button] button to view all pages, as shown in Figure M9.2.

3. Click the [button] button to print out the multipage PERT schedule as shown in Figures M9.3a through M9.3d.

4. To change back to the bar chart view, go to View, then Bar Chart, *or* press the

    F6 key, *or* simply click the [button] button.

5. Module 9 is complete. Save [button] the Delhi Medical Building Schedule project and answer the questions in the Schedule Analysis—Modules 8–9 from the printed schedule before moving on to Module 10. Turn the Schedule Analysis in to your instructor along with the multipage printouts of the two schedules.

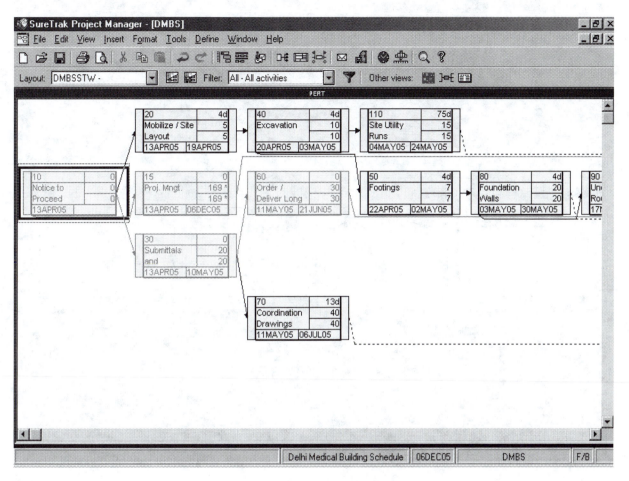

FIGURE M9.1

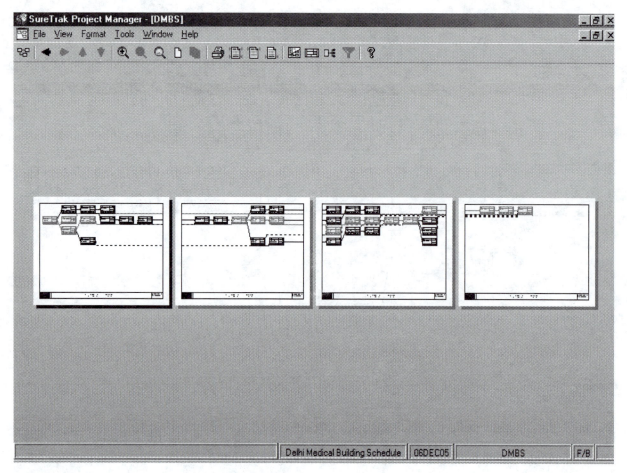

FIGURE M9.2

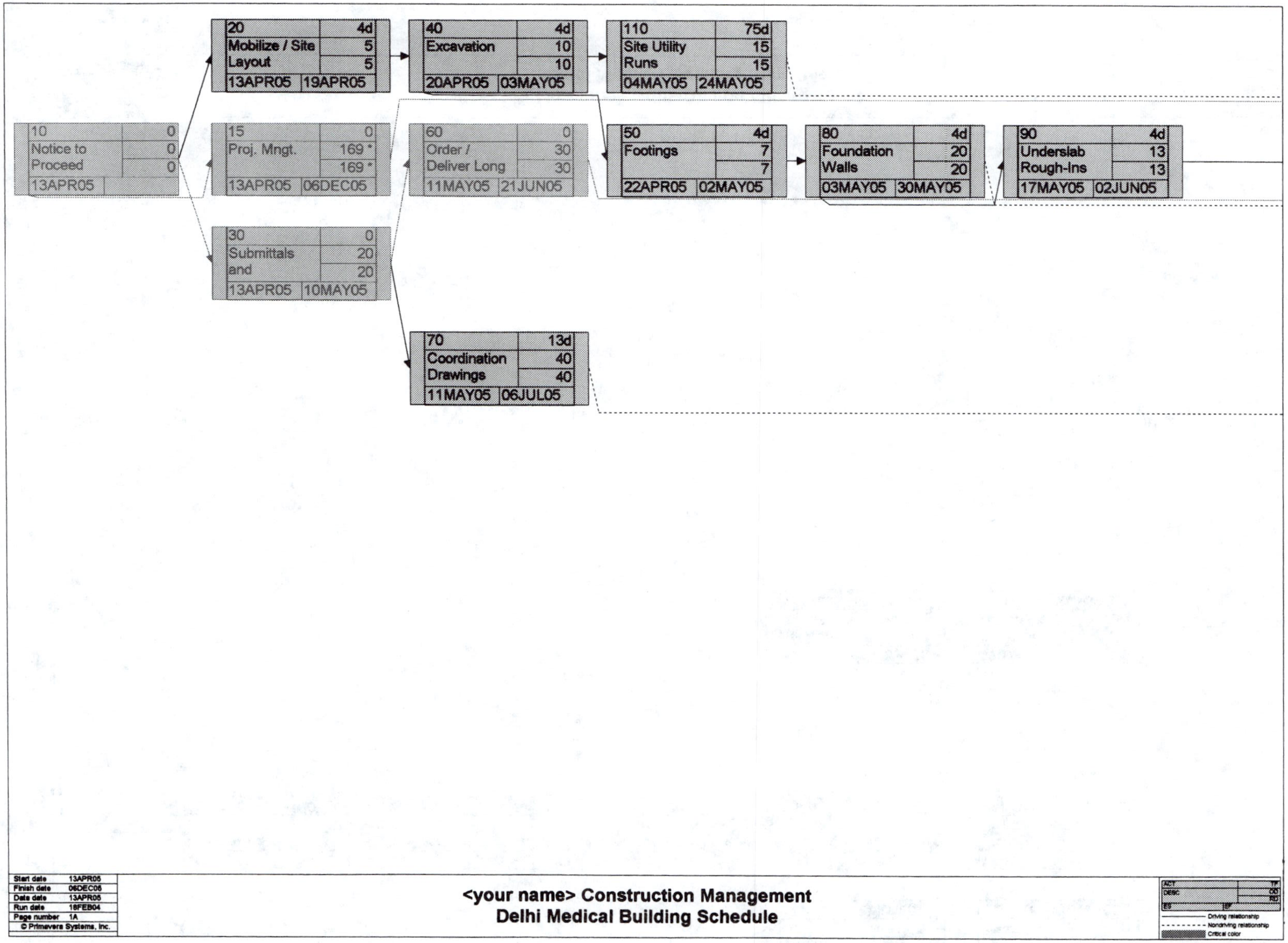

<your name> Construction Management
Delhi Medical Building Schedule

10		0
Notice to		0
Proceed		0
13APR05		

20	4d	5
Mobilize / Site		5
Layout		5
13APR05	19APR05	

40	4d	10
Excavation		10
		10
20APR05	03MAY05	

110	75d	15
Site Utility		15
Runs		15
04MAY05	24MAY05	

15		0
Proj. Mngt.		169 *
		169 *
13APR05	06DEC05	

60		0
Order /		30
Deliver Long		30
11MAY05	21JUN05	

50	4d	7
Footings		7
		7
22APR05	02MAY05	

80	4d	20
Foundation		20
Walls		20
03MAY05	30MAY05	

90	4d	13
Underslab		13
Rough-ins		13
17MAY05	02JUN05	

30		0
Submittals		20
and		20
13APR05	10MAY05	

70	13d	40
Coordination		40
Drawings		40
11MAY05	06JUL05	

Start date	13APR05
Finish date	06DEC05
Data date	13APR05
Run date	18FEB04
Page number	1A
© Primavera Systems, Inc.	

ACT		TF
DESC		OD
ES		EF

----- Driving relationship
---- Nondriving relationship
Critical color

FIGURE M9.3A

287

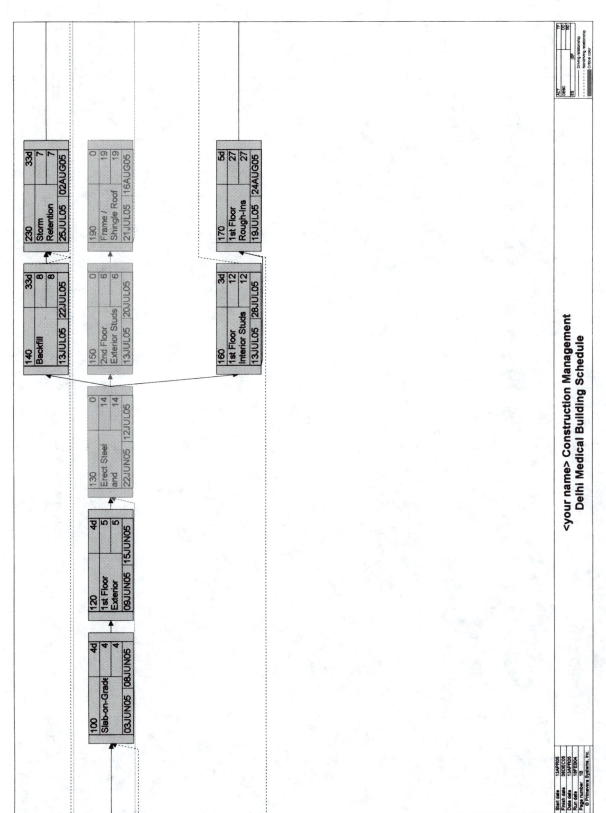

100		4d
		4
		4
Slab-on-Grade		
03JUN05	08JUN05	

120		4d
		5
		5
1st Floor		
Exterior		
09JUN05	15JUN05	

130		0
		14
		14
Erect Steel		
and		
22JUN05	12JUL05	

140		33d
		8
		8
Backfill		
13JUL05	22JUL05	

230		33d
		7
		7
Storm		
Retention		
26JUL05	02AUG05	

150		0
		6
		6
2nd Floor		
Exterior Studs		
13JUL05	20JUL05	

190		0
		19
		19
Frame /		
Shingle Roof		
21JUL05	16AUG05	

160		3d
		12
		12
1st Floor		
Interior Studs		
13JUL05	28JUL05	

170		5d
		27
		27
1st Floor		
Rough-Ins		
19JUL05	24AUG05	

<your name> Construction Management
Delhi Medical Building Schedule

ACT				TF
DESC				OD
ES		EF		RD
	Driving relationship			
	Nondriving relationship			
	Critical color			

Start date 13APR05
Finish date 06DEC05
Data date 13APR05
Run date 18FEB04
Page number 1B
© Primavera Systems, Inc.

FIGURE M9.3B

288

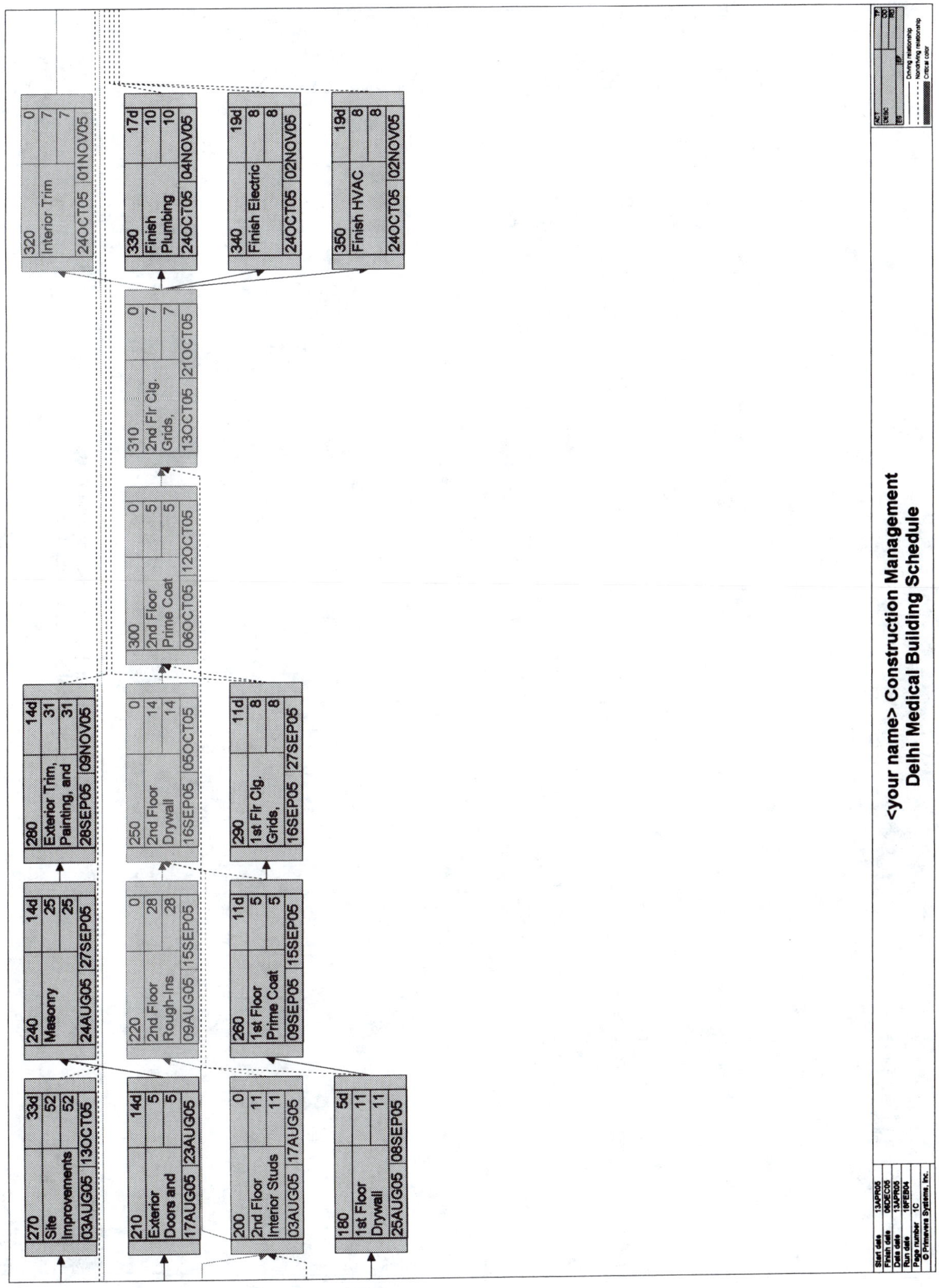
270
Site
Improvements
33d
52
52
03AUG05
13OCT05
240
Masonry
14d
25
25
24AUG05
27SEP05
280
Exterior Trim, Painting, and
14d
31
31
28SEP05
09NOV05
320
Interior Trim
0
7
7
24OCT05
01NOV05
210
Exterior Doors and
14d
5
5
17AUG05
23AUG05
220
2nd Floor Rough-Ins
0
28
28
09AUG05
15SEP05
250
2nd Floor Drywall
0
14
14
16SEP05
05OCT05
300
2nd Floor Prime Coat
0
5
5
06OCT05
12OCT05
310
2nd Flr Clg. Grids,
0
7
7
13OCT05
21OCT05
330
Finish Plumbing
17d
10
10
24OCT05
04NOV05
200
2nd Floor Interior Studs
0
11
11
03AUG05
17AUG05
260
1st Floor Prime Coat
11d
5
5
09SEP05
15SEP05
290
1st Flr Clg. Grids,
11d
8
8
16SEP05
27SEP05
340
Finish Electric
19d
8
8
24OCT05
02NOV05
180
1st Floor Drywall
5d
11
11
25AUG05
08SEP05
350
Finish HVAC
19d
8
8
24OCT05
02NOV05
<your name> Construction Management
Delhi Medical Building Schedule

FIGURE M9.3C

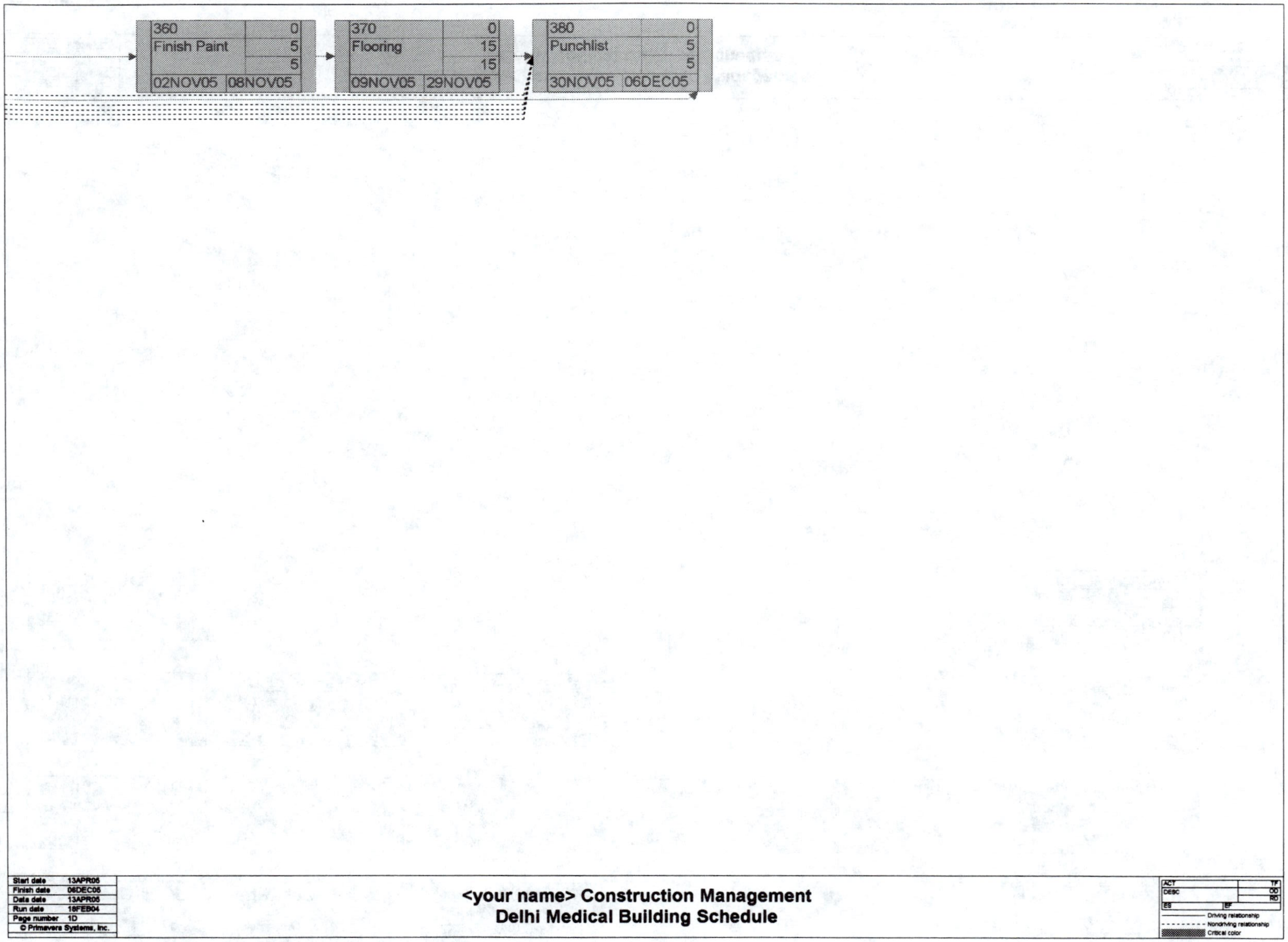

360		0
Finish Paint		5
02NOV05	08NOV05	5

370		0
Flooring		15
09NOV05	29NOV05	15

360		0
Punchlist		5
30NOV05	06DEC05	5

<your name> Construction Management
Delhi Medical Building Schedule

Start date	13APR05
Finish date	06DEC06
Data date	13APR05
Run date	18FEB04
Page number	1D
© Primavera Systems, Inc.	

ACT		TF
DESC		OD
ES	EF	RD

----- Driving relationship
------ Nondriving relationship
▓▓ Critical color

FIGURE M9.3D

SCHEDULE ANALYSIS
Delhi Medical Building Schedule

Name _____

After completing the Delhi Medical Building Schedule project, answer the following questions from the PERT schedule printout. Turn the Schedule Analysis in to your instructor along with the project schedule printout—PERT view of the Delhi Medical Building schedule.

1. What is the end date of the project? _____

    Name two places where you found it _____

    _____

2. What is the total project duration in days? _____ in months? _____

3. Is there a timescale shown on the schedule? **Yes No**

4. Are sightlines shown on the schedule? **Yes No**

5. Are the activities graphically connected to each other? **Yes No**

6. Can you tell what work is being performed on the fourth week of the project? **Yes No**

7. List all the critical activities of the schedule (*list by activity IDs*).

    _____

8. How do you know they are critical? List two ways you can tell which activities are critical.

    _____

9. How many critical paths are there on this schedule? _____

10. What activity information is shown inside each activity box?

    _____

    _____

11. Compare the PERT chart to the Bar Chart. Which do you like best? Which is easiest to read and understand? Explain why.

    _____

    _____

    _____

    _____

MODULE 10
Layouts—Saving, Applying, and Creating

Preface: At this point you have created two schedules. However, they may not have the look you want. In the next five modules, you will learn how to customize the look of a schedule. In SureTrak, the look of a schedule is called the *layout*.

In this module, you will learn more about layouts, about the default layout, how to save changes made to a layout (and how not to), how to apply an existing layout, and how to create a new layout.

You will re-open and use the GARG garage construction schedule project for the next five modules.

WHAT IS A LAYOUT?

The layout can be customized to sharpen the content and appearance of the onscreen displays and printed project reports. You can highlight different aspects of the project through layouts. The layout controls the visual elements of a project, including columns, sorting and grouping, footers and headers, rows, activity bars, the timescale, relationship lines, sightlines, screen colors, and resource profiles and tables.

Layouts do not control the position of the split bars, the display of the Activity Form, or the display of open windows.

Layouts created for one project can be applied to other projects. Additionally, SureTrak also comes with many useful prebuilt, customized layouts that you can apply to any project. You can use these layouts, modify them, or create your own.

THE DEFAULT LAYOUT

When you create a project, SureTrak automatically creates a layout using default settings. The name of the default layout is the four-character project name, followed by (STW-).

1. Open the garage construction schedule (GARG). Notice in the upper left-hand corner of the project window (Figure M10.1) that the layout of the project is shown as GARGSTW-. This is the default layout.

SAVING CHANGES TO THE LAYOUT

Whenever you save the project, you automatically save any changes you might have made to the layout. If you make changes to the layout, but don't save the project, those changes will be discarded.

2. To save the current layout you see on your screen, simply click the ■ button or go to File, Save. In Modules 11 through 13, you will make layout changes. At the end of each module, when you save the project, the changes you make will be saved.

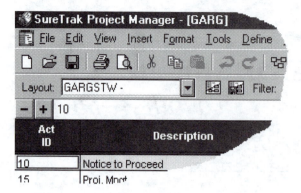

FIGURE M10.1

FIGURE M10.2

APPLYING AN EXISTING LAYOUT

SureTrak comes with many useful prebuilt, customized layouts that you can apply to any project. You can use these layouts, modify them, or create your own.

3. To apply an existing layout to your project, go to View, then Layouts . . . , or

   simply click the ▣ button to open the Layouts window (Figure M10.2). Notice that the window opens to the default [GARGSTW] layout. This layout currently has no description in the Description cell.

4. We are going to apply a different layout to the project—a *two-week lookahead layout*. Scroll up until you find the **2WEEKS–Next 2 weeks in zoomed timescale** layout. Single-click on it to highlight it (see Figure M10.3). Then click the

   Apply button.

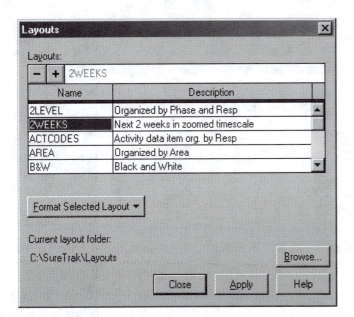

FIGURE M10.3

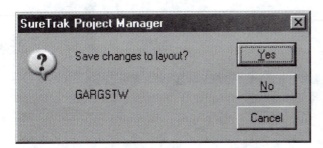

FIGURE M10.4

5. The new layout should appear. However, if you happened to make changes to the previous layout, a window will open (Figure M10.4), prompting you to save or abandon the changes you made to the current layout (**GARGSTW**) before opening the new layout (**2WEEKS**). Notice that the name of the current layout **GARGSTW** appears near the middle of this window. If you click **Yes**, changes you made to the **GARGSTW** layout will be saved before it gets replaced. If you click **No**, changes you made since the last time you saved will be discarded. Since you did not make any changes yet to the layout, it does not really matter what you click; however, click the **No** button just in case you accidentally changed something without knowing it.

6. The **2WEEKS** layout is now applied to the garage construction schedule project. Click the Print preview 🔍 button to see the entire schedule (Figure M10.5). This layout zooms in on the next two weeks of work, showing the work on a daily timescale, and then zooms out the remainder of

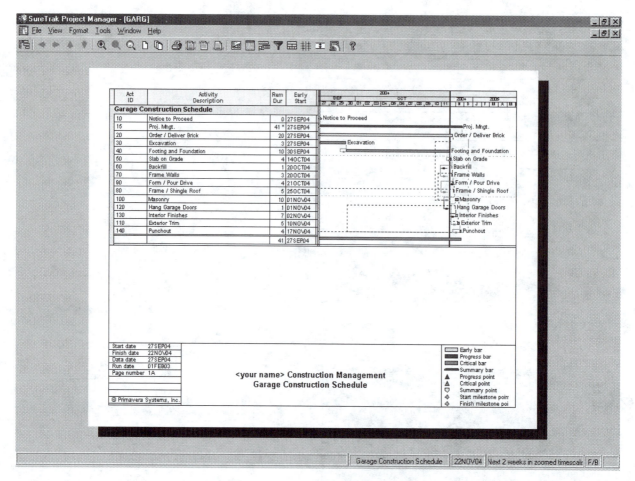

FIGURE M10.5

the work, showing it on a monthly timescale. It is a very popular layout used often in the industry. Many project managers will use this layout for the schedules they hand out to their subs at their weekly progress meetings.

7. Notice a few things about the layout. The activity columns are formatted differently. The footer has also changed. The layout description, Next 2 weeks in zoomed timescale, can be found in the bottom right-hand corner of the Print

preview window. Print out a copy of this schedule by clicking the button from the print preview. You will need to refer to this project schedule layout to answer some of the questions on the next *Schedule Analysis—Modules 10–14* at the end of Module 14. You will also turn in this schedule to your instructor along with the Schedule Analysis.

8. After printing out the 2WEEKS layout, reapply the GARGSTW default layout to

the schedule. To do this, go back to the bar chart view by clicking the

button. Click the button to open the Layouts window. Scroll back down

to the [GARGSTW] default layout and single-click it to highlight it.

Click Apply to return to the default layout and say No to saving changes, since you did not make changes to the 2WEEKS layout.

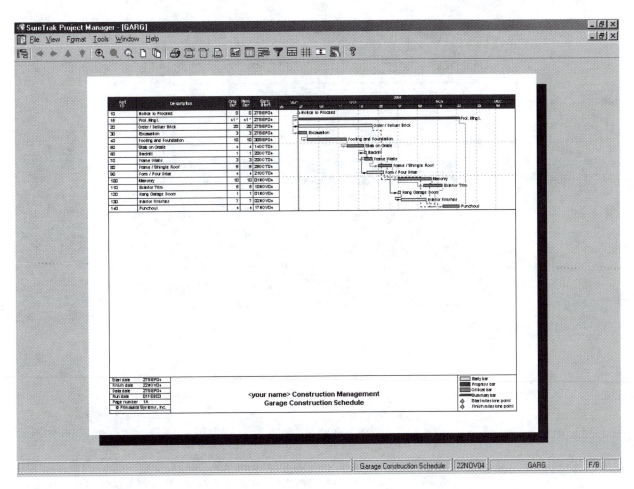

FIGURE M10.6

9. *Caution:* The prebuilt layouts that come with the software and any other layouts you create and save can be applied to any project. When you apply one of these layouts to a project and then make changes to it, you need to carefully decide if you want to save or discard those changes. If you do save the changes, **you are permanently changing that layout**. Therefore, when you apply that layout to a different project, you will see those changes there. If you want to keep the original layout intact, but still save the current layout with the changes you just made, save the current layout as a new layout and then you will have both the original layout and the newly changed current layout to use on future projects. Creating a new layout is discussed next in this module.

10. The original default layout should appear. Click the Print preview button to see the entire schedule (Figure M10.6).

CREATING A NEW LAYOUT

Once you get a schedule to look the way you want on a particular project, there is a good chance you will want to use that customized look on other projects. To do this, save these customized changes under a new layout name to use in the future. Additionally, the original layout will be left unchanged.

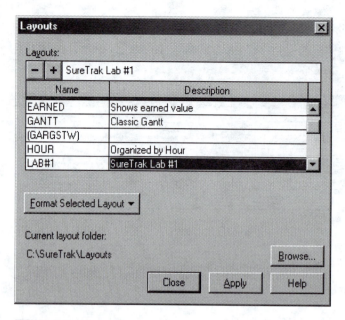

FIGURE M10.7

11. Create a new layout. You can create new layouts from the Bar Chart view or from print preview. Open the layouts window by going to <u>V</u>iew, then

    <u>L</u>ayouts, . . . or simply click the 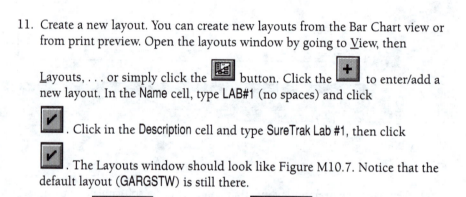 button. Click the 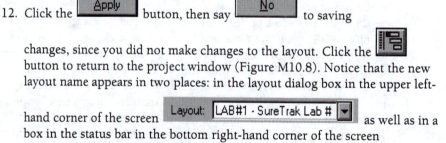 to enter/add a new layout. In the Name cell, type **LAB#1** (no spaces) and click

    . Click in the Description cell and type SureTrak Lab #1, then click

    . The Layouts window should look like Figure M10.7. Notice that the default layout (**GARGSTW**) is still there.

12. Click the Apply button, then say No to saving

    changes, since you did not make changes to the layout. Click the button to return to the project window (Figure M10.8). Notice that the new layout name appears in two places: in the layout dialog box in the upper left-

    hand corner of the screen Layout: LAB#1 - SureTrak Lab # as well as in a box in the status bar in the bottom right-hand corner of the screen

    SureTrak Lab #1 . See Figure M10.8. This is the layout you will customize in the next three modules.

13. Module 10 is complete. Save the garage schedule, which also saves changes made to the new layout. Move on to Module 11 to begin customizing the **LAB#1** layout.

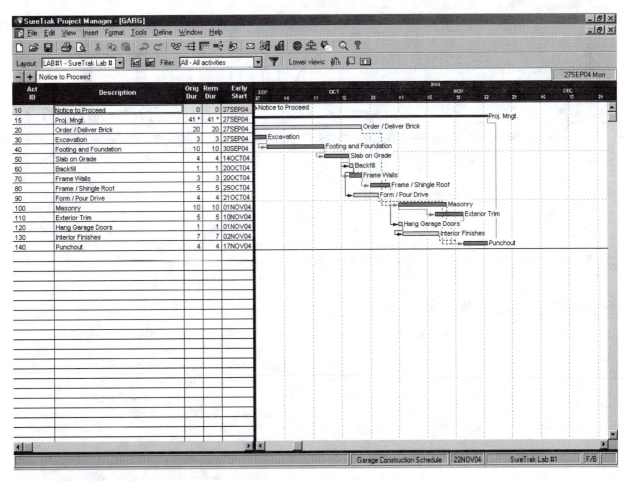

FIGURE M10.8

MODULE 11
Formatting Columns

Preface: In the next three modules you will customize the new layout, SureTrak Lab 1, that you created in the previous module.

In this module, you will learn how to format the activity columns of data that appear to the left of the bars in the project window. You will continue to use the GARG, the garage construction schedule project.

FORMATTING COLUMNS

1. Take a look at the left side (activity column area) of the schedule. Notice which columns are currently "turned on" and can be seen. There are more columns turned on, but you cannot see them because they are behind the bar chart area of the schedule. To see the rest of the columns, go up to the top of the schedule where the column headings meet the timescale. Notice the thick black line in between. This is called the Vertical Split Bar. Place the cursor precisely at this point

and notice that the cursor turns into a double-sided arrow (**↔**) when hovered over the split bar. Click and drag the split bar to the right to view the rest of the columns.

2. Now you can see all the columns that are turned on. In this module, you will turn some columns off, move one around, center most of the data, change the column widths, and format the font of the column headings. To make these changes, go to F*o*rmat, then C*o*lumns . . . (see Figure M11.1).

Note: All these changes will be made in this window; however, they will not take effect until you close the window.

3. Change the font of the column Title *f*ont to **Arial, bold italic, 9** by clicking the pull-down menu and formatting accordingly, as shown in Figure M11.2, then click OK to close the Font window <u>only</u>—be careful not to close the Columns window.

4. Remove the following columns by highlighting the column and clicking the

   ▭ button: **Remaining Duration, Late Start, Late Finish, Total Float, Percent Complete**, and **Resource**.

5. Insert the **Total Float** column back in-between Original Duration and Early Start. To do this, first insert a space by highlighting Early Start and clicking the

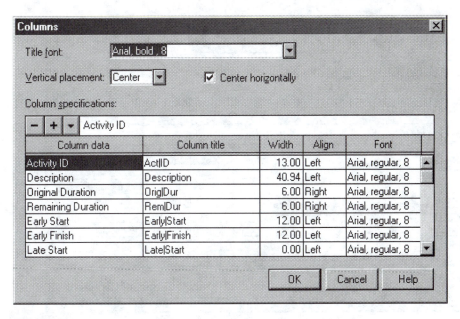

FIGURE M11.1

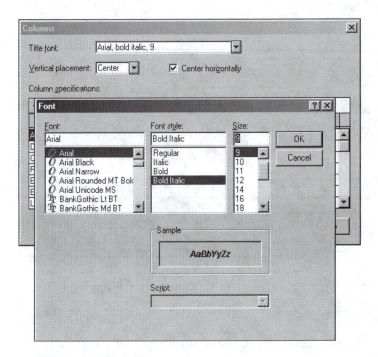

FIGURE M11.2

button. Then click the pull-down and select Total Float, as shown in Figure M11.3.

6. Align the data in all the columns to the Center except the Description (keep Left) and Budgeted Cost (keep Right) columns. Do this by highlighting the appropriate Align cell and using the pull-down menu as shown in Figure M11.4.

7. Change the column width of the Activity ID to 7.00 and the Description to 24.00. Leave the other columns as they were.

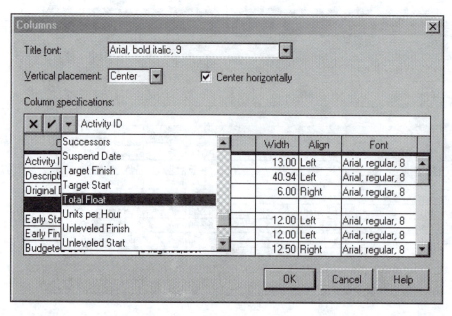

FIGURE M11.3

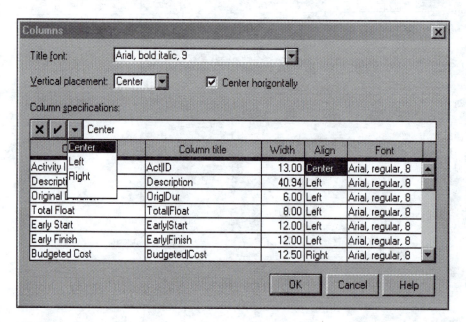

FIGURE M11.4

(F.Y.I.)

■ You can also adjust the width of the columns directly on the column heading with the mouse. Hover the cursor over the vertical line on the right side of the column title. When the mouse cursor changes to (↔), drag the line to the right or left to adjust the width. Be careful not to truncate the title of the column or the data in the column.

8. After making all the column format changes, the Columns window should look like Figure M11.5. Click the OK button to accept these changes.

9. To see the changes to all the columns, drag and drop the vertical split bar to the right side of the last column (Budgeted Cost), as shown in Figure M11.6.

10. Module 11 is complete. Save the garage schedule project and move on to Module 12.

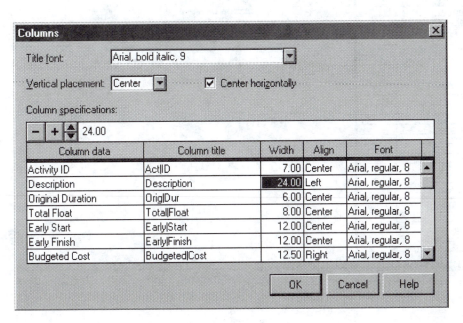

FIGURE M11.5

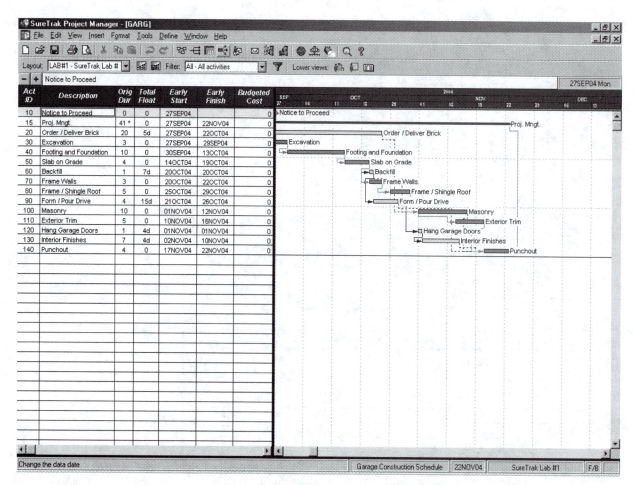

FIGURE M11.6

MODULE **12**
Sorting by Early Start

Preface: Look at the bars of the garage construction schedule and notice how they are laid out. They are currently laid out (sorted) in the order of their Activity IDs (10, 15, 20, 30, . . . through 140). As an example, notice here how

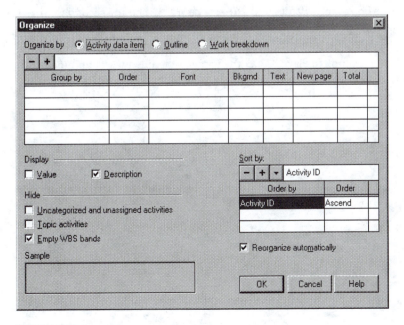

Form / Pour Drive follows Frame / Shingle Roof even though that work will happen first. Most people like the activity bars on the schedule to be sorted by the order in which the work is going to occur, in a cascading manner. To make the schedule look that way, you need to sort the activities by their early start.

In this module, you will learn how to sort the activities of a schedule by their early start.

SORTING BY EARLY START

1. Sort the schedule activities by their early start by opening the Organize window (Figure M12.1) and by going to Format, then Organize . . . , or

simply click the [⬛] button.

FIGURE M12.1

305

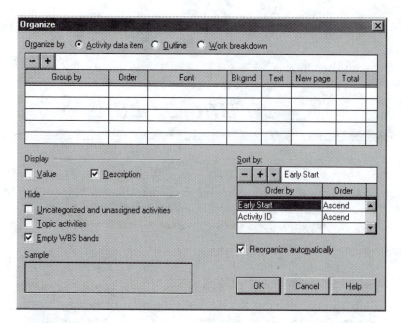

FIGURE M12.2

2. In the Sort by: section of the Organize window (right side of window, toward bottom), notice that the schedule is currently sorted by Activity ID. Click the ![+] button to add a blank space. Click the pull-down ![▼] button and select Early Start to add it as the primary sort. Activity ID will be the secondary sort. The Organize window should look like Figure M12.2.

3. Click ![OK] to resort the activity bars. Take a look at the bars again. They should be cascading down from left to right in order of their early start, as shown in Figure M12.3. Notice that when activities have the same early start date, as does #60—Backfill and #70—Frame Walls, then the secondary sort of Activity ID is applied.

4. Module 12 is complete. Save ![💾] the garage schedule project and move on to Module 13.

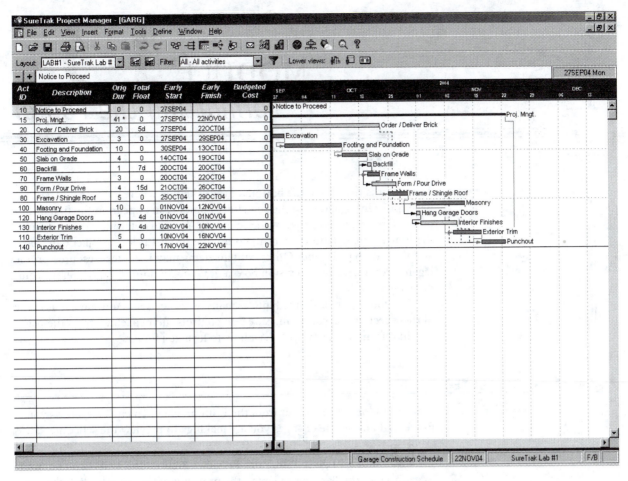

FIGURE M12.3

MODULE 13
Formatting the Footer

Preface: The footer is the area at the bottom of the schedule where you can add various descriptive information to the schedule. Footers can appear on the first or last page, all pages, or no pages of the schedule. You can determine the content of the footer. The default content items are the project title, a project dates box, and the bar chart legend. Other content items may include a resource profile legend, comments box, revision box, a drawing, and up to two different company logos.

    The footer can be divided into as many as six sections. You can use as many of these sections as you want. SureTrak controls their spacing across the page. In this module, you will learn how to format a footer.

FORMATTING THE FOOTER

1. It is best to format the footer from the Print preview screen. This allows you to see, right away, the changes you are making. To preview the schedule, click the ![button] button, or go to File, Print Preview (Figure M13.1). When you want to get back to the Bar Chart view in the project window, simply click the ![bar chart button] (bar chart) button. Make the following changes before you go back to the Bar Chart view. Notice that the three items currently in the footer are project dates, the project title, and the bar chart legend. They are the default footer items.

2. To format the footer, click the Define Footer ![button] button or go to File, Page Setup . . . , and then click the **Footer** tab. This will open the Page Setup window to the **Footer** tab (see Figure M13.2). You will make many changes to the footer in this window.

    Note: The changes will not take effect until you close the Page Setup window.

3. Start by changing the Default font to **Arial, bold, 10**. Do this by clicking the pull-down menu ![Default font: Arial, regular, 8] and making the appropriate selections, as shown in Figure M13.3. Click OK in the Font window *only*. The default font controls all of the font of the footer, except the font in the title block.

4. Notice that there are six footer sections to work with. They are shown in the middle of this window (refer back to Figure M13.2). Currently only three are being used. We will use the same three, and add one more that contains a logo.

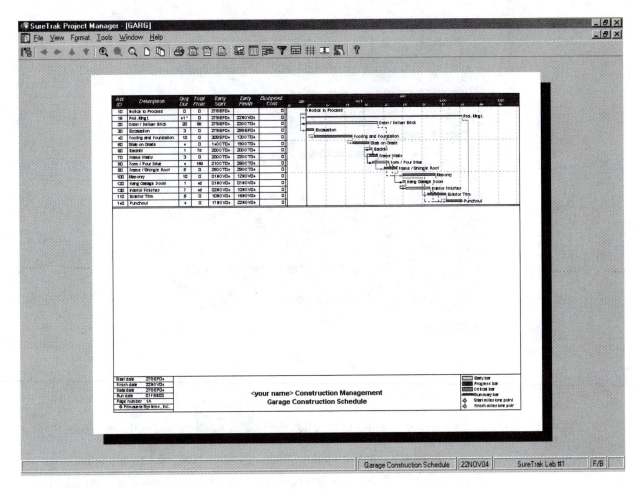

FIGURE M13.1

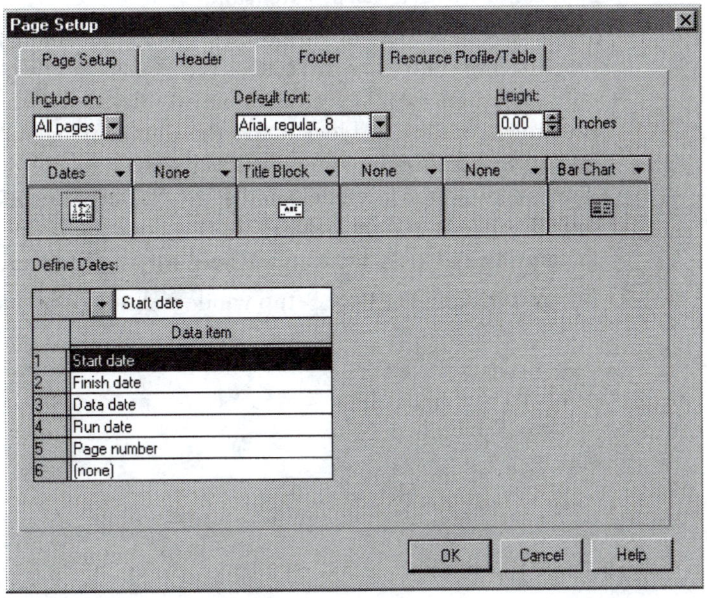

FIGURE M13.2

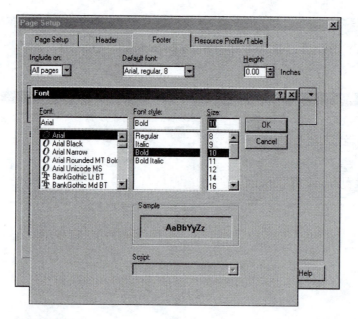

FIGURE M13.3

5. Next, add a logo into the fourth section. Use the pull-down menu in that section to select **Logo**. Click the Browse... button to find the logo. In the Browse for Logo File window, click the Up One Level button to get to the SureTrak file. This is where SureTrak stores the logos that are already in the software. Double-click on the pwpw file to send it to the preview window in the Browse for Logo File window, as shown in Figure M13.4. Notice the logo file has a (.bmp) extension. You can insert other logos from other applications with a (.bmp) extension.

6. The next step is to work with the Title Block section. Click into the Title Block section to see the three areas (Left, Center, and Right). You will work in only the center area. Leave the other two blank. Add the Number/Version of the project to the title block above the Company name. Do this by placing the cursor right in front of <Company name> and single-clicking. Click the pull-down menu in the Insert field and select **Number/Version**. Finally, change the Title Block font to **Arial, bold, 16**. This is done using the pull-down menu in the gray area directly beneath the field where you entered the Number, Version.

7. When complete, the Page Setup window should look like Figure M13.5.

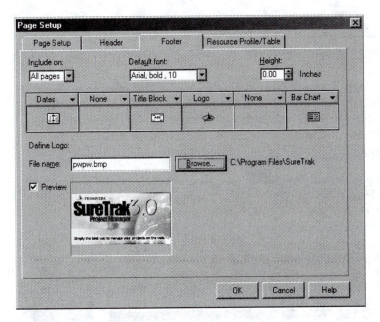

FIGURE M13.4

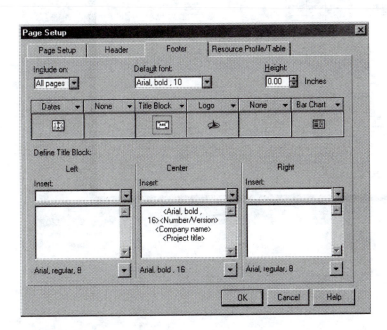

FIGURE M13.5

8. Click [OK] OK to close the Page Setup window and apply the various changes you just made to the footer. The footer should look like Figure M13.6.

9. Print out a copy of this schedule by clicking the button from the print preview. You will need to refer to this project schedule layout to answer some of the questions on the *Schedule Analysis—Modules 10.14* at the end of Module 14. You will also turn in this schedule to your instructor along with the Schedule Analysis.

10. Module 13 is complete. Save the garage schedule project and move on to Module 14.

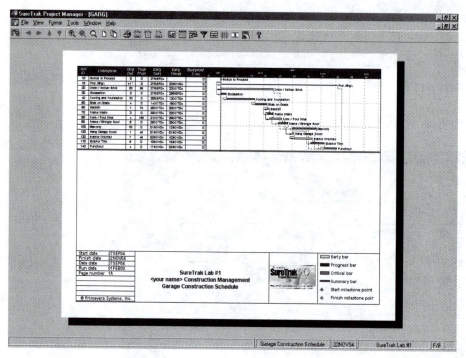

FIGURE M13.6

MODULE **14**
Formatting the Header

Preface: The header is the area at the top of the schedule where you can add various descriptive information to the schedule. Headers can appear on the first or last page, all pages, or no pages of the schedule. You can determine the content of the header. SureTrak's default setting places *no* content information in the header. This seems to be the preference of most people in the industry, *so you rarely see content information placed in the header.*

The header can display the same content items as the footer. They are the project title, important dates, the bar chart legend, a resource profile legend, comments section, revision box, a drawing, or up to two different company logos. The header can be divided into as many as six sections. You can use as many of these sections as you want. SureTrak controls their spacing across the page.

This module is *for your information* only; **you will <u>not</u> actually make changes to the header.** It details how to format a header. At the end of this module is the Schedule Analysis—Modules 10–14. Answer the questions and turn it in to your instructor, along with the 2WEEK layout from Module 10 and the LAB#1 layout from Module 13. When complete, move on to Module 15.

1. It is best to format the header from the Print preview screen. This allows you to see, right away, the changes you are making. To preview the schedule, click the ⬚ button, or go to File, Print Preview (Figure M14.1). When you want to get back to the Bar Chart view in the project window, simply click the ⬚ (bar chart) button. You will make *no changes* to the header in this module. Look at the schedule in the print preview, and notice that there is no header content (don't confuse the column headings or the schedule timescale with content of the header).

2. To format the header, click the Define Header ⬚ button or go to File, Page Setup . . . , and then click the **Header** tab. This will open the Page Setup window to the **Header** tab (see Figure M14.2). You will make *no changes* to the header in this module. Notice that none of the sections are filled.

   Note: If you did make changes, they would not take effect until you closed the Page Setup window.

3. Whenever you want to close a window that you *did not* make changes to, it is best to click ⬚ Cancel to close it; that way, if you accidentally did change something in the window, the change would not take effect. Click ⬚ Cancel to close the Page Setup window.

313

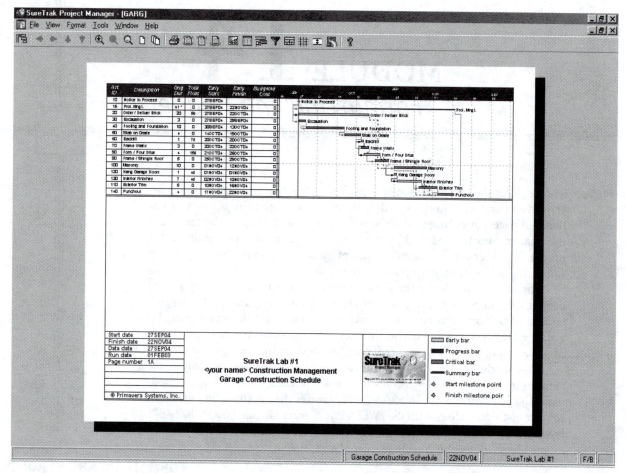

FIGURE M14.1

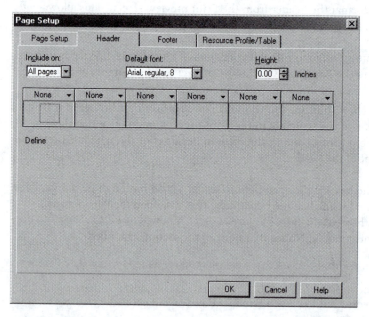

FIGURE M14.2

4. Module 14 is complete. Answer the questions on the *Schedule Analysis—Modules 10–14* and turn it in to your instructor, along with the 2WEEK layout from Module 10 and the LAB#1 layout from Module 13. When complete, move on to Module 15.

MODULES 10-14

SCHEDULE ANALYSIS
Garage Construction Schedule

Name _____

After completing Modules 10 through 14, answer the following questions from the **2WEEKS** and **SureTrak LAB #1** layouts of the garage construction schedule project schedule printouts. Turn the Schedule Analysis in to your instructor along with the two schedule printouts.

2WEEKS Layout:

1. What are the two timescale units shown on this layout? _____ _____

2. Name two places on the layout where you can find the name of the project.

    1. _____

    2. _____

3. Are the activities sorted by: **Activity ID** <u>or</u> **Early Start** (circle one)?

4. What activity columns are shown? _____

5. What does the long, continuous bar on the bottom represent? _____

SureTrak LAB #1 Layout:

6. Circle the smallest timescale increment shown on the schedule: **Days, Weeks,** or **Months**

7. How many footer sections are being used? _____

8. What activity has the greatest total float? _____ Is it critical? **Yes No**

                         Activity ID   # of Days

9. What information on the layout is in italics? _____

10. Are the activities sorted by: **Activity ID** <u>or</u> **Early Start** (circle one)?

Comparison of Both Layouts:

11. Do the bar chart legends in the footer of each layout show the same info.? **Yes No**

12. Do the project dates boxes in the footer of each layout show the same info.? **Yes No**

13. What additional title is shown and on what layout? _____ _____

                                    Title   Layout

14. Which layout shows sightlines: **2WEEKS** <u>or</u> **LAB#1** <u>or</u> **Both** (circle one)?

MODULE **15**
Renaming a Project

Preface: You can create a new project that is an exact copy of the active project as it exists at that moment by renaming it; that is, saving it under a new name.

There are many reasons that you might want to rename an existing project. If you are creating a new schedule that is similar to one that you have already created, it is easier to bring that one up and rename it, rather than start from scratch.

Or you may want to run *what if* scenarios with your schedule. As an example, you might want to see how much time is saved in your project schedule by working on Saturdays (we will be running this, and other calendar scenarios, in the next module). You would not want to make these changes to your original project schedule and take a chance of messing it up. It is better to rename the original schedule and make these changes to the new renamed schedule. Then, if the new schedule gets messed up—who cares? You will always have the original schedule to go back to.

In this module, you will open the garage construction schedule (GARG) project and rename it. You will then change the Number/Version, Project Title, and Layout name.

RENAMING A PROJECT

1. Open the garage construction schedule (GARG) project. (For detailed instructions on opening projects, see Module 7).

2. Rename this project by saving it with a different name. Do this by going to File, then Save As . . . . In the Save As window, enter **GAR1** for the new project name in the Project name: field, as shown in Figure M15.1.

3. Check two other things before saving. It is always a good idea to verify that the project Type: field says **Project Groups** and that the Current folder: shows the correct path to the folder that you want the project to be saved in. In our case it should be the default path of `C:\SureTrak\Projects` unless your instructor tells you differently.

4. After verifying the project type and folder path as described above, click the `OK` Ok button to save the project under the new filename. The project will appear as shown in Figure M15.2. Notice the new project name (GAR1) in the upper left-hand corner of the project window.

RENAMING THE NUMBER/VERSION, PROJECT TITLE, AND LAYOUT

When you rename a project, you usually also want to rename the Number/Version, Project Title, and Layout name; otherwise, your project will carry these names from the original project. Since we are going to perform different calendar scenarios on the GAR1 project, we will change the titles accordingly.

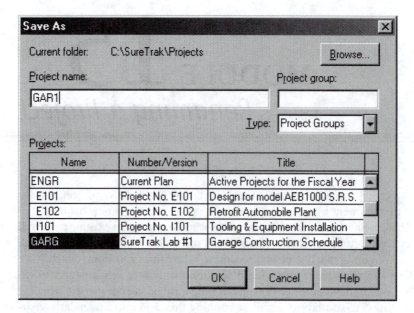

FIGURE M15.1

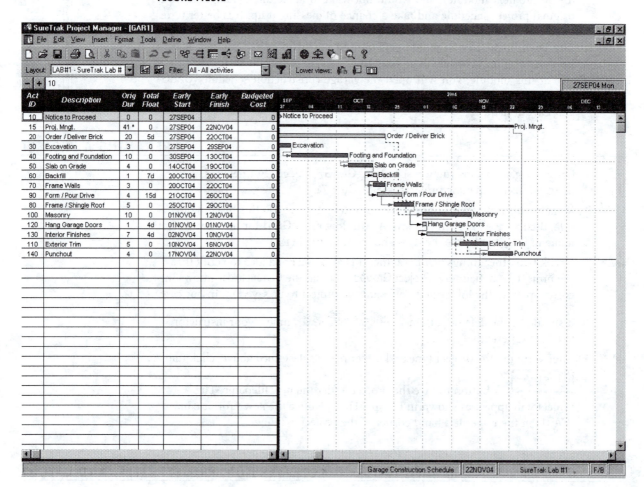

FIGURE M15.2

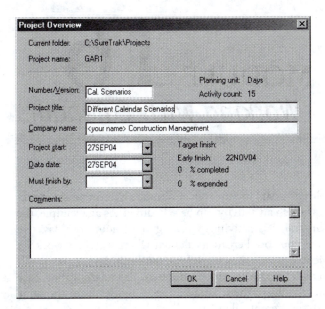

FIGURE M15.3

5. To change the Number/Version and Project Title, go to File, then Project Overview. . . . Change the Number/Version to **Cal. Scenarios** and the Project title to **Different Calendar Scenarios**. See Figure M15.3. Leave the other fields as is and click [OK]. Then click the 🖫 button to apply and save these changes.

6. There is one last change to make. The schedule is currently under the SureTrak Lab #1 layout. Create and apply a new layout for this scenario. Do this by following instructions #11 and #12 from Module 10, except type **DIFF_CAL** in the Name cell and **Different Calendar Scenarios** in the Description cell.

7. Module 15 is complete. Save 🖫 the GAR1 project, but leave it open and move on to Module 16 to perform what-if scenarios to the project.

MODULE 16
Working with Calendars

Preface: You can set up multiple calendars in SureTrak. Calendars determine the work-days and workhours on which an activity can be scheduled. As an example, the default calendar in SureTrak has activities working eight hours per day, five days per week. However, you could create a calendar where activities work six days per week or a calendar where they work four, ten-hour days.

You can define (create) up to thirty-one different calendars, called base calendars, and assign activities to them. In addition, activities from the same project can be assigned to different calendars.

There are three predefined calendars that automatically come with every new project you create. They are the Global, Normal workweek, and Seven 24-hr days calendars. They are discussed below.

In this module, you will work with the Global and Normal workweek calendars, add holidays to calendars, create a six-day workweek and a four-tens calendar, and assign calendars to activities. You will apply these calendar changes to the garage project, print out four different schedules of the project, and analyze their various effects.

GLOBAL CALENDAR

1. The global calendar is the basis for all other calendars in SureTrak. A change to the global calendar will change the settings on all *new* calendars you create. The global calendar is never assigned to activities; it is a behind-the-scenes calendar that controls the normal workdays, holidays, and worktimes of all new calendars. Additionally, any specific change to an *individual workday* made on the global calendar, such as creating a holiday, will be changed on *all* calendars, including ones you previously created. View the global calendar by going to Define, then Calendars. . . . The Global calendar will appear in the Calendars window (Figure M16.1).

NORMAL WORKWEEK CALENDAR

2. The Normal workweek calendar is the default calendar for all new projects. That is, whenever you create a new project, the activities in that project are automatically assigned to this calendar. Activities on this calendar work Monday through Friday, eight hours per day. View the Normal workweek calendar by going to Define, then Calendars. . . . Then click on calendar ID 1, the Normal workweek calendar as shown in Figure M16.2. Notice that the Sundays and Saturdays are XXX'ed out since work is not performed on these days. Notice in the Hours section of the window that all but eight hours of the day are XXX'ed out since work occurs only from 8 A.M. to 12 P.M. and from 1 P.M. to 5 P.M. After reviewing the Calendars window, click the ⬛ Close ⬛ button.

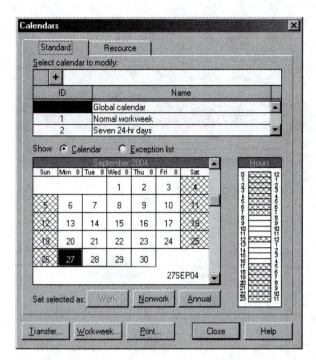

FIGURE M16.1

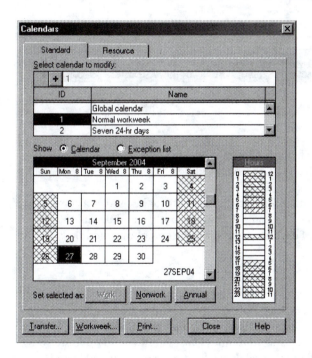

FIGURE M16.2

3. Your screen should currently show the GAR1 project schedule (Figure M16.3) with its activities on the Normal workweek calendar. Change the project title to Normal Workweek Calendar. To do this, go to File, then Project Overview . . . and type in **Normal Workweek Calendar** in the Project title field. Leave the

other fields as they were and click [OK]. Then click the [💾] button

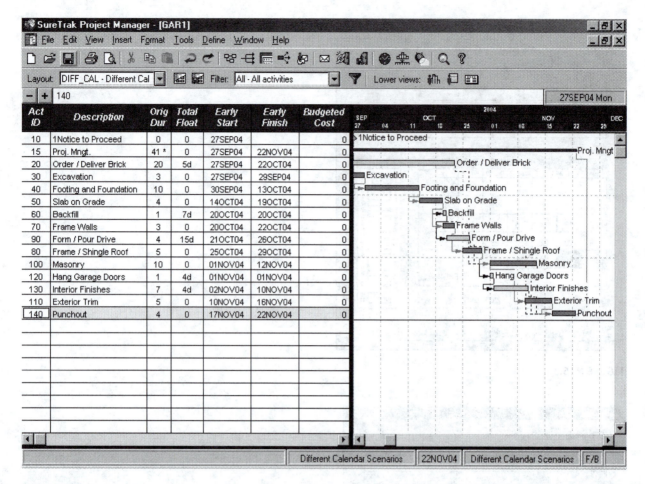

FIGURE M16.3

to apply and save these changes. (For more detailed instructions on changing the project title, see instruction #5 from Module 15).

Next, print out a copy of the GAR1 project schedule to be used as a comparison to the three different calendars you will generate in this module and to help answer questions from the Schedule Analysis at the end of this module.

ADDING HOLIDAYS TO CALENDARS

4. The three predefined calendars (Global, Normal workweek, and Seven 24-hr days) already contain three annual holidays: New Year's Day (January 1), U.S. Independence Day (July 4), and Christmas Day (December 25). We are going to add three more holidays to the global calendar for the years 2004 and 2005: Memorial Day (fourth Monday in May), Labor Day (first Monday in September), and Thanksgiving (fourth Thursday in November). Holidays and/or other nonwork days can be added to individual calendars or to the global calendar. If added to the global calendar, the holidays are automatically added to all existing and future calendars.

5. Start by adding Memorial Day in 2004 to the global calendar. First make sure that the Global calendar is chosen. Go to Define, then Calendars. . . . Scroll back to May of 2004 and highlight (single-click) the fourth Monday in May

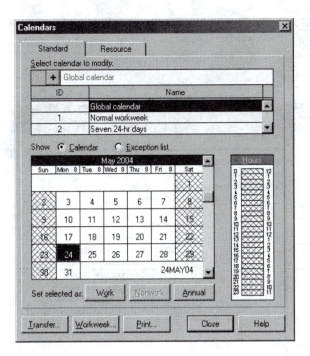

FIGURE M16.4

(May 24th). Next click the ⟨**Nonwork**⟩ button. Notice that the 24th is now XXX'ed out, as shown in Figure M16.4.

6. Add the remaining holidays to the Global calendar for 2004 and 2005. When complete, each year should have six holidays (including those that were predefined).

7. Verify that the holidays were also added to the Normal workweek calendar by selecting it and scrolling through 2004 and 2005. Notice that the holidays have either a G ⟨24⟩ or GA ⟨4⟩ inside each date box. The G signifies that this is a holiday carried over from the global calendar. The A signifies that the holiday is an annual holiday like the fourth of July, New Year's Day, or Christmas Day. After verifying the holidays, ⟨**Close**⟩ the Calendars window.

Since the GAR1 project's activities are on the Normal workweek calendar, the holidays you just added will be in effect on this schedule (Figure M16.5). That is, you *do not* have to specifically assign the holidays to the schedule activities.

8. Change the project title to *Schedule with Holidays*. To do this, go to File, then Project Overview . . . , and type in **Schedule with Holidays** in the Project title field. Leave the other fields as they were and click ⟨**OK**⟩. Then click the ⟨💾⟩ button to apply and save these changes. (For more detailed instructions on changing the project title, see instruction #5 from Module 15).

Next, print out a copy of the GAR1 project schedule (with holidays) to be used as a comparison to the other calendars you will generate in this module and to help answer questions from the Schedule Analysis at the end of this module.

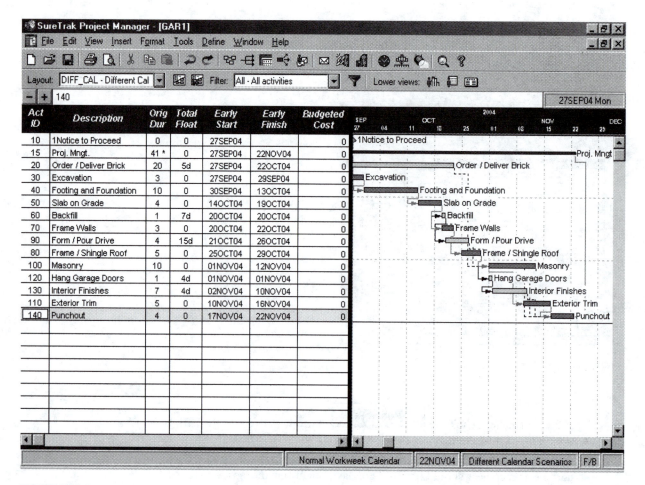

FIGURE M16.5

CREATING A CALENDAR (SIX-DAY WORKWEEK)

A construction project will often work Saturdays to get back on schedule or to get ahead. We are going to create a Six-day workweek calendar for the GAR1 project to see how much time will be saved by working Saturdays.

9. Create a Six-day workweek calendar by going to Define, then Calendars. . . . Click the ➕ button to add a calendar. Accept **3** for the **ID** number. You can enter up to sixteen alphanumeric characters for the calendar name. Enter **Six Day Workweek** for the Name, then click the ✔. The window should look like Figure M16.6.

10. Next click the **Workweek...** Workweek. . . button. In the Workweek window, click on Saturday, then click the **Work** Work button to make this a working day. Notice that the 24-hour work period (Figure M16.7) now shows eight hours of work on Saturday. To accept this and make Saturday a working day, click **OK**.

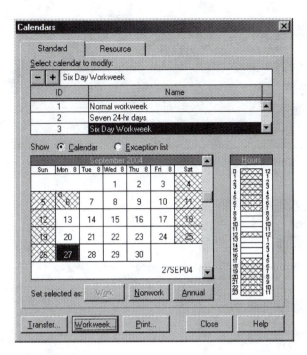

FIGURE M16.6

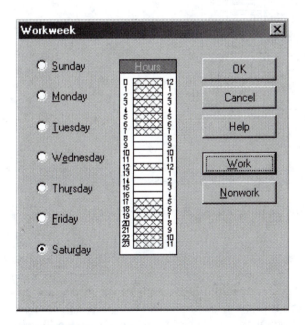

FIGURE M16.7

11. Say **No** to recalculating schedule dates according to the modified workweek (Figure M16.8).

Note: Saying **Yes** at this prompt would not have changed anything since no activities are currently assigned to the Six-day workweek calendar and no changes were made to the Global calendar.

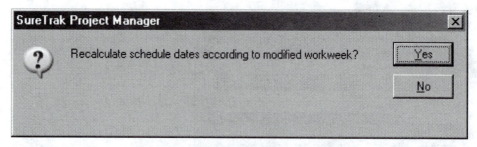

FIGURE M16.8

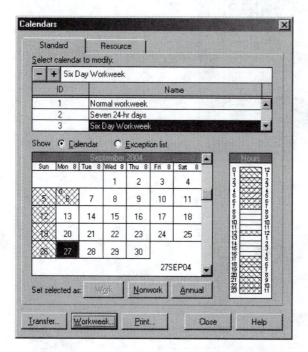

FIGURE M16.9

12. Notice that Saturdays are no longer XXX'ed out, as shown in Figure M16.9. Click the **Close** button to close the Calendars window.

ASSIGNING CALENDARS TO ACTIVITIES

The new Six-day workweek calendar is created, but it has not been assigned to any activities yet. The next step is to assign it to the activities of the GAR1 project to see how much it shortens the project end date compared to the project on the Normal workweek.

13. To assign calendars to activities, turn on the activity form by going to <u>V</u>iew, then <u>A</u>ctivity Form, *or* hitting the *F7* key, *or* simply clicking the 🖾 button.

14. Highlight the first activity (**Notice to Proceed**), then click the pull-down menu in the **Calendar** field to see all the available calendars (Figure M16.10). Click on the **3—Six Day Workweek** calendar to assign it to this activity, as shown in Figure M16.10. Rather than using the pull-down, menu you could have simply typed a 3 in the **Calendar** field to change the calendar ID for that

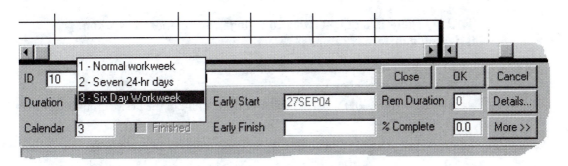

FIGURE M16.10

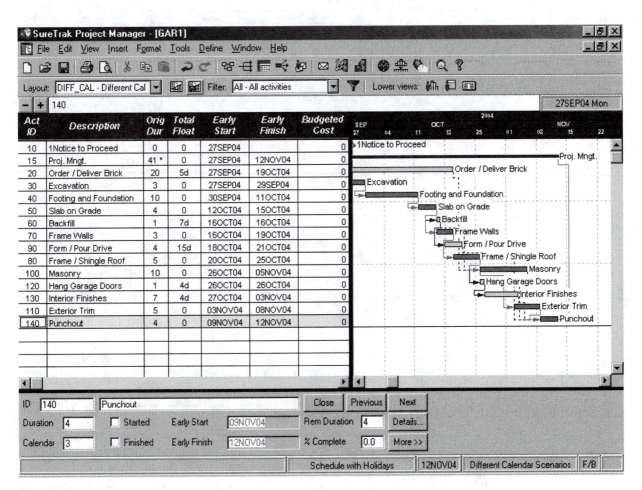

FIGURE M16.11

activity. Click [OK] and move on to the Next activity by clicking the

[Next] Next button. Rather than clicking OK, then Next for each activity, you could simply click on (highlight) the next activity; this will automatically accept the changes made to the previous activity.

15. Assign the Six-day workweek calendar to the remainder of the activities. When complete, the project schedule should look like Figure M16.11.

(F.Y.I.)   There is a quicker way to change the calendar IDs when assigning a different calendar to activities.

■ Temporarily add the Calendar column to the activity columns (see Module 11 if you forgot how).

■ Then, change all the calendar IDs in the column to the desired number as shown below.

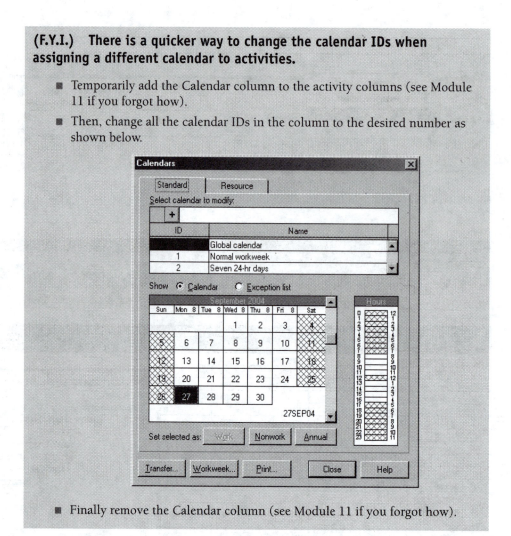

■ Finally remove the Calendar column (see Module 11 if you forgot how).

16. Change the project title to Six-Day Workweek. To do this, go to File, then Project Overview, . . . and type in **Six Day Workweek** in the Project title field.

Leave the other fields as they were and click [OK]. Then click the

[💾] button to apply and save these changes. (For more detailed instructions on changing the project title, see instruction #5 from Module 15).

Next, print out a copy of the **GAR1** project schedule (on the six-day workweek) to be used as a comparison to the other calendars you will generate in this module and to help answer questions from the Schedule Analysis at the end of this module.

CREATING A CALENDAR (FOUR-TENS)

Before creating the Four, ten-hour day calendar, you have to make changes to the Global calendar. Since the Global calendar is the basis for all new calendars created, it must be changed to a four, ten-hour format. You will do this in two steps: change the workday to ten hours, and then change the workweek to four days.

17. Open the Calendar window (Define, Calendars . . .) and open the Global Workweek window as shown in Figure M16.12 by clicking the

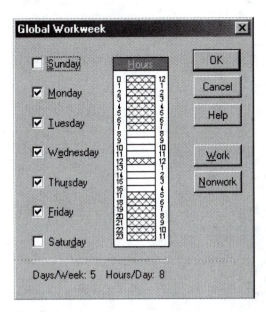

FIGURE M16.12

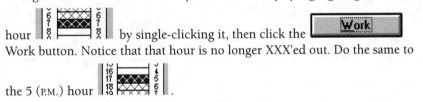

Workweek... button. Notice that the workweek is currently set at five, eight-hour days.

18. Change the Global calendar workday to a ten-hour day by highlighting the 7 (A.M.) hour by single-clicking it, then click the **Work** button. Notice that that hour is no longer XXX'ed out. Do the same to the 5 (P.M.) hour .

19. Next, in this same window, change the Global calendar workweek to a four-day, Monday through Thursday workweek by unchecking ☑ **Friday** . When complete, notice the Global Workweek is set to four, ten-hour days, as shown in Figure M16.13. Click **OK** to accept these changes and close the window.

20. Say **No** to recalculating schedule dates according to the modified workweek (Figure M16.14).

Note: Even though you said **No** at this prompt, you may have noticed that some of the project information has changed. The project duration changed to thirty-three days, most of the activity durations changed, and all of the non-zero total floats changed. These changes would have been identical if you had said **Yes** at the prompt. The schedule changed, reflecting the global change to ten-hour days (this is what the schedule would look like on five, ten-hour days). The schedule is about half-accurate right now. You need to create and assign the Four-Tens calendar (in the next two steps) to the activities to make it completely accurate.

21. Create a Four, ten-hour day calendar by clicking the ➕ button to add a calendar. Accept 4 for the ID number. You can enter up to sixteen alphanumeric characters for the calendar name. Enter Four Tens for the

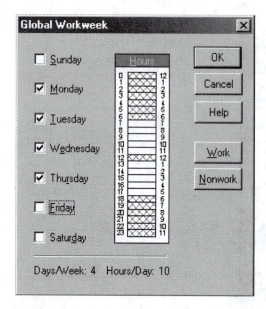

FIGURE M16.13

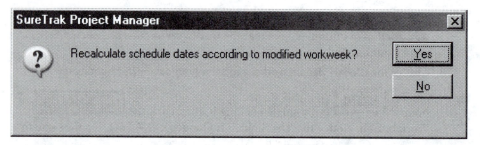

FIGURE M16.14

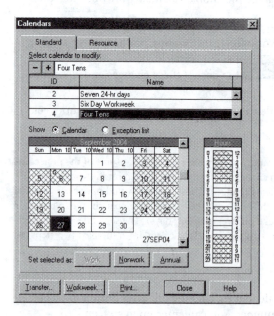

FIGURE M16.15

Name, then click the 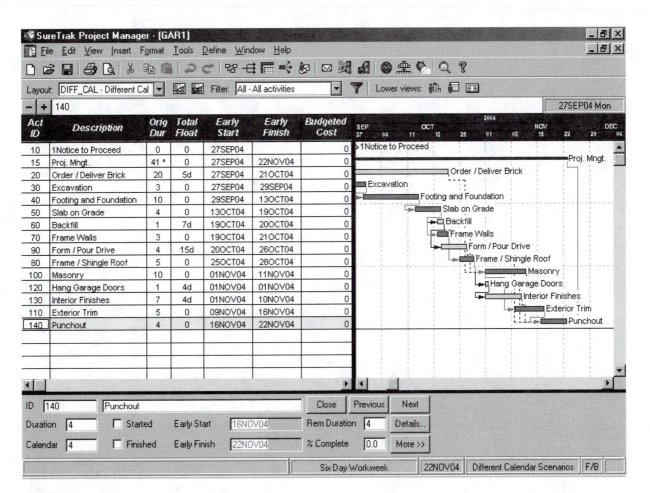 button. The window should look like Figure M16.15.

22. Assign the Four-tens calendar to all the activities the same way you previously assigned the Six-day workweek calendar. When complete, the project schedule should look like Figure M16.16.

23. Change the project title to Four Tens. To do this, go to <u>F</u>ile, then Project Overvie<u>w</u>, . . . and type in **Four Tens** in the Project <u>t</u>itle field. Leave the other fields as they were and click OK . Then click the button to apply and save these changes. (For more detailed instructions on changing the project title, see instruction #5 from Module 15).

   Next, print out a copy of the GAR1 project schedule to see the effect of the Four-tens calendar on the schedule, to be used as a comparison to the other calendars you generated in this module, and to help answer questions from the Schedule Analysis at the end of this module.

24. Module 16 is complete. Save the GAR1 project. Answer the questions on the *Schedule Analysis—Module 16* and turn it in to your instructor along with the four (4) printouts of the GAR1 project schedules: Normal workweek calendar, Holidays calendar, Six day workweek calendar, and Four tens calendar. When complete, move on to Module 17.

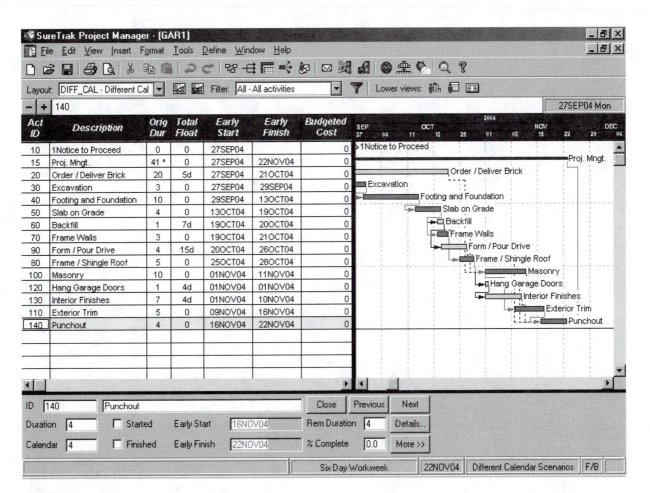

FIGURE M16.16

MODULE 16

SCHEDULE ANALYSIS
Garage Construction Schedule

Name _____

After completing Module 16, answer the following questions from the **Holidays**, **Six-day workweek**, and **Four-tens** calendars as they compare to the Normal workweek calendar of the garage construction schedule project (GAR1) schedule printouts. Turn the Schedule Analysis in to your instructor, along with all four printouts of the schedule on the various calendars.

Holidays Calendar:

1. Did the schedule end date change when holidays were added to the calendar? **Yes   No**

2. If yes, what is the new end date? _____ If no, why didn't it change? _____

   _____

Six-Day Workweek Calendar:

3. Did the schedule end date change with a six-day workweek? **Yes No**

4. If yes, what is the new end date? _____ If no, why didn't it change? _____

   _____

5. Did the total project duration (total working days—see duration of Proj. Mngt.) change ?
   Yes   No

6. If yes, what is the new project duration? _____ days. If no, why didn't it change?

   _____

7. Did the critical path change? **Yes   No**

Four-Tens Calendar:

8. Did the total project duration change? **Yes   No** If yes, what to? _____ days.

9. Did the critical path change? **Yes   No**

10. What other areas of the schedule changed? List: _____

    _____

11. The end date of the Normal workweek and the Four-tens calendars were the same. Was that a coincidence or should you expect them to be the same? Explain. _____

    _____

12. If the end date is the same, what is the advantage of working with a Four-tens calendar ?
    Explain. _____

    _____

MODULE 17
Activity Codes

Preface: Activity codes allow you to organize project activities into various groups. As an example, you may want to show which project activities your company is performing with your own forces and which you are subcontracting out. Or you might want to sort the activities by responsibility of individuals within your company. Projects are often grouped in numerous ways such as by phases of the project, floor levels in a building, or pour areas of a concrete deck. Activity coding allows you to group activities in these many different ways.

Additionally, you can organize activity codes within other activity codes in a nested fashion. For instance, you could group your project first by the contractor performing the work (your company or a sub) and then, second, subgroup by the responsible individual within your company. That is what we will do in this module.

There are four predefined default activity codes that automatically come with every new project you create. They are Responsibility, Area, Phase, and Mail. You can create additional codes (up to twenty) or replace the default codes with others that are more relevant to your projects.

In teaching this software for many years to my students at Cincinnati State and to the industry, I have found that this is one of the most difficult pieces of the software to remember. Working with activity codes is not difficult; however, the process is long with multiple steps. There are *three* distinct steps involved. They are:

1. Define (create) the activity codes and their values.
2. Assign the codes to the appropriate activities.
3. Group the activities.

In this module, you will define (create) a contractor activity code, adapt the default responsibility code, assign these codes to the appropriate activities, and organize the project according to these codes. Additionally, you will learn how to add the project title above all of the activities and how to sort activities within the activity codes. You will apply these activity codes to the garage project, open the garage project, and rename it.

To get a preview of what the project schedule will look like when this module is complete, look at Figure M17.1. Notice that the project title is on top followed by the two groupings (also called bands) of the contractor activity code, and within that, the activities are grouped by responsibility. Finally, within the responsibility bands, the activities are sorted by early start, then Activity ID.

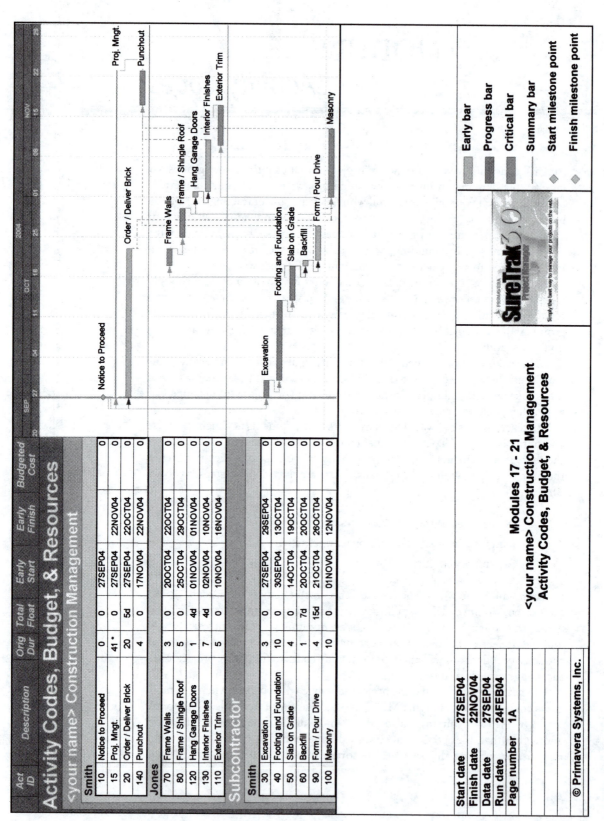

Activity Codes, Budget, & Resources

\<your name\> Construction Management

Act ID	Description	Orig Dur	Total Float	Early Start	Early Finish	Budgeted Cost
Smith						
10	Notice to Proceed	0	0	27SEP04		0
15	Proj. Mngt.	41 *	0	27SEP04	22NOV04	0
20	Order / Deliver Brick	20	5d	27SEP04	22OCT04	0
140	Punchout	4	0	17NOV04	22NOV04	0
Jones						
70	Frame Walls	3	0	20OCT04	22OCT04	0
80	Frame / Shingle Roof	5	0	25OCT04	29OCT04	0
120	Hang Garage Doors	1	4d	01NOV04	01NOV04	0
130	Interior Finishes	7	4d	02NOV04	10NOV04	0
110	Exterior Trim	5	0	10NOV04	16NOV04	0
Subcontractor						
Smith						
30	Excavation	3	0	27SEP04	29SEP04	0
40	Footing and Foundation	10	0	30SEP04	13OCT04	0
50	Slab on Grade	4	0	14OCT04	19OCT04	0
60	Backfill	1	7d	20OCT04	20OCT04	0
90	Form / Pour Drive	4	15d	21OCT04	26OCT04	0
100	Masonry	10	0	01NOV04	12NOV04	0

		Early bar
		Progress bar
		Critical bar
		Summary bar
	◆	Start milestone point
	◆	Finish milestone point

Modules 17 - 21
\<your name\> Construction Management
Activity Codes, Budget, & Resources

Start date	27SEP04
Finish date	22NOV04
Data date	27SEP04
Run date	24FEB04
Page number	1A

© Primavera Systems, Inc.

FIGURE M17.1

In the next few modules you will be working with the garage construction schedule (GARG) project. But rather than working with the original project, rename it as described below.

1. Open the garage construction schedule (GARG) project. Rename it by saving it with a different name. Do this by going to File, then Save As. . . . In the Save As window, enter GAR2 for the new project name in the Project name: field (for more detailed instructions on renaming projects, see Module 15). Remember, it is always a good idea to verify that the project Type: field says Project Groups and that the Current folder: shows the correct path to the folder that you want the project to be saved in. In our case it should be the default

   path of `C:\...\SureTrak\Projects` unless your instructor tells you differently. After verifying the project type and folder path as previously described, click

   the `OK` button to save the project under the new filename.

2. Next, change the Number/Version and Project Title in the Project overview window (File, then Project Overview. . .). Change the Number/Version to Modules 17.21 and the Project title to Activity Codes, Budget, & Resources.

   Leave the other fields as they were and click `OK`. Then click the

   button to apply and save these changes.

3. Finally, create and apply a new layout for this project. Do this by following instructions #9 and #10 from Module 10, except type MOD17-21 (no spaces) in the Name cell and Act. Codes, Budget, & Resources in the Description cell.

First off, we will create the activity code used to group the project activities into those being performed by your company and those that are subbed out.

4. To create an activity code, go to Define, then Activity Codes, . . . to open the Activity Codes window (see Figure M17.2). Notice the four predefined default activity codes in the window. These same codes appear in the bottom left-hand corner of the activity form. Open the activity form to view these

   codes by clicking the button and then clicking the `More >>` button to completely expand the form. Notice the codes in the bottom left-hand corner (Figure M17.3).

5. Click the button in the Activity Codes window to add a code. In the

   Name field type in **CNTR** and click the button. Set the Length field to 1.

   In the Description field, type in **Contractor**, then click the button (see Figure M17.4). The contractor activity code has been defined; click

   `Close` Close to accept it. Notice that the CNTR code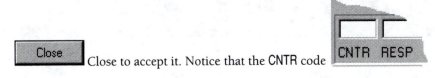

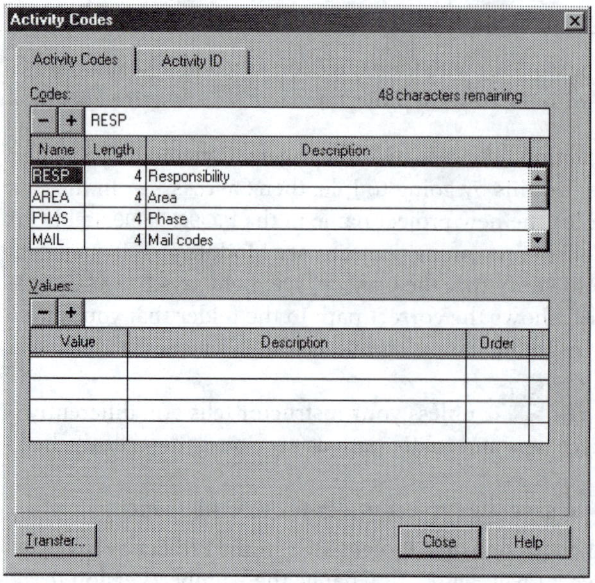

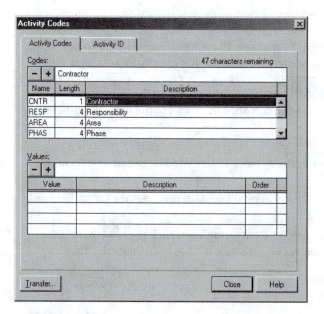

FIGURE M17.2

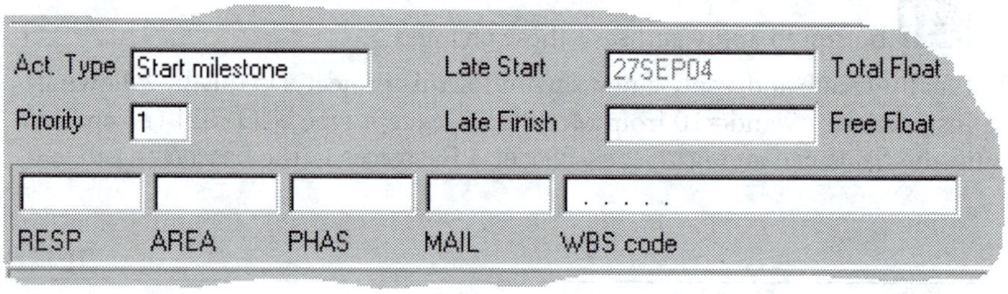

FIGURE M17.3

FIGURE M17.4

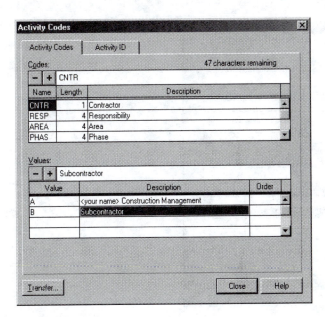

FIGURE M17.5

is now showing in the activity form. It is listed first because you input it in front of the other codes.

6. The next step is to assign <u>V</u>alues: to the codes. For example, we said earlier that the work on this project is either going to be performed by your company or by subcontractors. Therefore, the Contractor code will have those two values. To insert these values, re-open the Activity Codes window (<u>D</u>efine, <u>A</u>ctivity Codes. . .). Make sure the Contractor code is highlighted.

Click in the Value field and insert an A in this field, then click the button. Enter <your name> Construction Management (up to forty-eight characters) in the Description field, then click . Enter the second value beneath with B in the Value field and Subcontractor in the Description field.

SureTrak will sort the code by its values alphanumerically. In this case, we want our company's activities to be listed before the subcontractor's, so the values are in the right order, since A comes before B. If you wanted the values ordered differently, you would use the Order field and order the values numerically in the order you preferred. When complete with the Contractor code, the Activity Codes window should look like Figure M17.5.

We also want to group the project by responsibility. In your company you have two people who are responsible for this project. Smith is the superintendent and is responsible for the overall project and all the subs. Jones is your carpenter foreman and is responsible for most of the work your company is doing with your crews. Rather than create a new code, we will use the predefined default Responsibility code. You will just have to assign Smith and Jones as its values.

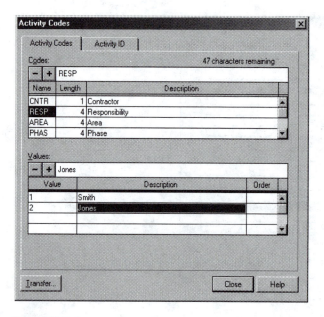

FIGURE M17.6

7. Highlight (click on) the RESP code to select it. Click in the Value field and insert a 1 in this field, then click the 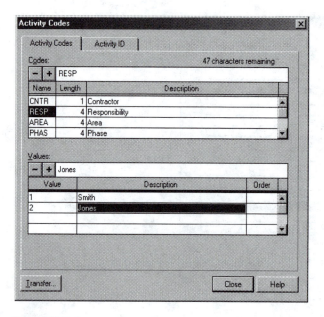 button. Enter Smith in the Description field, then click ▣. Enter the second value beneath with a 2 in the Value field and Jones in the Description field. We used a 1 and 2 (rather than an A and B) in the Value field just to illustrate this option. You may also find it less confusing later when you assign the Contractor and Responsibility codes to the activities. When complete with the Responsibility code, the Activity Codes window should look like Figure M17.6.

8. You are now ready to assign the appropriate activity codes to the activities. [Close] Close the Activity Codes window.

ASSIGNING ACTIVITY CODES

Now that the codes are created, the next step is to assign the appropriate codes and values to the activities. One of the advantages of drawing the project schedule out by hand first is that you can include various bits of information about the project there as you did in Module 1. Use the hand-drawn schedule from Module 1, shown in Figure M17.7. Notice that the contractor (<your company>/subcontractor) and responsibility (Smith/Jones) project information is shown. You will use this information to assign the appropriate codes and values to the activities in the next step.

9. You will assign the codes and values to the activities using the activity form. Open the form by clicking the ▦ button and expand it by clicking the **More >>** button. Select (single-click) the first activity, Notice to Proceed, then click down into the CNTR activity code field and click the pull-down button ▼ to show the two values that you just created for the Contractor activity code (see Figure M17.8). Click **A—<your name> Construction**

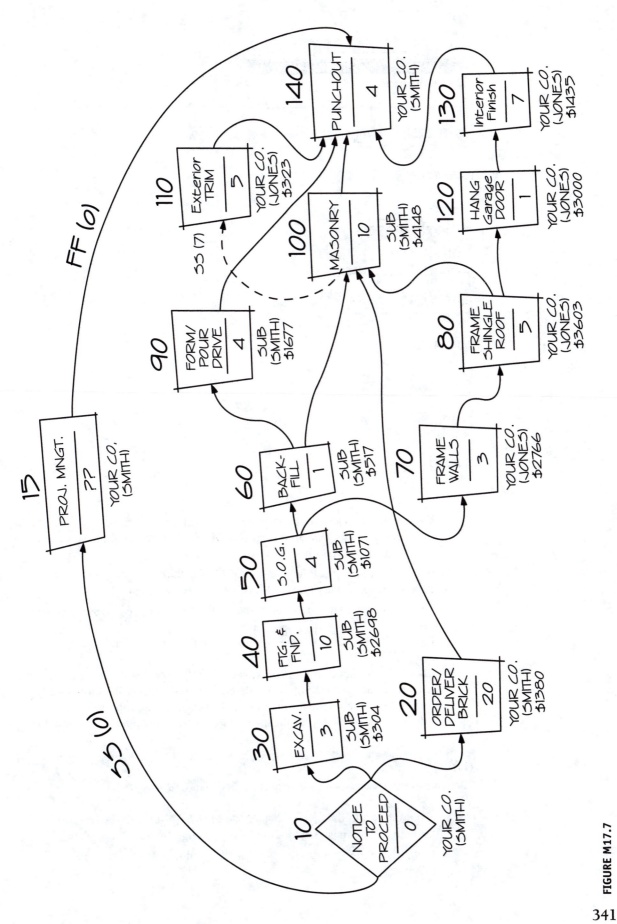

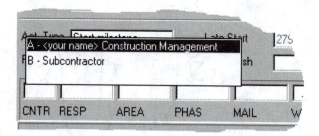

FIGURE M17.8

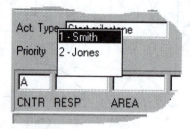

FIGURE M17.9

FIGURE M17.10

Management to select your company for the value of the Contractor code for this activity. Notice that an A is entered in the field. You could have simply entered the letter A, rather than using the pull-down.

10. Next, click in the RESP field and assign **1—Smith** (or simply enter the number 1) as the responsible individual for this activity (see Figure M17.9).

11. The assigned activity codes for Notice to Proceed should be entered as shown in Figure M17.10. Click OK to accept these entries, then click Next to move on to the next activity, Proj. Mngt. (or save time by moving straight to the next activity by single-clicking it—which will automatically accept the entries made to the previous). Assign the appropriate codes and values to Proj. Mngt. Repeat this procedure for the remainder of the activities.

(F.Y.I.)

There is a quicker way to assign activity codes and values to activities.

- Temporarily add the CNTR—Contractor and RESP—Responsibility columns to the activity columns (see Module 11 if you forgot how).
- Next, assign the appropriate values in each column as shown on the following page.

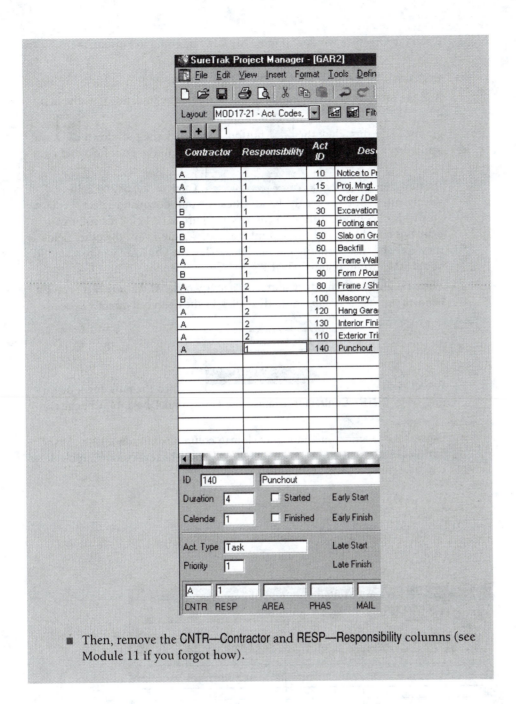

■ Then, remove the CNTR—Contractor and RESP—Responsibility columns (see Module 11 if you forgot how).

GROUPING THE ACTIVITIES BY ACTIVITY CODES

Now that the appropriate activity codes and values have been assigned to the activities, the next step is to group the activities accordingly. You will group the project first by the Contractor code (your company or sub) and then second, subgroup the activities within the Contractor bands by the Responsibility (Smith or Jones) code. Additionally, you will add the project title above all of the activities and sort the activities within each band by early start, total float, and Activity ID.

12. Open the Organize window (Figure M17.11) by going to Format, then Organize, . . . or simply clicking the 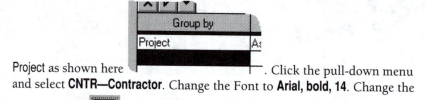 button.

13. Add the project title to the top of all the activities by inserting it as the first group. To do this, click the ⊞ button. Then click the pull-down ▼ and scroll down to select (click on) **Project**. Next click in the Font field and click the pull-down to select ⬚Font⬚. Click in the Bkgrnd field to select a different color for the band. Click the pull-down and select the dark green (third column, fifth row) color (see Figure M17.12). This color will print out on a black and white printer as a dark gray. Leave the other fields as they are. The first grouping is complete. So far, the Organize window should be set as shown in Figure M17.13.

14. The next group will be the Contractor activity code. *Make sure this is added beneath the* Project *group.* To do this, click in the open cell directly beneath

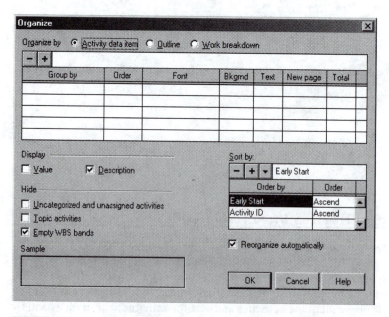

Project as shown here . Click the pull-down menu and select **CNTR—Contractor**. Change the Font to **Arial, bold, 14**. Change the Bkgrnd color to ⬚ medium gray (fourth column, sixth row). Click in the Text field and use the pull-down menu to change the text color from black to white (eighth column, sixth row).

FIGURE M17.11

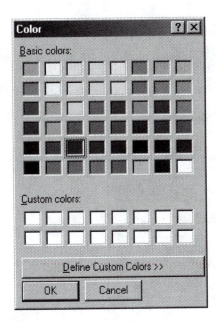

FIGURE M17.12

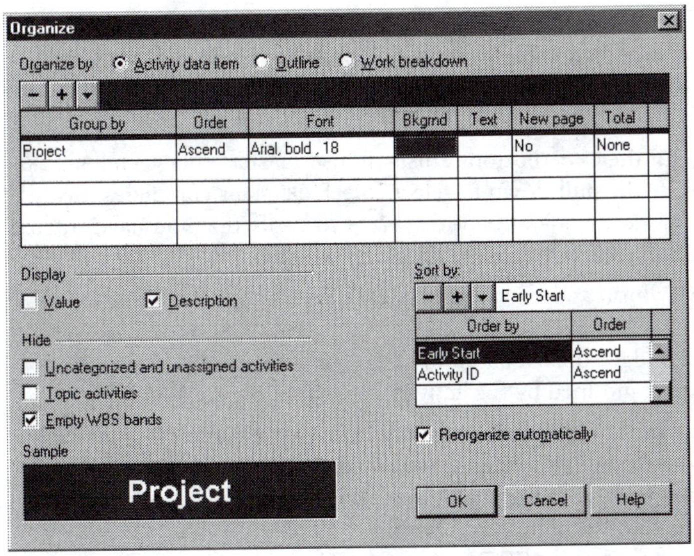

FIGURE M17.13

15. The last group will be the responsibility activity code. *Make sure this is added beneath the* CNTR—**Contractor** group. To do this, click in the open cell directly beneath CNTR—Contractor as you previously did. Click the pull-down menu and select **RESP—Responsibility**. Change the Font to **Arial, bold, 10**. Change the

    Bkgrnd color to ⬜ light gray (sixth column, sixth row). Click in the Text field and use the pull-down menu to change the text color from white to black (first column, sixth row).

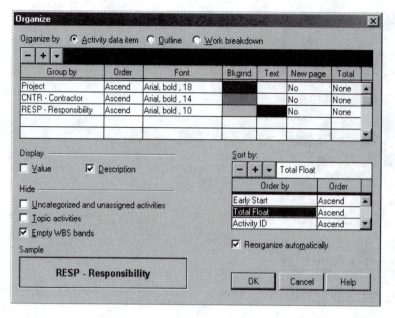

FIGURE M17.14

16. The final setting to make is in the Sort by: field. This field will sort the activities within each band. The current sort probably reads Early Start, then Activity ID. We want to insert Total Float in-between. To do this, select (click on) Activity ID, then hit the ⊞ button. This will insert a space between Early Start and Activity ID. Use the pull-down to select **Total Float**. This completes the entries in this window. Look at Figure M17.14 to verify that you have entered all the information correctly into the Organize window.

17. Close the activity form and move the vertical split bar (thick black line) to the right of the Budgeted Cost column. Click the ▣ Print preview button to view the project grouped by the activity codes (see Figure M17.15).

18. Print out a copy of the GAR2 project schedule to view the project grouped by the activity codes. It will also be used to answer questions from the *Schedule Analysis—Modules 17–21* at the end of Module 21 and will be turned in to your instructor along with the Schedule Analysis.

19. Module 17 is complete. Save ▤ the GAR2 project. Move on to Module 18.

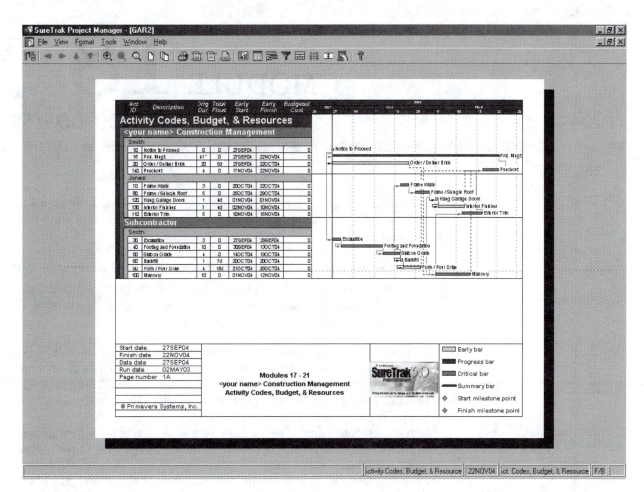

FIGURE M17.15

Preface: SureTrak allows you to assign costs to activities. From these costs, the software can project the cash flow of the project. There are two main ways to input the cost of an activity.

1. The cost of an activity can be input as an exact *lump sum,* or
2. The cost of an activity can be generated from the hourly unit costs of the *resource(s)* needed to complete the activity. This will be covered in the next module.

Combo: Additionally, an activity's cost may be entered as a combination of the two. For example, you could enter the material needed for an activity as a lump sum amount and combine that with the activity's labor and equipment resource costs (calculated from the hourly unit cost of each resource multiplied by the number of hours the activity will take to complete).

In this module, you will assign lump sum costs to activities of the garage construction schedule project. Specifically, you will assign costs to the activities that the subcontractors are performing (the sub bids) and you will assign the material costs for the activities that your company is performing. The labor and equipment costs for the work your company is performing will be entered later as resources in Module 19.

You will continue to work with the garage construction schedule project, specifically GAR2, for this module. Use the hand-drawn project schedule shown in Figure M18.1. Notice that budgeted costs are shown beneath most of the activities. This is another example of the tremendous amount of information that can be shown on a hand-drawn schedule. These same budgeted costs are shown in Table M18.1.

ASSIGNING LUMP SUM COSTS TO ACTIVITIES

When you assign a lump sum cost to an activity in SureTrak, the software spreads that cost equally across the activity's duration. For example, the material cost to frame the walls is $2,766. That amount will be assigned to activity 70—Frame Walls, which has a three (3)-day duration and occurs 20OCT04 through 22OCT04. Therefore, the $2,766 will be spread across those three days at $922 each day.

1. To assign lump sum costs to activities, go to View, Activity Detail, and then Costs to open the Costs window. Select activity 20—Order / Deliver Brick, since that is the first activity to have a cost assigned to it (see Figure M18.2).
2. Click in the cell to the right of the word Resource to enter a name for the resource (SureTrak treats money as a resource). Resources cannot be assigned to activities unless they are first given a name in the Resource Dictionary.

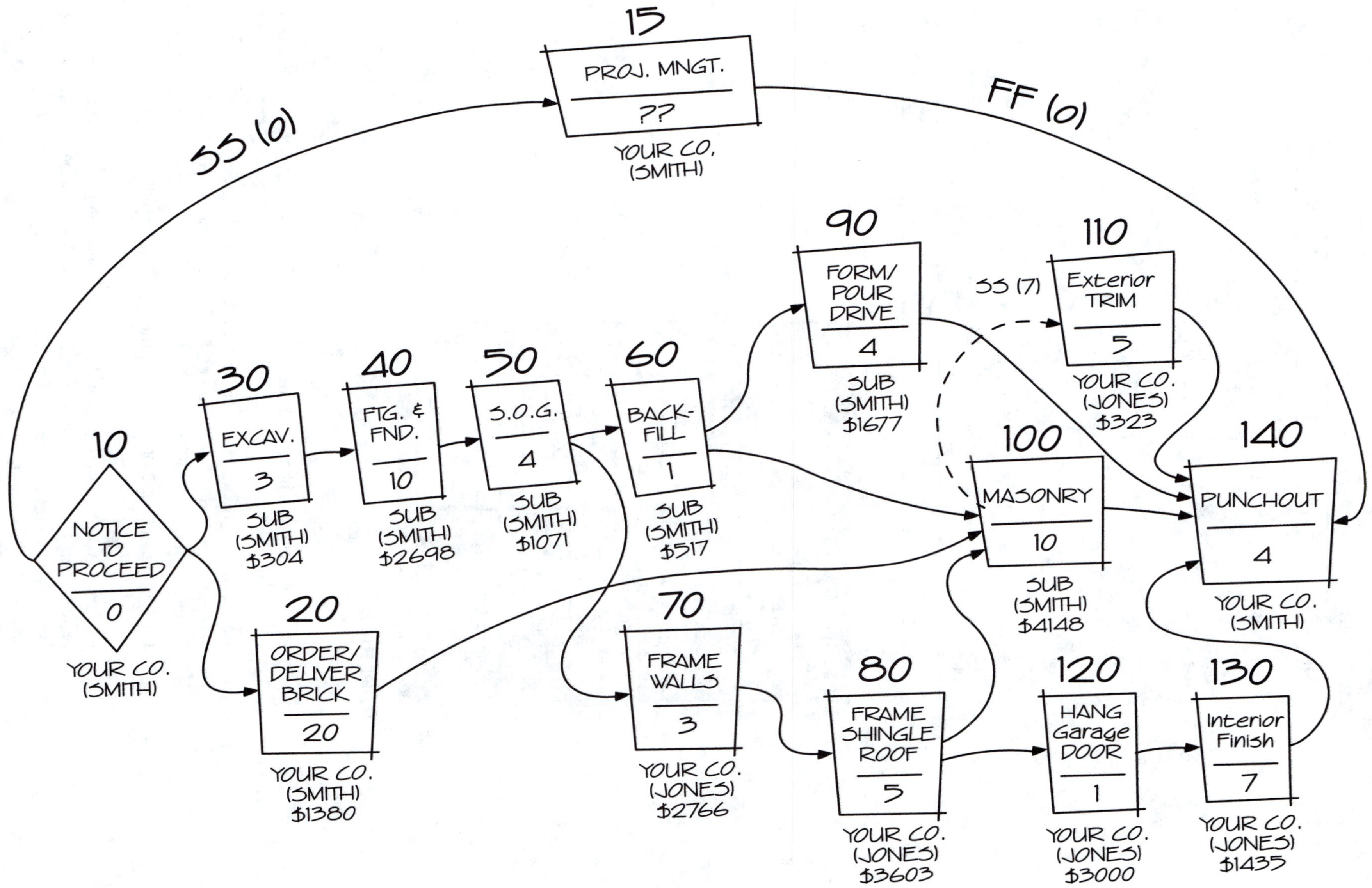

15
PROJ. MNGT.
??
YOUR CO, (SMITH)
SS (0)
FF (0)
10
NOTICE TO PROCEED
0
YOUR CO. (SMITH)
30
EXCAV.
3
SUB (SMITH) $304
40
FTG. & FND.
10
SUB (SMITH) $2698
50
S.O.G.
4
SUB (SMITH) $1071
60
BACK-FILL
1
SUB (SMITH) $517
90
FORM/ POUR DRIVE
4
SUB (SMITH) $1677
SS (7)
110
Exterior TRIM
5
YOUR CO. (JONES) $323
100
MASONRY
10
SUB (SMITH) $4148
140
PUNCHOUT
4
YOUR CO. (SMITH)
20
ORDER/ DELIVER BRICK
20
YOUR CO. (SMITH) $1380
70
FRAME WALLS
3
YOUR CO. (JONES) $2766
80
FRAME SHINGLE ROOF
5
YOUR CO. (JONES) $3603
120
HANG Garage DOOR
1
YOUR CO. (JONES) $3000
130
Interior Finish
7
YOUR CO. (JONES) $1435

FIGURE M18.1

TABLE M18.1

Activity ID	Description	Cost
10	Notice to Proceed	
15	Proj. Mngt.	
20	Order / Deliver Brick	$ 1380
30	Excavation	$ 304
40	Footing and Foundation	$ 2698
50	Slab on Grade	$ 1071
60	Backfill	$ 517
70	Frame Walls	$ 2766
80	Frame / Shingle Roof	$ 3603
90	Form / Pour Drive	$ 1677
100	Masonry	$ 4148
110	Exterior Trim	$ 323
120	Hang Garage Doors	$ 3000
130	Interior Finishes	$ 1435
140	Punchout	
Total		$22,922

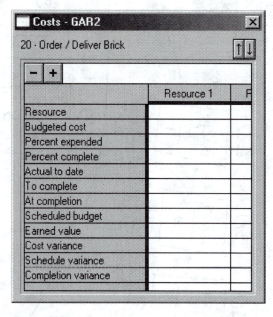

FIGURE M18.2

However, they can be named "on-the-fly" in other windows including the

Costs window; therefore, enter (type in) **COST** here. Click the [✔] button to accept this resource. The resource *COST* has now been added to the Resource Dictionary for this project.

3. Click in the At completion cell. Enter the cost of the brick (1380) in this cell.

Click the [✔] button to accept this amount. Notice that the amount prefills above. That is why we enter the amount in the At completion cell—to avoid entering it two other times. When this activity is complete, the Costs window should look like Figure M18.3.

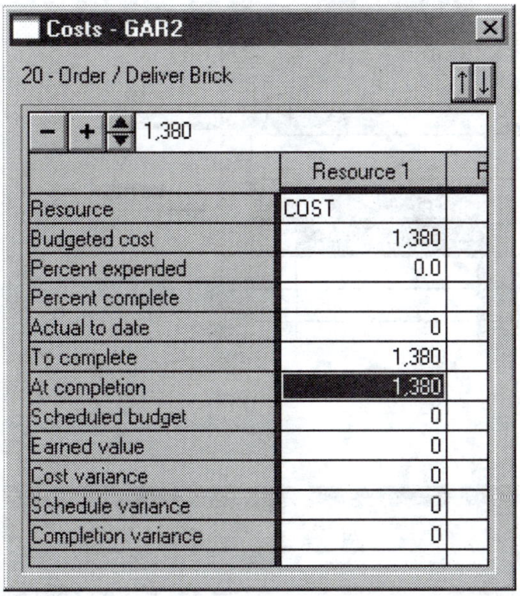

FIGURE M18.3

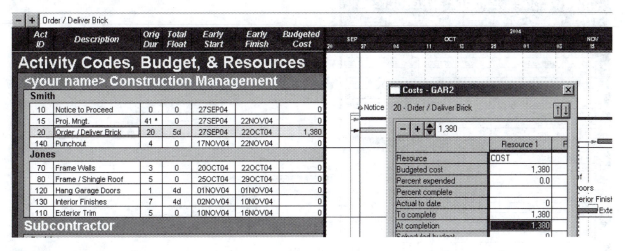

FIGURE M18.4

4. Notice that the cost for this activity is also shown in the Budgeted Cost column on the project schedule. You may have to move the Costs window and the thick black vertical split bar to see it (see Figure M18.4).

5. Move on to the next activity. Use the [↓] button in the upper right-hand corner of the Costs window to move to the next activity and the

[↑] to move back up.

Be Aware: The activities are no longer in numeric order, so make sure you enter the correct cost for each activity. Arrow down to activity **70—Frame Walls**. Click in the cell next to the word **Resource**. Rather than typing in the resource (**COST**), select it using the pull-down menu since it is now in the resource dictionary (see Figure M18.5). Enter the cost **2766** for this activity in the **At completion** cell.

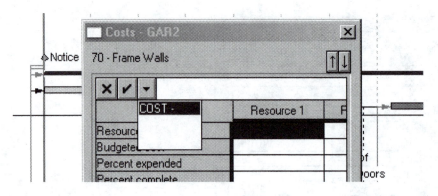

FIGURE M18.5

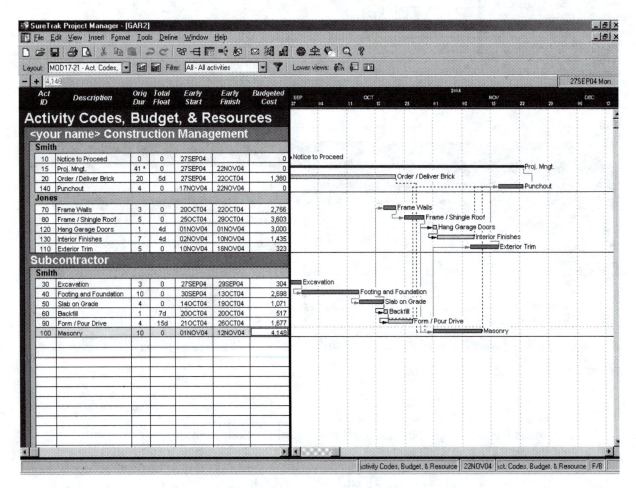

FIGURE M18.6

6. Using the same procedure, enter the appropriate costs for the remainder of the activities. Close the Costs window when complete. Check the costs you entered on your schedule with those in the Budgeted Cost column in Figure M18.6.

7. Module 18 is complete. Save ![save icon] the GAR2 project. Move on to Module 19 to input the labor and equipment resources.

MODULE **19**
Resources

Preface: A resource can be anything it takes to get the job done, such as labor, equipment, materials, management, cash, and so on—really anything that is needed to accomplish work. SureTrak has powerful resource scheduling and management capabilities. It allows you to assign various resources to project activities and track and control them throughout the project. However, before resources can be assigned to project activities, the resources must be defined for that project; that is, you have to tell the computer what resources your company has available for that project. When a project is created, there are no defined resources in its Resource Dictionary.

We will continue to use the garage construction schedule project (GAR2) for this module. You will define various resources for the GAR2 project, then assign labor, management, and equipment resources to the activities that your company is performing.

DEFINING RESOURCES

The only resource we have used so far on this project is cash (in the previous module). Therefore, you need to tell the computer what resources your company has for this project and how much they cost your company at an hourly rate. Table M19.1 lists various labor resources and one equipment resource (scaffolding). The hourly rate for the scaffolding is based on the rental rate, per hour, for 50 linear feet of common bricklayers scaffolding, one level high. In SureTrak, all resource calculations are driven by hourly rates. Following the directions below, enter the resources in Table M19.1 into the Resource Dictionary for the (GAR2) project.

1. To enter the resources, go to <u>D</u>efine and then <u>R</u>esources . . . to open the Define Resources window (Figure M19.1).

2. Notice that the COST resource is already there (you created that resource on the fly in the previous module). Start by creating the carpenter resource. Click

TABLE M19.1

Resource	Abbreviated Description	Cost Per Hour
Carpenter	CRPN	$23.89
Carpenter Foreman	CRPN FOR	$28.55
Carpenter Helper	CRPN HLP	$18.10
Laborer Class 1	LAB CL 1	$16.26
Laborer Class 2	LAB CL 2	$12.68
Brick Mason	MASON	$28.46
Project Manager	PROJMGR	$57.04
Assistant Project Manager	PROJMGRA	$48.44
Project Superintendent	PROJSUP	$42.20
Scaffolding	SCAFFOLD	$ 2.00

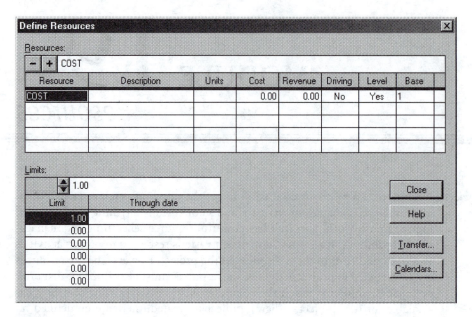

FIGURE M19.1

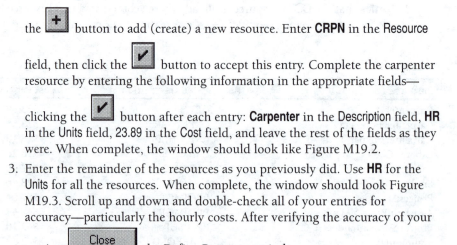

FIGURE M19.2

the button to add (create) a new resource. Enter **CRPN** in the Resource

field, then click the button to accept this entry. Complete the carpenter resource by entering the following information in the appropriate fields—

clicking the button after each entry: **Carpenter** in the Description field, **HR** in the Units field, 23.89 in the Cost field, and leave the rest of the fields as they were. When complete, the window should look like Figure M19.2.

3. Enter the remainder of the resources as you previously did. Use **HR** for the Units for all the resources. When complete, the window should look Figure M19.3. Scroll up and down and double-check all of your entries for accuracy—particularly the hourly costs. After verifying the accuracy of your

entries, Close the Define Resources window.

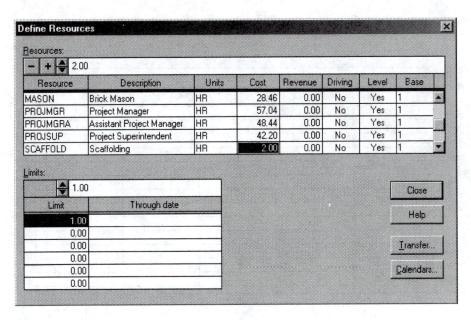

FIGURE M19.3

TABLE M19.2

Activity	Resources Needed	Total Budgeted Cost
70 Frame Walls	Carp Fore., (3) Carpenters, Carp Helper, Lab Class 1	$5,996
80 Frame / Shingle Roof	Carp Fore. (1/4th), (3) Carpenters, Lab Class 1, Lab Class 2	$7,913
120 Hang Garage Doors	Carp Fore. (3/4th), (2) Carpenters, Lab Class 1	$3,684
130 Interior Finishes	Carp Fore. (1/2lf), (3) Carpenters, (2) Lab Class 1	$8,069
110 Exterior Trim	Carp Fore. (1/4th), (3) Carpenters, (2) Lab Class 2, (1) Scaffolding	$4,570

ASSIGNING RESOURCES TO ACTIVITIES

Now that the computer knows what resources your company has available for this project, the next step is to assign resources to certain activities that are being performed by your company.

Remember: You have already assigned subcontractor costs to the subactivities and material costs to activities your company is performing as **Cost** resources in the previous module.

Table M19.2 shows the activities that require labor and/or equipment resources, the resources needed, and the total cost of the activity (*including the material cost assigned in the previous module*). This cost should match the one that appears on the schedule in the budgeted cost column if you did it right.

Following the directions below, assign the resources in Table M19.2 to the activities listed.

4. Start with activity #70—Frame Walls, so highlight it by single-clicking on it. Next, go to View, Activity Detail, and then to Resources to open the Resources window (Figure M19.4).

5. We will enter the carpenter foreman resource first. Notice that the COST resource is already there. (*Be very careful not to accidentally delete the COST resource from the activity—if you do, you will have to add the material cost*

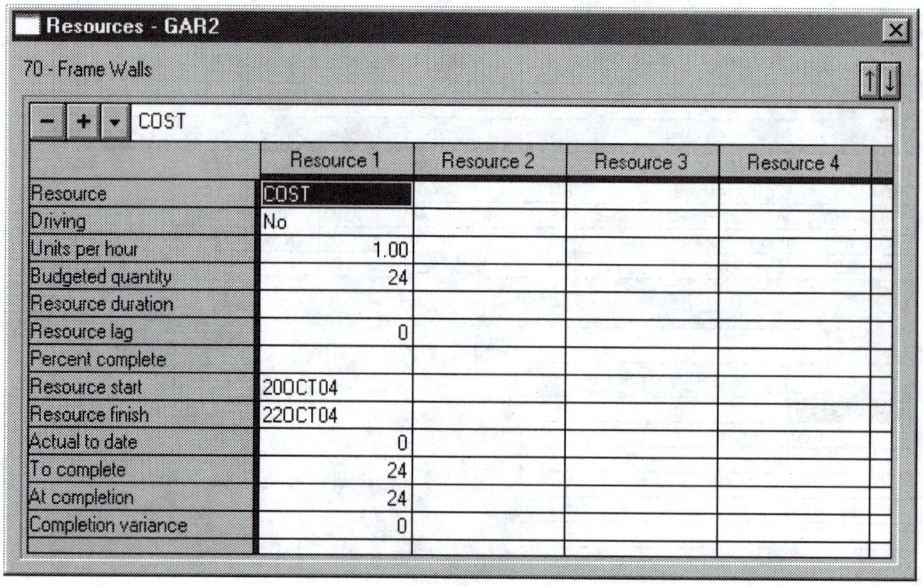

FIGURE M19.4

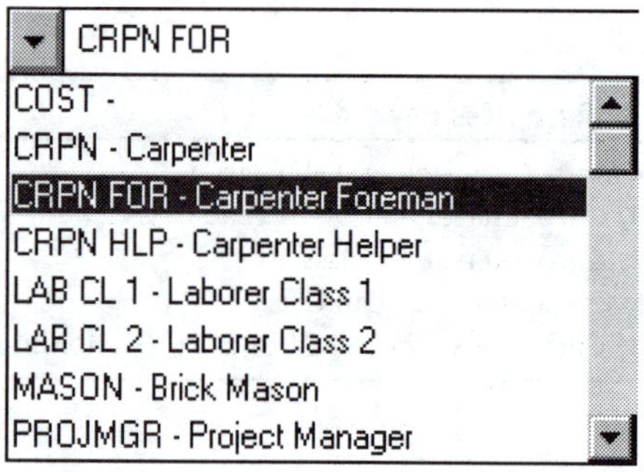

FIGURE M19.5

($2,766) *back in [see Module 18].*). Click in the **Resource 2** cell *to the right* of the COST resource. Use the pull-down menu to see the resources that you have just added to the dictionary (Figure M19.5). Click on **CRPN FOR— Carpenter Foreman** to enter this resource.

Note: Notice that the Units per hour cell defaults to one. This means that there is only one of that resource (that is, [1] carpenter foreman) working on that activity. Also notice that the **Budgeted quantity** cell defaults to the number of total hours that that resource will expend throughout the entire duration of the activity. Therefore, the carpenter foreman will have a budgeted quantity of 24 hours (that is, *[1 carpenter foreman]*[8 hours per day]*[3-days duration]*). The carpenter foreman resource for activity #70—Frame Walls has been entered. Move on to the next instruction to enter the remainder of the resources for this activity.

6. To enter the carpenter resource, click in the **Resource 3** cell and use the pull-down to select **CRPN–Carpenter**. Since we need three (3) carpenters working on this activity, enter a 3 in the Units per hour cell. Notice that the Budgeted quantity cell changed to 72 hours (that is, *[3 carpenters]*[8 hours per day]*[3-days duration]*). Next, click in the **Resource 4** cell and use the pull-down menu to select **CRPN HLP—Carpenter Helper**. Complete the resource entries for this

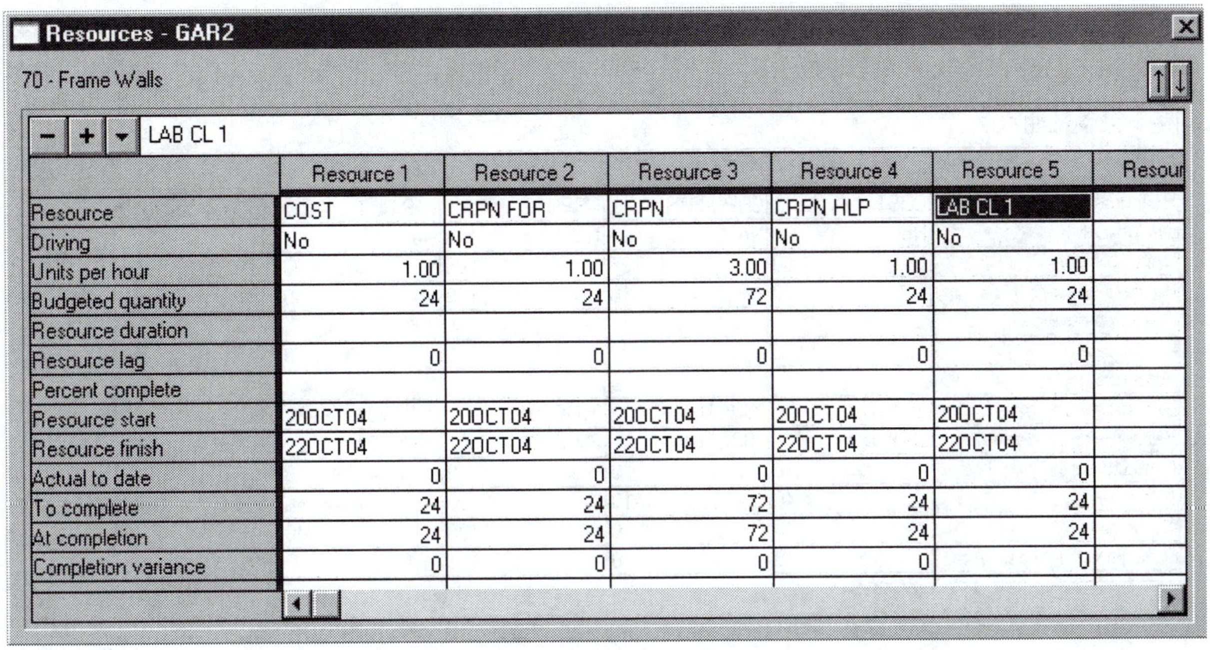

FIGURE M19.6

activity by entering **LAB CL 1—Laborer Class 1** in the Resource 5 cell (you may have to widen the Resources window to get to that cell). When complete, the Resources window for activity #70—Frame Walls should look like Figure M19.6. Now look at the Budgeted Cost column on the schedule for this activity (you may have to move the Resources window to see it). Verify that it shows the accurate amount ($5,996) for this activity. If it does not, ask your instructor for help.

7. Use the ⬆⬇ arrows in the Resource window to move around from activity to activity *or* simply click on the activity you want to move to. Go to the #80—Frame / Shingle Roof activity. Enter the resources for this activity, beginning with the **CRPN FOR—Carpenter Foreman** in the Resource 2 cell. The carpenter foreman is spending only one-fourth of his/her time each day on this activity. To input this amount, enter 0.25 in the Units per hour cell, then click the

   ✔ button to accept this entry. Notice that the Budgeted quantity cell has changed to 10 hours (that is, *[1 carpenter foreman]* *[2 hours per day]* *[5-days duration]*). Enter the remainder of the resources (3 carpenters, a laborer class 1, and a laborer class 2) for this activity. When complete, the Resources window for activity #80—Frame / Shingle Roof should look like Figure M19.7. Verify that the Budgeted Cost column on the schedule shows ($7,913) as the amount for this activity. If it does not, ask your instructor for help.

8. Next, go to the #120—Hang Garage Door activity. Enter the resources for this activity. Remember that the carpenter foreman is spending only three-fourths of his/her time each day on this activity. When complete, the Resources window for activity #120—Hang Garage Door should look like that shown in Figure M19.8. Verify that the Budgeted Cost column on the schedule shows ($3,684) as the amount for this activity. If it does not, ask your instructor for help.

9. Next, go to the #130—Interior Finishes activity. Enter the resources for this activity. Remember that the carpenter foreman is spending only one-half of

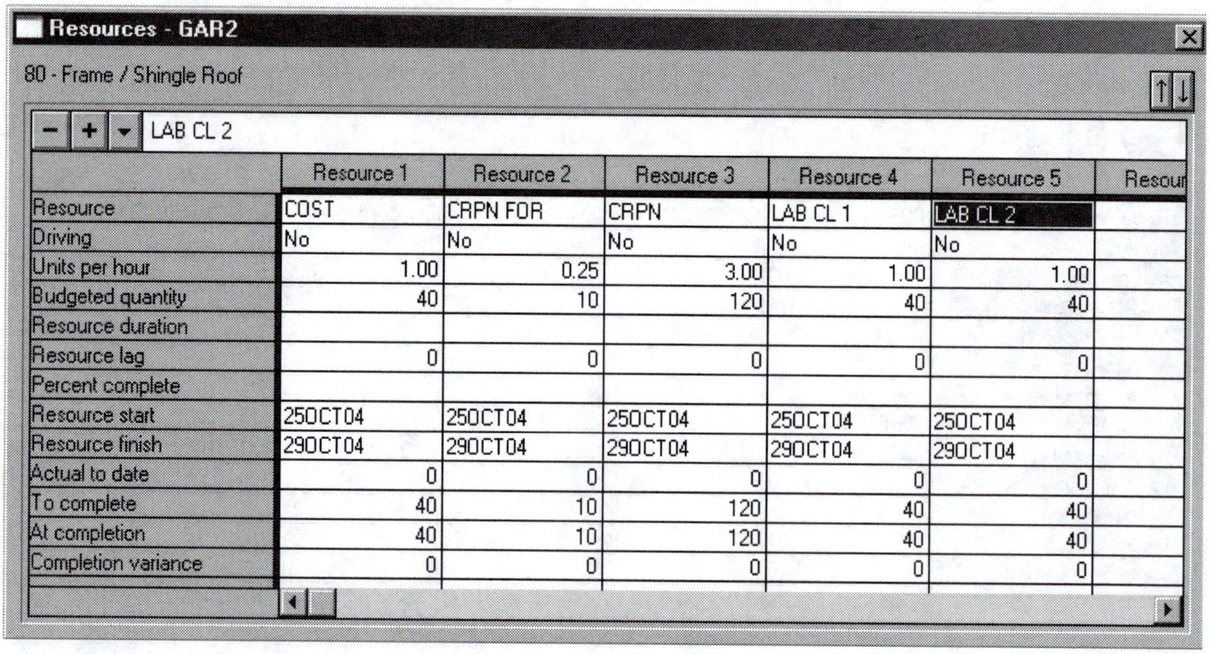

Resources - GAR2 ✕

80 - Frame / Shingle Roof ↑↓

− + ▼ LAB CL 2

	Resource 1	Resource 2	Resource 3	Resource 4	Resource 5	Resour
Resource	COST	CRPN FOR	CRPN	LAB CL 1	LAB CL 2	
Driving	No	No	No	No	No	
Units per hour	1.00	0.25	3.00	1.00	1.00	
Budgeted quantity	40	10	120	40	40	
Resource duration						
Resource lag	0	0	0	0	0	
Percent complete						
Resource start	25OCT04	25OCT04	25OCT04	25OCT04	25OCT04	
Resource finish	29OCT04	29OCT04	29OCT04	29OCT04	29OCT04	
Actual to date	0	0	0	0	0	
To complete	40	10	120	40	40	
At completion	40	10	120	40	40	
Completion variance	0	0	0	0	0	

FIGURE M19.7

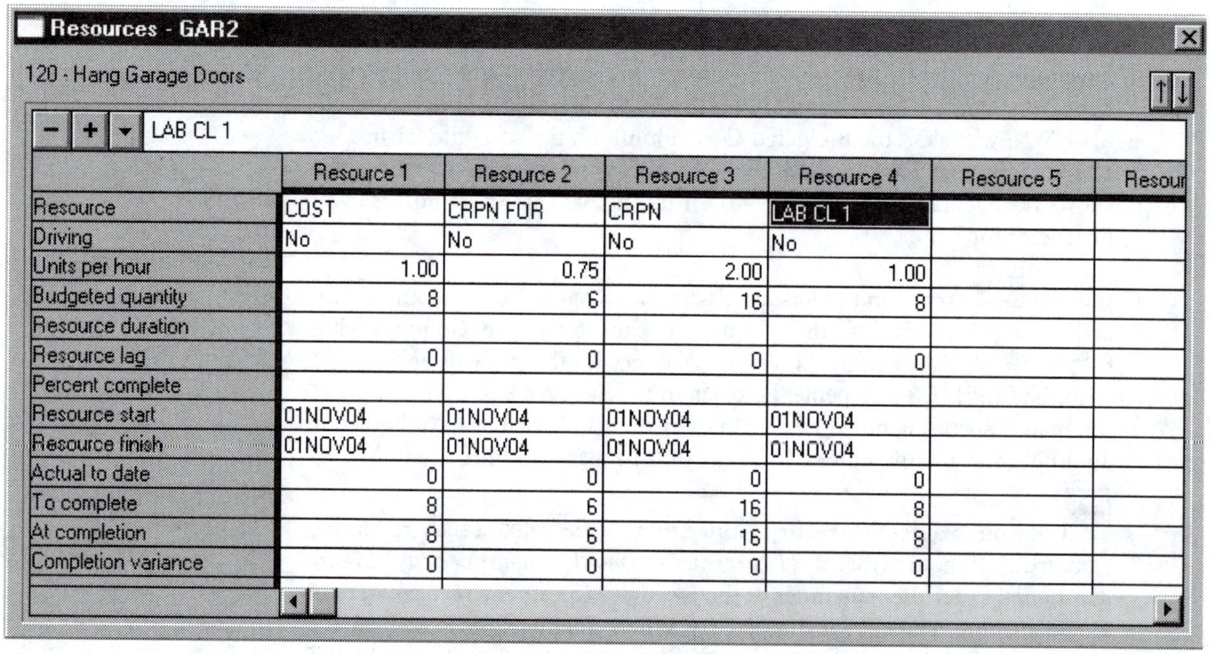

Resources - GAR2 ✕

120 - Hang Garage Doors ↑↓

− + ▼ LAB CL 1

	Resource 1	Resource 2	Resource 3	Resource 4	Resource 5	Resour
Resource	COST	CRPN FOR	CRPN	LAB CL 1		
Driving	No	No	No	No		
Units per hour	1.00	0.75	2.00	1.00		
Budgeted quantity	8	6	16	8		
Resource duration						
Resource lag	0	0	0	0		
Percent complete						
Resource start	01NOV04	01NOV04	01NOV04	01NOV04		
Resource finish	01NOV04	01NOV04	01NOV04	01NOV04		
Actual to date	0	0	0	0		
To complete	8	6	16	8		
At completion	8	6	16	8		
Completion variance	0	0	0	0		

FIGURE M19.8

his/her time each day on this activity. When complete, the Resources window for activity #130—Interior Finishes should look like Figure M19.9. Verify that the Budgeted Cost column on the schedule shows ($8,069) as the amount for this activity. If it does not, ask your instructor for help.

10. Next, go to the #110—Exterior Trim activity. Enter the resources for this activity. Remember that the carpenter foreman is spending only one-fourth of his/her time each day on this activity and that this activity has scaffolding as a resource. Accept the default of 1 in the Units per hour cell for scaffolding—this

Resources - GAR2

130 - Interior Finishes

2.00

	Resource 1	Resource 2	Resource 3	Resource 4	Resource 5	Resour
Resource	COST	CRPN FOR	CRPN	LAB CL 1		
Driving	No	No	No	No		
Units per hour	1.00	0.50	3.00	2.00		
Budgeted quantity	56	28	168	112		
Resource duration						
Resource lag	0	0	0	0		
Percent complete						
Resource start	02NOV04	02NOV04	02NOV04	02NOV04		
Resource finish	10NOV04	10NOV04	10NOV04	10NOV04		
Actual to date	0	0	0	0		
To complete	56	28	168	112		
At completion	56	28	168	112		
Completion variance	0	0	0	0		

FIGURE M19.9

Resources - GAR2

110 - Exterior Trim

SCAFFOLD

	Resource 1	Resource 2	Resource 3	Resource 4	Resource 5	Resour
Resource	COST	CRPN FOR	CRPN	LAB CL 2	SCAFFOLD	
Driving	No	No	No	No	No	
Units per hour	1.00	0.25	3.00	2.00	1.00	
Budgeted quantity	40	10	120	80	40	
Resource duration						
Resource lag	0	0	0	0	0	
Percent complete						
Resource start	10NOV04	10NOV04	10NOV04	10NOV04	10NOV04	
Resource finish	16NOV04	16NOV04	16NOV04	16NOV04	16NOV04	
Actual to date	0	0	0	0	0	
To complete	40	10	120	80	40	
At completion	40	10	120	80	40	
Completion variance	0	0	0	0	0	

FIGURE M19.10

will provide for the cost of renting a section of scaffolding, one level high, around two sides of the building. That way, the laborers can be moving one side while the carpenters are on the other. When complete, the Resources window for activity #110—Exterior Trim should look like Figure M19.10. Verify that the Budgeted Cost column on the schedule shows ($4,570) as the amount for this activity. If it does not, ask your instructor for help.

MORE ON ASSIGNING RESOURCES

In addition to the labor and equipment resources previously assigned, add the following resources to the Project Management (#15) and Punchout (#140) activities using the instructions below. Many of the resources are not full, eight-hour-per-day type resources, so they may be a bit tricky to input. As an example, on the Punchout (#140) activity below, the assistant project manager will work a total of four hours (two walk-throughs @ two hours per walk-through) on the punchout.

11. Enter the following resources for the Project Management (#15) activity. The project will require about a half-hour per day of the project manager's time. Since the project is forty-one days long, a half-hour per day would be equal to 20.5 total hours of the project manager's time throughout the entire project. This amount can be entered directly into the To Complete cell; however, this cell will not accept decimals, so round up and enter 21 into this cell. Notice that the Budgeted quantity cell also changed to 21 and that the Units per hour cell changed to 0.06, which is one-sixteenth of an eight-hour day.

In addition to the project manager, the assistant project manager will be on-site about two hours per day and the superintendent will be there full-time. When complete, the Resources window for activity Project Management (#15) should look like Figure M19.11. Verify that the Budgeted Cost column on the schedule shows ($19,012) as the amount for this activity. If it does not, ask your instructor for help.

12. Enter the following resources for the Punchout (#140) activity. During punchout the superintendent spends about two-thirds of the day, with a carpenter by his/her side about half that time. To input this, enter 0.66 in the Units per hour cell for the superintendent and 0.33 in the Units per hour cell for the carpenter. The assistant project manager will spend around two hours per walk-through and it usually takes two walk-throughs (for a total of four hours) to get a building punched out. To enter this, enter 4 directly

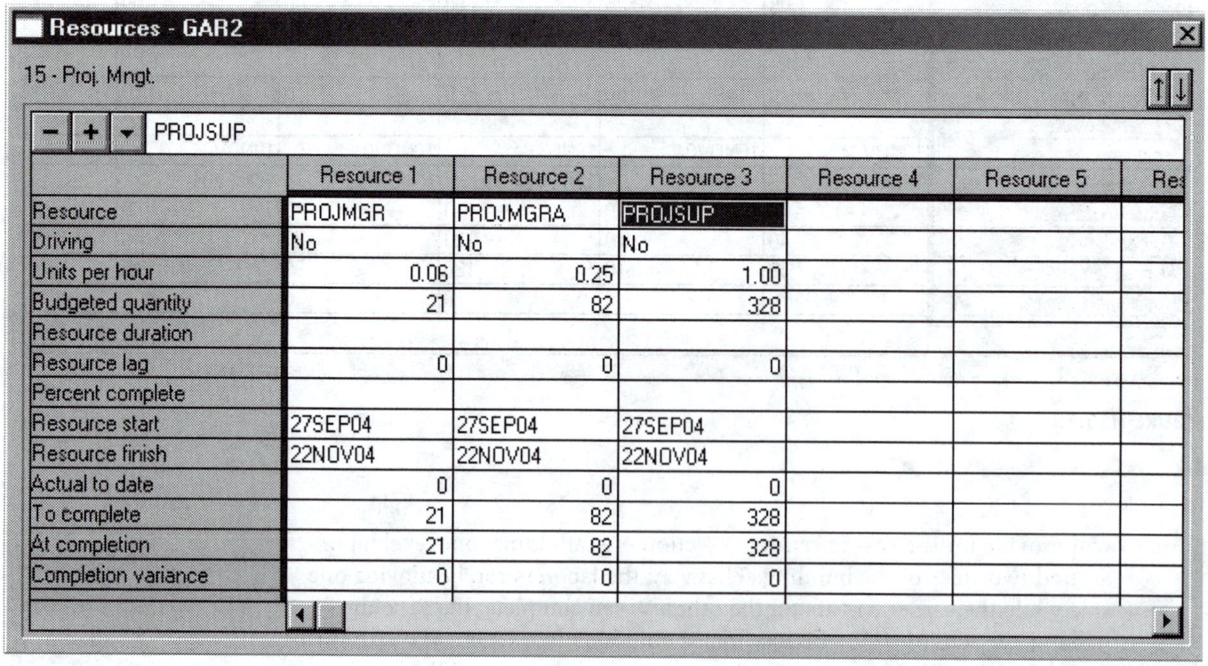

Resources - GAR2

15 - Proj. Mngt.

PROJSUP

Resource	Resource 1	Resource 2	Resource 3	Resource 4	Resource 5	Res
Resource	PROJMGR	PROJMGRA	PROJSUP			
Driving	No	No	No			
Units per hour	0.06	0.25	1.00			
Budgeted quantity	21	82	328			
Resource duration						
Resource lag	0	0	0			
Percent complete						
Resource start	27SEP04	27SEP04	27SEP04			
Resource finish	22NOV04	22NOV04	22NOV04			
Actual to date	0	0	0			
To complete	21	82	328			
At completion	21	82	328			
Completion variance	0	0	0			

FIGURE M19.11

	Resource 1	Resource 2	Resource 3	Resource 4	Resource 5	Res
Resource	PROJSUP	CRPN	PROJMGRA	PROJMGR		
Driving	No	No	No	No		
Units per hour	0.66	0.33	0.13	0.03		
Budgeted quantity	21	11	4	1		
Resource duration						
Resource lag	0	0	0	0		
Percent complete						
Resource start	17NOV04	17NOV04	17NOV04	17NOV04		
Resource finish	22NOV04	22NOV04	22NOV04	22NOV04		
Actual to date	0	0	0	0		
To complete	21	11	4	1		
At completion	21	11	4	1		
Completion variance	0	0	0	0		

Resources - GAR2

140 - Punchout

FIGURE M19.12

into the **To Complete** cell for the assistant project manager resource. Finally, the project manager will spend an hour reviewing the punchout paperwork, so enter a 1 directly into the **To Complete** cell for the project manager resource.

When complete, the Resources window for activity Punchout (#140) should look like Figure M19.12. Verify that the Budgeted Cost column on the schedule shows ($1,394) as the amount for this activity. If it does not, ask your instructor for help.

13. You are now finished inputting the project resources. Your project schedule should look like Figure M19.13. The only thing that has really changed is the amount in the Budgeted Cost column on the schedule. The next two modules will explain how to illustrate the budget and resource information in various ways.

14. Module 19 is complete. Save the GAR2 project. Move on to Module 20 to view the project cash flow and other graphical displays of the project resources.

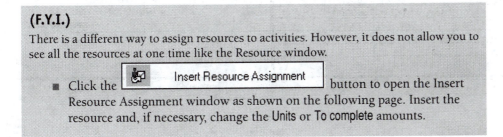

(F.Y.I.)

There is a different way to assign resources to activities. However, it does not allow you to see all the resources at one time like the Resource window.

- Click the   **Insert Resource Assignment**   button to open the Insert Resource Assignment window as shown on the following page. Insert the resource and, if necessary, change the **Units** or **To complete** amounts.

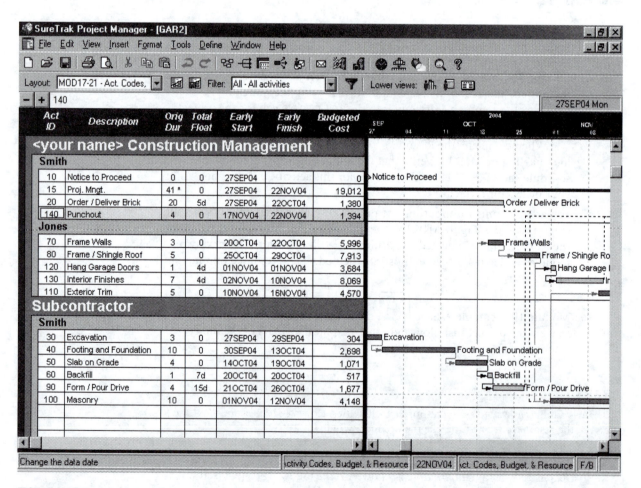

FIGURE M19.13

Preface: SureTrak allows you to track resource information either graphically with resource profiles or numerically in a tabular form with resource tables. The profiles and tables in SureTrak can display many types of resource information including quantities, costs, revenues, net profit, and budget in many different ways. You can view this data for a specific resource, all resources, or any combination of resources. Profiles and tables can reflect this data for a selected activity, several selected activities, or all activities. Resource management is one of the greatest strengths of SureTrak.

In this module, you will work with resource profiles to display the resources from the GAR2 project. You will work with resource tables in the next module. We will be covering only a few of the more common profiles in this module. However, you will learn enough to investigate the many other available profiles on your own.

PROJECT CASH FLOW

The most important resource needed in construction is cash. The contractor typically does not have all the cash available to build the entire project, but rather counts on receiving progress payments (usually monthly) from the owner to recoup costs as the project is being built. Similarly, the owner typically does not have all the cash available to pay for the entire project, but rather will borrow the funds from a bank, or other institution, in the form of a construction loan which is later paid off with permanent financing. In both cases, it is very important to monitor the flow of cash throughout the project.

Additionally, some project managers use cash flow as a way of monitoring the construction progress. Cash flow is a very accurate indicator of how much work is scheduled to be put in place for a specific period of time. For example, if the project schedule says that the cash flow for a particular month is to be $2 million, but only $1.5 million of construction was put in place that month, there's a problem.

The first resource profile you will create is a histogram and cumulative curve of the project cash flow shown in weekly increments.

1. To view the cash flow of the project (or any other resource), you need to turn on the resource profile on the screen. To do this, go to View, Resource

    Profile, or simply click the ▥ button. Notice in Figure M20.1 that a histogram resource profile appears on the bottom of the project window directly beneath the activities and uses the same timescale that the activities use. The profile is currently displaying the default settings for resource profiles. To see the total project cash flow, you need to select the appropriate resources and change some format settings.

2. Currently the profile is only displaying the COST resource. Remember, this is the resource we used to input the material costs back in Module 18 and, therefore, the profile includes only material costs. To see the total project cash flow, you need to select all the project resources. Do this by using the pull-down

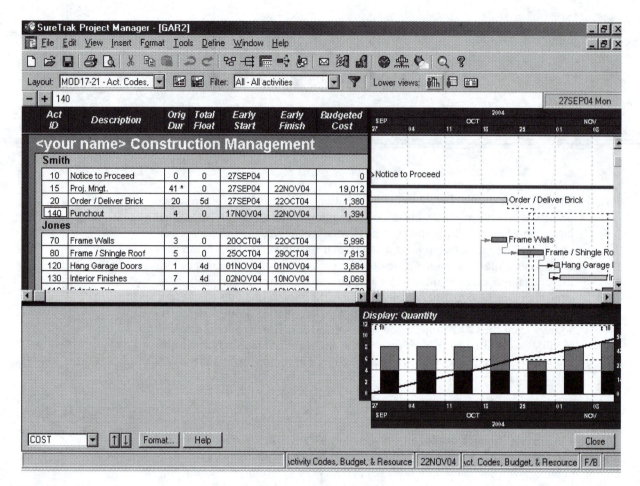

FIGURE M20.1

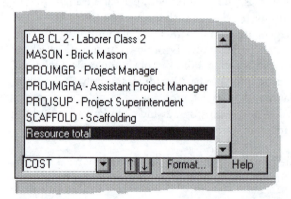

FIGURE M20.2

menu in the bottom left-hand corner of the screen and scrolling down to select **Resource total**, as shown in Figure M20.2.

3. The next step is to change a setting of the resource profile. To do this, click

the [Format...] button near the bottom of the window or go to Format, Resource Profile/Table . . . to open the Format Resource Profile/Table window, as shown in Figure M20.3.

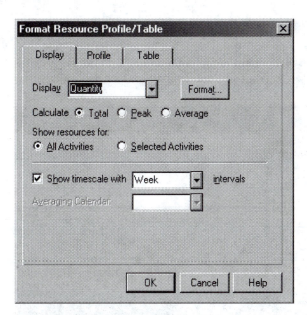

FIGURE M20.3

4. Notice that there are three tabs in this window. Click on each to review what is in each tab and see what different settings are available. The Display tab allows you to choose what type of resource information you want to display in the profile or table, while the Profile and Table tabs allow you to format the profile or table.

5. To show the project cash flow we need to select the appropriate resource information. Go back to the Display tab and in the Display field, use the pull-down menu and select **Budget**. This displays the budgeted cash flow throughout the project based on the early start dates of the project activities. Leave the other fields at their default settings since we want the cash flow to be calculated on

   the *total* budget, for *all activities*, in *weekly* intervals. Click the [OK] button to display the profile.

6. The profile is displayed, but we need to also turn on the resource legend for the profile. To do this, go to View, then click Resource Legend to toggle on the legend. Using the double-sided arrow $(\leftrightarrow)$, reshape the legend to the size shown with the profile in Figure M20.4.

7. The weekly cash flow for the project is now displayed in the profile. Let's analyze the profile. Resource profiles are dynamic; that is, they will automatically change as the project schedule is changed and refined. Additionally, project information can easily and quickly be extracted from the profiles. To illustrate, go to the sixth week in the profile and **left-click** anywhere in the blue histogram bar for that week. The cash flow *for that week* will appear in a window (Figure M20.5) showing the amount of $12,687. This amount is the accumulated budget for the four activities (#15, #100, #120, and #130) that are working that week. Next, **right-click** on the same bar and the cumulative cash flow *for the project* ($45,836) will appear (see Figure M20.5). This amount is the cumulative cash flow of all of the project activities that have occurred up to, and including, that week.

Note: You will need to come back to this profile and repeat these steps to answer questions in the *Schedule Analysis—Modules 17–21*, at the end of Module 21.

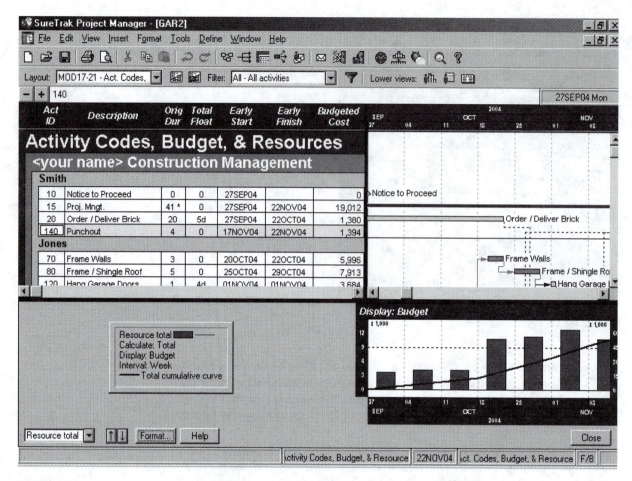

FIGURE M20.4

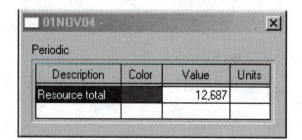

FIGURE M20.5

PRINTING RESOURCE PROFILES

You cannot print a resource profile (or table) if it is not turned on in the print preview—even though it might be turned on in the project window. Follow the instructions below to turn on, format to one page, and print out the GAR2 project with a cash flow resource profile.

8. Click the ⬚ button to go to the print preview. Notice that the resource profile is not there. In the print preview, click the ⬚ button or go to File, Page Setup . . . to open the Page Setup window. Click the Resource Profile/Table

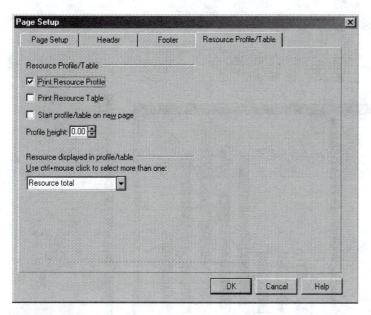

FIGURE M20.6

tab and 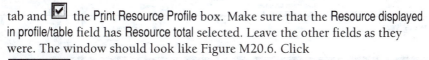 the Print Resource Profile box. Make sure that the Resource displayed in profile/table field has Resource total selected. Leave the other fields as they were. The window should look like Figure M20.6. Click

    [OK] to turn on the resource profile.

9. The resource profile is turned on, but you probably cannot see it. That is because it is on the second page. Notice that the View Page Below

    buttons in the upper left-hand corner of the screen is lit up. Click on it to see page two (Figure M20.7) and the cash flow resource profile. SureTrak will place resource profiles and tables below the last activity of the schedule—if there is enough room. If there is not enough room, it automatically puts it on page two, as was the case here.

10. The profile is disproportionately large. Our next step is to make it smaller and to get it to fit onto the first page. The first thing to do is make more room for the profile by reducing the footer height. To do this, go back to the Page

    Setup ( ) window and to the Footer tab. The default height of zero allows for the footer height to be scaled to a height based on what information is placed inside the footing. Change this height to 1.25 inches as shown

    Height:
    [1.25] Inches

    (you will have to manually type it in). Click

    [OK] . The profile still does not fit onto the first page. The next step is to reduce the height of the profile. Go back to the Resource Profile/Table tab in the Page Setup window and change the Profile height: to 1.50 inches as

    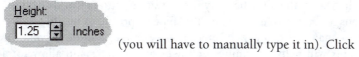

    shown   Profile height: [1.50] . Then click [OK] . The cash flow resource profile should now be on the first page with the project schedule, as shown in Figure M20.8.

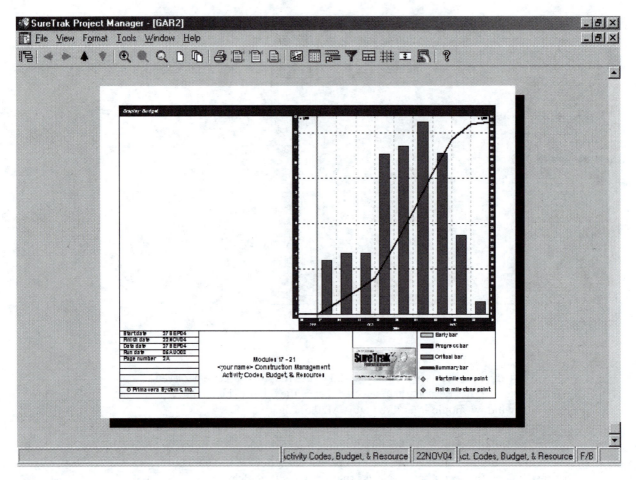

FIGURE M20.7

11. Print a copy of the GAR2 project schedule with the cash flow resource profile. It will be used to answer questions on the *Schedule Analysis—Modules 17–21* at the end of Module 21 and turned in with the analysis.

12. Save the GAR2 project. This will also save the formatting changes you made to the resource profile in the print preview.

OTHER RESOURCE PROFILES

Another common type of resource profile used is that of an individual resource. The profile we will create will show the daily use of the carpenters working on the project. A project manager might want to create this type of profile to quickly and accurately determine how many carpenters (or any other resource) will be needed throughout the project. This will help determine peak uses of resources and allow for advanced planning.

13. Create the profile of an individual resource by first selecting the resource. Start in the project window (not the print preview). If it is not already there,

turn on (click the button) the resource profile. Using the pull-down menu in the bottom left-hand corner, select the **CRPN—Carpenter** resource.

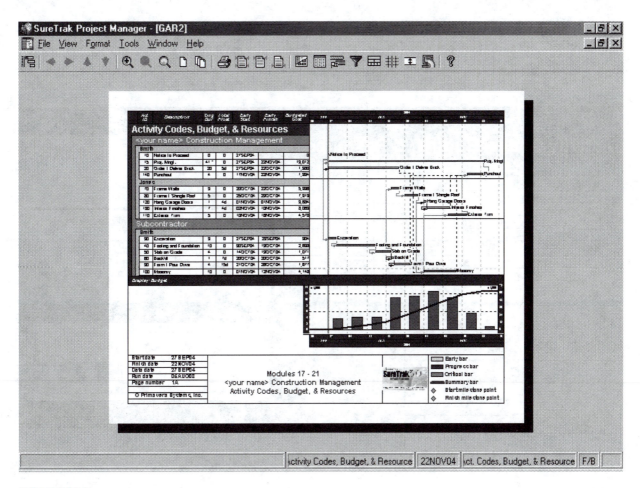

FIGURE M20.8

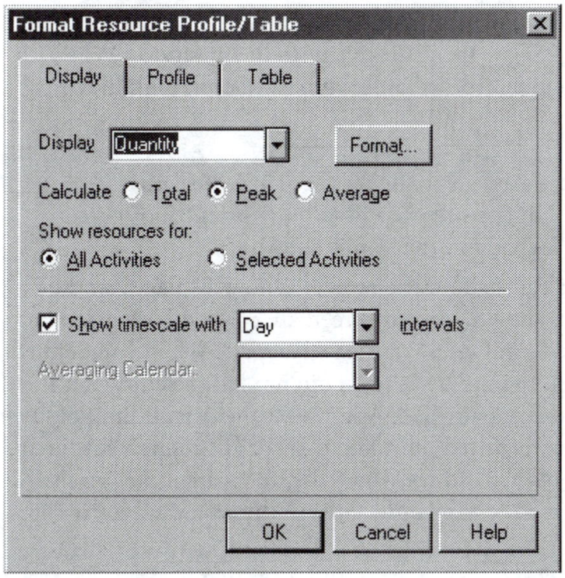

FIGURE M20.9

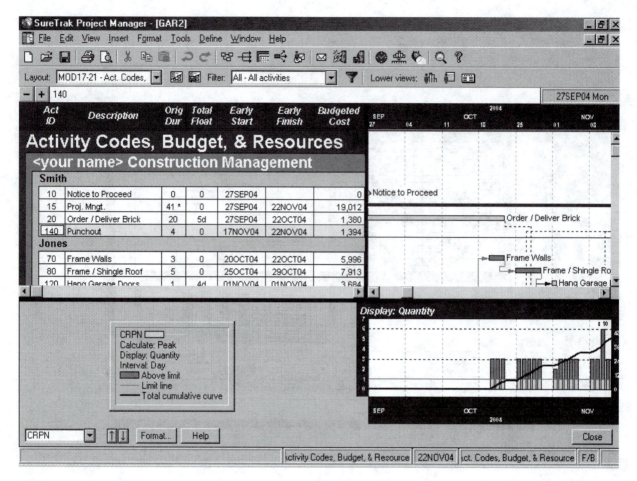

FIGURE M20.10

14. Next, open the Format Resource Profile/Table window (click the

    [Format...] button near the bottom of the window). In the Display tab and in the Display field, use the pull-down and select **Quantity**. Select **Peak** for the calculation of the resource. Show the timescale with **Day** intervals. When complete, the Format Resource Profile/Table window should look like Figure M20.9.

15. Click the [OK] button to display the profile. Then, turn on and reshape the resource legend to the size shown with the profile in Figure M20.10. Make sure all the legend information is showing.

16. The daily use of carpenters throughout the project is now displayed in the profile. Notice that the bars shown on your screen are colored both green and red and separated by the red limit line. Why is it that way? When you defined (created) the resources back in Module 19, you did not tell the computer how many of each resource your company had. As a result, the default limit of (1) resource kicked in. Therefore, the red limit line is set at (1) and any resource bar above that level is colored red. To see where the limits are input, go to Define, then Resources . . . and to the Limits: area in the window. Notice the default is [1].

17. Review the values/content of the carpenter profile. **Left-click** on any histogram bar. The number of carpenters needed for that day will appear in

the window (disregard the unit HR). Next, **right-click** on any bar and the cumulative number of hours expended up to, and including, that day will appear in the window (oddly enough, without a unit).

Note: You will need to come back to this profile and repeat these steps to answer questions in the *Schedule Analysis—Modules 17–21* at the end of Module 21.

16. Click the button to go to the print preview. Notice that the resource profile has to be changed here to show the individual resource of the carpenters. Click the button to open the Page Setup window. Click the Resource Profile/Table tab. Make sure the Print Resource Profile box is . Use the pull-down in the Resource displayed in profile/table field to select CRPN—Carpenter. Leave the other fields as they were and click to show the carpenter resource in the print preview screen.

17. The resource profile and project schedule should all be on one page. If not, go back and follow instructions #9 and #10, in this module, to get both onto one page. Print a copy of the GAR2 project schedule with the carpenter resource profile. It will be used to answer questions on the *Schedule Analysis—Modules 17–21* at the end of Module 21 and turned in with the analysis.

18. Save the GAR2 project. This will also save the formatting changes you made to the resource profile in the print preview.

19. Module 20 is complete. Move on to Module 21 to learn about resource tables.

MODULE 21
Resource Tables

Preface: SureTrak allows you to track resource information either graphically with resource profiles or numerically in a tabular form with resource tables. The profiles and tables in SureTrak can display many types of resource information including quantities, costs, revenues, net profit, and budget in many different ways. You can view this data for a specific resource, all resources, or any combination of resources. Profiles and tables can reflect this data for a selected activity, several selected activities, or all activities. Resource management is one of the greatest strengths of SureTrak.

In the previous module you worked with resource profiles. In this module, you will be working with resource tables. A resource table is the tabular equivalent to a resource profile. That is, resource tables track and illustrate resource information from a project in a numeric, tabular, spreadsheet format.

You will work with resource tables to display the resources from the GAR2 project. We will be covering only a few of the more common tables in this module. However, you will learn enough to investigate the many other tables on your own.

PROJECT CASH FLOW

The most important resource needed in construction is cash. The contractor typically does not have all the cash available to build the entire project, but rather counts on receiving progress payments (usually monthly) from the owner to recoup costs as the project is being built. Similarly, the owner typically does not have all the cash available to pay for the entire project, but rather will borrow the funds from a bank, or other institution, in the form of a construction loan, which is later paid off with permanent financing. In both cases, it is very important to monitor the flow of cash throughout the project.

Additionally, some project managers use cash flow as a way of monitoring the construction progress. Cash flow is a very accurate indicator of how much work is scheduled to be put in place for a specific period of time. For example, if the project schedule says that the cash flow for a particular month is to be $2 million, but only $1.5 million of construction was put in place that month, there's a problem.

The first resource table you will create is one that shows the project cash flow in weekly increments. It will illustrate the same cash flow information that was graphically shown in the profile you created in the previous module.

1. To view the cash flow of the project (or any other resource) in a resource table, you need to turn on the resource table on the screen. To do this, go to

   <u>V</u>iew, Reso<u>u</u>rce Table, or simply click the ▣ button. Notice in Figure M21.1 that a table appears showing the carpenter resource on a daily timescale. This table is displaying the settings from the last resource profile in the previous module. To see the project cash flow, you need to select the appropriate resources and change some format settings.

372

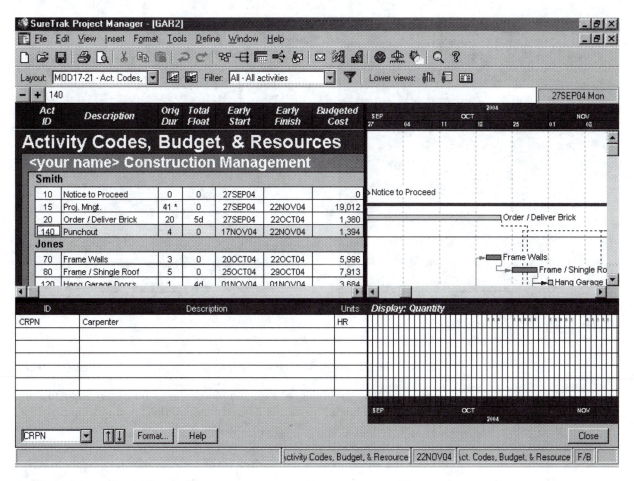

FIGURE M21.1

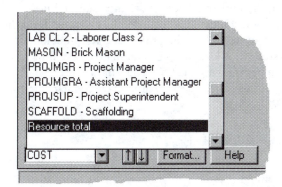

FIGURE M21.2

2. To see the total project cash flow, you need to select all the project resources. Do this by using the pull-down menu in the bottom left-hand corner of the screen and scrolling down to select **Resource total**, as shown in Figure M21.2.

3. The next step is to change some settings of the resource table. Click the

   Format...   button near the bottom of the window or go to Format, Resource Profile/Table, to open the Format Resource Profile/Table window. In the Display tab, go to the Display field and use the pull-down to select **Budget**.

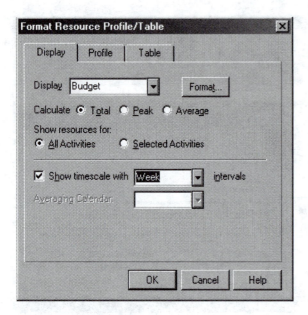

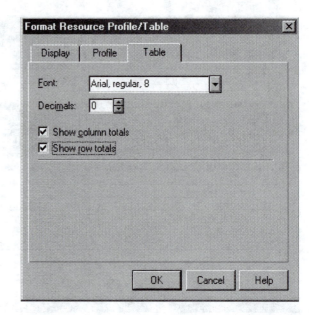

FIGURE M21.3

Select **Total** for the calculation of the resource. Show the timescale with **Week** intervals. Next, go to the Table tab and the boxes for **Show column totals** and **Show row totals**. The Display tab and Table tab settings should match those in Figure M21.3.

4. Click the ☐ OK button to display the table, as shown in Figure M21.4.

5. The weekly cash flow for the project is now displayed in the table. Let's analyze it. Like resource profiles, the resource tables are dynamic; that is, they will automatically change as the project schedule is changed and refined. Additionally, project information can easily and quickly be extracted from the tables. To illustrate, go to the sixth week in the project and **right-click** in the cell that has the weekly cash flow of $12,687. The cumulative cash flow for the project ($45,836) will appear (Figure M21.5). This amount is the cumulative cash flow of all of the project activities that have occurred up to, and including, that week.

Note: You will need to come back to this profile and repeat these steps to answer questions in the *Schedule Analysis—Modules 17–21* at the end of this module.

PRINTING RESOURCE TABLES

You cannot print a resource table (or profile) if it is not turned on in the print preview—even though it might be turned on in the project window. Follow the instructions below to turn on, format to one page, and print out the GAR2 project with a cash flow resource table.

6. Click the ☐ button to go to the print preview. Notice that a resource profile from the previous module is there. Click the ☐ button or go to File, Page Setup . . . to open the Page Setup window. Click the Resource Profile/Table tab to uncheck (☐) the Print Resource Profile and to ☑ the Print Resource

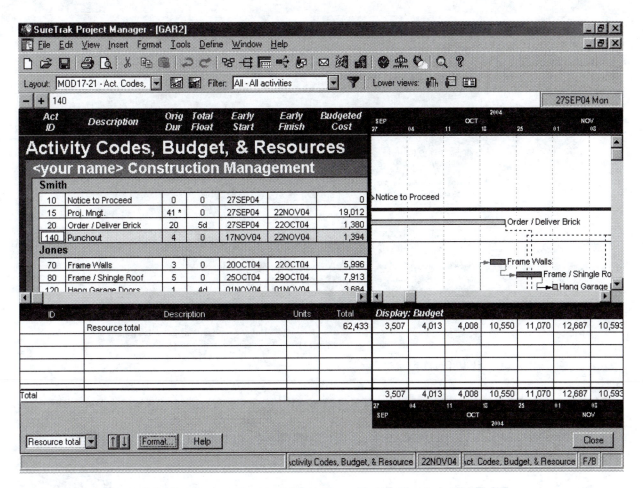

FIGURE M21.4

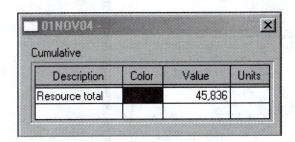

FIGURE M21.5

Table box. Change the Profile <u>h</u>eight: back to **0.00**. Make sure that the Resource displayed in profile/table field has **Resource total** selected. The window should look like Figure M21.6. Click OK to turn on the resource table.

7. The resource table is turned on and fits onto one page. Since the table had just one row, it fit immediately onto one page with the project schedule, as shown in Figure M21.7.

8. Print a copy of the **GAR2** project schedule with the cash flow resource table. It will be used to answer questions on the *Schedule Analysis—Modules 17–21* at the end of this module and will be turned in with the analysis.

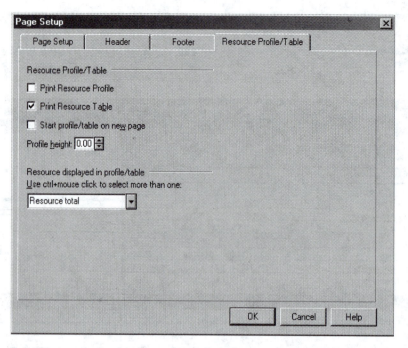

FIGURE M21.6

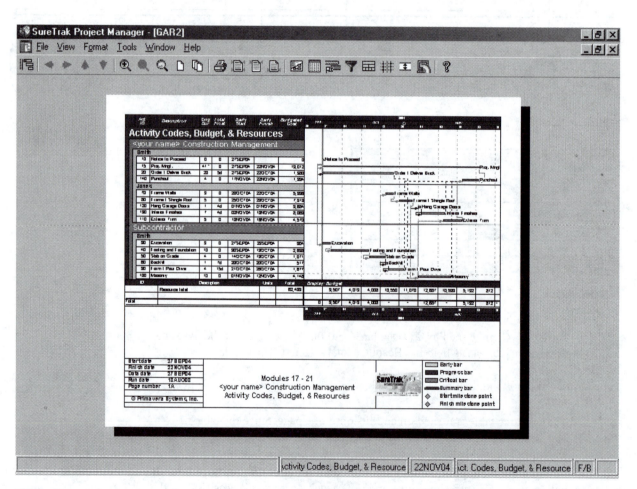

FIGURE M21.7

9. Save ⊞ the GAR2 project. This will also save the formatting changes you made to the resource profile in the print preview.

OTHER RESOURCE TABLES

As in the previous module, the next table you will create will be an individual resource table of the carpenter requirements throughout the project. This table will show the daily use of the carpenters working on the project. A project manager might want to create this type of table to quickly and accurately determine how many carpenters (or any other resource) will be needed throughout the project. This will help determine peak uses of resources and allow for advanced planning.

10. Create the table of an individual resource by first selecting the resource. Start in the project window (not the print preview). If it is not already there, turn on (click the ⊞ button) the resource table. Using the pull-down menu in the bottom left-hand corner, select the **CRPN—Carpenter** resource.

11. Next open the Format Resource Profile/Table window (click the  Format... button near the bottom of the window). In the Display tab, go to the Display field and use the pull-down menu and select **Quantity**. Select **Peak** for the calculation of the resource. Show the timescale with **Day** intervals. When complete, the Format Resource Profile/Table window should look like Figure M21.8.

12. Click the  OK button to display the table. Notice that the table is there, but asterisks appear in the cells rather than numbers. The cells are not wide enough for the numbers to appear on your computer screen since the table's timescale interval is in days. **This is often the problem of resource tables with daily time intervals.** However, the cells may be wide enough for the numbers to appear on your printout. Go to the print preview to see (click

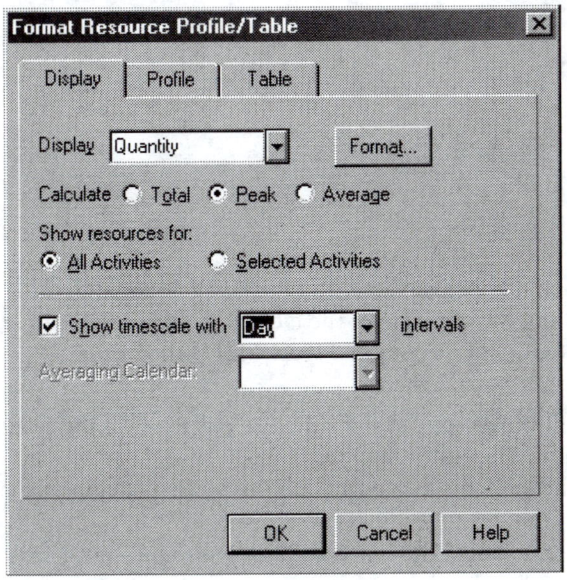

FIGURE M21.8

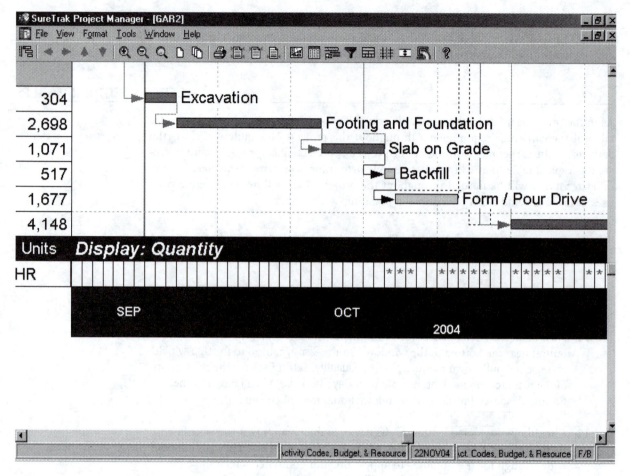

FIGURE M21.9

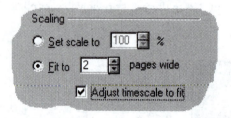

FIGURE M21.10

the ⬚ button) if the asterisks are still there. You may have to zoom in on the table. Do this by hovering the cursor over the table. The cursor will turn into a magnifying glass (Q). Click to zoom in. Figure M21.9 shows the zoomed-in table; the asterisks are still there.

13. Since the print preview still shows asterisks, the next step is to make the cells wider so the numbers can fit. The easiest way to do this is to widen the timescale by fitting the schedule onto two pages. Do this by first clicking the

View Single Page ⬚ button to zoom the schedule back out to full size. Next,

open the Page Setup window by clicking the ⬚ button. Go to the Scaling

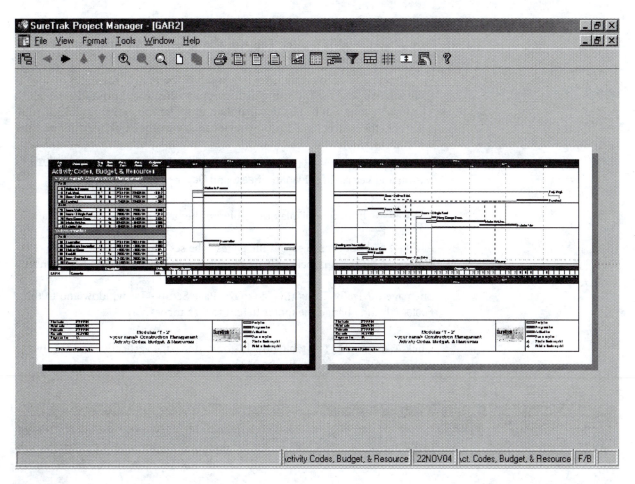

FIGURE M21.11

area on the Page Setup tab and mark ⦿ the Fit to **2** pages wide field and check

☑ the Adjust timescale to fit box. The settings should match those in

Figure M21.10. Leave the other fields as they were and click [OK]. The

schedule is now on two pages. Click the View All Pages 🗂 button to see both pages, as shown in Figure M21.11. Notice that the numbers appear in the cells. You may have to zoom in on the table as you did before in step 12.

14. The daily use of carpenters throughout the project is now displayed in the table. Notice on your screen that the numbers are mostly red and a few are black. Why is that? When you defined (created) the resources back in Module 19, you did not tell the computer how many of each resource your company had. As a result, the default limit of (1) resource kicked in. Therefore, any resource requirement above that level is colored red. (To see where the limits are input, go to Define, then Resources . . . and to the Limits: area in the window. Notice the default is [1].)

15. Print a copy of the GAR2 project schedule with the carpenter resource table. It will be used to answer questions on the *Schedule Analysis—Modules 17–21* at the end of this module and will be turned in with the analysis.

16. Save ⊞ the GAR2 project. This will also save the formatting changes you made to the resource table.

    The next table to create is one showing all the project resources on a daily interval. Use the following instructions to create and print out the table. The instructions will be less detailed than those for the previous table. If you get stuck, the instructions for the previous table might be of help, or you can ask your instructor for help.

17. Go back to the project window and select All resources. Click the `Format...` button and verify that **Quantity**, **Peak**, and **Day** are selected. Click the

    `OK` button to display the table. In the print preview, click the View

    All Pages 🗗 button to see all the pages. The schedule has to be on two pages *wide* so the numbers will appear in the cells, but it should be on only

    one page vertically. To fix this, go to the Page Setup 🖫 window and to the Footer tab and change the footer height to 0.75 inches.

    Click `OK`. The table now fits onto one page vertically (and still two pages wide), as shown in Figure M21.12.

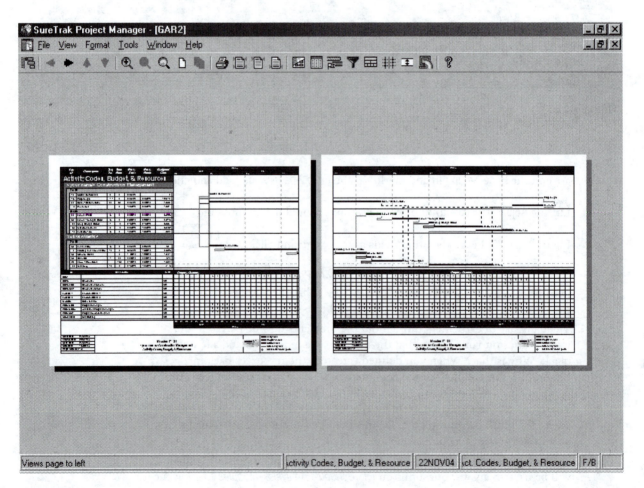

FIGURE M21.12

18. Print a copy of the GAR2 project schedule with all the resources in a table. It will be used to answer questions on the *Schedule Analysis—Modules 17–21* at the end of this module and will be turned in with the analysis.

19. Save 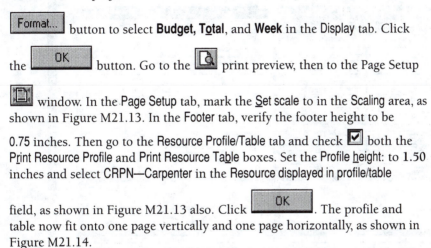 the GAR2 project. This will also save the formatting changes you made to the resource table.

COMBINED RESOURCE PROFILES AND TABLES

SureTrak gives you the ability to create and print out a resource profile combined with a resource table of the same resource. Both tables will not appear on the screen, but will appear in the print preview and will print out. The last schedule you will create will display a profile and table of the weekly cash flow of the carpenter resource throughout the entire project. Use the following instructions to create this schedule.

20. Go back to the project window and select **CRPN—Carpenter**. Click the

Format... button to select **Budget, Total**, and **Week** in the Display tab. Click

the OK button. Go to the print preview, then to the Page Setup

window. In the Page Setup tab, mark the Set scale to in the Scaling area, as shown in Figure M21.13. In the Footer tab, verify the footer height to be

0.75 inches. Then go to the Resource Profile/Table tab and check ☑ both the Print Resource Profile and Print Resource Table boxes. Set the Profile height: to **1.50** inches and select CRPN—Carpenter in the Resource displayed in profile/table

field, as shown in Figure M21.13 also. Click OK. The profile and table now fit onto one page vertically and one page horizontally, as shown in Figure M21.14.

21. Print a copy of the GAR2 project schedule displaying the weekly cash flow of the carpenter resource in both a profile and table. It will be used to answer

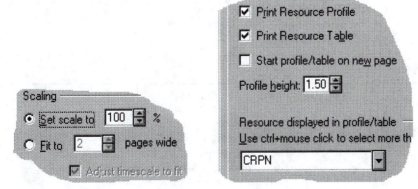

FIGURE M21.13

questions on the *Schedule Analysis—Modules 17–21* at the end of this module and will be turned in with the analysis.

22. Save ![save icon] the GAR2 project.

23. Module 21 is complete. Answer questions on the *Schedule Analysis—Modules 17–21* at the end of this module and turn it in, along with the project schedule printouts that you have prepared from Modules 17 through 21 and from question 12 in the Schedule Analysis. The printouts are listed in Table M21.1.

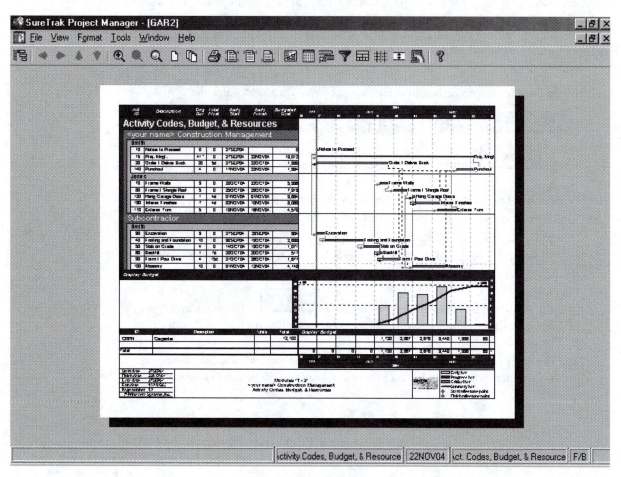

FIGURE M21.14

TABLE M21.1

Module 17	Activity codes printout
Module 20	Total project weekly cash flow profile
	Daily carpenter requirement profile
Module 21	Total project weekly cash flow table
	Daily carpenter requirement table (2 pages)
	Daily requirement of all resources table (2 pages)
	Weekly carpenter cash flow profile/table
Schedule Analysis (#12)	Weekly project management overhead cash flow profile

Name _____

After completing Modules 17–21, answer the following questions from the GAR2 schedule and the various schedule printouts you created. Turn the Schedule Analysis in to your instructor along with the project schedule printouts you have prepared from Modules 17 through 21 listed in Table M21.1.

Based on the work you performed with activity codes, budgeted costs, and resources throughout Modules 17–21, answer the following two questions.

1. Did the end date of the project schedule change? **Yes   No**
2. Did the critical path of the project schedule change? **Yes   No**

Activity Codes (Mod. 17):

3. Identify the sorting sequence (1 through 6) of the activities after the GAR2 schedule was organized and sorted in Module 17 (1 for highest, 2 for second-highest, 3 for third-highest, etc.).

_____ Activity ID, _____ Project, _____ Early Start, _____ Contractor, _____ Total Float, _____ Responsibility.

Budgeted Costs (Mod. 18): (circle one)

4. The budgeted costs were entered as a **Lump Sum** *or* as a function of the activity's **Duration**

Resource Profiles (Mod. 20): (You may have to recreate the cash flow and carpenter profiles to answer questions.)

5. What is the weekly cash flow for the fourth week of the project? $ _____
6. What is the cumulative cash flow up to and including the fourth week of the project? $ _____
7. What is the total cash flow for the entire project? $ _____
8. From the carpenter profile, determine the peak requirement of carpenters. How many are needed at the peak? _____ On what date(s) is the peak needed? _____

9. List the activities (list IDs) that are using carpenters that day(s) _____ Of those listed, which are critical? _____

10. How would you handle this peak need for carpenters? _____

11. What is the total cumulative use of carpenters for the entire project? _____ What is the unit for this total? _____ How was the total calculated? (show calc.) _____

12. Create and turn in with the analysis a printout of the GAR2 project schedule, on one page, including a resource profile showing the weekly cash flow throughout the entire project of the project manager, assistant project manager, and superintendent resources. This type of profile would be used to display the project management overhead costs of a project. *Extra Credit:* You will receive extra credit if you can figure out how to get the resource legend to display in the footer. *Hint:* . Answer the following questions from the printout.

What is the total cash flow of these three (3) resources throughout the entire project? $ _____

What is the typical weekly cash flow of these resources for most weeks? $ _____

Resource Tables (Mod. 21): (You may have to recreate the cash flow, carpenter, and resource tables to answer questions.)

13. Determine from the weekly cash flow table how much money will be spent on the total project up to the point right before the garage doors are hung. $ _____

14. Why are most numbers on the daily carpenter resource table in red? _____

15 Why do zeros appear in some cells while others are left blank on the carpenter resource table? _____

16. Determine from the table displaying all the resources which resource(s) is not being used _____

17. What activity(s) is the scaffolding resource being used with? _____

18. In the combined profile/table, what is the total budget for the carpenter cash flow? $ _____

19. What week in the project has the highest cash flow for the carpenter resource? _____

What is the cash flow amount for that week? $ _____

What is the hourly rate (cost) for the carpenter resource? $ _____ per hour.

Based on the cash flow amount from the week above and the hourly rate (cost) for the carpenter resource, calculate how many total hours of the carpenter resource is required for that particular week. (show calc.) _____ hours.

MODULE 22
Target Schedules

Preface: Once you have created, reviewed, and refined the project schedule, it is important to lock-in the schedule as the project baseline. It will become the schedule that the project is measured against, providing a way to compare actual progress to the original plan.

Baseline schedules are sometimes referred to as a master project schedule, milestone schedule, or simply as the original schedule. SureTrak calls the baseline schedule the target schedule and calls the activity dates target dates. Target dates are simply the original early start, early finish, late start, and late finish activity dates of the original project schedule. They allow you to compare your updated actual start and finish dates to the target (original schedule) dates.

In this module, you will rename the GAR2 project to **GART** (T–for Target), create the target schedule, then print out a copy of this schedule with the target bars included. The target schedule will be used in the next module when you create reports, and in Module 25 when you update the project with progress.

RENAMING THE PROJECT

1. If it is not already opened, open the GAR2 project.

2. (Refer to Module 15 for more detailed instructions for renaming a project.) Rename this project by going to File, Save As. . . . In the Project name: field, enter **GART** for the new project name. Check two other settings before saving. Verify that the project Type: field says **Project Groups** and that the Current folder: shows the correct path to the folder that you want the project to be saved in. In our case it should be the default path of `C:\...\SureTrak\Projects` unless your instructor tells you differently. After verifying the project type and folder path as previously described, click `OK` to save the project under the new filename. Notice the new project name (GART) in the upper left-hand corner of the project window.

3. Go to File, then Project Overview . . . to match to change the Number/Version and Project Title. Change the Number/Version to **Target Schedule** and the Project title to **Garage Construction Project**. Leave the other fields as they were and click `OK`. Then click the 💾 button to apply and save these changes.

4. There is one last change to make. The schedule is currently under the Act. Codes, Budget, & Resources layout. Create and apply a new layout for the target schedule. Do this by following instructions #9 and #10 from Module 10, except type **TRGT_SCH** in the Name cell and **Target Schedule** in the Description cell.

5. The project is renamed. Save the GART project to save the changes you made to the layout and move on to the next instruction to create the target schedule.

CREATING THE TARGET SCHEDULE

6. To create the target schedule, go back to the project window (if not already there) and then go to Define, then Target Dates, . . . to open the Target Dates window, as shown in Figure M22.1.

7. Target schedules are almost always based off the early dates of the original schedule; therefore, accept the default of Early dates. We want the target schedule to include all the project activities, so accept the default of All activities and click OK.

8. To see target dates, turn on those two columns. Do this by going to Format, Columns . . . to open the Columns window. Insert the **Target Start** column directly after the Early Start column. Insert the **Target Finish** column directly after the Early Finish column. Finally, highlight the **Budgeted Cost** column and click the button to remove it. When complete, the columns window (showing only the lower six "turned-on" columns) should match that shown in Figure M22.2. Click OK.

9. Move the vertical split bar (see Figure M22.3) to the right to display all the columns. Click the button to turn off the resource table, if it is still turned on. The columns that should be displayed are shown in Figure M22.4.

10. Additionally, we will display the target dates in the form of a bar. To do this, go to Format, Bars, . . . to open the Format Bars window. Scroll down to the Target bar data item and make the target bars visible by checking the visible column as shown in Figure M22.5. Click OK. The yellow target bars will appear.

11. Go to the print preview. Click the View All Pages button. The resource profile and table may still be there from the previous module. To

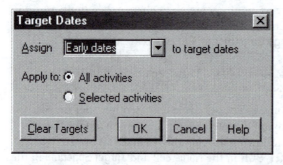

FIGURE M22.1

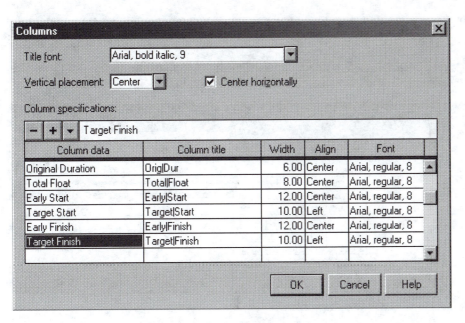

FIGURE M22.2

FIGURE M22.3

turn them off, click the [icon] button or go to File, Page Setup . . . and then to

the Resource Profile/Table tab to uncheck ([icon]) the Print Resource

Profile and Print Resource Table boxes. Click [OK]. The schedule may be
two pages wide. To get it onto one page, go back to the Page Setup window

and to the Scaling area on the Page Setup tab and mark [icon] the Fit to 1 pages

wide field and check [icon] the Adjust timescale to fit box. The print preview of the
target schedule should match that shown in Figure M22.6.

12. Print a copy of the GART target project schedule. It will be used to answer
    questions on the *Schedule Analysis—Modules 22–23* at the end of the next
    module and will be turned in with the analysis.

13. Save [icon] the GART project. This will also save the formatting changes you
    made to the schedule.

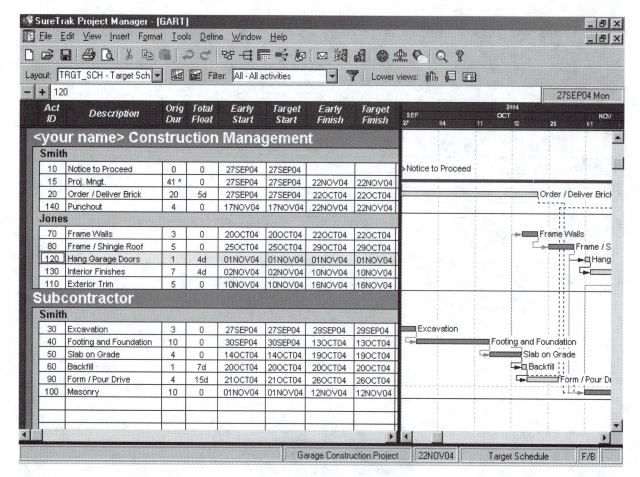

FIGURE M22.4

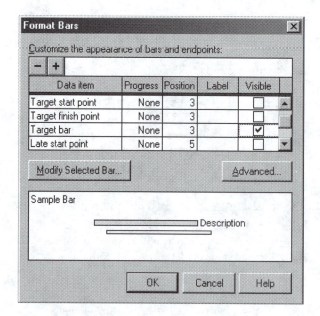

FIGURE M22.5

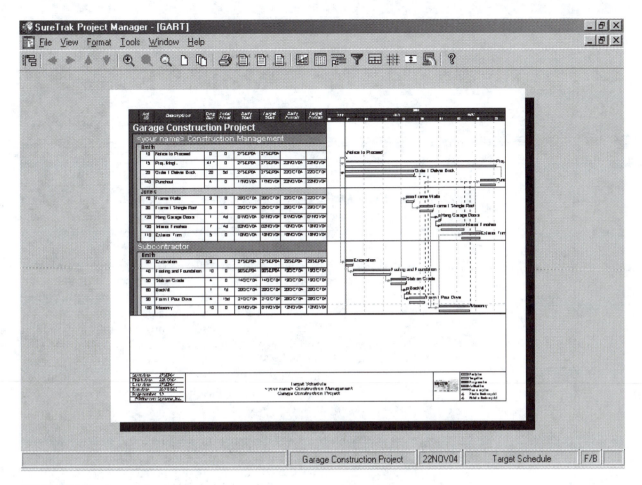

FIGURE M22.6

MODULE 23
Reports

Preface: SureTrak has a feature that displays project information in a tabular format called reports. Project owners, executives, managers, and others are often interested in viewing project information in this form. Sometimes a tabular format is a more convenient way for you, and others from the project team, to monitor and control project data. Additionally, you may need to create your own customized report for your record keeping, to update the project, or to show and detail project status. SureTrak allows you to create reports illustrating nearly any combination of project data with nearly any combination of setup features.

Reports in SureTrak can be just tabular, containing only information from activity columns, while others may also include the graphical display of the bar chart and/or a resource profile/table. Some reports are specific to the PERT view. SureTrak comes with forty-five different prebuilt reports that you can customize or apply as is, or you can build your own customized report from scratch. They can be saved and applied to other projects.

You can print a single report or series of reports that you bundled together—a valuable timesaver if you use the same report(s) in many different projects *or* if you use the same report(s) many times in the same project.

In this module, you will assign one pre-built report and create three different customized reports for the GART target schedule, a Classic Schedule Report, a Schedule Status Report, and a Two-Week Lookahead. The Schedule Status Report will be used in Module 25 when you update the project with progress.

APPLYING A PRE-BUILT REPORT

1. If it is not already opened, open the GART project.

2. Select a prebuilt report by going to Tools, then Reports . . . to open the Reports window, as shown in Figure M23.1. Scroll up and down in the window to review the prebuilt reports that came with the software. When done reviewing the report descriptions, scroll to the **BUD1—Budgeted costs**

   report. Select it by single-clicking it and then clicking the [Apply] button. The report is now loaded in the project window (see Figure M23.2). Notice that the layout changed to BUDGET—Shows budgeted costs. Reports all have a predefined layout. Notice also that the bar chart is still visible in the project window. This won't show up on the report. To see what the printed hard copy

   of the report will look like, go to the print preview [icon] to preview the report. Figure M23.3 shows the preview of the report.

3. Click the [icon] button to print out a copy of the Budgeted Costs Report. It will be used to answer questions on the *Schedule Analysis—Modules 22–23* at the end of this module and will be turned in with the analysis.

390

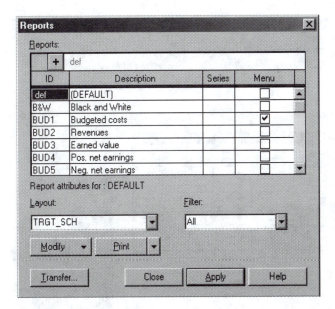

FIGURE M23.1

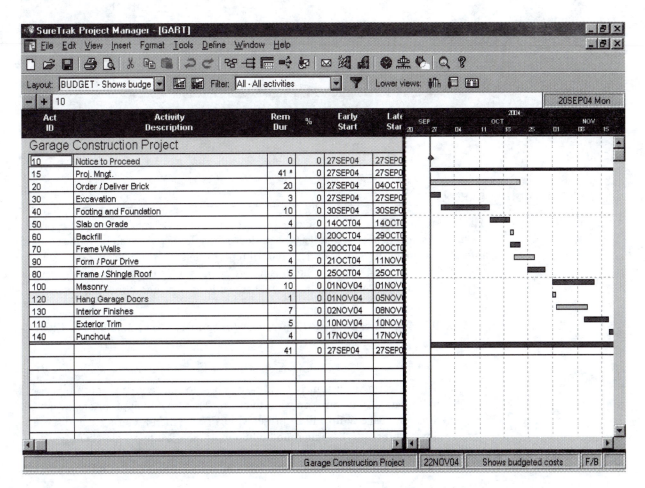

FIGURE M23.2

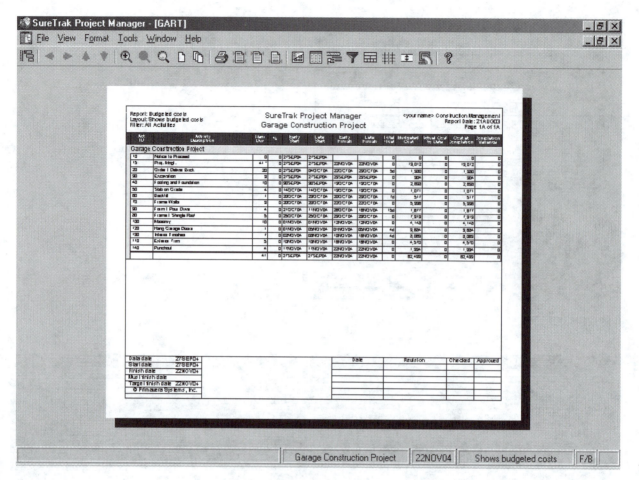

FIGURE M23.3

CLASSIC SCHEDULE REPORT

The next report will be a customized report we will call the Classic Schedule Report—a traditional schedule report that lists the project schedule's activities along with standard information about the activities. This type of report is usually sorted by the early start of the activities. We are going to create this report by pulling up one of SureTrak's prebuilt reports and then customizing it by adding some information and removing others.

4. If it is not already opened, open the **GART** project. Go back to the Bar Chart view in the project window by clicking the [button] button.

5. When creating a customized report, it is best to start with a prebuilt report that resembles the one you want to create. That way, an appropriate layer, filter, and page setup will be preset. Go to Tools, then Reports . . . and scroll down to the **SCH1—Schedule by ES** report. Select it by single-clicking it.

Next, click the [+] button to add a new report. Enter **CLSC** as the report ID, then click [✓]. Click in the Description cell and enter **Classic Schedule**

Report as the description, then click [✓]. The report is ready to apply. The

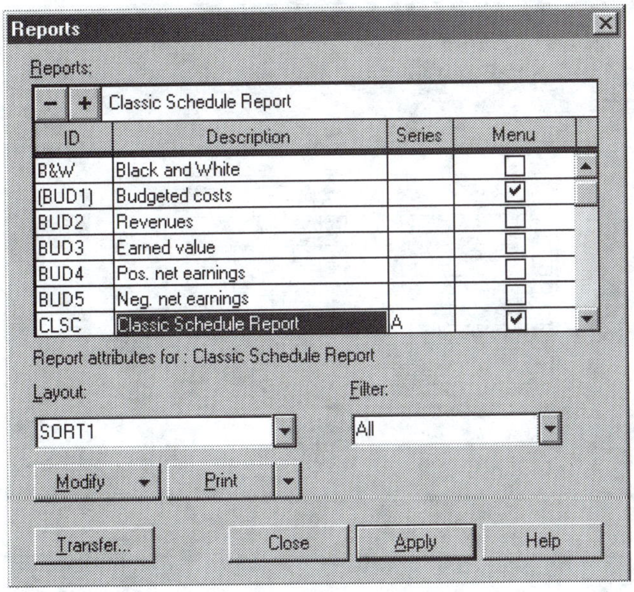

FIGURE M23.4

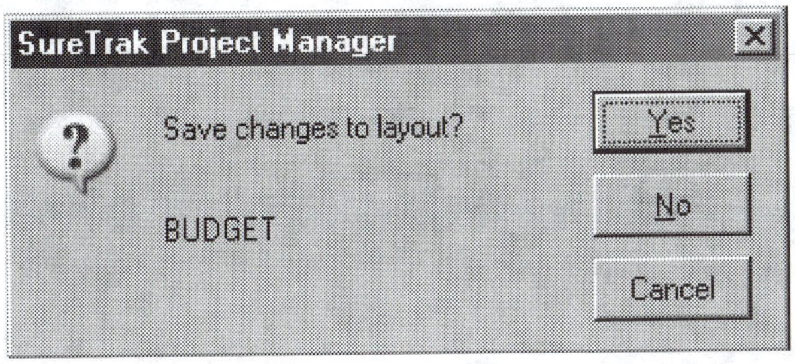

FIGURE M23.5

Reports window should match that in Figure M23.4. Click the [Apply] button. Since you did not make any changes to the previous Budget report, click [No] to saving changes to the layout (see Figure M23.5). The report is now loaded in the project window.

6. To preview the report, go to [🔍] print preview. Customize the report, starting with the columns. Go to Format, Columns . . . , or simply click the [▦] button. Change the column width of the Description column to 30 and the Late Start and Late Finish columns to 12. Show only the following columns in this exact order: Activity ID, Description, Original Duration, Remaining Duration, Percent Complete, Total Float, Early Start, Early Finish, Late Start, Late Finish, and Budgeted Cost. **Center** all data except Description (left) and Budgeted Cost (right). Click [OK].

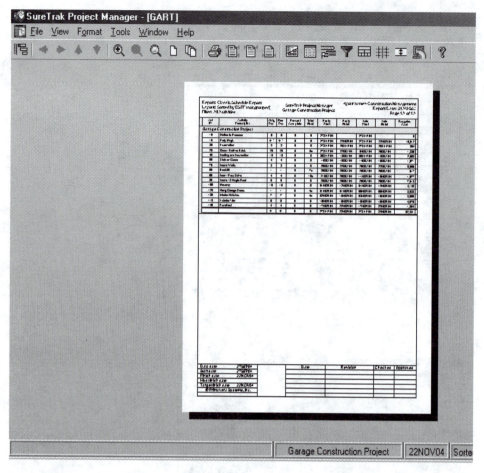

FIGURE M23.6

7. Next, click the [icon] button to open the Header tab in the Page Setup window and change the Default font: from Regular to Bold. Click [OK]. The Classic Schedule Report is complete (see Figure M23.6).

8. Click the [icon] button to print out a copy of the Classic Schedule Report. It will be used to answer questions on the *Schedule Analysis—Modules 22–23* at the end of this module and will be turned in with the analysis.

9. Save [icon] the GART project. This will also save the Classic Schedule Report you just created, along with the formatting changes you just made. Read the following note about reports and layouts.

REPORTS AND LAYOUTS

Every report in SureTrak, whether prebuilt or custom built, has a predefined layout. When you make changes to the report, you are actually making changes to the layout, not the report.

Additionally, if those changes are saved, they will carry through to any other project *or* report that that layout is applied to. Therefore, when you apply a layout to a project or report and then make changes to it, you need to carefully decide if you want to save or discard those changes. If you do save the changes, **you are permanently chang-ing that layout.** Therefore, when you apply that layout to a different project, you will see those changes there. If you want to keep the original layout intact, but still save the cur-rent layout with the changes you just made, save the current layout as a new layout and then you will have both the original layout and the newly changed current layout to use on future projects. Creating a new layout was discussed in Module 10.

SCHEDULE STATUS REPORT

An important part of project management is recording the project's progress. The Sched-ule Status Report is a useful worksheet created for monitoring the progress of the sched-ule and updating the project. A project manager, superintendent, or foreman can use this report to keep track and handwrite in the actual dates to track the progress of the activ-ities, then use those dates to periodically update the project in SureTrak.

10. If it is not already opened, open the GART project. Go back to the Bar Chart

    view in the project window by clicking the [⊞] button.

11. Like the previous report, start with the SCH1—Schedule by ES report as the basis of this report. Go to <u>T</u>ools, then <u>R</u>eports . . . scroll down, and select the

    SCH1—Schedule by ES report. Click the [+] button to add a new report.

    Enter **STAT** as the report ID, then click [✔]. In the Description cell, enter

    Schedule Status Report as the description, then click [✔]. Click the

    [Apply] button. If prompted, say [Yes] to save changes to the layout. The report is now loaded in the project window.

12. Go to the [🔍] print preview, then to [🖨] the Page Setup window, and change the Orientation to **La<u>n</u>dscape**. In the Header tab, change the Defa<u>u</u>lt font:

    from Regular to **Bold**. Click [OK].

13. Format the columns [▦], showing only the following columns in this order: Activity ID, Description, Original Duration, Remaining Duration, Percent Complete, Total Float, Target Start, Actual Start, Target Finish, and Actual Finish. Center all data except the Description, which you will keep left. Decrease the column width of the Activity ID column to 6 and the Description column to 25. Increase the column width of the Actual Start and Actual Finish columns to

    15. Click [OK].

14. Notice how wide the Percent Complete column is. It is this wide to fit its

    column title. Reopen the Columns window [▦] and reduce its column title by clicking in its Column title cell and changing it to Perc|Comp (the vertical line | can be found with the \ on the keyboard, usually above the *Enter* key).

    Then decrease the width of the cell to 6. Click [OK].

15. By reducing some of the column widths, we have created a large blank area on the right side of the worksheet. We are going to turn that into a remarks column. However, SureTrak does not have a Remarks column to select.

Therefore, we need to create it. Reopen the Columns window ▦ one more time and scroll down below the Actual Finish column. Click in the Column data cell beneath it, then use the ▼ pull-down to select Log Text 1 for that cell. In the Column title cell, type in Remarks as the title. Change the width of this cell to 70. The Column window should match that shown in Figure M23.7.

Click OK . The Remarks column should fill up nearly the rest of the report.

Note: If the Remarks column spills onto a second page (horizontally), reduce the width of its cell until the report fits back onto one page.

16. The final adjustment to make is to increase the row height. This will make it easier to handwrite the actual dates onto the worksheet. To do this, go to Format, then Row Height . . . or simply click the ⬍ button to open the Row Height window. First uncheck ☐ the Automatic size field, then increase the Row height in points: to 23. The Row Height window should match that shown in Figure M23.8. Click OK . The activities should fill up nearly the rest of the report.

Note: If they spill onto a second page (vertically), reduce the row height until the report fits back onto one page.

The Schedule Status Report is complete (see Figure M23.9).

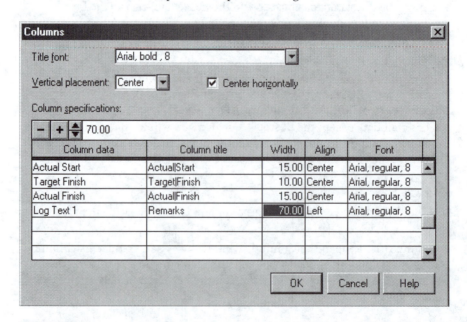

FIGURE M23.7

FIGURE M23.8

(F.Y.I.)

■ Different printers have different print margins. For this reason, a report or schedule may not fit onto the number of pages specified in this text—even though you have entered the correct settings. In this case, simply adjust the settings appropriately until the schedule or report fits onto the correct number of pages.

---

17. Click the 🖨 button to print out a copy of the Schedule Status Report. It will be used to answer questions on the *Schedule Analysis—Modules 22–23* at the end of this module and will be turned in with the analysis.

18. Save 💾 the GART project. This will also save the Schedule Status Report you just created, along with the formatting changes you just made.

THREE-WEEK LOOKAHEAD REPORT

The last report will be similar to the Two-Week Lookahead layout you applied to the GARG schedule back in Module 10. However, rather than zooming in on two weeks, this report will zoom in on three. This type of report is often passed out in contractor progress meetings to help everyone involved focus on the tasks at hand.

19. If it is not already opened, open the GART project. Go back to the Bar Chart view in the project window by clicking the ▦ button. Open the Reports window and apply the **def DEFAULT** report. Then use the Layouts: pull-down menu to select the **2WEEKS—Next 2 weeks in zoomed timescale** layout.

20. Create a new layout by going to View, then Layouts . . . , or simply click the ▦ button (if you need to, you can refer back to the detailed instructions in Module 10). Click the ➕ button and in the Name cell, type **3WEEKS** (no spaces) and click ✔. In the Description cell, type **Three-Week Lookahead,**

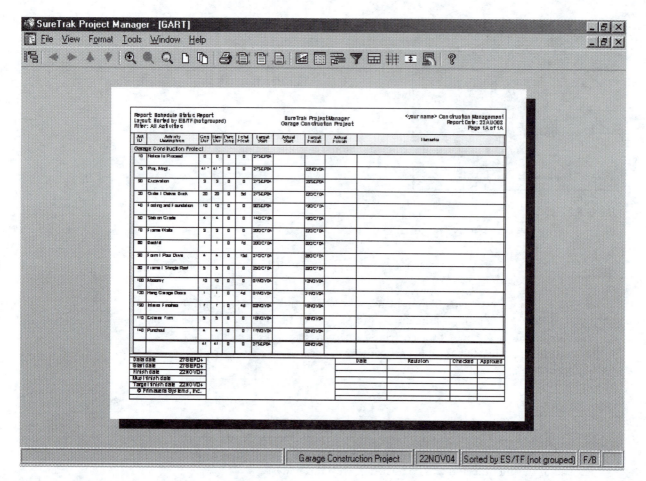

FIGURE M23.9

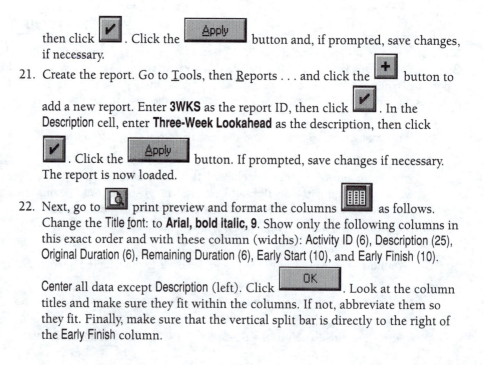

then click ✔. Click the **Apply** button and, if prompted, save changes, if necessary.

21. Create the report. Go to Tools, then Reports . . . and click the ➕ button to add a new report. Enter **3WKS** as the report ID, then click ✔. In the Description cell, enter **Three-Week Lookahead** as the description, then click ✔. Click the **Apply** button. If prompted, save changes if necessary. The report is now loaded.

22. Next, go to 🔍 print preview and format the columns ▦ as follows. Change the Title font: to **Arial, bold italic, 9**. Show only the following columns in this exact order and with these column (widths): Activity ID (6), Description (25), Original Duration (6), Remaining Duration (6), Early Start (10), and Early Finish (10).

Center all data except Description (left). Click **OK**. Look at the column titles and make sure they fit within the columns. If not, abbreviate them so they fit. Finally, make sure that the vertical split bar is directly to the right of the Early Finish column.

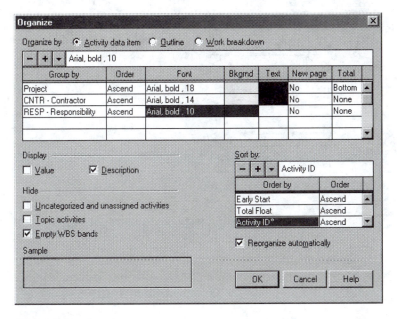

FIGURE M23.10

23. Go to Format, then Organize . . . to open the Organize window. Change the settings in the **Group by**, **Font**, and **Order by** sections of the window to match what is shown in Figure M23.10. Leave the rest of the settings as they were, and click [OK] .

24. Next, change the zoomed timescale to three weeks. To do this, open the Timescale window by going to Format, Timescale . . . or simply clicking the [image] button. From there, open the Zoomed Timescale window by clicking the [Settings...] button. In the **End date:** field, change the days from 14 to 21 (type in 21, do not use the pull-down). The Zoom Timescale window should look like Figure M23.11. Click [OK] . Then click [OK] again.

25. Go to the page setup [image] and mark ⦿ the **Set scale to** field. Click [OK] . Notice that the activity bars do not fill up the entire page. To fill up the page with the bars, go back to page setup and mark ⦿ the **Fit to 1 pages wide** and ☑ the **Adjust timescale to fit** box. Click [OK] .

26. Go to the Row Height window [image] and uncheck ☐ the **Automatic size** field if it is not unchecked, then increase the **Row height in points:** to 20. Click [OK] . The activities should fill up nearly the rest of the report.

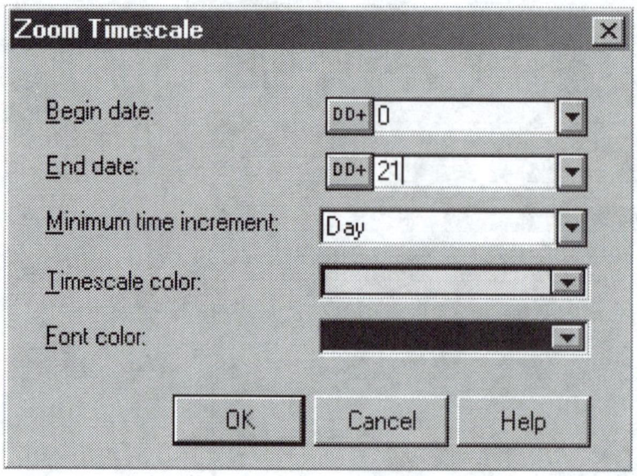

FIGURE M23.11

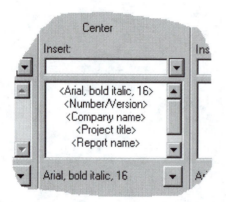

FIGURE M23.12

Note: If the activities spill onto a second page (vertically), reduce the row height until the report fits back onto one page.

27. Next, click the  button to open the **Footer** tab in the Page Setup window to add the report description (report name), **Three-Week Lookahead** to the title

block. Click anywhere in the  to open the three (left, center, right) title block sections. Place the cursor below the **<Project title>** line in the **Center** section, then using the pull-down, insert the **<Report name>** as shown in Figure M23.12. Next, go to the font pull-down directly beneath the **Center** section and change the font to **Arial, bold italic, 16** (see Figure M23.12). Then, near the top of the **Footer** tab, change the **Height:** to 1.00

Inches. The **Footer** settings are complete. Click **OK**.

28. The Three-Week Lookahead Report is complete (see Figure M23.13).

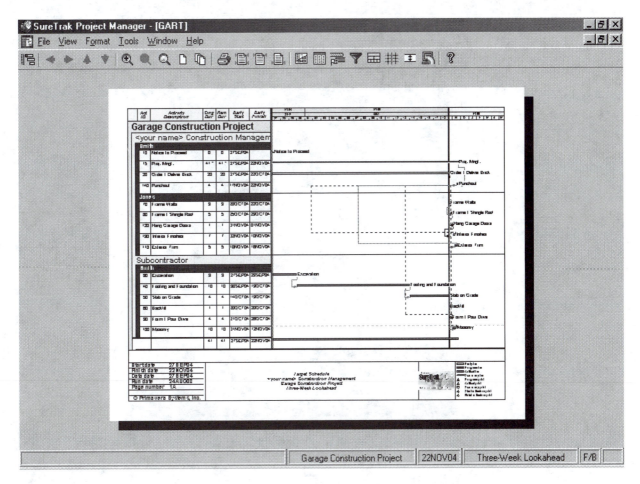

FIGURE M23.13

29. Click the 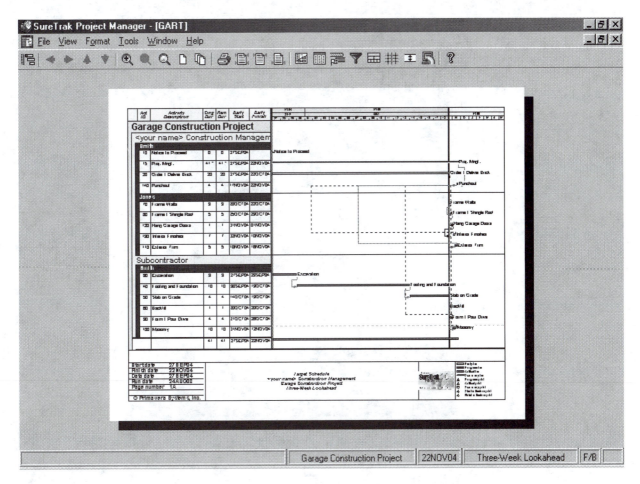 button to print out a copy of the Three-Week Lookahead Report. It will be used to answer questions on the *Schedule Analysis—Modules 22–23* at the end of this module and will be turned in with the analysis.

30. Save the GART project. This will also save the Three-Week Lookahead Report you just created, along with the formatting changes you just made.

RUN REPORT MENU

SureTrak allows for up to twenty reports to be listed on its Run Report menu. This menu, directly off the Tools menu, provides for quick and easy access to your more frequently used reports.

31. Go to Tools, then Run Report (see Figure M23.14) to see the reports that are currently listed there. Notice that the Classic Schedule Report and the Schedule Status Report are already there. That's because both were based off the Schedule by ES report that was already on the menu.

32. Add the Three-Week Lookahead report to the Run Report menu by opening the Reports window (Tools, Reports . . .) and checking the Menu box next to

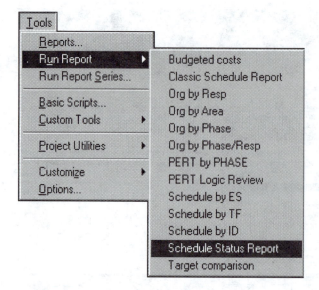

FIGURE M23.14

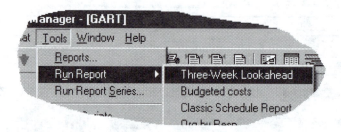

FIGURE M23.15

the report. Go back to the menu and verify that the report was added (see Figure M23.15).

33. Module 23 is complete. Answer the questions on the *Schedule Analysis— Modules 22–23* and turn it in to your instructor, along with the four (4) printouts of the GART project schedule reports: Budgeted Costs, Classic Schedule Report, Schedule Status Report, and the Three-Week Lookahead. When complete, move on to Module 24.

SCHEDULE ANALYSIS
Garage Construction Schedule

Name _____

After completing Modules 22 and 23, answer the following questions from the **Budgeted Costs Report, Classic Schedule Report, Schedule Status Report,** and the **Three-Week Lookahead Report.** Turn the Schedule Analysis in to your instructor, along with all four printouts of the reports.

Budgeted Costs Report:

1. Circle the project information that appears in the header of the report.

Company name	Finish date	Project name	Page count
Report ID	Number/Version	Percent Complete	Report name

2. How are the activities on the report sorted? _____

Classic Schedule Report:

3. This report includes late start and late finish dates. Would you give it to your subcontractors? If **Yes,** explain why _____

   _____

   If **No,** explain why not _____

   _____

4. Can you tell from this report which activities are critical?　**Yes　No**
   If **Yes,** explain how _____

Schedule Status Report:

5. List two places on the report where the total project duration can be found. _____

   _____

6. Is the total project budget shown on the report?　**Yes　No**　If Yes, what is the total?
   $_____

Three-Week Lookahead Report:

7. What is the timescale unit of the zoomed section of the bar chart on the report?

   _____

8. What is the timescale unit of the non-zoomed section of the bar chart on the report?

   _____

9. This report is intended to be used as a tool to help focus, in detail, on the next few weeks of work. What other information do you think would be helpful to be placed on this report?

   _____

   _____

MODULE 24
Multi-Phase Projects

Preface: Very often in construction, projects have multiple phases of the same type of work. An example would be a multistory building where each level is pretty much like the other and has the same activities required to complete it. Or a project might involve two or more of the same building being built. Rather than retyping all the activities multiple times, SureTrak allows you to enter the activities once, copy them, rename them, and then tie them all together with the appropriate schedule logic.

For this multi-phase project, we will continue to use the garage construction schedule from previous modules as the reference project—specifically, we will use the GAR2 project. However, instead of scheduling the construction of one garage, we are going to schedule the construction of two similar garages. We will create a project schedule that will attempt to minimize the total project duration of constructing both buildings. For example, when the foundation crew is done with the foundation of the first garage, they would go directly onto the foundation of the second garage. This project schedule will be very similar to the fourth CPM manual schedule (to build five houses—with five crews) we worked with in Chapters 6 and 7 of this text.

In this module, you will create a new project, learn how to transfer resources, and copy and paste activities. You will learn about milestone activities and how to work with the logic of a multi-phased project.

CREATE THE PROJECT

Follow the instructions below to create the project we will use for the multi-phase project. More detailed instructions for creating a project can be found in Module 2, if need be.

1. To create a new project, go to the File command, and click New . . . , or simply click the ☐ icon. If it appears, click No to the Project KickStart Wizard. The New Project window will open. Verify that the Current folder: path reads C:\...\SureTrak\Projects , unless your instructor tells you to use a different path.

Enter **GARM** (the M is for multi-phase) as the Project name. Use the **_DEFAULT** template for this project, so tab past this field. Select **Project Groups** as the project Type if it is not already selected. Click Day for the planning unit as shown Planning Unit: ○ Hour ● Day and do not Add this new project to a project group, so tab past that field. Enter **Multi-Phase Proj** in the Number/Version field. Note that your instructor may want you to enter something different. Enter **04MAY05** for the Start date for this project. *Do not* enter a Must finish by date.

405

New Project

Current folder: C:\SureTrak\Projects   Browse...

Project name: GARM

Template: _DEFAULT

Type: Project Groups

Planning Unit: ○ Hour   ● Day

☐ Add this new project to a project group

Group: _____   Project ID: _____

Number/Version: Multi-Phase Proj

Start date: 04MAY05

Must finish by: _____

Project title: Multi-Phase Garage Project

Company name: <your name> Construction Management

OK   Cancel   Help

FIGURE M24.1

Tab past this field. Enter **Multi-Phase Garage Project** for the Project title. Enter *<your name>* **Construction Management** for the Company name.

2. The project information has been entered. Carefully verify that your entries match those shown in Figure M24.1. After verifying your entries, click

OK   to create the project.

TRANSFERRING RESOURCES

When you create (define) resources, activity codes, calendars, and so forth for a project, they are defined *only* for that project. To help illustrate this point, go to Define, Resources. Notice that there are no resources in the window of the GARM project—even though you defined them for a previous project.

Rather than retyping all those resources back in, SureTrak allows you to transfer them into your current project from another. Additionally, if you are copying activities from a different project—which we are about to do—into your current project, only the resources (or activity codes, calendars, etc.) assigned to the copied activities will transfer over. Therefore, you might end up with an incomplete group of resources. It is a recommended practice to transfer all the resources over first from the other project, then copy the activities.

We will transfer over the resources from the GAR2 project into the GARM project. Later on in this module, when you copy activities from the GAR2 project into the GARM project, all the resources will be transferred over. This discussion and the instructions about transferring resources are also valid with the four (4) other Defined items: Calendars, Activity Codes, WBS Codes, and Target Dates.

3. To do this, go to Define, Resources . . . to open the Define Resource window.

Click the   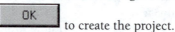   button to open the Transfer Resources window. Start near the bottom of the window in the project Type: field and use the pull-

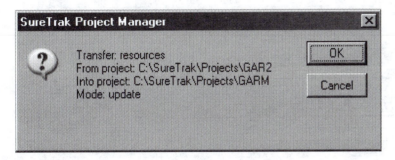

FIGURE M24.2

FIGURE M24.3

FIGURE M24.4

down menu to choose **Project Groups**. The Current folder: probably reads

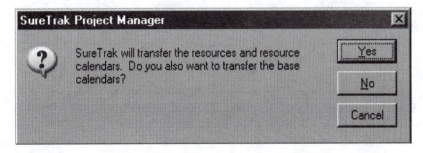 . If not, click the 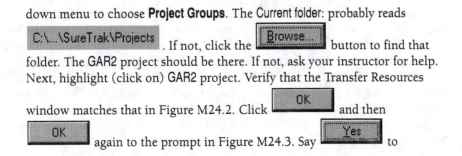 button to find that
folder. The GAR2 project should be there. If not, ask your instructor for help.
Next, highlight (click on) GAR2 project. Verify that the Transfer Resources

window matches that in Figure M24.2. Click **OK** and then

OK again to the prompt in Figure M24.3. Say **Yes** to

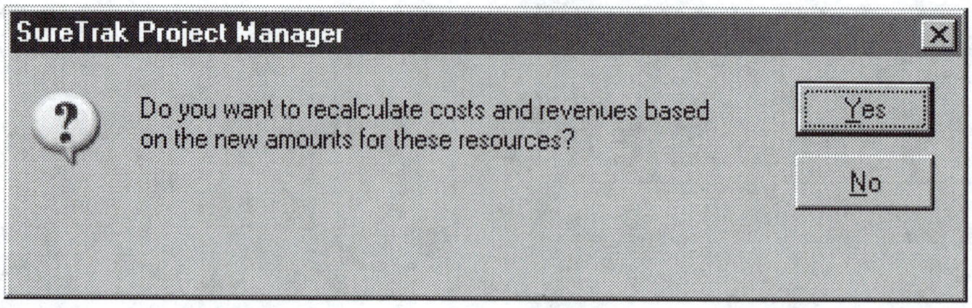

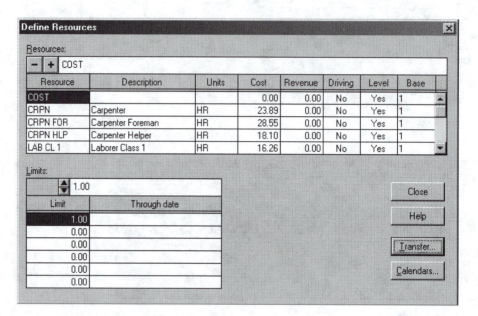

FIGURE M24.5

FIGURE M24.6

transferring the base calendars prompt, as shown in Figure M24.4. For the next prompt, shown in Figure M24.5, it does not really matter how you answer it since the resource amounts have not changed. If you would have changed the hourly cost of a resource and resource costs were already calculated, then it would matter. For now, say [Yes] to recalculating costs and revenues. The resources from the GAR2 project have now transferred into the GARM project, as shown in Figure M24.6.

COPYING ACTIVITIES

SureTrak allows you to copy one or more activities from one project and paste them into the same project or into a different project. This can save significant time entering data. When you copy activities, the description, duration, logic, and other activity information copies over with the activity and you have the option to change the Activity ID.

Definable information such as resources (including costs), calendars, activity codes, and so forth will copy over as well. However, if you are pasting activities into a different project, it is a good practice to transfer the definable information into the different project before you copy and paste the activities. This is what you just did in this module. Following this practice will ensure that all the definable information gets transferred, not just that assigned to the copied activities.

FIGURE M24.7

Organize   [×]

Organize by   ⦿ Activity data item   ○ Outline   ○ Work breakdown

–	+						
Group by	Order	Font	Bkgrnd	Text	New page	Total	
							▲
							▼

Display
☐ Value   ☑ Description

Hide
☐ Uncategorized and unassigned activities
☐ Topic activities
☑ Empty WBS bands

Sample

Sort by:

–	+	▼	Activity ID

Order by	Order
Activity ID	Ascend ▲
	▼

☑ Reorganize automatically

OK	Cancel	Help

FIGURE M24.8

We will copy activities from the GAR2 project and paste them into the GARM project.

4. Re-open the GAR2 project. The GARM project should already be opened. To go back and forth from one project to the other, use the *lower* (the upper minimizes the entire SureTrak program) of the two Minimize [–] buttons in the upper right-hand corner of the project window. When both projects are minimized, their icons will appear (see Figure M24.7) in the bottom left-hand corner of the project window.

5. Maximize [□] the GAR2 project and remove all organization (Project, CNTR, RESP), then sort by Activity ID. To do this, go to Format, then Organize . . . or simply click the [▦] button to open the Organize window. Click the [–] button to remove the Project, CNTR, and RESP groups. Then go to the Sort by: field and click the [–] button to remove the Early Start and Total Float sorts,

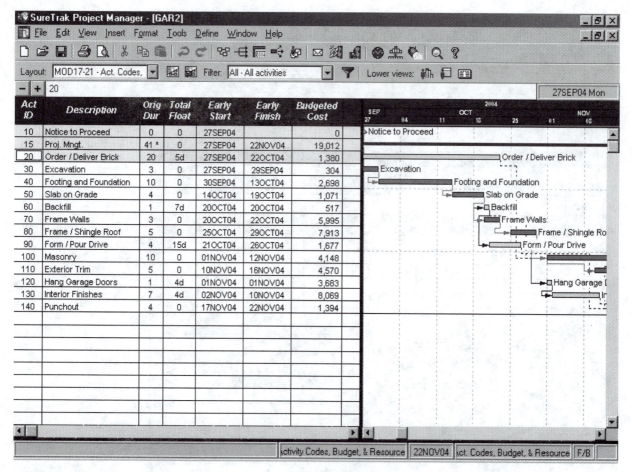

FIGURE M24.9

leaving only Activity ID in the Sort by: field. Verify that the Organize window matches that shown in Figure M24.8, then click [OK].

6. If a resource profile or resource table still appears in the project window, turn it off by clicking the appropriate button, [image] or [image]. You are now ready to copy activities from the GAR2 project (see Figure M24.9).

To create the schedule for the multi-phase garage project, you will copy two sets of activities from the GAR2 project and paste them into the GARM project for the two buildings. However, some activities like Notice to Proceed (10) and Project Management (15) relate to the whole project, not to each building, and therefore would only be copied once. Additionally, there would *not* be an Order / Deliver Brick (20) activity for each building; you probably would order all the brick at once. Therefore, those three activities will be copied together first and only once.

7. To do this, go to the GAR2 project and select those three activities. Do this by single-clicking the first activity, 10, then hold down the *Control* (Ctrl) key on the keyboard to select (single-click) the other two, 15 and 20. Notice on your screen that they are highlighted in blue. They are shown in Figure M24.9.

8. Next, go to **Edit**, then **Copy Activity** to copy these activities to the clipboard. Minimize the GAR2 project and maximize the GARM project. Insert these

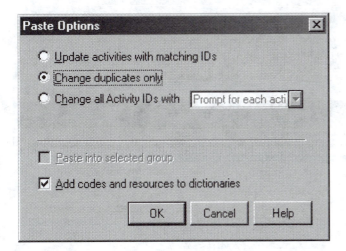

FIGURE M24.10

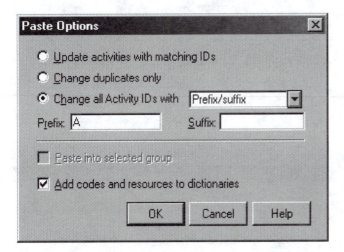

FIGURE M24.11

activities into the new project by clicking **Edit**, then **Paste Activity**. . . . The Paste Options window appears (Figure M24.10) and gives you some choices as to how to handle this paste. We will accept the defaults and click

      OK   . Notice the three activities have been pasted into the GARM project and are numbered in order.

9. Now we will copy the remainder of the activities, 30 through 140, twice. Go back to the GAR2 project and select these activities by single-clicking activity 30, hold down the **Shift** key on the keyboard, and single-click activity **140**. Notice on your screen that all the activities in-between are highlighted in blue (selected). Next, go to **Edit**, then **Copy Activity**, to copy these activities onto the clipboard. Go to the GARM project and paste these activities into the project by clicking **Edit**, then **Paste Activity**. . . . The Paste Options window appears again. We want to use the same activity IDs, but this time we will assign the prefixes A and B in front of each to represent the two garages. Mark the

    ⊙ **Change all Activity IDs with** button. In the field to the right, use the pull-down menu to choose **Prefix/suffix**. Enter an A (for Garage A) in the Prefix: field that just came up. The Paste Options window should match that in Figure M24.11.

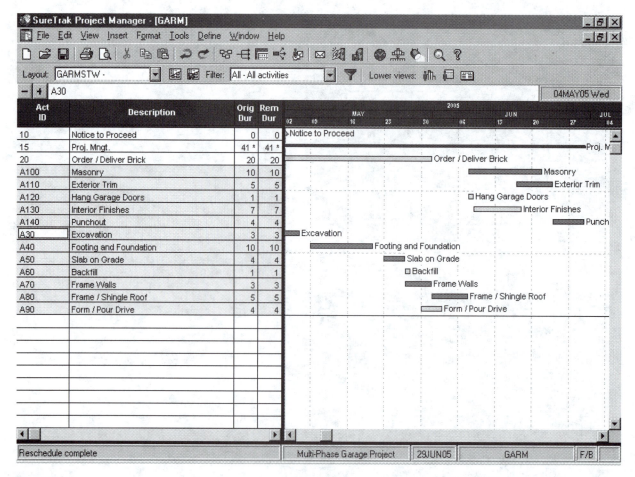

FIGURE M24.12

10. Click [OK] to paste activities **30** through **140**. Notice that the activities appear with the **A** prefix, but probably not in the order you expected (see Figure M24.12).

Note: SureTrak pasted these activities in a strictly alphanumeric order. In that order, **A100** through **A140** comes before **A30** because a (1) comes before a (3). Don't worry about this now; when we sort the project by early start later, this order will not matter.

11. Paste the same group of activities (30 through 140) from the **GAR2** project to the **GARM** project for the second garage. Unless you have copied something else, those same activities should still be on the clipboard. Therefore, click **Edit**, then **Paste Activity**. . . . The Paste Options window appears again. Enter an **B** (for Garage B) in the P̲refix: field this time. Click [OK]. After this step, the GARM project should have twenty-seven activities: **10, 15, 20, A30–A140,** and **B30–B140** (see Figure M24.13). Notice that the logic for each group of garage activities is still intact, but the two buildings are not logically tied together, yet. As the schedule stands now, both garages are being built at the same time. That is not the plan for this project since we are using only one crew for each activity. Eventually, we will fix that situation.

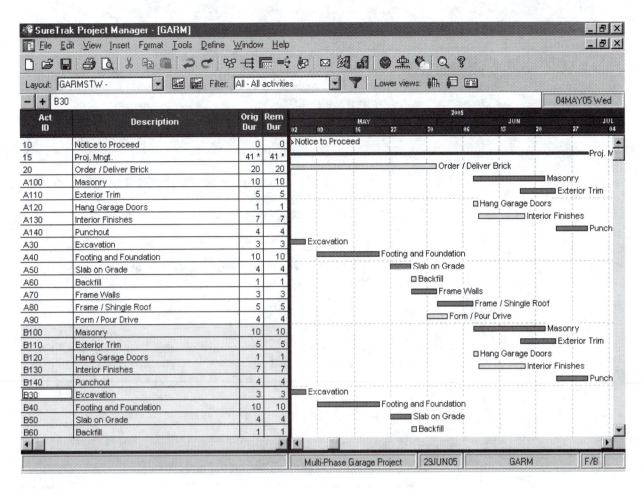

FIGURE M24.13

ADDING ACTIVITIES TO AN EXISTING PROJECT

When working with an existing project, it is often necessary to add additional activities to it and tie them in to the current logic of the project. We will add a project complete milestone to the multi-phase garage project.

12. To add an activity to an existing project, open the project and simply click the **+** button, then change the Activity ID by highlighting it and typing in the ID of your choice. In our case, change the ID from **B150** to **25**, then click the ✔ button to accept the new ID. In the Description cell next to the ID,

enter **Project Complete** as the description and click ✔. This activity will be

a finish milestone, so we have to open the activity form ▦, and click the

More >> button. Click in the Act. Type field and use the pull-down to

select **Finish milestone** as the activity type. Click OK. The activity is now added to the project.

THE LOGIC OF A MULTI-PHASE PROJECT

The logic of a project tells the computer what activities follow what. We did this earlier in Module 4 using the successors window. Adding or changing logic to an existing project is no different than adding the logic to a new project. In this module we need to add more logic to this multi-phase project.

Excavation (A30) on the first building is followed by Footing and Foundation (A40) on the first building. That logic came over from the GAR2 project. All the logic from the group of activities copied over. However, we still need to tie the two buildings together with logic. For example, when Excavation (A30) on the first building is complete, excavation can begin on the *second* building, so the activity Excavation (B30) should be added as a successor of A30. Similarly, Footing and Foundation (B40) will follow (will be a successor of) Footing and Foundation (A40), B50 (Slab on Grade) will be a successor to A50 (Slab on Grade) and so on.

13. Begin to input the logic that will tie the construction schedule of the two garages together. Go to <u>V</u>iew, Activity <u>D</u>etail, and open the <u>S</u>uccessors window (detailed instructions about working with successors can be found in Module 4). Start with the first activity listed for building A, which is Masonry

   (A100). Use the arrows to select it, as shown in Figure M24.14. **This next line is extremely important!** To add a successor, you must click <u>*below*</u> the last successor currently in the window—in this case, that would be **A140**.

   Then click the button. The window, as shown in Figure M24.15, is

   ready to accept the next successor. Using the pull-down , select **Masonry (B100)** as a successor to A100, as shown in Figure M24.16.

   The reason it is so important to click <u>*below*</u> the last successor before inserting the next successor can be illustrated by looking at Figure M24.14. Notice that successor A110 is highlighted. If you inserted a successor now, it would *take the place of* A110 and completely change the logic of the schedule. Furthermore, you may not even know the error was made. This is the most frequent and most disruptive mistake students make. Even after a warning, many students still make this mistake.

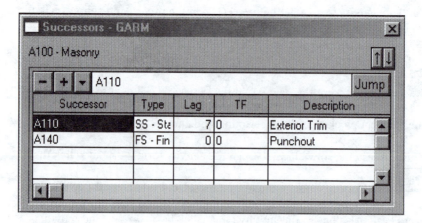

FIGURE M24.14

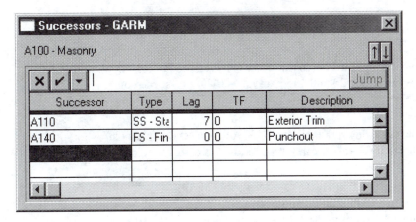

FIGURE M24.15

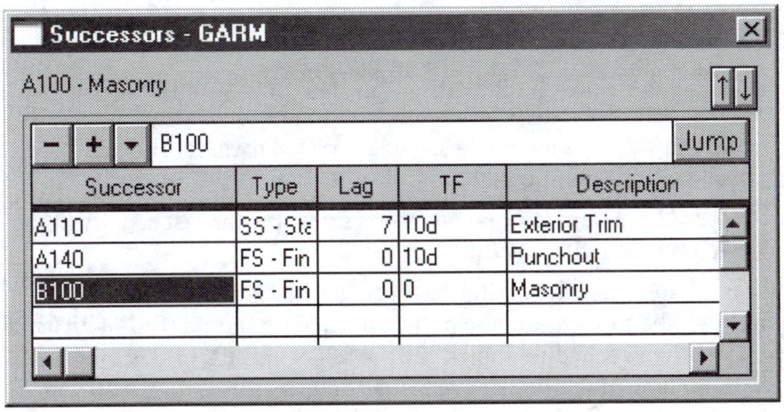

FIGURE M24.16

Once you detect a problem with the logic of the schedule, it can be very difficult to find. Therefore, be extremely careful as you input the remainder of the successors for the multi-phase project.

14. Click the [↓] down arrow to move on to the next activity, Exterior Trim (A110). Click below the successor A140 and add activity **Exterior Trim (B110)**.

Click the [↓] down arrow to move on to the next activity, Hang Garage Doors (A120). Click below the successor A130 and add activity **Hang Garage Doors (B120)**. Continue in this fashion until you have assigned a successor for all the A building activities. Make sure you move down in order of how the activities are listed (this will help ensure that you don't miss one)—the last activity to receive a successor being A90—Form / Pour Drive. To help avoid mistakes, be very careful and deliberate as you input the remaining successors. When complete, the two buildings will be logically tied together.

Note: Since building **B** is the last building, it will not have successors from another building, as did building **A**. When complete, I would *strongly suggest* that you check the logic that you just input by arrowing back up through the activities.

The next step is to tie the activities that relate to the whole project (the first four activities 10, 15, 20, and 25) to the rest of the schedule.

15. Arrow ⬆ up until Notice to Proceed (10) is in the Successors window. Click below successor 20 and add **Excavation (A30)** as a successor.

16. Arrow ⬇ down to Proj. Mngt. (15). Add **Project Complete (25)** as its successor. Notice that the relationship type in the successors window defaults to a

Type	Lag
FF - Fini	0 51

Finish-to-Finish relationship with a zero lag . This is because the activity Project Complete (25) is a finish milestone.

17. The brick must arrive at the site in time for the masonry to begin on the first

building, even though we are ordering all the brick together, so arrow ⬇ down to Order / Deliver Brick (20) and add **Masonry (A100)** as its successor.

18. The Project Complete (25) activity is a finish milestone and will start as soon as the *last* garage punchout is complete, so go down to Punchout (B140) and add **Project Complete (25)** as its successor.

19. Project Complete (25) should have *no successors* since it is the last activity of the schedule. Go up to it and verify this.

20. The logic is complete for the multi-phase garage project. The total project duration should be **51** days and the project finish date should read **14JUL05**. If this is not what your schedule shows, see the following (F.Y.I.) box for instructions on how to review your schedule. Your instructor can help you with this review. If your schedule is correct, close the Successors window and move on to the next instruction.

(F.Y.I.)

Follow the steps below to review a project schedule when you suspect that it is inaccurate or you know it is because you have a previous accurate version of the schedule.

1. If you have an accurate version of the schedule, compare total floats of each activity. This may quickly point out the problem area.

2. Make sure the activity durations are correct.

3. Carefully review the activity logic through the Successors window.

4. Check the calendar ID of each activity. An activity(s) may have been placed on a different calendar, thereby changing the project.

5. Check the Constraints window to see if unwanted constraints were placed on any activity.

6. Go to the Define Resources window (Define, then Resources . . .) and check the Driving column. If a resource is driving, it will change activity durations.

7. Finally, if all else fails, you could close the project without saving changes. This would bring you back to the point of your last save—and in the process, possibly remove a mistake you made that you cannot find.

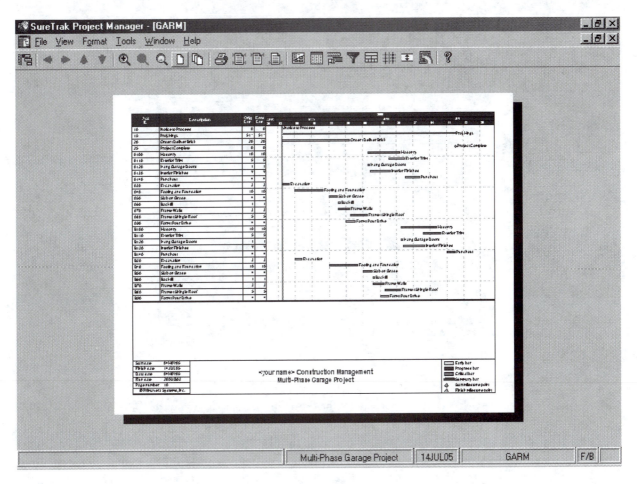

FIGURE M24.17

21. Preview the multi-phase garage project schedule at the [icon] print preview (see Figure M24.17). We still have a few more things to do to the schedule. Your schedule might spill onto two pages horizontally. For now, don't worry about it—we'll deal with that later.

22. Customize the schedule starting with the columns. Go to Format, Columns . . . or simply click the [icon] button. Show only the following columns in this exact order with the correct column width (shown in parentheses after column title): Activity ID (**8**), Description (**25**), Original Duration (6), Total Float (6), Early Start (12), Early Finish (12), and Budgeted Cost (**12**). Center all data except Description (left) and Budgeted Cost (right). Click

    [OK]. Go back to the project window [icon] and move the vertical split bar to the right edge of the Budgeted Cost column.

23. Now that the budgeted costs are in view, take a look at that column. Notice that the costs copied over with the activities. One cost that needs to be increased is the cost for the brick. It currently has the same amount there from the previous (GAR2) project. You need to double that. Go to View, Activity Detail, then Costs to open the Costs window (detailed instructions of

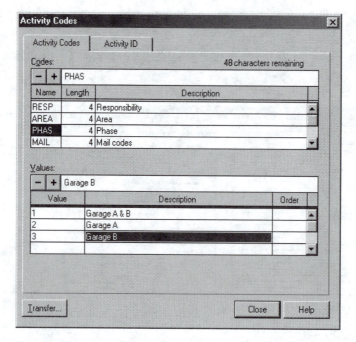

FIGURE M24.18

inputting costs can be found in Module 18). Go to the Order / Deliver Brick (20)

activity and enter 2760 in the At completion cell, then click ☑ .

24. Using activity codes, organize the schedule (detailed instructions for defining, assigning, and organizing with activity codes can be found in Module 17). Start by defining a code for the multi-phases of the project. Go to Define, then Activity Codes . . . to open the Activity Codes window. Highlight the **PHAS** code and in the Values: field below enter on the first line a 1 for the value and **Garage A & B** for the description; on the second line enter a 2 for the value and **Garage A** for the description; and on the third line enter a 3 for the value and **Garage B** for the description. When complete, verify that your Activity

Codes window matches that in Figure M24.18. Then ⬚Close⬚ the window.

25. Assign the appropriate value to each activity. To do this, open the activity

form ⬚ , and click the ⬚More >>⬚ button. Go to the first activity, Notice to Proceed (10), and click inside the **PHAS** field at the bottom of the activity form. Use the pull-down or simply enter a 1 in this field (see Figure M24.19). Continue assigning values to each activity—assigning a 1 to activities (10, 15, 20, and 25), a 2 to the activities that start with an A, and a 3 to the activities

that start with a B. When complete, ⬚Close⬚ the activity form.

26. Organize the schedule. Open the Organize window ⬚ (Format, Organize . . .) and Group by **Project**, then **PHAS—Phase**. Change the Font for the Project to **Arial, bold, 14** and for the PHAS—Phase to **Arial, bold, 10**. In the Sort by: field, sort by **Early Start, Total Float**, and then by **Activity ID**. Leave the rest of the

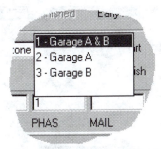

FIGURE M24.19

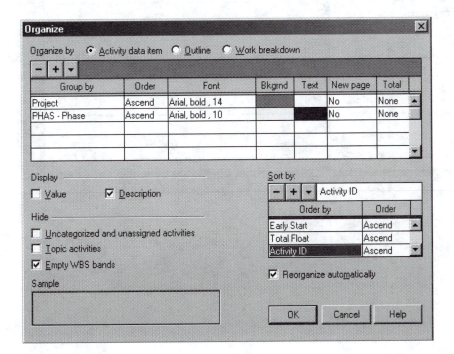

FIGURE M24.20

settings as they were. Verify that your Organize window matches that shown

in Figure M24.20. Then click [OK].

27. Turn on the relationship lines [⊞], if they are not already on.

28. Preview the schedule [🔍] (see Figure M24.21). Your schedule probably is
on two pages horizontally. Click the View All Pages [▥] button to see both.

29. Go to the page setup [▤] and mark ◉ the Fit to **1** pages wide and ☑ the

Adjust timescale to fit box. Click [OK].

30. Next, click the [▤] button to open the Footer tab in the Page Setup window
and type in for the footer Height: **0.50** Inches. This will help make room for the

cash flow profile. Click [OK].

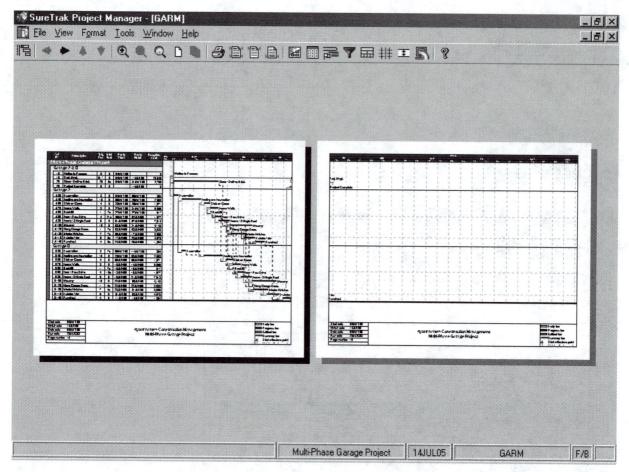

FIGURE M24.21

Now that the project schedule is complete, evaluate the schedule by preparing a project cash flow resource profile, a resource table detailing all the carpenter resources, and a schedule report.

31. Prepare a resource profile of the project cash flow (detailed instructions about creating resource profiles can be found in Module 20). Go back to the project window ▨ and turn on the resource profile ▥. Select **Resource total** in the bottom left-hand corner of the screen, then click the Format... button. In the Display tab, in the Display field, select **Budget**. Click the OK button to display the profile.

32. Go back to the print preview ▨. Click the ▨ button. Click the Resource Profile/Table tab and ☑ the Print Resource Profile box. Make sure that the Resource displayed in profile/table field has **Resource total** selected. Change the

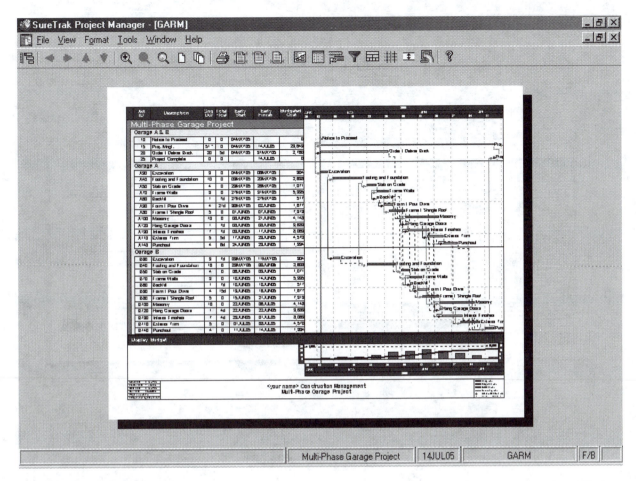

FIGURE M24.22

Profile height: to 0.75 inches. Then click OK . The cash flow resource profile should now be on the first page with the project schedule, as shown in Figure M24.22.

33. Click the button to print out a copy of the multi-phase garage project with the cash flow resource profile. It will be used to answer questions on the *Schedule Analysis—Module 24* at the end of this module and will be turned in with the analysis.

34. Save the GARM project. This will also save the changes you just made. Move on to create a resource table.

35. Prepare a resource table of the three carpenter resources: carpenter, carpenter foreman, and carpenter helper (detailed instructions about creating resource tables can be found in Module 21). Go back to the Bar Chart view in the project window . Turn on the resource table. Using the pull-down menu in the bottom left-hand corner and holding the *Control* (**Ctrl**) key down on the keyboard, select the **CRPN—Carpenter, CRPN—Carpenter Foreman, and CRPN—Carpenter Helper** resources. Click the Format... button and in the Display tab,

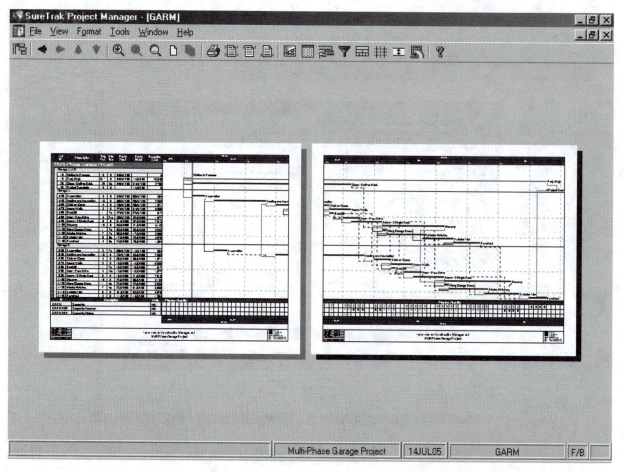

FIGURE M24.23

go to the Display field and select **Quantity**. Select **Peak** for the calculation

of the resource and Show the timescale with **Day** intervals. Click the [OK]

button to display the table. Go to the print preview 🔍 and open the Page

Setup window 🗒 . Go to the Scaling area on the Page Setup tab and mark

◉ the Fit to **2** pages wide field and check ☑ the Adjust timescale to fit box.

Click [OK] . Click the View All Pages 🗗 button to see both pages, as
shown in Figure M24.23.

36. Click the 🖨 button to print out a copy of the multi-phase garage project
    with the carpenters resource table. It will be used to answer questions on the
    Schedule Analysis—Module 24 at the end of this module and will be turned in
    with the analysis.

37. Save 💾 the GARM project. This will also save the changes you just made.
    Move on to create a report.

38. Prepare a Classic Schedule Report (detailed instructions about creating reports can be found in Module 23). Go back to the Bar Chart view in the project window 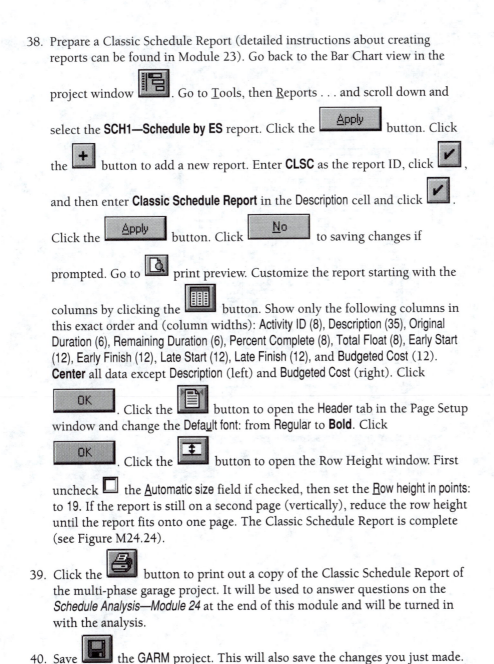. Go to <u>T</u>ools, then <u>R</u>eports . . . and scroll down and select the **SCH1—Schedule by ES** report. Click the [Apply] button. Click the [+] button to add a new report. Enter **CLSC** as the report ID, click [✔], and then enter **Classic Schedule Report** in the Description cell and click [✔]. Click the [Apply] button. Click [No] to saving changes if prompted. Go to [🔍] print preview. Customize the report starting with the columns by clicking the [▥] button. Show only the following columns in this exact order and (column widths): Activity ID (8), Description (35), Original Duration (6), Remaining Duration (6), Percent Complete (8), Total Float (8), Early Start (12), Early Finish (12), Late Start (12), Late Finish (12), and Budgeted Cost (12). **Center** all data except Description (left) and Budgeted Cost (right). Click [OK]. Click the [📄] button to open the Header tab in the Page Setup window and change the Defa<u>u</u>lt font: from Regular to **Bold**. Click [OK]. Click the [⬍] button to open the Row Height window. First uncheck [☐] the <u>A</u>utomatic size field if checked, then set the <u>R</u>ow height in points: to 19. If the report is still on a second page (vertically), reduce the row height until the report fits onto one page. The Classic Schedule Report is complete (see Figure M24.24).

39. Click the [🖨] button to print out a copy of the Classic Schedule Report of the multi-phase garage project. It will be used to answer questions on the *Schedule Analysis—Module 24* at the end of this module and will be turned in with the analysis.

40. Save [💾] the GARM project. This will also save the changes you just made.

41. Module 24 is complete. Answer the questions on the *Schedule Analysis—Module 24* and turn it in to your instructor, along with the three (3) printouts of the GARM project schedules showing project cash flow, carpenter resources, and the Classic Schedule Report. When complete, move on to Module 25.

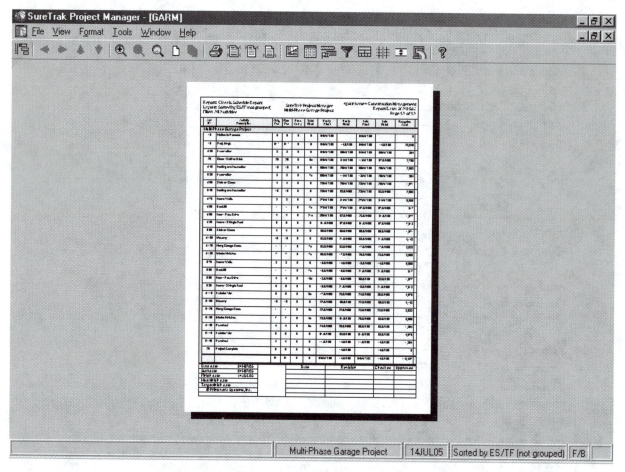

FIGURE M24.24

MODULE 24

SCHEDULE ANALYSIS
Multi-Phase Garage Project

Name _____

After completing Module 24, answer the following questions from the GAR2—garage construction project as it compares to the GARM—multi-phase garage project schedule, as well as from the project cash flow profile, carpenter resource table, and the Classic Schedule Report. Turn the Schedule Analysis in to your instructor along with all three printouts.

1. How many more *workdays* did it take to build two garages rather than one? _____ days.

2. How many more *calendar days* did it take to build two garages rather than one? _____ days.

3. Did the activities that were critical on the first garage change, at all, when the schedule went from building one garage to building two? **Yes No**

4. Are the critical activities on the first garage the same as the critical activities on the second? **Yes No**

Project Cash Flow Profile:

5. Since the project went from one garage to two identical garages, did the price double?
   Yes No

   If yes, explain why _____

   If no, explain why not _____

6. What is the total cash flow for the entire multi-phase garage project? $ _____

7. What week has the highest cash flow? _____, and how much is it?
   $_____

8. List the budgeted cost for *#15—Proj. Mngt.* on both projects? $ _____ **GAR2**
   $_____ **GARM** If the budgeted cost for *#15—Proj. Mngt.* is correct on the first project, write the calculation that proves that the budgeted cost is correct for the second.

   _____

Carpenter Resource Table:

9. At any point is the carpenter resource below its limit? **Yes No**   If yes, how far is it below the limit? _____, and on what day(s) (list dates) _____

10. At any point is the carpenter foreman resource above its limit? **Yes No**   If yes, how far is it above the limit? _____, and on what day(s) (list dates) _____

11. At any point is the carpenter helper resource above its limit? **Yes No**   If yes, how far is it above the limit? _____, and on what day(s) (list dates) _____

Classic Schedule Report:

12. Which activity has the highest float? (list ID) _____, and what is the float? _____ days.

MODULE 25
Updating the Schedule

Preface: A primary benefit of computerized CPM scheduling is the ability to accurately and quickly recalculate the schedule based on how updated information, surprise events, change orders, and/or shifting priorities affect the rest of the project.

Construction managers often update projects periodically (weekly, biweekly, monthly, and so on). They use the updated schedule to reflect current status, to identify areas of concern, as a tool to look ahead at work to come, and to evaluate alternative courses of action to help meet project goals.

Some companies use updating to keep historical records of each period of a project. Each updated schedule may be saved as a record of the project's progress, so over the course of the project, many schedules may be created.

In this module, you will learn how to update a schedule by showing actual work progress on a number of activities. You will work with the garage construction target schedule (GART). You will first manually update the Schedule Status Report, based on a given progress scenario. From that you will update the schedule on SureTrak. Then, from the newly updated schedule, you will create a new Schedule Status Report to be used for the next update.

NAMING AND SAVING CONVENTIONS FOR UPDATES

Before updating the schedule, you should always create a new schedule for the update and *always* leave the original target schedule intact as the baseline to compare against. As the construction manager creates the updates periodically, he/she will want to save them, possibly for a number of years, as a historical record. Each project may eventually have numerous schedules to be managed and saved. I strongly recommend adopting the following two conventions for naming and saving updates:

1. Use a two (2)-letter and two (2)-number naming convention for the four-character project names. Let the two letters represent the name of the project. For example, a project being built at Cincinnati State would use the letters CS. Then, let the two numbers represent the sequence of updates, such as 01, 02, and so on. Therefore, the first update would be CS01, then CS02, and CS03, and so on. Using this convention allows the manager to quickly and accurately identify the updates.

2. The next item to address is the storage of the saved updates. Since these updates may need to be saved for several years, it would be smart for the construction manager to keep them all in one place. I would suggest creating a folder off the C: drive named Projects. Then, create a folder off the Projects folder using the two-letter designation above for each individual project the construction manager builds, where he/she can store the original target schedule and all the updates for those individual projects. For example, the Cincinnati State project folder would be labeled CS, or the garage folder could be labeled GR, as shown in Figure M25.1.

427

FIGURE M25.1

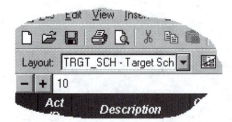

FIGURE M25.2

Follow the directions below to open and rename the GART project to GR01 for the first update. Refer to Module 15 for more detailed instructions for renaming a project.

1. Open the GART target schedule. Make sure that the **TRGT_SCH—Target Schedule** layout is selected. If not, use the pull-down menu in the upper left-hand corner to select it (see Figure M25.2). If the layout isn't there (because it wasn't saved earlier), you will have to recreate it following instructions #8 through 11 in Module 22.

2. Rename the project by going to File, Save As . . . . In the Project name: field, enter **GR01** for the new project name. Check two other settings before saving. Verify that the project Type: field says **Project Groups** and that the Current folder: shows the correct path to the folder that you want the project to be saved in. In our case it should be the default path of C:\...\SureTrak\Projects unless your instructor tells you differently. After verifying the project type and folder path as previously described, click OK to save the project under the new filename. Notice the new project name (GR01) in the upper left-hand corner of the project window.

3. Go to File, then Project Overview. . . . Change the Number/Version to **First Update** since this is our first update in this text. You normally would use the Number/Version to clearly define the time period of each update. For example, if you were updating a project monthly, you would probably want to title the Number/Version of succeeding updates, APR 05' Update, MAY 05' Update, JUN 05' Update, and so forth. Remember, you only have sixteen characters for the Number/Version title.

Leave the project title and other fields as they were and click OK. Then click the [save] button to apply and save these changes.

TRACKING PROJECT PROGRESS

One of the main responsibilities of the construction manager is to track the project's progress. Once a project has begun, you will want to update the progress of the schedule. You will do this by tracking the progress that has occurred on each schedule activity. When tracking progress, there are only three (3) possible situations for each activity. They are listed below with the appropriate tracking information to input onto the Schedule Status Report.

1. *Activity is complete.* Record the actual start and actual finish date of the activity.

2. *Activity is in progress.* Record the actual start date of the activity *and* enter your estimate for the remaining duration of the activity.

3. *Activity has not started.* There is nothing to record yet for this activity.

The Schedule Status Report was specifically designed to be used as a worksheet for construction management personnel to track project progress. You will use the Schedule Status Report that you created in Module 23 (see Figure M25.3) to first update the project manually. You will do this by filling in the report based on the progress detailed in the scenario in Table M25.1. The report will be filled in by hand and turned in to your instructor.

Scenario: It is morning of the eighth day of the project, Wednesday, October 6th, 2004. The project started on time and has worked seven (7) days so far. Individual activity information is detailed below and is current as of the close of work yesterday.

4. Use the information in Table M25.1 to manually update (handwrite-in) the Schedule Status Report shown in Figure M25.3. Fill the **Actual Start** and **Actual Finish** dates that have occurred into the report in the appropriate boxes for the activities that have made progress. Fill in the remaining duration (**Rem|Dur**) for all activities that are in progress. Write down important information in the **Remarks** column. When you are finished manually updating the report, move on to the discussion of the data date to complete the report.

WHAT IS THE DATA DATE?

The data date is the date through which the project is current; that is, the project is current *as of* the data date. Before the first update, the project start date is the data date. After the project starts, the data date changes each time you update the project. You decide the date to which you are updating it and make that date the new data date.

TABLE M25.1

Act.	Description	Status
10	Notice to Proceed	Project started on time (9/27).
15	Proj. Mngt.	Started w/ NTP and will finish with the project because it's a hammock activity.
20	Order / Deliver Brick	Ordered on time (9/27) and expected to be delivered on time—per Jim, 10/1 e-mail.
30	Excavation	Started on time (9/27) and finished one day late due to weather (9/30).
40	Footing and Foundation	Started one day late (10/1), has worked three (3) days, but still has nine (9) days remaining.

Data Date: Wednesday, October 6, 2004

The data date may differ from the date on which you enter the update information. For example, you can enter update information on a Monday for a data date as of the previous Friday; the resulting update will show progress as of that Friday.

If you are working with a daily schedule, the data date is always in the morning. For example, to update a project as of Tuesday night, make Wednesday morning the data date; since no work took place overnight, it is the same point in time as far as the schedule is concerned.

Complete filling out the Schedule Status Report. The report will be used later in the module when you update the schedule in SureTrak. It will also be turned in to your instructor at the end of the module.

5. Strike through the old information and write down the new **Data date** for the project in the left side of the footer. Write your initials in the **Approved** section of the revision box. The Schedule Status Report is complete. Construction managers should keep these handwritten status reports in a file as a historical record. You will use yours to update the project in SureTrak, <u>and later turn it in to your instructor at the end of the module.</u>

UPDATING THE PROJECT

Now that you have copied and renamed the target project, tracked the progress on the project, and wrote it down on the Schedule Status Report, you are ready to update the project. Here are a few things to remember about updating.

- Updates should only be performed on projects with defined target dates. You created the **GART** target schedule back in Module 22 for this reason.

- Your first update is always an update to the target schedule. After that, you will update the updates. That is, the second update will be an update to the first update, the third update will be an update to the second update, and so on.

- Always create a new project for each new update before entering the update information. Use the naming and saving conventions discussed earlier in this module.

- There are no set rules for how frequently you should update, although your contract with the owner may specify this.

- If your project schedule never seems to be accurate, you may not be updating enough, or the scope of your activities may be too broad—you should divide activities into smaller ones.

- If you spend too much time updating, the scope of your activities may be too narrow, or you may simply be updating too often.

- Always turn off the Automatic Schedule Calculation feature before you update, then turn it back on after the update is complete. **This is extremely important!**

- Always uncheck the setting in the bottom right-hand corner of the organize window (F<u>o</u>rmat, <u>O</u>rganize. . .), then turn it back on (recheck it) after the update is complete.

As discussed earlier in the module, there are only three (3) possible update situations for all activities. They are listed next with the appropriate instructions for input into SureTrak for the schedule update.

Report: Schedule Status Report
Layout: Sorted by ES/TF (not grouped)
Filter: All Activities

SureTrak Project Manager
Garage Construction Project

<your name> Construction Management
Report Date: 03SEP03
Page 1A of 1A

Act ID	Activity Description	Orig Dur	Rem Dur	Perc Comp	Total Float	Target Start	Actual Start	Target Finish	Actual Finish	Remarks
Garage Construction Project										
10	Notice to Proceed	0	0	0	0	27SEP04				
15	Proj. Mngt.	41 *	41 *	0	0	27SEP04		22NOV04		
30	Excavation	3	3	0	0	27SEP04		29SEP04		
20	Order / Deliver Brick	20	20	0	5d	27SEP04		22OCT04		
40	Footing and Foundation	10	10	0	0	30SEP04		13OCT04		
50	Slab on Grade	4	4	0	0	14OCT04		19OCT04		
70	Frame Walls	3	3	0	0	20OCT04		22OCT04		
60	Backfill	1	1	0	7d	20OCT04		20OCT04		
90	Form / Pour Drive	4	4	0	15d	21OCT04		26OCT04		
80	Frame / Shingle Roof	5	5	0	0	25OCT04		29OCT04		
100	Masonry	10	10	0	0	01NOV04		12NOV04		
120	Hang Garage Doors	1	1	0	4d	01NOV04		01NOV04		
130	Interior Finishes	7	7	0	4d	02NOV04		10NOV04		
110	Exterior Trim	5	5	0	0	10NOV04		16NOV04		
140	Punchout	4	4	0	0	17NOV04		22NOV04		
		41	41	0	0	27SEP04		22NOV04		

Data date	27SEP04
Start date	27SEP04
Finish date	22NOV04
Must finish date	
Target finish date	22NOV04

© Primavera Systems, Inc.

	Date	Revision	Checked	Approved

FIGURE M25.3

1. *Activity is complete.* Enter the actual start and actual finish date of the activity. If the activity was completed prior to this update, you do not need to update it again.

2. *Activity is in progress.* Enter the actual start date of the activity *and* enter your estimate for the remaining duration of the activity.

3. *Activity has not started.* There is nothing to update yet for this activity, even if the activity should have already started.

SureTrak offers several methods of inputting the update information for the activities. In this text we will update the activities individually using the activity form. This method of updating is exact, rather than estimated, which is the case with other methods, and it is very straightforward. We will use this method exclusively, because it is the most accurate, most thorough, and least complicated method for updating.

After you have filled in, by hand, the Schedule Status Report with the update information, it should look like Figure M25.4.

BEGIN THE UPDATE

Update the GR01 project. Before you update, there are always two automatic settings you need to turn off.

6. Go to Tools, then Schedule . . . and in the bottom of the Schedule window, turn ⦿ Off the Automatic Schedule Calculation, as shown in Figure M25.5. Without this turned off, updating the schedule can become extremely confusing. Leave the other settings as they were and click OK .

7. Second, click the button (Format, Organize . . .) to open the Organize window. Turn off (uncheck) the ☐ Reorganize automatically setting in the bottom right-hand corner of the window. This will keep the activities from moving all around as you update. Leave the other settings as they were and click OK . You are now ready to update.

8. You are now ready to begin the update. Turn on the activity form by clicking the button, pressing F7, or going to View, Activity Form.

9. Select the activity, Notice to Proceed. Check the ☑ Started box. Since this activity started on time, you do not have to change the Actual Start date in that field. Notice that the ☑ Finished box is grayed out. Since this activity is a start milestone, there is no finish information to update. The activity form should match Figure M25.6. Click OK .

   Notice that the date in the Early Start column has an A after it, as shown here 27SEP04 A . The A signifies that the date in the cell is an actual date. Notice that down in the activity form, the titles of the Early Start and Early Finish fields have changed to Actual Start and Actual Finish, since these are actual dates. Move on to the next activity by clicking Next .

Report: Schedule Status Report
Layout: Sorted by ES/TF (not grouped)
Filter: All Activities

SureTrak Project Manager
Garage Construction Project

<your name> Construction Management
Report Date: 31AUG03
Page 1A of 1A

Act ID	Activity Description	Orig Dur	Rem Dur	Perc Comp	Total Float	Target Start	Actual Start	Target Finish	Actual Finish	Remarks
Garage Construction Project										
10	Notice to Proceed	0	0	0	0	27SEP04	9/27			
15	Proj. Mngt.	41 *	41 *	0	0	27SEP04	9/27	22NOV04		
30	Excavation	3	3	0	0	27SEP04	9/27	29SEP04	9/30	HELD UP BY WEATHER
20	Order / Deliver Brick	20	20	0	5d	27SEP04	9/27	22OCT04		EXPECTED ON TIME – PER 1% E-MAIL
40	Footing and Foundation	10	10/9	0	0	30SEP04	10/1	13OCT04		WORKED (5) DAYS – BUT STILL (9) LEFT
50	Slab on Grade	4	4	0	0	14OCT04		19OCT04		
70	Frame Walls	3	3	0	0	20OCT04		22OCT04		
60	Backfill	1	1	0	7d	20OCT04		20OCT04		
90	Form / Pour Drive	4	4	0	15d	21OCT04		26OCT04		
80	Frame / Shingle Roof	5	5	0	0	25OCT04		29OCT04		
100	Masonry	10	10	0	0	01NOV04		12NOV04		
120	Hang Garage Doors	1	1	0	4d	01NOV04		01NOV04		
130	Interior Finishes	7	7	0	4d	02NOV04		10NOV04		
110	Exterior Trim	5	5	0	0	10NOV04		16NOV04		
140	Punchout	4	4	0	0	17NOV04		22NOV04		
		41	41	0	0	27SEP04		22NOV04		

Data date	~~27SEP04~~ 10/6/04			
Start date	27SEP04			
Finish date	22NOV04			
Must finish date				
Target finish date	22NOV04			
© Primavera Systems, Inc.				

	Date	Revision	Checked	Approved
				J.V.B.
				10/6/04

FIGURE M25.4

434

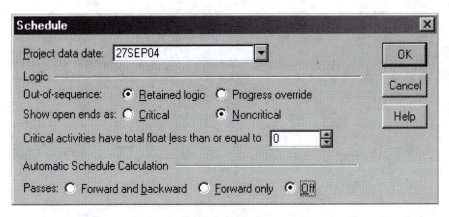

FIGURE M25.5

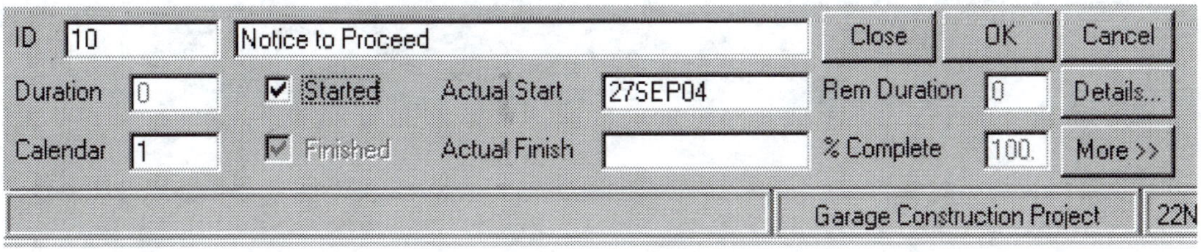

FIGURE M25.6

10. The next activity is **Project Management**. Because it is a hammock activity, its start and finish are totally dependent on other activities and, therefore, cannot be updated. Click [Next] to move on to the next activity.

11. The **Order / Deliver Brick** activity is selected. Check the ☑ Started box. Since this activity started on time, you do not have to change the actual start date in that field. Estimate the remaining duration of the activity. The brick is expected to be delivered on time and the activity has progressed 7 days, so far. Since the original duration of the activity was 20 days, the remaining duration will be 20 − 7 = 13 days. Click in the **Rem Duration** field and type in 13. The activity form should match Figure M25.7. Click [OK]. Notice that after clicking okay, the **% Complete** automatically changed to 35.0.

12. Go down to the **Excavation** activity and single-click it to select it. Check the ☑ Started box; again, since this activity started on time, you do not have to change the actual start date in that field. Check the ☑ Finished box. Since this activity actually finished one (1) day late, enter the actual finish date by clicking in the **Actual Finish** field. Then, use the pull-down calendar and double-click on the 30th to enter **30SEP04** as the actual finish date in the **Actual Finish** field. The activity form should match Figure M25.8. Click [OK].

   Since this activity is now complete, a few things have changed. The date in the Early Finish column has an A after it now since it is also an actual date. Notice that the Rem Duration automatically changed to 0, the % Complete changed to 100, and both are now grayed-out. Additionally, notice as shown

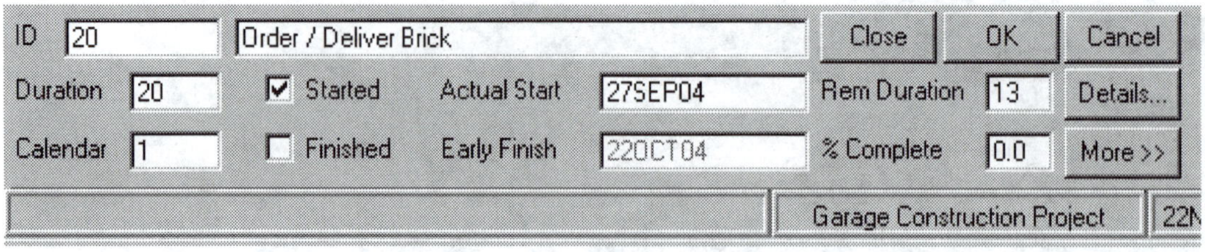

FIGURE M25.7

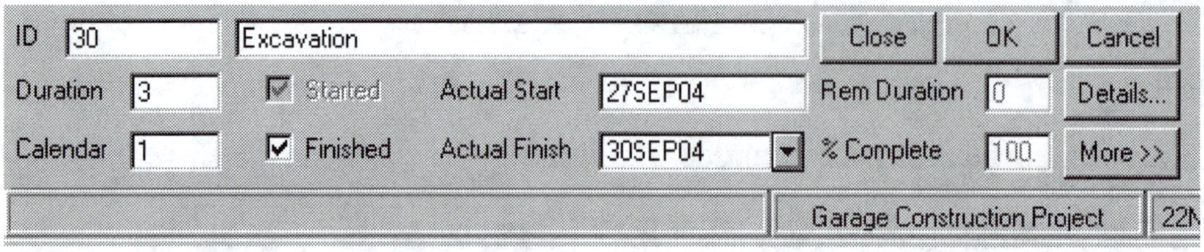

FIGURE M25.8

here _____ that the activity bar shown on your screen for Excavation is now blue. Blue is the color SureTrak uses to signify work progress. Finally, notice that the blue bar extends past the yellow target bar. This is because the activity actually finished one day later than the target finish date.

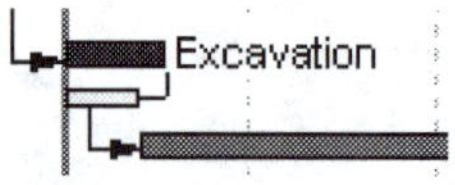

13. The last activity to update is Footing and Foundation. Select it. Check the

 ☑ Started box. This activity started a day later than expected, on October 1st, so enter that start date by clicking in the Actual Start field and using the pull-down calendar to enter **01OCT04** as the actual start date. The original duration of this activity was 10 days and it has worked three full days, so far. However, the work is not proceeding as fast as you expected and you believe it will still take nine (9) days to complete from this point, so enter a 9 in the Rem Duration field. The activity form should match Figure M25.9. Leave the other fields as

they were and click [OK]. For now the activity is showing a negative float of one day (–1d) in the total float column. This will change when you enter the data date and recalculate the schedule. That is the next step.

You have now entered all the tracked progress from the Schedule Status Report. The updating is complete, but the schedule is not accurate. You still need to enter the data date and recalculate the schedule.

14. Go to Tools, then Schedule . . . . In the Project data date field, use the pull-down menu to select **06OCT04** as the data date. After inserting the data date,

choose [● Forward and backward] in the Automatic Schedule Calculation field. The Schedule window should match Figure M25.10. Leave the other fields as they

were and click [OK]. The schedule will recalculate based on the data date and updated activity information.

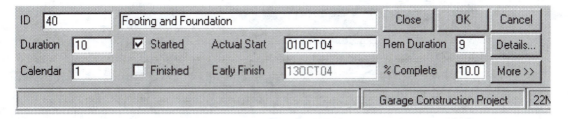

FIGURE M25.9

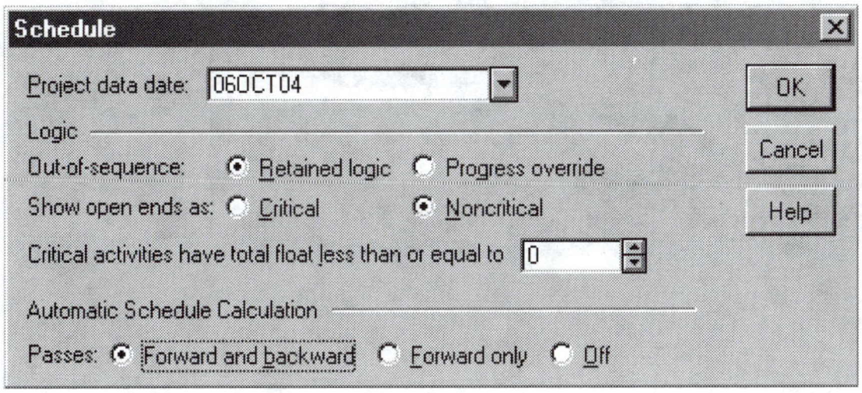

FIGURE M25.10

15. Next, click the ▦ button (F<u>o</u>rmat, <u>O</u>rganize . . .) to open the Organize window. Turn back on (check) the ☑ Reorganize automatically setting in the bottom right-hand corner of the window. Then remove **Total Float** from the <u>S</u>ort by: field by selecting it and clicking the ⊟ button. Leave the other settings as they were. The Organize window should match Figure M25.11. Click OK .

16. Go to F<u>o</u>rmat, <u>C</u>olumns . . . to add the **Remaining Duration** and **Percent Complete** columns directly after the Original Duration column (detailed instructions for formatting columns can be found in Module 11). Change the column titles for each to **Rem|Dur** and **%|Comp**. Align the data to the **Center** in both. Change the column width for Remaining Duration to 6, % Complete to 7, and Total Float to 7. The Columns window should match Figure M25.12. Click  OK . Drag the vertical split bar to the right of the Target Finish column to uncover all columns.

17. Click 🔍 print preview to view the updated schedule. Click the 📄 button to open the Footer tab in the Page Setup window to open the  Title Block ▼ sections. Remove the **\<Report name\>** from the title block and verify that the three titles remaining are \<Number/Version\>, \<Company name\>,

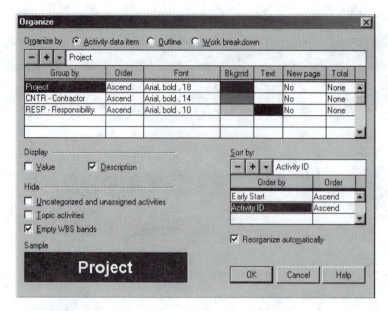

FIGURE M25.11

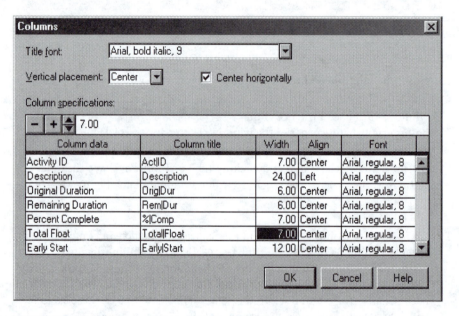

FIGURE M25.12

and <Project title>, in that order. Next, go to the font pull-down menu directly beneath the Center title block section and verify the font to be Arial, bold, **16**. Then, near the top of the Footer tab, change the Height: to **0.00** Inches. The

Footer settings are complete. Click [OK]. The First Update is complete and should match that shown in Figure M25.13.

18. Click the 🖨 button to print out a copy of the first update (GR01) of the garage construction project schedule. It will be used to answer questions on

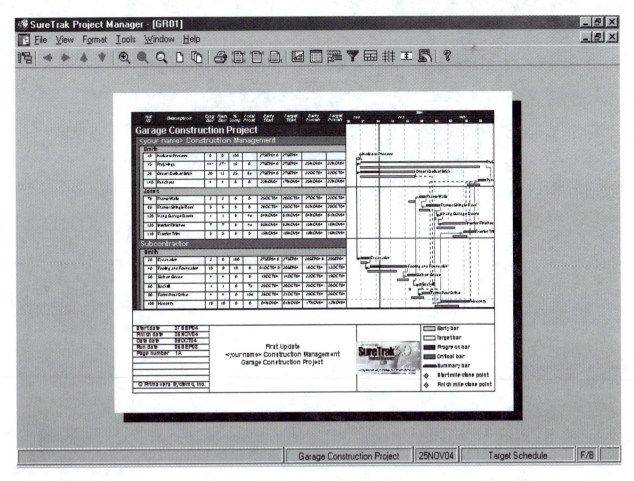

FIGURE M25.13

the *Schedule Analysis—Module 25* at the end of this module and will be turned in with the analysis.

19. Save 💾 the GR01 project. This will also save the changes you just made.

UPDATED SCHEDULE STATUS REPORT

Now that the GR01 project schedule has been updated, you will want to create a new Schedule Status Report to use as a worksheet to track the continued progress of the project for the next update. Use the following instructions to create a Schedule Status Report that shows the status updates after the first update.

The original Schedule Status Report that you created back in Module 23 was created for the target project (GART). When you created the GR01 project for the first update, you made an exact copy of the GART project. Therefore, the Schedule Status Report (from GART) should be included in the list of reports for the GR01 project. This will allow you to pull up the existing report and apply it to the updated project, saving you the numerous steps it took to create it. There will be only a few changes to make.

20. If it is not already opened, open the GR01 project. Go back to the Bar Chart view in the project window by clicking the 🗐 button.

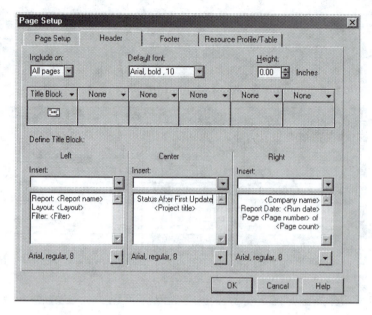

FIGURE M25.14

21. Apply the Schedule Status Report to the GR01 project by going to Tools, then Reports . . . to open the Reports window. Scroll down toward the bottom and select (highlight by single-clicking) the **STAT** report. Click the 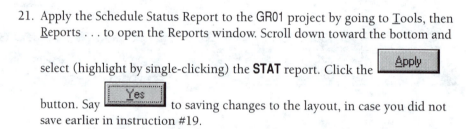 button. Say [Yes] to saving changes to the layout, in case you did not save earlier in instruction #19.

22. Go to the [🔍] print preview to view the report. Zoom in on the report to view the activities near the top. Notice that some activities were moved around. **Notice to Proceed** and **Excavation** were moved below Proj. Mngt. and Order / Deliver Brick. They were moved because they are complete now and no longer have total float; and this report is sorted by early start and then by *total float*.

    To keep this from happening and to sort this report to look more like the previous Schedule Status Report, go to Format, Organize . . . to open the Organize window. In the Sort by: area of the window, click on **Total Float** and click the [−] button to remove it from the sort sequence. Click [OK].

23. Change a title in the header by clicking the [📄] button (or go to File, Page Setup . . . , Header tab) to open the Header tab of the Page Setup window. In the Center section of the Title Block, the first title is SureTrak Project Manager. Replace that with the title **Status After First Update**. The Header tab should match Figure M25.14. Click [OK].

24. The Schedule Status Report with the Status After First Update is complete (see Figure M25.15) and is ready to be used as a worksheet to track the continued progress of the project for the next update. You will use this report to perform a second update in the *Schedule Analysis—Module 25*.

Report: Schedule Status Report
Layout: Sorted by ES/TF (not grouped)
Filter: All Activities

Act ID	Activity Description	Orig Dur	Rem Dur	Perc Comp	Total Float	Target Start	Actual Start	Target Finish	Actual Finish	Remarks
	Garage Construction Project									
10	Notice to Proceed	0	0	100		27SEP04	27SEP04			
15	Proj. Mngt.	44 *	37 *	16	0	27SEP04	27SEP04	22NOV04		
20	Order / Deliver Brick	20	13	35	8d	27SEP04	27SEP04	22OCT04		
30	Excavation	3	0	100		27SEP04	27SEP04	29SEP04	30SEP04	
40	Footing and Foundation	10	9	10	0	30SEP04	01OCT04	13OCT04		
50	Slab on Grade	4	4	0	0	14OCT04		19OCT04		
60	Backfill	1	1	0	7d	20OCT04		20OCT04		
70	Frame Walls	3	3	0	0	20OCT04		22OCT04		
90	Form / Pour Drive	4	4	0	15d	21OCT04		26OCT04		
80	Frame / Shingle Roof	5	5	0	0	25OCT04		29OCT04		
100	Masonry	10	10	0	0	01NOV04		12NOV04		
120	Hang Garage Doors	1	1	0	4d	01NOV04		01NOV04		
130	Interior Finishes	7	7	0	4d	02NOV04		10NOV04		
110	Exterior Trim	5	5	0	0	10NOV04		16NOV04		
140	Punchout	4	4	0	0	17NOV04	27SEP04	22NOV04		
		44	37	15	0	27SEP04	27SEP04	22NOV04	22NOV04	

Date	Revision	Checked	Approved

Data date	06OCT04
Start date	27SEP04
Finish date	25NOV04
Must finish date	
Target finish date	22NOV04

© Primavera Systems, Inc.

FIGURE M25.15

441

25. Click the button to print out a copy of this report. It will be used to perform a second update in the *Schedule Analysis—Module 25* at the end of this module and will be turned in with the analysis.

26. Save the GR01 project. This will also save the changes you just made to the Schedule Status Report.

27. Module 25 is complete. Answer the questions on the *Schedule Analysis— Module 25* and turn it in to your instructor, along with the following four printouts: (1) Schedule Status Report filled in, by hand, with tracking that was used for the first update; (2) the updated GR01 project schedule; (3) the second Schedule Status Report that was just printed out and is to be used for the second update in the *Schedule Analysis;* and (4) the second updated GR02 project schedule that you will create in the *Schedule Analysis—Module 25*. When complete, move on to Module 26.

MODULE 25

SCHEDULE ANALYSIS
Updated Garage Project

Name _____

After completing Module 25, answer the following questions from the GR01—updated garage project schedule and the related Schedule Status Reports. Additionally, you will perform the second update of the project. The analysis is worth 200 points.

First Update: (100 points)

Answer the following questions from the first update (GR01) as compared to the target schedule (GART).

1. Did the end date of the project change? **Yes No**
   If yes, to what date? _____

2. Did the total project duration change? **Yes No**
   If yes, from what to what? _____ to _____

3. Did the critical path of the project change? **Yes No**
   If yes, what new activities are critical? (list IDs only) _____

4. What was the original start date for #140—Punchout? _____ and what is the current start date for this activity? _____

5. What is the current percent complete of the updated project? _____ %. Where did you find this percentage? _____

6. Did the total float of activity #20—Order / Deliver Brick change with the update?
   Yes No
   If yes, from what to what? _____ to _____

7. Did the total float of activity *#70—Frame Walls* change with the update? **Yes No**
   If yes, from what to what? _____ to _____

8. Some activities are behind schedule. How is that graphically shown on the schedule?
   _____
   _____

9. How is the progress of activities graphically shown on the schedule? _____

10. How is the data date graphically shown on the schedule? _____ and where else does it appear on the schedule? _____
    _____

Second Update: (100 points)

Based on the scenario and instructions presented below, perform the second update on the garage project (GR01). Refer to the instructions from the previous modules, if need be.

Scenario:

It is morning of October 27th, 2004. The project has been updated once and is ready for its second update. Individual activity information is detailed below and is current as of the close of work yesterday.

Act.	Description	Status
20	Order / Deliver Brick	Brick is still not in, but will be delivered in two (2) days per Tom Burns' phone call yesterday
40	Footing and Foundation	Finished on 10/15—a day earlier than estimated on the previous update
50	Slab on Grade	Started (10/18) since foundation got done, finished on (10/21)
60	Backfill	Started (10/22) since the slab got done and it finished on the same day (10/22)
70	Frame Walls	Also started (10/22) and took only two days to complete instead of three, finished (10/25)
90	Form / Pour Drive	Started (10/25) and has two (2) days remaining per Paul De Nu, the concrete contractor
80	Frame / Shingle Roof	Started (10/26), worked 1 day and is not expected to go as long, and so has only three (3) days left

Data Date: Wednesday, October 27, 2004

a. Begin the second update by creating a new project **GR02,** number/version **Second Update.**

b. Fill in, by hand, the tracking information detailed in the scenario above into the Schedule Status Report that is titled "Status After First Update" (Figure M25.15).

c. Using the status report you just filled in from the progress scenario, update the GR02 project in SureTrak. Remember to first turn *off* the **Forward and backward** pass and **Reorganize automatically** settings (see instructions #6 and #7 in Module 25 for details).

d. After the second update is performed, turn the settings above back on. The schedule is updated. Now create a new Schedule Status Report entitled, "Status After Second Update."

e. Answer the questions below comparing the updated GR02 schedule to the GR01 schedule.

f. **Turn in the following:** (1) this analysis, (2) the first Sched. Status Report (Fig. M25.3) with the handwritten first update info., (3) the GR01 (first update) schedule, (4) the second Sched. Status Report (Fig. M25.15) with the handwritten second update info., and (5) the GR02 (second update) schedule.

11. Did the end date of the project change?   **Yes No**
    If yes, to what date? _____

12. Did the total project duration change?   **Yes No**
    If yes, from what to what? _____ to _____

13. Did the critical path of the project change?   **Yes No**
    If yes, what new activities are critical? (list IDs only) _____

14. What is the current percent complete of the updated project? _____ %.

15. Did the total float of activity *#20—Order / Deliver Brick* change with the update?
    Yes No
    If yes, from what to what? _____ to _____

16. Did the total float of any other non-critical activity(s) change with the update (list all below)? **Yes   No**
    If so, what activity (list ID only) _____ and from what to what? _____ to
    _____

    If so, what activity (list ID only) _____ and from what to what? _____ to
    _____

    If so, what activity (list ID only) _____ and from what to what? _____ to
    _____

MODULE 26
Revising Schedules

Preface: In the previous twenty-five modules, you have been working with schedule information that was set and did not change. You may have changed many things on the schedule, such as calendars, the layout, or resources, but the activities, logic, and durations stayed the same. However, it is common in construction for schedules to change. We saw that take place in Chapter 8 with the Delhi Medical Building Construction Schedule.

In this module you will learn to revise schedules. This is a very real-world exercise.

REVISING SCHEDULES

1. Using the First Draft of the Delhi Medical Building Construction Schedule that came with the textbook, create this schedule in SureTrak. Feel free to display the schedule to your liking. Print the schedule out on C-size or D-size paper. Your instructor will have to help you with the settings.

2. Using the Revised Construction Schedule that came with the textbook, revise the First Draft Schedule. Do not create the revision schedule from scratch; rather, rename the First Draft Schedule and change the schedule according to the changes that took place in the revision exercise. Print the schedule out on C-size or D-size paper. Your instructor will have to help you with the settings.

3. Module 26 is complete. Turn both printouts in to your instructor.

MODULE 27
Capstone Project

Preface: Create a schedule of the USA Volleyball Centers in SureTrak.

CAPSTONE SCHEDULE

1. Using your completed USA Volleyball Centers Construction Schedule that you created in Chapter 8, create this schedule in SureTrak. Feel free to display the schedule to your liking. However, you are expected to showcase your knowledge of the software. Print the schedule out on C-size or D-size paper. Your instructor will have to help you with the settings.

2. Module 27 is complete. Turn the printout in to your instructor.

Appendix A

Delhi Medical Building
Project No. 140-427-00

SPECIFICATIONS

TABLE OF CONTENTS

Title Page
Table of Contents

Bidding and Contract Requirements

Division 1

Section 00010 - Invitation to Bid   00010-1
Section 00012 - Description of Work   00012-1 thru 3
Section 00100 - Instructions to Bidders   00100-1 thru 7
Section 00300 - Bid Form   00300-1 thru 3
Section 00400 - General Conditions   00400-1
Section 00500 - Supplementary General Conditions   00500-1 thru 10
Section 01020 - Project Procedures   01020-1 thru 5
Section 01030 - Cutting and Patching   01030-1 thru 4
Section 01400 - Allowances   01200-1 thru 2
Section 01500 - Alternates   01500-1
Section 01700 - Project Closeout   01700-1 thru 3

Division 2

Section 02110 - Site Clearing   02110-1 thru 2
Section 02110 - Hot Mixed Asphalt Paving   02511-1 thru 3
Section 02200 - Earth Work   02200-1 thru 3
Section 02900 - Landscape   02900-1 thru 5

Division 3

Section 03300 - Cast in Place Concrete   03300-1 thru 5

Division 4

Section 04200 - Unit Masonry   04200-1 thru 9

Division 5

Section 05120 - Structural Steel   05120-1 thru 2
Section 05310 - Steel Deck   05310-1 thru 2
Section 05500 - Metal Fabrications   05500-1 thru

Division 6

Section 06100 - Rough Carpentry   06100-1 thru 4
Section 06200 - Finish Carpentry   06200-1 thru 3
Section 06402 - Interior Architectural Woodwork   06402-1 thru 4

Delhi Medical Building
Project No. 140-427-00

Section 06192 - Prefabricated Wood Trusses   06192-1 thru

Division 7

Section 07110 - Sheet Membrane Waterproofing   07110-1 thru 4
Section 07160 - Bituminous Damp-proofing   07160-1 thru 3
Section 07175 - Water Repellents   07175-1 thru 2
Section 07200 - Insulation   07200-1
Section 07240 - Exterior Insulation and Finish
                Systems   07241-1 thru 3
Section 07311 - Asphalt Shingles   07311-1 thru 2
Section 07511 - Built Up Asphalt Roofing   07511-1 thru 2
Section 07600 - Flashing and Sheet Metal   07600-1
Section 07900 - Joint Sealers   07900-1 thru 4

Division 8

Section 08110 - Steel Doors and Frames   08110-1 thru 2
Section 08211 - Flush Wood Doors   08212-1 thru 3
Section 08212 - Panel Wood Doors/Sidelights   08212-1 thru
Section 08410 - Aluminum Entrances and
                Storefronts   08410-1 thru 5
Section 08610 - Wood Windows   08610-1
Section 08710 - Finish Hardware   08710-1 thru 2
Section 08800 - Glass and Glazing   08800-1
Section 08525 - Aluminum Architectural Windows   08525-1 thru

Division 9

Section 09250 - Gypsum Drywall   09250-1 thru 4
Section 09270 - Gypsum Board Shaft Wall Systems   09270-1
Section 09511 - Acoustical Panel Ceilings   09511-1 thru 2
Section 09650 - Resilient Flooring   09650-1 thru 2
Section 09680 - Carpeting   09680-1 thru 3
Section 09900 - Painting   09900-1 thru 8
Section 09950 - Wallcovering   09950-1 thru 4

Division 10

Section 10800 - Toilet and Bath Accessories   10800-1 thru 2

Division 14

Section 14240 - Hydrolic Elevators   14240-1 thru

Division 15

Section 15010 - General Provisions Mechanical   15010-1 thru 11
Section 15050 - Basic Materials and Methods   15050-1 thru 14

Section 15180 - Insulation   15180-1 thru 5
Section 15400 - Plumbing Systems   15400-1 thru 5
Section 15450 - Plumbing Fixtures and Trim   15450-1 thru 4
Section 15500 - Fire Protection-Base Bid   15500-1 thru 4
Section 15550 - Fire Protection-Alternate FP-1   15550-1 thru 7
Section 15602 - Heating   15600-1 thru 3
Section 15650 - Refrigeration   15650-1 thru 2
Section 15702 - Heating Air Conditioning Systems
                Piping   15702-1
Section 15764 - Air Handling and
                Conditioning   15764-1 thru 2
Section 15800 - Air Distribution   15800-1 thru 9
Section 15903 - Controls   15903-1 thru 4
Section 15990 - Balancing   15990-1 thru 3

<u>Division 16 - Electrical</u>

Section 16010 - General Provisions Electrical   16010-1 thru 8
Section 16050 - Basic Materials and Methods
                Electrical   16050-1 thru 16
Section 16400 - Service and Distribution   16400-1 thru 6
Section 16500 - Lighting   16500-1 thru 4
Section 16740 - Telephone System   16740-1 thru 2

<u>Appendix</u>

G.J. Thelen & Associates Geotechnical Report

Delhi Medical Building
Project No. 140-427-00

SECTION 00012 - DESCRIPTION OF WORK

PART I - GENERAL

1.1   SCOPE

    A.   The following is a description of the work for the Delhi Medical Building.

        The proposed project is a two story office building and the completion of three (3) tenant suites. Included in this work are site improvements such as parking lots, retaining walls, and site drainage. The building is approximately 10,000 SF with one interior stairway and an elevator. The Form of Proposal lists separate costs for each tenant and other building improvements and alternates. These costs are for book keeping purposes only. The entire contract for construction will be awarded to a single General Contractor.

    B.   This summary should in no way be construed as being all inclusive. It is issued as a guide to aid in the assignment of work. If <u>conflicts</u> regarding <u>assignment</u> of work exist between the drawing notes and these descriptions, the <u>Description of Work will take precedence.</u>

    C.   CONTRACT DOCUMENTS

        The Contract Documents shall include the agreement, surety bonds, if required, specifications as herein listed under Table of Contents and the following list of Contract Drawings and their sub-titles. The work shall conform with the listed drawings and such additional and supplemental drawings as may be issued in amplication thereof.

SCHEDULE OF DRAWINGS

DRAWING NO.	TITLE
A-1	Site Plan/Details
A-2	First Floor Plan
A-3	Second Floor Plan
A-4	Finish Schedule
A-5	Door Schedule/Details
A-6	Exterior Elevations
A-7	Building Sections

A-8	Wall Sections/Details
A-9	Wall Sections/Details
A-10	Casework
A-11	Casework
A-12	Interior Elevations/Details
A-13	Reflected Ceiling Plans
S-1	Foundation/Second Floor Framing Plan
S-2	Roof Framing/Details/Schedules
ME-1	Site Utilities
P-1	Plumbing Floor Plans, Schedule, Legend, Isometrics, Schematics & Notes
E-1	Electric Lighting – Floor Plans
E-2	Electric Power – Floor Plans
E-3	Electric Schedules and Details
M-1	Mechanical Floor Plans
M-2	Mechanical Schedules and Details

D. The following provisions form a part of the Work Description and apply to each Contractor's Scope of Work.

1. All work is to comply with the rules and regulations of governing bodies having jurisdiction. Work shall be performed by skilled tradesmen having experience performing the work.

2. This Contractor shall not interfere with the traffic flow and activities associated with the adjacent office building and condominium projects. All construction deliveries and access to the sites will be from Rapid Run. Parking will not be permitted on any of the adjacent drives for contractors vehicles. All parking must be on Dr. Stephens property.

3. Contractors shall examine the conditions under which the work is to be installed and notify the Architect in writing of any discrepancies or conditions detrimental to proper performances of the work. This Contractor is not to proceed until the required corrections are accomplished.

4. Provide and maintain an effective safety program and conform to all Federal and Local safety codes.

5. This Contractor is responsible to review the site and be familiar with all existing conditions within and around the projects including local conditions

Delhi Medical Building
Project No. 140-427-00

and requirements.

6.   Provide all other trades all information (drawings, diagrams, templates, embedments) in other related work necessary for the coordination of the work.

7.   Where new work connects with existing, do all necessary cutting and fitting required to make a satisfactory connection with the work to be performed under these Sections so as to leave the entire work in a finished and workmanlike condition. Furnish all labor and materials to this end, whether or not shown or specified. All measurements must be verified at the building.

8.   Each Contractor shall at all times maintain a clean and safe passageway for the Owner, personnel, students and residents.

9.   Each Contractor shall field verify dimensions, materials and conditions of the existing building, interface same as detailed, and coordinate with work of other trades.

10. Benchmarks, control lines and elevations will be provided by the General Contractor. Each Contractor is responsible for all detailed layout, grade and stakes from the indicated benchmark and control points required for proper location and coordination of work.

11. Each Contractor is to coordinate all work with the work of other trades through the General Contractor for proper function and sequence to avoid construction delays.

END OF SECTION 00012

DESCRIPTION OF WORK   00012 - 3

Delhi Medical Building
Project No. 140-427-00

SECTION 00300 - BID FORM

Submit in Duplicate
All Blanks Shall Be Filled In

Delhi Medical Building

Bids Received: 2:00 PM EST   Date:

                                        JUNE 21, 2002

To: Champlin/Haupt, Inc.
       Architect

In response to your request for bids and in compliance with the
Contract Requirements, the undersigned proposes to furnish all
labor, materials and equipment, freight, rigging, all supervision,
coordination, all related incidentals necessary to perform the:

Delhi Medical Building

In strict accordance with the Project Manual and the Drawings dated
_____, including Addenda numbered _____, through ____
____ inclusive, prepared by Architects - Champlin/Haupt, Inc.

Bidder, in submitting this proposal, the undersigned agrees that
the Bid will not be withdrawn for a period of 90 consecutive
calendar days following the date of Bid Opening; further, that if
a Notice to Proceed or if prepared Agreement provided by the Owner
is received at the business address identified below, within the
above named 90 day period, the undersigned will, within ten days of
such receipt, acknowledge acceptance of the contract award and will
execute and deliver the Agreement; the Performance, Labor and
Materials Payment Bond if required; the Certificates of Insurance;
Workmen's Compensation and will proceed in accordance with
requirements of the Contract Documents for this project and have
the Project at substantial completion on or before April 1, 2003.

BID FORM   00300 - 1

Delhi Medical Building
Project No. 140-427-00

I.   PRICING

A.   Item 1 - Base Bid for all work shown on the drawings and
      described in the specifications for the Delhi Medical
      Building.

      Bidder agrees to perform all work for the lump sum of

      _____ Dollars ($)

B.   Item 2 - Hydraulic elevator as specified in Section 14240, the
      concrete pit, and all electric work required for installation
      of pumps and controllers.

      Bidder agrees to deduct this work for the lump sum of

      _____ Dollars ($)

C.   Item 3 - Interior "build-out" of First Floor Physician Suite
      titled   Work includes all
      partitions, ceilings, casework, finish materials, electric,
      plumbing, HVAC ductwork and fire protection. Work not
      included here which remains a part of the base bid includes
      exterior building shell, all public corridor spaces and
      finishes, HVAC equipment, slab on grade, Second Floor slab and
      roof construction including the gypsum board at the bottom of
      the wood trusses. Interior drywall on exterior walls is
      considered a part of the tenant "build-out".

      Bidder agrees to deduct this work for the lump sum of

      _____ Dollars ($)

D.   Item 4 - Interior "build-out" of the Second Floor Physicians
      Suite titled   Work includes all
      partitions, ceilings, casework, finish materials, electric,
      plumbing, HVAC ductwork and fire protection. Work not
      included here which remains a part of the base bid includes
      exterior building shell, all public corridor spaces and
      finishes, HVAC equipment, slab on grade, Second Floor slab and
      roof construction including the gypsum board at the bottom of
      the wood trusses. Interior drywall on exterior walls is
      considered a part of the tenant "build-out".

      Bidders agrees to deduct this work for the lump sum of

      _____ Dollars ($)

BID FORM   00300 - 2

E.   Item 5 - Interior "build-out" of the Second Floor suite titled
The Christ Hospital Pre Admission Testing. Work includes all
partitions, ceilings, casework, finish materials, electric,
plumbing, HVAC ductwork and fire protection.   Work not
included here which remains a part of the base bid includes
exterior building shell, all public corridor spaces and
finishes, HVAC equipment, slab on grade, Second Floor slab and
roof construction including the gypsum board at the bottom of
the wood trusses.   Interior drywall on exterior walls is
considered a part of the tenant "build-out".

Bidders agrees to deduct this work for the lump sum of

_____ Dollars ($)

F.   Item 6 - In lieu of the wood, double hung windows shown on the
drawings and specified herein, provide aluminum windows and
glazing as specified in the Section titled <u>Alternates</u>.

Bidder agrees to provide all labor and materials required by
this alternate for a (deduct or add) lump sum of

_____ Dollars ($)

G.   Item 7 - Total Building Fire Protection System: This work
provides for a complete sprinkler system throughout the
building.   Reference is made to Section 15550 of the
specifications.

Bidder agrees to add this work and deduct amount of Base Bid
Fire Protection Work, for the lump sum of

_____ Dollars ($)

H.   Item 8 - Ductwork: Substitute fiberglass ductwork in lieu of
insulated sheet metal.

_____ Dollars ($)

II.   <u>QUALIFICATIONS</u>

Item 1. State any qualifications to Bidders Proposal. _____

_____

_____

_____

_____

III. Changes

    Item 1   Work performed by this Contract for lump sum change proposals. Add to new field cost for overhead and profit $_____

    Item 2   Work performed by the Contractor's Sub-contractors: Add to net field cost for overhead and profit
        $_____

    Item 3   Work performed by this Contractor on a time and materials basis: Add to net field cost for overhead and profit
        $_____

IV. BONDS

    A.   To supply a 100% Performance Bond and a labor and Material Payment Bond: Add $_____ to Base Bid.

    B.   Name of Surety _____

V.   SIGNATURE OF BIDDER   DATE_____1991

                                NAME OF FIRM_____

                                _____

                                BY_____

                                TITLE_____

                                BUSINESS ADDRESS_____

                                _____

                                STATE OF INCORPORATION_____

Note: If bidder is corporation, write state of incorporation under signature and, if a partnership, give full name of all partners.

BID FORM   00300 - 4

Delhi Medical Building
Project No. 140-427-00

IV.   SUBSTITUTIONS

Item 1.   Although substitutions may be accepted by the
Owner, they will not be considered in arriving at
the base bid price.

We submit the following substitutions to the plans
and specifications:

Item   Manufacturer   Add/Deduct

_____

_____

_____

_____

END OF SECTION 00300

Delhi Medical Building
Project No. 140-427-00

SECTION 01400 - ALLOWANCES

Selected materials and equipment, and in some cases, installation are included in Contract Documents by allowances. Allowances are established to defer selection until more information is available. Other requirements will be issued by a Change Order.

The following are allowances required to be included in the contractors lump sum proposals.

Landscape $10,000.00

Scope: This work is the completed landscape of the Delhi Office Building Property. Included is all plantings and trees, bad preparation, mulching and other natural features. These beds and trees are schematically shown on the Site Plan. Areas shown to be finished graded and seeded are part of the base bid and not a part of this allowance.

Signage   Interior $1,000.00
                                                  Exterior $2,000.00

Selection and Purchase: At the earliest feasible date after Contract award, advise the Architect of the date when selection and purchase of each product or system described by an allowance must be completed to avoid delay.

> When requested by the Architect, obtain proposals for each allowance for use in making final selections; include recommendations that are relevant to performance of the Work.

> Purchase products and systems from the designated supplier.

Submittals: Submit proposals for purchase of products or systems included in allowances, in the form of Change Orders.

> Submit invoices or delivery slips to indicate quantities of materials delivered for use in fulfillment of each allowance.

Inspection: Inspect products covered by an allowance promptly upon delivery for damage or defects.

Preparation: Coordinate materials and installation for each allowance with related materials and installations to ensure that each allowance item is integrated with related construction activities.

ALLOWANCES   01400 - 1

Delhi Medical Building
Project No. 140-427-00

SECTION 01500 - ALTERNATES

An Alternate is an amount proposed by Bidders and stated ont he Bid Form for certain items that may be added to or deducted from Base Bid amount if the Owner decides to accept a corresponding change in either the amount of construction to be completed, or in the products, materials, equipment, systems or installation methods described in Contract Documents.

Coordination: Coordinate related work and modify or adjust adjacent work as necessary to ensure that work affected by each accepted alternate is complete and fully integrated into the Project.

Notification: Immediately following Contract award, prepare and distribute to each party involved, notification of the status of each alternate.   Indicate whether alternates have been accepted, rejected or deferred for consideration at a later date.   Include a complete description of negotiated modifications to alternates.

Schedule: A "Schedule of Alternates" is included at the end of this Section.   Specification Sections referenced in the Schedule contain requirements for materials and methods necessary to achieve the work described under each alternate.

> Include as part of each alternate, miscellaneous devices, accessory objects and similar items incidental to or required for a completed installation whether or not mentioned as part of the alternate.

SCHEDULE OF ALTERNATES:

Alternate A-1 (Item 2 on the Bid Form)
Hydraulic elevator as specified in Section 14240.   The Alternate Bid is a deduct for all construction and equipment related to the elevator including concrete pit, ladder, sump, and all electric work required for installation of pumps and controllers.

Alternate A-2 (Item 6 on the Bid Form)
In lieu of double hung wood windows shown on the drawings and specified, provide aluminum windows as specified in Section 08525 Aluminum Architectural Windows and Section 08800 Glass and Glazing.

Alternate P-1 (Item 7 on the Bid Form)
Provide a complete sprinkler system throughout the building as specified in Section 15550.

ALTERNATES   01500 - 1

Delhi Medical Building
Project No. 140-427-00

<u>Alternate H-1</u> (Item 8 on the Bid Form)
Provide fiberglass ductwork specified in Section 15800 Air Distribution in lieu of metal ductwork.

END OF SECTION 01500

ALTERNATES   01500 - 2

SECTION 04200 - UNIT MASONRY

General:

Unit Masonry Standard: Comply with ACI 530.1/ASCE 6 "Specification for Masonry Structures", except as otherwise indicated.

System Performance Requirements: Provide unit masonry that develops the installed compressive strengths (f'm) indicated.

Submittals: In addition to product data for each different masonry unit, accessory, and manufactured product indicated, submit the following:

Samples of each different exposed masonry unit, colored masonry mortar, and accessories.

Material certificates for each different masonry product required.

Fire Performance Characteristics: Where indicated, provide materials and construction identical to those of assemblies whose fire resistance has been determined per ASTM E 119 by a testing and inspecting organization by equivalent concrete masonry thickness, or by another means, as acceptable to authorities having jurisdiction.

Products:

Clay Masonry Units: Comply with the following requirements:

Size: Provide bricks manufactured to the following actual dimensions:

Modular Standard: 2 1/4" x 3 5/8" x 7 5/8"

Provide special molded shapes where indicated and for application requiring brick of form, size and finish on exposed surfaces which cannot be produced from standard brick sizes by sawing.

For sills, caps and similar applications resulting in exposure of brick surfaces which otherwise would be concealed from view, provide uncored or unfrogged units with all exposed surfaces finished.

SECTION 06192 - PREFABRICATED WOOD TRUSSES

PART 1 - GENERAL

Standards: Comply with N.F.P.A. "National Design Specifications" and with TPI standards including "Quality Standard for Metal Plate Connected Wood Trusses", "Commentary and Recommendations for Handling and Erecting Wood Tresses", "Commentary and Recommendations for Bracing Wood Trusses" and the following:

"Design Specification for Metal Plate Connected Wood Trusses".

"Design Specification for Metal Place Connected Parallel Chord Wood Trusses".

Submittals: In addition to product date for tress components submit the following:

Shop drawings showing sizes, design values, materials and dimensional relationships of components as well as bearing and anchorage details.

To extent engineering design consideration are fabricator's responsibility, submit design analysis and test reports indicating truss performance characteristics and compliance with requirements.

Provide shop drawings which have been signed and stamped by a structural engineer licensed to practice in jurisdiction where trusses will be installed.

Certification, signed by officer of fabricating firm, indicating trusses comply with project requirements.

Handle and store trusses with care and to comply with TPI recommendations to avoid damage from bending, overturning or other cause.

PART 2 - PRODUCTS

Lumber: Provide lumber S4S, S-Dry unless otherwise indicated grade marked, complying with PS 20 and requirements indicated.

Lumber Species: See Section 06100.

Lumber Grade: See Section 06100.

PREFABRICATED WOOD TRUSSES   06192 - 1

Stress Rating: Provide lumber which has been graded or tested and certified to comply with stress ratings indicated.

Fb = 1850 psi.
E = 1,800,000 psi.

Metal Connector Plates: Metals and thickness as indicated, but not less than thickness indicated below:

Hot-Dip Galvanized Sheet Steel: ASTM A 446, Grade A, G60, 0.036".

Fasteners and Anchorages: Of size, type, material and finish suited to application shown.

Fire-Retardant Treatment: Provide pressure impregnated lumber with fire-retardant chemicals to comply with AWPA C20 for Interior Type A treatment. Identify treated material with appropriate classification marking of UL or other testing and inspection agency acceptable to authorities having jurisdiction. Inspect each piece of treated lumber after drying and discard damaged or defective pieces.

Fabrication: Fabricate and assemble trusses to provide units of configuration indicated, with closely fitted joints and connector plates securely fastened to wood members.

PART 3 - EXECUTION

Installation:

Install trusses to comply with TPI referenced standards and other indicated requirements.

END OF SECTION 06192

Delhi Medical Building
Project No. 140-427-00

SECTION 07110 - SHEET MEMBRANE WATERPROOFING

General:

This section specifies sheet membrane waterproofing.

Types of sheet waterproofing specified in this section include the following:

Rubberized asphalt sheet waterproofing.

Product Data: Submit product data and general recommendations from waterproofing materials manufacturer for types of waterproofing required. Include data substantiating that materials comply with requirements.

Manufacturer: Obtain primary waterproofing materials of each type required from a single manufacturer, to greatest extent possible. Provide secondary materials only as recommended by manufacturer of primary materials.

Project Conditions: Proceed with work after substrate construction, openings, and penetrating work have been completed.

Start waterproofing and associated work only when existing and forecasted weather conditions will permit work to be performed in accordance with manufacturers' recommendations and warranty requirements.

Warranty: Submit a written warranty, executed by manufacturer, agreeing to replace or repair sheet membrane waterproofing that fails in materials or workmanship within the specified Warranty period.   Warranty includes responsibility for removal and replacement of other work that conceals sheet waterproofing. This Warranty shall be in addition to and not a limitation of other rights the Owner may have against the Contractor under the Contract Documents.

Warranty period is 5 years after date of Substantial Completion.

Products:

Rubberized Asphalt Sheet Waterproofing: Self-adhering membrane of rubberized asphalt integrally bonded to polyethylene sheeting, formed into uniform flexible sheets of thickness shown, or not less

SHEET MEMBRANE WATERPROOFING   07110 - 1

than 56 mils if no thickness is shown, complying with the
following:

Tensile Strength: 250 psi min; ASTM D 412.

Ultimate Elongation: 300 percent min; ASTM D 412.

Brittleness Temperature: minus 25 deg F (minus 32 deg C); ASTM
D 746.

Hydrostatic Head Resistance: 150 feet min.

Water Absorption: Not more than 0.5 percent weight gain after
48 hours of immersion at 70 deg F (21 deg C); ASTM D 570.

Available Products: Subject to compliance with requirements,
products that may be incorporated in the work include, but are
not limited to, the following:

   Bituthene; W. R. Grace & Co.

Adhesives: Provide types of adhesive compound and tapes
recommended by waterproofing sheet manufacturer, for bonding to
substrate (if required), for waterproof sealing of seams in
membrane, and for waterproof sealing of joints between membrane
and flashings, adjoining surfaces and projections through
membrane.

Primers: Provide type of concrete primer recommended by
manufacturer of sheet waterproofing material for applications
required.

Flashing Materials: Except as otherwise indicated, provide
types of flexible sheet material for flashing as recommended by
waterproofing sheet manufacturer.

Protection Board: Provide type of protection board recommended
by waterproofing sheet manufacturer.   Include adhesives
recommended by manufacturer.

Execution:

Preparation: Comply with manufacturer's instruction for surface
preparation.

Apply primer to concrete and masonry surfaces at rate recommended

Delhi Medical Building
Project No. 140-427-00

by manufacturer of primary waterproofing materials. Prime only area that will be covered by WP membrane in same working day; reprime areas not covered by WP membrane within 24 hours.

<u>Installation</u>: Comply with manufacturer's instructions for handling and installation of sheet waterproofing materials.

> <u>Coordinate installation</u> of waterproofing materials and associated work to provide complete system complying with combined recommendations of manufacturers and installers involved in work.

> Schedule installation to minimize period of exposure of sheet waterproofing materials.

> <u>Extend waterproofing sheet and flashings</u> as shown to provide complete membrane over area indicated to be waterproofed. Seal to projections through membrane and seal seams. Bond to vertical surfaces and also, where shown or recommended by manufacturer, bond to horizontal surfaces.

> <u>Install protection board</u> over completed membrane, complying with manufacturer's recommendations for both waterproofing sheet and protection course materials.

<u>Cleaning</u>: After completion, remove any masking materials and stains from exposed surfaces caused by waterproofing installation.

<u>Protection</u>: Provide protection of completed membrane during installation of work over membrane and throughout remainder of construction period. Do not allow traffic of any type on unprotected membrane.

END OF SECTION 07110

SECTION 08610 - WOOD WINDOWS

<u>General</u>: This Section includes the following window types:

    Double hung Window Units.
    Non-Operative (Fixed) Window Units.

<u>Glazing requirements</u>, including factory glazing, are specified in Division 8 section "Glass and Glazing."

<u>Performance Grade Classification</u>: Provide wood windows that comply with requirements of NWWDA I.S. 2 for performance grade 20.

<u>Standards</u>: Performance requirements for wood windows are those specified in NWWDA I.S. 2 "Industry Standard for Wood Window Units."

<u>Testing</u>: Manufacturer's stock units of each grade of wood window shall have been tested by a recognized testing agency, in accordance with ASTM E 283 for air infiltration, ASTM E 547 for water penetration and ASTM E 330 for structural performance.

<u>Performance Requirements</u>: Each window unit shall comply with the following performance requirements:

    <u>Air Infiltration</u>: Not more than 0.34 cfm per sq. ft. of overall frame area at an inward test pressure of 1.57 lbf per sq. ft.

    <u>Water Penetration</u>: No water penetration at an inward test pressure of 2.86 lbf per sq. ft.

    <u>Structural Performance</u>: No glass breakage, damage to hardware, or permanent deformation that would impair operation or residual deflection greater than 0.4 percent of the span at a positive and negative test pressure of 20 lbf per sq. ft.

<u>Submittals</u>: Submit the following:

    <u>Product data</u>, including standard construction details, dimensions, profiles, finishes, hardware and accessories.

Shop drawings, including wall elevations, unit elevations, glazing details, and full-size details of typical composite members.

Wood Window Standard: Comply with NWWDA I.S. 2.

Safety Glass Standard: Comply with ANSI Z97.1 and testing requirements of 16 CFR 1201 for category II materials.

Glazing Standards: Comply with Flat Glass Marketing Association (FGMA) "Glazing Manual" and "Sealant Manual."

Insulating Glass Certification Program: Provide insulating glass units permanently marked on spacers or one component pane of units with the label of the Insulating Glass Certification Council.

Design Criteria: Drawings indicate sizes, profiles and dimensional requirements. Units with minor deviations may be accepted, provided deviations do not detract from the design concept or performance.

Products: Provide windows produced by one of the following:

  Vinyl Clad Wood Window Units:

    Anderson Corp.
    Marvin

Materials: Comply with NWWDA I.S. 2.

Wood: Ponderosa Pine or other clear fine-grain lumber, kiln-dried to moisture content of 6 to 12 percent at time of fabrication, free of visible finger-joints, blue stain, knots, pitch pockets and surface checks larger than 1/8-inch deep by 2-inches wide.

  Lumber shall be water repellent preservative treated after machining in accordance with NWWDA I.S. 4.

Vinyl Cladding: Manufacturer's bonded cladding on exterior exposure of wood members, consisting of rigid polyvinyl chloride sheath, complying with ASTM D 1784, Class 14344-C, not less than 35-mil average thickness, permanent white paintable finish.

SECTION 14240 - HYDRAULIC ELEVATORS

<u>General</u>:

<u>Submittals</u>:   Submit the following:

   <u>Product Data</u>:   Manufacturer's complete technical product data
   indicating capacities, sizes, performances, operations, safety
   features, controls, finishes and similar data.

   <u>Shop Drawings</u>:   Plans, elevations, and details showing,
   dimensional data, service at each landing, and interfaces with
   other work including loading on structure.

   <u>Samples</u>:   Submit samples of exposed finishes (excluding
   primed-for-paint finish).

   <u>Certificates and Permits</u>:   Obtain and furnish required
   inspection/acceptance certificates and operating permits as
   required by jurisdictional authorities.

<u>Regulatory Requirements</u>:   In addition to local governing
regulations, comply with ASME/ANSI A17.1, "Safety Code for
Elevators and Escalators."

<u>Maintenance and Operating Manual</u>:   Furnish bound copies of
maintenance and operating manual, including operating and
maintenance instructions, emergency information, spare parts list
and similar information.

<u>Demonstration</u>:   Instruct Owner's personnel in operation and
maintenance of elevators.

<u>Maintenance Service</u>: Provide 12 months of complete maintenance, on
a monthly site visit/preventive maintenance basis, starting on date
of Substantial Completion.

<u>Products</u>:

<u>Elevator Manufacturer</u>:   The Building has been planned around the
Dover Corp. "Fleetwood 21-H" pre-engineered elevator.   Other
manufacturers may be acceptable provided they meet this
specification.

<u>Elevator Performance</u>:   Comply with the following:

Delhi Medical Building
Project No. 140-427-00

Hydraulic Power Unit: Manufacturer's standard belt-drive, nonpulsating, constant-displacement unit with single-speed electric motor, muffler and solenoid-operated valves.   Locate motor, pump, tank, and control system equipment in Elevator Machine Room.

Hydraulic Machines and Elevator Equipment: Manufacturer's standard single-acting under-the-car hydraulic plunger-cylinder unit for the elevator.   Provide complete with steel casing and waterproofed well cylinder.

Plunger Unit: Manufacturer's standard holeless direct-lift telescoping hydraulic plunger unit for each elevator.

Power Supply: 208 volt a.c., 3-phase, 60 Hertz, (refer to Div. 16 sections).

Capacity and Speed: 2,100 lbs.; 100 feet per minute.

Landings and Travel: Floors 1 and 2; 12'-0" travel.

Elevator Control System: Provide industry-recognized automatic operation of the following type as defined in Code, which responds to momentary pressing of signal buttons and to other signals and devices.

Single automatic operation.

Devices and Equipment: Provide the following:

Automatic Two-Way Leveling Device: Provide with leveling tolerance of 1/4-inch for travel either direction.

Load-Weighing Device: Including automatic loaded car by-pass, automatic loaded car early-dispatch, and overload protection with audible warning.

Power Door Operator: Provide car door operator with inter-connection to hoistway doors, checking action, and hand operation of car door for power failure.

Door Edge Protection Device: Provide retractable astragal device on leading edges of elevator entrance doors to automatically reopen doors upon contact with an obstructing object.

Electronic Photo-Eye Device: Provide dual beam electronic photo-eye device to reopen doors upon interruption of beam by obstructing object. Provide with 15-second timed cut-out.

Signal Equipment: Provide mfr.'s standard signal equipment and graphics system, for the required control and operation of elevators. Provide stainless steel exposed metal surfaces, with illuminated translucent signals.

Provide hall bell and lanterns (up and down) for each entrance.

Provide position indicator in each car.

Provide flush-mounted telephone box in each car, with printed instructions on door and rough-in wiring for telephone handset.

Provide emergency alarm bell, located within building as indicated, with button in each car. Comply with Code.

Car Enclosures: Provide manufacturer's standard car enclosures, or units fabricated by firm specializing in elevator car enclosures. Include walls, ceiling, lighting, car ventilation, car heating (if needed), doors, emergency car access panels, hardware, accessories and finish on walls, ceilings and floor. Provide the following finishes where indicated:

Front Panel: Brushed Stainless Steel.

Wall Panels: Plastic laminate paneling, NEMA LD3 0.05-inch thick, color and pattern as selected by Architect from manufacturers standard selections. Provide horizontal panel style as manufactured by Dover.

Ceiling Finish: Steel paneling with baked enamel finish.

Lighting: Cove light option as manufactured by Dover.

Floor Finish: Prepare platform to receive wood finish. See Finish Schedule.

Doors/Frames: Hollow metal, baked enamel finish. Match size and function of hoistway entrances.

Handrails: Contoured oak - continuous at back and side panels.

Sill: Extruded aluminum.

Protective Blanket Lining: Full-height, heavy cotton duck, padded and quilted, removable, with brass grommets. Provide permanent hooks in car.

Hoistway Entrances: Provide manufacturer's standard hoistway entrances, or units fabricated by firm specializing in elevator hoistway entrances; comply with ASME/ANSI A17.1 requirements.

Construction: 16 ga. mechanically joined frames and 18 ga. flush-welded door panels; sound-deadened.

Frame Finish: Baked enamel.

Door Finish: Baked enamel.

Sills: Extruded aluminum.

Style/Function: Single-leaf, horizontal sliding.

Execution:

Installation: Comply with Code and shop drawing requirements. Install hoistway entrances for each elevator plumb with each other and aligned properly with hoistway. Install guide rails for uniform, close tolerance of car door with hoistway entrances. Install sills after car installation, and align with car sill.

Testing: Before elevators are placed into use, perform acceptance tests as required and recommended by Code and governing authorities. Review test results with Owner, and submit record copy.

END OF SECTION 14240

Index

A

Activities, 75. *See also* Drawing;
    Dummy activities;
    Excavation activity;
    Foundation; Hammock
    activity; Up-fronts; Work
    item activity
  addition, 249–252. *See also*
    Projects
  assignation, 77, 78
  calendars, assignation, 326–328
  categories, 77, 85
  connections, 88–89
  copying, 408–413
  definition, 77–79
  descriptions, 77, 85
  detail, 77, 80–81
  duration, 76, 95–105
    equation, 99
    resource change, 83
  EF, 154
    calculation, 149–150
    start-to-start relationships,
      inclusion, 152–155
  ES, 154
    calculation, 151–152
    start-to-start relationships,
      inclusion, 152–155
  free float, definition, 170–173
  grouping, 343–347
  guidelines, 81–84
  identification, 76–87
  IDs, 77, 85–86, 128, 143, 315
    change, 249
  information, 77, 86–87, 251
  lag, 88, 91–95
  LF, 160–166
    start-to-start relationships,
      inclusion, 161–166
    successors, inclusion,
      161–166
  logic, 88–89
  LS, 160–166
    start-to-start relationships,
      inclusion, 161–166
    successors, inclusion,
      161–166
  lump sum costs, assignation,
    348–352
  measurement, 77–79
  progress, observation/
    measurement, 81–83
  relationships, 88–91

resources
  assignation, 355–359
  consumption, 77
scheduling. *See* Sites
sequence, 78
sequencing logic, 76, 87–95, 128
sorting, ES usage, 305–307
start/finish, 78
starting/stopping point, 81
start-to-start relationships,
  inclusion, 152–155
TF, 167–168
time consumption, 77
time-scaling, 127
types, 77, 79–80
work
  continuousness, 81
  scope, 77–78
Activity codes, 335
  assignation, 340–343
  creation, 406
  defining, 337–340
Activity-on-arrow (AOA),
  62, 124–125
  advantages/disadvantages, 125
Activity-on-node (AON), 62, 124, 126
  advantages/disadvantages, 126
Added cost, perception, 10
Addenda, definition, 46
ADM. *See* Arrow Diagramming
  Method
Advanced Technology and Learning
  Center (ATLC), 70
Adversarial relationship. *See* Owners;
  Owners/contractors; Team
  members
  absence, 10
Agency construction management,
  6, 8–10
  advantages, 10
  characteristics, 9–10
  disadvantages, 10
Air conditioning. *See* Heating
  ventilation air conditioning
Allowances, definition, 209
Alternates, definition, 209
AOA. *See* Activity-on-arrow
AON. *See* Activity-on-node
Approvals, 145, 275
Architects, 23
  project team, 9
  role, 6, 10, 11
  team leaders, 9, 11

Arrow Diagramming Method
  (ADM), 125
ATLC. *See* Advanced Technology
  and Learning Center
At-risk construction management, 6,
  10–12
  advantages, 11–12
  characteristics, 11
  disadvantages, 12
Automatic save feature, 272
Award contracts, 57

B

Backfill, 143, 239
Backward pass
  calculation, 156–166
  initiation, 157
Bar charts (Gantt charts), 62–64
  network diagramming, contrast,
    124
Bidding documents, 100
Bidding phase, 8, 35, 45–47
Bids
  competitiveness, 7, 16, 18
  documents, 100
  estimate, 100
  form, 208, 209
  opening, 57
  package, 276
    schedule, 57–60, 275
  prices, competitiveness, 18
Board of directors, 24, 25
Bonding problems, 10
Bricks, 211
  cleaning, 33
  delivery, 239, 250
  order/deliver, 144
Budgeted costs, 348
Budgets. *See* Projects; Target budget
  accuracy, 12
  information, 87
  measurement, 86
  overruns, 8
Builders, 23–24. *See also* Master
  builder
  conflict. *See* Designer
Building
  component, 85
  construction projects, 211
  enclosed, 79
  envelope, 70
  footprint, 40
  foundation, 70

sections, usage, 205
skin, 58
Business, disruption, 72
Buttons, addition. *See* Toolbar

C

Calendars. *See* Globe calendar;
  Workweek calendar
  assignation. *See* Activities
  creation, 324–326, 406
    four-tens, 328–331
  holidays, addition, 322–324
  usage, 320
Capstone project, 224, 450
  USA Volleyball Centers, 229,
    231–238
    construction schedule,
      creation, 229
Casework, 211. *See also* First floor;
  Second floor
Cash flow. *See* Projects; Total project
  cash flow
  problems, 2, 4
  small companies, impact, 5
Changes
  increase, 73
  order, definition, 48
Checks/balances
  absence, 14
  system, 7
CM. *See* Construction manager
CMP. *See* Corrugated metal pipe
Codes. *See* Activity codes
Columns, formatting, 300–304
Company
  impact. *See* Construction
  size, contract value
    (relationship), 5
Competition, absence (perception),
  12, 14
Completion. *See* Substantial
  completion
Computerized schedule,
  accuracy/reliability,
  123–124
Condensing units (CUs), 205
Connecting activities, 128–129
Construction. *See* Outdoor
  construction
  contracts. *See* Owners
  types, 15–20
  coordination, need, 74
  cost risk, 7

design, multiple entities (impact), 3
document, 35, 40, 43–45, 57
expertise, 7, 10, 12–13
industry, 1
    risk, 2–5
locked-in price, 4
management. *See* Agency construction management; At-risk construction management; Pure construction management
firm, hiring, 11
modularization, 53
multiple companies, impact, 4
multiple contracts, 9
parties/members, involvement, 21
phase, 35, 47–49
price lock-in, 2
projects. *See* Building
providing, 13
safety concerns, 5
schedule, 57, 60–62. *See also* First draft construction schedule; Garage; Revised construction schedule
    creation, 201, 212–218. *See also* Capstone project
separation. *See* Design
size, enormity, 4
start, 7, 57
team, formation, 54
work, division, 59
Construction manager (CM), 21, 23
    construction effort, direction, 9
    formation, 9
    owner action, 10
    project team, 9, 11
Construction projects
    3-D object creation, 2-D plans (usage), 3
    initiation, 211
    repetition, lack, 3
    scheduling, 106–111, 113–114, 116–117, 119
Consultants. *See* Subconsultants
Contingency, definition, 47
Continuous overtime, impact, 104–105
Contracting. *See* General contracting
    traditional method, 6
Contractors. *See* Trade contractors
    advantages, 72
    adversarial relationship. *See* Owners/contractors
    disadvantages, 74
    marked-up price, payment, 19
    number, 73
    overhead, knowledge, 17
    performance agreement, 15, 19
    profit, 16
        knowledge, 17. *See also* Owners
    risk, 16, 17
    selection criteria, 16–18
    shared risk. *See* Owners/contractors
Contracts. *See* Cost plus a fee contract; Guaranteed maximum price contract; Lump sum contract; Time/material contract; Unit price contract

combinations, 19–20
negotiation, 16, 18, 19
number, 73
price, basis, 16
trust, 17, 18
types. *See* Construction
unit prices, basis, 18
value, 2
    relationship. *See* Company
Contractual relationships, 7
Coordination drawings, 145, 211, 275
    definition, 209
Corrugated metal pipe (CMP), 204–205
Cost commitment, 13
Cost plus a fee contract, 18
    characteristics, 18
Costs. *See* Budgeted costs
CPM. *See* Critical path method
Critical path, 166–173
    definition. *See* Projects
Critical path method (CPM)
    calculations, 126, 147–148, 170
    completion, 172
    performing, 186
    capabilities, 147
    network calculation
        in-class exercises, 174–185
        student exercises, 186–200
Curtain wall, trade contractors, 30
CUs. *See* Condensing units

D
Data
    dates, 429–430
Dates. *See* Locked-in dates
Days (unit, usage), 96
Design. *See* Electrical; Incomplete designs/documents; Interiors; Plumbing; Schematic design; Specialty designs; Start design
    changes, increase, 73
    completion, problems, 73
    conflicts, 73
    construction
        separation, 7
        transition, 12, 13
    coordination, need, 73
    development, 40, 43, 57
    documents, completion, 18
    firm, direction, 13
    influence, 53
    multiple entities, 2
    phase, 8, 11, 35, 40–47. *See also* Predesign phase
    potential. *See* Overdesign
    problems, 73
    providing, 13
    requirement, 7
Design-bid-build, 6
    timing method, 71
Design/build entity, 13
Design/build (project delivery system), 12–14
    advantages, 13
    characteristics, 13
    disadvantages, 14
Design/build team, 13
Design/builder, formation, 13
Designer, builder (conflict), 14
Disks, project (saving), 269–271

Documents. *See* Bidding documents; Bids; Construction; Incomplete designs/documents
    completion. *See* Work
        problems, 73
    misinterpretation, 104
    requirement, 7
    review, 201–210
Doors, 211
    in-class exercise. *See* First floor; Second floor
Drawing. *See* Precedence network diagram; Relationship types
    activities, 128–129
    definition. *See* Coordination drawings
    example. *See* Network
    importance. *See* Network
    in-class exercises. *See* Network diagrams
    review, 201–207
    student exercises. *See* Network diagrams
Dryvit, 203
Drywall, 33, 213. *See also* First floor; Floors; Second floor
    usage, 217
Ductwork, 32
Dummy activities, 126
Duration, 75. *See also* Hammock activity; Locked-in duration; Projects
    assignation, 99–103
    calculation, 99–103
        in-class exercise, 105, 112, 115, 118, 120–122
    determination, factors, 95, 97–98
    factors, 95, 102–105
    resource change. *See* Activities

E
Early finish (EF), 148–150. *See also* Hammock activity
    calculation. *See* Activities
Early start (ES), 148, 151–152. *See also* Hammock activity
    calculation. *See* Activities
    usage. *See* Activities
Earthwork, 31, 58
EF. *See* Early finish
EIFS. *See* Exterior insulation finish system
Electrical. *See* Mechanical electrical plumbing; Underground electrical
    designs, 28
    equipment, 211
    rough-in, 59, 144
    subconsultants, 27
    trade contractors, 30
    work, 143
Elevations
    plans, usage. *See* South wall structural elevation plans
    usage, 203. *See also* Entry elevations
Elevators, 211
End nodes, 141
End of day conventions, 149
End users, 24, 25
Engineers. *See* Site engineers; Structural engineers

Entry elevations, usage, 206
Equipment
    availability, 98
    installation, 33
    maintenance, 54
    productivity, 103
    resources, 88–89
ES. *See* Early start
Estimation
    expertise, 12, 13
    guides, 101
Excavation, 58, 60, 143–144. *See also* Mass excavation
    activity, 221
    start, 275
Existing layouts, application, 294–297
Expedited materials, delivery (scheduling), 54
Experience. *See* Managers
    impact, 100, 101
Expertise, estimation, 8, 10
Exterior insulation finish system (EIFS), 203, 217
Exteriors
    doors/windows, 144, 275
    finishes, 213
        usage, 217
    lighting, 32
    sheathing. *See* First floor
    studs. *See* First floor
        in-class exercise. *See* Second floor
    trim, 143, 145, 259
    walls, 144
        framing, 143, 239

F
Fabrication, scheduling, 54
Fast-tracking
    advantages, 72
    disadvantages, 72–74
    explanation, 68–74
Favoritism, avoidance, 7
FF. *See* Finish-to-finish; Free float
Field verification, 18
Financing, 57
    costs, saving, 72
Finishes, 70
    usage. *See* Exteriors; Interiors
Finish-to-finish (FF)
    activities, 256
    free float, 171
    relationships, 90–92
Finish-to-start (FS)
    activities, 256
    free float, 170–171
    relationships, 89
        lag, inclusion, 92
Fire protection, 32
Fire-separated space, 203
First draft construction schedule, 212–219, 229
    questions, 217
    revision. *See* Revised construction schedule
First floor
    casework, 225
    drywall, 145
    exterior sheathing, 112
    exterior studs, 112, 145
    interior

doors/hardware, in-class
    exercise, 118
    partitions, in-class exercise, 115
layout, 225
plans, usage, 203–204
prime coat, 145, 225
rough-ins, 145
Flashing, 32
Float. *See* Free float; Shared float;
    Total float
Flooring, 32
Floors, 58
    ceiling grids, 276
    drywall, 276
    exterior studs, 275
    interior studs, 275
Footers, formatting, 308–312
Footings, 58, 60, 143–145, 275
Footprint. *See* Building
Formatting. *See* Footers; Headers
Formwork, 32
Forward pass
    calculation, 148–156
    initiation, 149
Foundation, 58, 60, 143–144, 213.
        See also House
    activities, 214–215
    plans, usage, 206–207
    trade contractors, 30
    walls, 145, 275
Frame. *See* Structural frame
Framing. *See* House
    plans, usage. *See* Roof; Second floor
Free float (FF). *See* Finish-to-finish
        activities; Finish-to-start
        activities; Start-to-finish
        activities; Start-to-start
    definition. *See* Activities
    usage, 170–173
FS. *See* Finish-to-start

G
Gantt charts. *See* Bar charts
Garage
    construction schedule (analysis),
        242, 267, 315, 333,
        383–384, 403, 445–447
    completion, 260
    printing, 264
    doors, 239
    project, 256. *See also* Multi-phase
        garage project
    renaming, 337
    schedule analysis, 315, 333
Gas piping, 32
GC. *See* General contractor
General contracting, 6–8, 11
    advantages, 7
    characteristics, 6–7
    disadvantages, 7–8
General contractor (GC), 21, 23
Glass, 211
Globe calendar, 320
GMP. *See* Guaranteed maximum price
Grand opening, 58
    phase, 35, 50–51
Guaranteed maximum price
        (GMP), 15
    addition, 18
    contract, 16–17
        characteristics, 16–17
Gut feelings, 99, 101

H
Hammock activity, 80, 133, 144
    duration, 156
    EF, 156
    ES, 156
    LF, 166
    LS, 166
    start, 253, 276
Hard drives, project (saving), 269
Hardware, 211
    in-class exercises. *See* First floor;
        Second floor
Headers, formatting, 313–314
Heating ventilation air conditioning
        (HVAC), 28, 43
    completion, 145
    contractors, 216
    equipment, 211
    rough-in, 59–61, 144
    subconsultants, 27
    trade contractors, 30
Holidays, addition. *See* Calendars
Hours (unit, usage), 96
House
    exterior/interior finish, 143
    foundation, 143
    framing, 143
HVAC. *See* Heating ventilation air
        conditioning
Hybrids, 6
    project delivery system, 14
Hydraulic elevators, 208, 210

I
Icons, addition. *See* Toolbar
i-j Diagramming method, 125
Incomplete designs/documents, 73
Indirect costs, saving, 72
Insulation, 33
Interiors
    design, 28–29
    exercises. *See* First floor; Second
        floor interior
    finishes, 59, 213, 221
        usage, 217, 225
    partitions, 59, 143–144
    rough-ins, 221
        usage, 222–225
    studs, 213
        usage, 216–217
    subconsultants, 27
    trade contractors, 30
    trim, 276

J
Job layout, 123

L
Labor
    agreement restrictions, 104
    productivity, 103
Lag, 133. *See also* Activities
    definition, 91
    inclusion. *See* Finish-to-start
        activities
Landscaping, 31, 59, 143
Late finish (LF), 156–161. *See also*
        Activities; Hammock
        activity
Late start (LS), 156–158. *See also*
        Activities; Hammock
        activity

Layouts. *See* Sites
    application, 293–299. *See* Existing
        layouts
    changes, saving, 293–294
    creation, 293, 297–299
    default, 293
    definition, 293
    interaction. *See* Reports
    renaming, 317–319
    saving, 293–299
LF. *See* Late finish
Locked-in dates, 99, 102
Locked-in duration, 99, 102
Locked-in price. *See* Construction
Logic, 75
    adding, 256–261
Lookahead report. *See* Three-week
        lookahead report
LS. *See* Late start
Lump sum contract, 10, 15–16
    characteristics, 16
    impact. *See* Single lump sum
        contract
    type, usage, 7
Lump sum costs, assignation. *See*
        Activities

M
Management philosophy. *See*
        Projects
Managers, experience, 103
Masonry, 143–145. *See also* Unit
        masonry
    in-class exercise, 105, 120
    trade contractors, 30
Mass excavation, 70
Master builder, 13
Materials, 15, 89
    availability, 98, 103–104
    contract. *See* Time/material
        contract
    delivery, scheduling. *See*
        Expedited materials
    purchase. *See* Owners
    suppliers, 21, 33
        formation, 54
Mechanical electrical plumbing
        (MEP), 43, 70
    rough-ins, 213, *222*
        usage, 216–217
    site plans, usage, 204–205
Membranes, 32
MEP. *See* Mechanical electrical
        plumbing
Milestones, 41
    activity, 143–145, 275
    definition, 57
    examples, 79
    schedule, 57–58
Minimum total project
        duration, 148
Minutes (unit, usage), 96
Mistakes, erasure, 227
Modularization, 104. *See also*
        Construction
Money, saving, 72
Months (unit, usage), 96
Multi-phase garage project (schedule
        analysis), 425–426
Multi-phase projects, 405
    creation, 405–406
    logic, 414–424

Multiple companies, impact. *See*
        Construction

N
Network. *See* Program evaluation
        and review technique
    calculation
        in-class exercises. *See* Critical
            path method
        student exercises. *See* Critical
            path method
    diagramming
        contrast. *See* Bar charts
        methods, 124–127
    drawing, 128
        example, 129–134
        importance, 123–124
    schedule, 148
        drawing, 239–241
Network diagrams, 123
    definition, 124–127
    drawing. *See* Precedence
    in-class exercises, 134–140
    student exercises, 141–145
Non-finish-to-start activities,
        calculations, 127
Notice to proceed, 79, 143–144
    activity, 249, 253, 257
Number/version, renaming, 317–319

O
Object creation (3-D), 2-D plans
        (usage). *See* Construction
        projects
Occupancy, certificate, 58
Outdoor construction, 4, 103
Outside sources, usage, 101
Overdesign, potential, 73
Overhead, knowledge. *See*
        Contractors
Overtime, 98
    impact. *See* Continuous overtime
Owners, 21–22. *See also* Private
        owner; Public owner
    action. *See* Construction
        manager
    construction contract, 7
    design/builder, adversarial
        relationship, 14
    groups, 21, 24–26
    materials, purchase, 12
    move-in, 57
    needs, 73
    project
        cost savings, 12
        team, 9, 11, 13
    representatives, 7, 24, 26
    risk, 19
Owners/contractors
    adversarial relationship, 18
    profit, knowledge, 18
    shared risk, 17

P
Package schedule. *See* Bids
Painting, 33
Parking garage, 70
Partitions. *See* Interiors
    in-class exercises. *See* First floor;
        Second floor
Passes, calculation. *See* Backward
        pass; Forward pass

PDM. *See* Precedence diagramming method
PERT. *See* Program evaluation and review technique
Phone wiring, 32
Physical work, type, 35
Planning, 53–56
    scheduling, contrast, 53–54
    unit, 95–97
    usage, 53
Plans
    2-D, usage. *See* Construction projects
    usage. *See* First floor; Foundation; Mechanical electrical plumbing; Roof; Second floor; Site plans
Plumbing. *See* Mechanical electrical plumbing; Underground plumbing
    completion, 145, 276
    designs, 28
    rough-in, 59, 144
    subconsultants, 27
    trade contractors, 30
Potéa, 205
Pre-built report, application, 390–392
Precedence
    diagrams, 65
    method, 62
    network diagram, drawing, 128–134
Precedence diagramming method (PDM), 124, 126–127
    advantages/disadvantages, 127
Preconstruction phase, 11
Predesign phase, 8, 11, 35–40
Prefabricated wood trusses, 208, 210
Preference, connection, 89
Price lock-in. *See* Construction
Prime contractors, 10
Private owners, 22
Productivity. *See* Equipment; Labor
    factors, 95, 103–105
    rates, 100–101
    relationship. *See* Quantity
Products, outdoor construction, 2
Profit
    knowledge. *See* Contractors
    maximization, resourcing (usage), 97–98
Program evaluation, 36
Program evaluation and review technique (PERT), 62, 64–66
    networks, 125
    project window, change, 284–290
    view, 284
Programming, initiation, 57
Project delivery
    acceleration, 13
    systems, 5–15. *See also* Design/build; Hybrids
    usage. *See* Projects
Projects
    activities, addition, 413
    arrangements, 20
    budgets, 47
    cash flow, 363–366, 372–374. *See also* Total project cash flow

ceiling cost. *See* Total project ceiling cost
closeout, 58, 59
closing, 269, 272
complete, significance, 79
completion, 58, 79, 217–218
complexity, 80–81
cost. *See* Total project cost
    risk, 9
    savings. *See* Owners
creation, 242, 244–246. *See also* Multi-phase projects
critical path, definition, 168–170
3-D object creation, 2-D plans (usage). *See* Construction projects
    definition, 35
    duration, 156. *See also* Minimum total project duration
    evolution, 35
fast-tracking, 8, 10, 13, 16–18
    non-allowance, 17
    prediction, 55–56
financial risk, 13
flow, 126
goals/objectives, 36
groups, 273
history, impact, 101–102
information, 147
    awareness, 81
initial budget, 56
initial completion date, 56
interface, 55
management, 143–145, 239
    activity, 262
    philosophy, 81
multiple parties, involvement, 104
opening, 273–274
phase, 85
progress, tracking, 429
renaming, 317, 385–386
saving, 246–248, 269–272. *See also* Disks; Hard drives
    file name, change, 271–272
    folder, change, 272
schedule preparation, 81
scheduling. *See* Construction projects
size, enormity, 104
table of contents, usefulness, 208
team, 21–24
    approach, fostering, 10, 12
title, renaming, 317–319
uniqueness, 2, 104
updating, 430–433
window, change. *See* Program evaluation and review technique
workflow, 127
Property management phase, 35, 50–51
Prototype, absence, 2–3
Public owner, 22
Punchlist, 145, 252, 258
Punchout, 58, 59, 143, 239
Pure construction management, 9

Q
Quantity. *See* Work
    productivity, relationship, 99–101
    take-off, 99–100

R
Redo buttons, 272
Reimbursed cost, fee percentage, 19
Relationship lag, 256–257
Relationship types, 256–257
    drawing, 129
Repetitiveness, absence, 2
Reporting requirements, meeting, 83–84
Reports, 390. *See also* Schedule; Three-week lookahead report
    application. *See* Pre-built report
    layouts, interaction, 394–395
    menu. *See* Run report menu
Request For Information (RFI), 48
Resources, 353. *See also* Equipment
    assignation, 360–362. *See also* Activities
    change. *See* Activities
    consumption. *See* Activities
    defining, 353–355
    measurement, 86
    profiles, 363, 368–371
        printing, 366–368
    tables, 372
        printing, 374–382
    transfer, 406–408
Resourcing, usage. *See* Profit
Responsibility
    level, 87
    single source, 13
Retaining wall, 70
Reviews. *See* Documents; Drawing; Specification review
    technique. *See* Program evaluation and review technique
Revised construction schedule, 221–225, 227, 229
    questions, 223
Revised draft construction schedule, 218–222
RFI. *See* Request For Information
Roofing, trade contractors, 30
Roofs, 58, 213
    framing, 143, 239
    plans, usage, 207
    shingling, 143, 239
    trusses/sheathing, 215
Rough-ins. *See* Electrical; First floor; Heating ventilation air conditioning; Plumbing; Second floor; Underslab
    usage. *See* Interiors; Mechanical electrical plumbing
Run report menu, 401–402

S
Safety, 88
    concerns, 2, 72, 98. *See also* Construction
    practices, 104
Saving
    feature. *See* Automatic save feature
    process. *See* Projects
Scaffolding, 32
Schedule. *See* Bids; Construction; First draft construction schedule; Milestones
    accuracy/reliability. *See* Computerized schedule

analysis, 219, 227, 265. *See also* Garage; Multi-phase garage project
    components, 86
    computerization, 123–124
    creation, 271. *See also* Construction; SureTrak schedule
    drawing, 275–276. *See also* Network
    evolution, 56–62
    expertise, 8, 13
    hand drawing, 239–241
    preparation. *See* Projects
    printing, 264–266
    purpose, 80
    report, 392–394
    revision. *See* Revised construction schedule
    status report, 395–397
        updating. *See* Updated schedule status report
    types, 62–68
    uncontamination, 271
    updating, 427
    usage/involvement, 80
Scheduling, 53, 56–62
    contrast. *See* Planning
    expertise, 10, 12
    usage, 53
Schematic design, 40–43, 57
Screen captures, creation, 263
Second floor
    casework, 145
    ceiling grids, 145
    doors, 145
    drywall, 145
    exterior studs/sheathing, 145
        in-class exercise, 120–121
    framing plans, usage, 206–207
    hardware, 145
    layout, 225
    plans, usage, 204
    prime coat, 145
    rough-ins, 145
Second floor interior
    doors/hardware, in-class exercise, 122
    partitions, in-class exercise, 121
    studs, 145
Seconds
    fractions (unit, usage), 96–97
    unit, usage, 96–97
Sections, 206–208
    usage. *See* Building sections; Wall sections
Security, 32
Sequencing logic. *See* Activities
SF. *See* Start-to-finish
Shared float, 167
Sheathing. *See* First floor; Roof
    in-class exercise. *See* Second floor
Sheet membrane waterproofing, 208, 210
Sheets, examples, 203–207
Shift combinations, 54
Shift work, 98
Shingling. *See* Roofs
Shoring, 31
Single lump sum contract, impact, 16

Sites
  activities, scheduling, 54
  engineers, 27
  improvements, 276
  layouts, 145, 275
  plans, usage, 204. *See also*
    Mechanical electrical
    plumbing
  subconsultants, 27
  utilities, 58, 143
  runs, 145, 275
Sitework, 59, 213–216
  trade contractors, 30
Six-day workweek, creation,
  324–326
Size, enormity, 2
Skin, 213
  application, 215–216
Slab-on-deck, 145, 225, 275
Slab-on-grade, 143–145, 239, 275
Slabs, 58
Small companies, impact. *See*
  Construction
Software, opening, 242–244
Sorting, ES usage. *See* Activities
South wall structural elevation
  plans, usage, 207
Specialty designs, 29
Specification review, 207–210
Spellcheck, usage, 252–255
SS. *See* Start-to-start
Start design, 57
Start nodes, 141
Start-to-finish (SF) activities, 256
  free float, 172–173
  relationships, 91, 92, 94–95
Start-to-start (SS)
  activities, 256
  free float, 171
  inclusion. *See* Total float
  activity relationships, 89–90
  lag, inclusion, 92
  relationships, 133. *See also*
    Activities
  successors, 161–162, 168, 171
Start-up phase, 35, 49–50
Status report. *See* Schedule
Steel, 211
  erection, 32, 144, 275
  fabrication, 32
Stone, 211

Stonework, 32
Storm retention, 145
Structural engineers, 27–28
Structural frame, 58, 70, 213, 215
Structural subconsultants, 27
Structure, trade contractors, 30
Studs. *See* First floor
  in-class exercise. *See* Second floor
  usage. *See* Interiors
Subconsultants, 21, 26–29. *See also*
  Electrical; Interiors;
  Plumbing; Sites; Structural
Subcontractor, multiple markups
  (reduction), 10
Subframes, 32
Submittals, 145, 275
Substantial completion, 79
Successors
  addition, 256
  inclusion. *See* Activities
Supervisor responsibility. *See* Work
Suppliers. *See* Material suppliers
SureTrak
  modules, 65, 134
  schedule, creation, 276–283
  usage, 250

T
Table of contents, usefulness. *See*
  Projects
Target budget, 35
Target schedules, 385
  renaming, 386–389
Team members, adversarial
  relationships, 7
Tenants, 24–25
TF. *See* Total float
Three-dimensional objects,
  derivation. *See* Two-
  dimensional plans
Three-week lookahead report,
  397–401
Time, 15
  availability, 97
  consumption. *See* Activities
  saving, 72, 124
Time/material contract, 19
  characteristics, 19
Time-scaled logic diagram, 62, 66–68
Toolbar, buttons/icons (addition),
  261–263

Tools, availability, 98
Topping out, 79
Total float (TF), 167–168. *See also*
  Activities
  calculation, start-to-start activities
    (inclusion), 168
Total project cash flow, 87
Total project ceiling cost, 16
Total project cost (TPC), 16, 18, 47
  knowledge, 17, 19
Total project duration. *See* Minimum
  total project duration
TPC. *See* Total project cost
Trade contractors, 10, 21, 30–33, 101
  formation, 54
  input, 99, 102–103
Trusses, 211. *See also* Prefabricated
  wood trusses; Roof
Turnkey delivery concepts, 13
Two-dimensional plans, 3-D object
  derivation, 2

U
Underground electrical, 221–222
Underground plumbing, 32,
  221–222
Underslab
  rough-ins, 145
  utilities, 144
Undo buttons, 272
Unit masonry, 208, 209
Unit price, 15
Unit price contract, 17–18
  characteristics, 17–18
Updated schedule status report,
  439–443
Updates
  initiation, 433–439
  naming/saving conventions,
    427–428
Updating. *See* Projects; Schedule
Up-fronts, 213–214
  activities, 211–212
  definition, 210
  identification, 210–212
USA Volleyball Centers. *See*
  Capstone project
Utilities, 31. *See also* Sites; Underslab

V
Value, measurement, 86

Ventilation. *See* Heating ventilation
  air conditioning
Version, renaming. *See*
  Number/version

W
Wall sections, usage, 205–206
Waterproofing. *See* Sheet membrane
  waterproofing
WBS. *See* Work breakdown structure
Weeks (unit, usage), 96
Window captures, creation, 263
Wood trusses. *See* Prefabricated
  wood trusses
Wood windows, 208, 210
Work. *See* Shift work
  area
    congestion, 104
    overcrowding, 98
  continuousness. *See* Activities
  crews, 85
  description, 208
  division. *See* Construction
  location, 85
  packages, 60
    dissection, 10
  packaging, definition, 59
  performance, 85
    agreement, 18
    identification, 81
  quantity, 99–100
  restrictions, 104
  scope, 16. *See also* Activities
    defining, 18, 77
    interface, 74
  supervisor responsibility, 85
Work breakdown structure (WBS),
  77, 84
Work item activity, 79
Workday analysis, 54
Workflow. *See* Projects
Working area, impact, 89
Workweek
  calendar, 320–322
  creation. *See* Six-day workweek

Y
Years (unit, usage), 96